CORPOREAL MOVEABLES

IN

SCOTS LAW

CORPOREAL
MOVEABLES
IN
SCOTS LAW

By

D. L. CAREY MILLER, B.A., LL.B., LL.M., Ph.D.
Senior Lecturer in the Department of Jurisprudence,
University of Aberdeen

Published under the auspices of
THE SCOTTISH UNIVERSITIES LAW INSTITUTE

W. GREEN
Edinburgh
1991

First published in 1991

ISBN 0 414 00962 2

A catalogue record for this book
is available from the British Library

Typeset by LBJ Enterprises Limited, Chilcompton and Tadley.
Printed in Great Britain by Hartnolls Limited, Bodmin

PREFACE

THIS book is intended to cover the general principles of the law of property applying to corporeal moveables in respect of acquisition, protection (or remedies), security and reservation of title. Limits had to be set within the wide and diverse area of the law having a bearing upon corporeal moveables. The notion of real or proprietary rights is strong in the system of property in Scots law and the scope of my treatment is intended to reflect this. But the subject is open to various approaches and I would particularly draw attention to the coverage of matters pertaining to moveables in the late Professor J. M. Halliday's *Conveyancing Law and Practice in Scotland,* published in this series.

The common law of Scotland relating to moveable property is distinctive. Partly through the reception of Roman law, it represents a system of property founded upon a strong underlying basis of principle. The Institutional writings, reflecting this, have much to offer. I have tried to make good use of them. In this regard, I should explain that I use the fourth (1839) edition of Bell's *Principles* because it was the last prepared by the author himself.

My general approach to the sources has been with a view to emphasising the principles which are important to much of the law covered. I have tried to give priority to material — whether from case law or other sources — which explains or illustrates the working of the system. On this basis I have sought to include material to the end of 1990.

A number of people have given me very valuable assistance in my work but I alone am responsible for the errors and imperfections of the book. The intitial drafts of certain chapters were read by fellow academics Professor W. M. Gordon, Judith Pearson, Professor G. D. MacCormack and David Sellar. The final manuscript was referred by the Scottish Universities Law Institute to Lord Clyde and Professor Gordon. I am most grateful to all the above for their very helpful comments. I would also like to record special thanks to my Aberdeen colleague Stephen Girvin for his much appreciated help in the tasks of checking and in the preparation of the tables and index.

Acknowledgments are also due to Professor W. W. McBryde for his involvement as Director of the Scottish Universities Law Institute, to Peter Nicholson of Greens, with whom the idea of the book was conceived in 1987, and to Rosemary Campbell of Greens for her work after submission of the manuscript.

Department of Jurisprudence   D. L. CAREY MILLER
Old Aberdeen
May 1, 1991

CONTENTS

CHAPTER 12: RESERVATION OF TITLE

General Matters

TABLE OF CASES

TABLE OF STATUTES

TABLE OF STATUTORY INSTRUMENTS

TABLE OF ABBREVIATIONS

Gloag and Henderson — W. M. Gloag and R. C. Henderson, *Introduction to the Law of Scotland* (9th ed. by A. B. Wilkinson and W. A. Wilson, 1987).

Gloag and Irvine, *Rights in Security* — W. M. Gloag and J. M. Irvine, *Law of Rights in Security, Heritable and Moveable including Cautionary Obligations* (1897, reprinted 1987).

Gordon, *Criminal Law* — G. H. Gordon, *The Criminal Law of Scotland* (2nd ed., 1978, Supp., 1984).

Gordon, *Scottish Land Law* — W. M. Gordon, *Scottish Land Law* (1989).

Gordon, *Studies in the Transfer of Property by Traditio* — W. M. Gordon, *Studies in the Transfer of Property by Traditio* (1970).

Gow, *Mercantile Law* — J. J. Gow, *The Mercantile and Industrial Law of Scotland* (1964).

Graham Stewart, *The Law of Diligence* — J. Graham Stewart, *A Treatise on the Law of Diligence* (1898).

Gretton, *Inhibition and Adjudication* — G. L. Gretton, *The Law of Inhibition and Adjudication* (1987).

Grotius, *De Jure Belli ac Pacis* — Hugo Grotius, *De Jure Belli ac Pacis Libri Tres* (1625).

Halliday, *Conveyancing* — J. M. Halliday, *Conveyancing Law and Practice in Scotland*, Vols. I (1985), II (1986), III (1987), IV (1989).

Hume — G. C. H. Paton (ed.), *Baron David Hume's Lectures 1786–1822* (Stair Society Publications, Vol. III, 1952).

Kames, *Elucidations* — H. Home, Lord Kames, *Elucidations Respecting the Common and Statute Law of Scotland* (1800).

McBryde, *Bankruptcy* — W. W. McBryde, *Bankruptcy* (1989).

McBryde, *Contract* — W. W. McBryde, *The Law of Contract in Scotland* (1987).

McBryde and Downie, *Petition Procedure in the Court of Session* — W. W. McBryde and N. J. Downie, *Petition Procedure in the Court of Session* (2nd ed., 1988).

MacDonald, *Succession* — D. R. MacDonald, *An Introduction to the Scots Law of Succession* (1990).

Maclaren, *Court of Session Practice* — J. A. Maclaren, *Court of Session Practice* (1916).

McMillan, *Bona Vacantia* — A. R. G. McMillan, *The Law of Bona Vacantia in Scotland* (1936).

Maher and Cusine, *Diligence* — G. Maher and D. J. Cusine, *The Law and Practice of Diligence* (1990).

Maxwell, *Court of Session Practice* — D. Maxwell, *The Practice of the Court of Session* (1980).

Meston, *The Succession (Scotland) Act 1964*	M. C. Meston, *The Succession (Scotland) Act 1964* (3rd ed., 1982).
Napier, *Prescription*	M. Napier, *Commentaries on the Law of Prescription in Scotland* (2nd ed., 1854).
New Perspectives in the Roman Law of Property	P. Birks (ed.), *New Perspectives in the Roman Law of Property* (1989).
Rankine, *Landownership*	J. Rankine, *The Law of Landownership in Scotland* (4th ed., 1909, reprinted 1986).
Rankine, *Personal Bar*	J. Rankine, *A Treatise on the Law of Personal Bar in Scotland* (1921).
Scot. Law Com.	Scottish Law Commission, Memorandum No. 24, *Corporeal Moveables: General Introduction and Summary of Provisional Proposals* (1976); Memorandum No. 25, *Corporeal Moveables: Passing of Risk and Ownership* (1976); Memorandum No. 26, *Corporeal Moveables: Some Problems of Classification* (1976); Memorandum No. 27, *Corporeal Moveables: Protection of the Onerous Bona Fide Acquirer of Another's Property* (1976); Memorandum No. 28, *Corporeal Moveables: Mixing, Union and Creation* (1976); Memorandum No. 29, *Corporeal Moveables: Lost and Abandoned Property* (1976); Memorandum No. 30, *Corporeal Moveables: Usucapion or Acquisitive Prescription* (1976); Memorandum No. 31, *Corporeal Moveables: Remedies* (1976).
Smith, *Property Problems in Sale*	T. B. Smith, *Property Problems in Sale* (1978).
Smith, *Short Commentary*	T. B. Smith, *Short Commentary on the Law of Scotland* (1962).
Spencer Bower and Turner, *Estoppel by Representation*	G. Spencer Bower and A. K. Turner, *The Law Relating to Estoppel by Representation* (3rd ed., 1977).
Stair	James Dalrymple, 1st Viscount Stair, *Institutions of the Law of Scotland* (Tercentenary (6th) ed. by D. M. Walker, 1981).
Stair Memorial Encyclopaedia	Sir Thomas Smith *et al.* (eds.), *The Laws of Scotland: Stair Memorial Encyclopaedia* (1987–).
St Clair and Drummond Young, *The Law of Corporate Insolvency in Scotland*	J. B. St Clair and J. E. Drummond Young, *The Law of Corporate Insolvency in Scotland* (1988).
Voet, *ad Pandectas*	J. Voet, *Commentarius ad Pandectas* (1698–1704).
Walker, *Civil Remedies*	D. M. Walker, *The Law of Civil Remedies in Scotland* (1974).
Walker, *The Law of Prescription and Limitation of Actions in Scotland*	D. M. Walker, *The Law of Prescription and Limitation of Actions in Scotland* (3rd ed., 1981, Supp., 1985).

Walker, *Principles*   D. M. Walker, *Principles of Scottish Private Law*, Vol. III (4th ed., 1989).

Wilson, *The Law of Scotland Relating to Debt*   W. A. Wilson, *The Law of Scotland Relating to Debt* (1982).

CHAPTER 1

NATURE AND SCOPE OF RIGHTS IN MOVEABLES

Basis of heritable/moveable distinction

Scots law recognises a distinction between immoveable and move- **1.01**
able things; on the one hand, land, and what pertains to land, and, on
the other hand, all other forms of property, which are designated
"moveable."[1] According to Stair[2] the distinction is between a moveable
thing, "which by its nature and use is capable of motion," and
immoveables, "the earth, sea and things fixed to the earth." However,
the distinction becomes one between the more closely defined category
of immoveable property and other things.

Technically, the distinction is between heritable and moveable
property. The terminology has its basis in a fundamental aspect of the
common law of succession; land, and rights in land, passed to the heir-
at-law and were accordingly designated heritage or heritable property
while moveables went to the executor for distribution to the next-of-
kin. Stair,[3] after referring to the various forms immoveable property
may take, notes that the items concerned "are called heritable,
because they descend not to executors, to whom only moveables befal,
but to heirs."[4]

In the modern law of succession the distinction no longer has a
central rôle but nonetheless remains important.[5] From the point of
view of the general scope of the distinction two trends are evident.
First, the category of heritable property has come to encompass rights
of a permanent nature not necessarily connected with land.[6] Secondly,
the category of incorporeal moveable property has expanded.[7] But the
subject of corporeal moveables remains essentially a category of things
with a physical existence which are not classified as heritable property.[8]

---

[1] See Bell, *Prin.*, § 636.
[2] II.i.2.
[3] *Ibid.*
[4] See also Erskine, II.ii.3; Bell, Prin., §§ 636, 1283, 1470.
[5] Following the recommendations of the Mackintosh Committee on Succession (1951,
Cmd. 8144) the heir-at-law's feudal right to heritable property was abolished by the
Succession (Scotland) Act 1964 which, by and large, assimilated the two classes of
property for the purposes of succession. See Meston, *The Succession (Scotland) Act
1964*, pp. 13–14. As to the continuing importance of the distinction to the modern law of
succession see Gordon, *Scottish Land Law*, paras. 1.29–1.37.
[6] See Gordon, *Scottish Land Law*, para. 1.02.
[7] *Ibid.*, paras. 1.25–1.27.
[8] See below, paras. 1.05–1.08.

2

NATURE AND SCOPE OF RIGHTS IN MOVEABLES

Importance of the heritable/moveable distinction

1.02 In various areas of the law different rules apply depending upon whether one is dealing with heritable or moveable property.[9] Although governed by the same fundamental principles the acquisition of rights—both personal and real—proceed on a different technical basis in relation to land and moveable items.[10] The following are some instances of the division in other contexts. In succession legal rights—which cannot be avoided by testamentary act—apply only in respect of the deceased's moveable estate.[11] The rules of diligence—providing for execution against a debtor's property—differ depending upon whether the property concerned is heritable or moveable; Scots law speaks of inhibition and adjudication in relation to land and arrestment and poinding in respect of moveable property.[12] The distinction is also important in the ways in which the law deals with a bankrupt estate.[13] In keeping with most systems the Scottish rules of private international law treat issues differently depending upon whether immoveable or moveable property is involved.[14]

Terminology

1.03 The Scottish Law Commission, in a memorandum published in 1976, advocated the abandoning of the designation "heritable" and its replacement with the word "immovable": "nothing of value would be lost, and much in the way clarity would be gained, were 'immovable' to replace "heritable" in legal usage."[15]

---

[9] See, generally, Bell, *Prin.*, § 1470. Regarding the continuing importance of the category of heritable property see Gordon, *Scottish Land Law*, paras. 1.28–1.55.

[10] The law requires contracts in respect of heritage to be in writing (Stair, I.x.9; Erskine, III.ii.2; *Goldston* v. *Young* (1868) 7 M. 188 at p. 192; Gordon, *Scottish Land Law*, para. 12.56) and, of course, the real right of ownership can only be acquired on a derivative basis through conveyance in the requisite form: since the Land Registration (Scotland) Act 1979 this includes the requirement of registration in respect of land situate within the geographical area covered by the legislation. Although the distinction between the acquisition of rights in heritable and moveable property is, in general, clearly maintained, an exception may apply in the case of heritable subjects sold together with moveable items in a *universitas* predominantly moveable in nature. In *Allan* v. *Millar*, 1932 S.C. 620, it was held that a personal right was acquired over the heritables concerned in such a case even though the unitary contract did not comply with the requirements of form appropriate to heritage. From a policy point of view it is difficult to accept this decision. The value and importance of immoveable property justifies requirements of form; a position not outweighed by commercial considerations which, in the case of consumer moveables, demand ease and speed of contract. The contractual compromise of severance would appear to have been a more appropriate solution.

[11] See Bell, *Prin.*, §§ 1582, 1591; Macdonald, *Succession*, paras. 4.12–4.14.

[12] See Bell, *Prin.*, §§ 2273, 2284, 2299, 2306; see generally Graham Stewart, *The Law of Diligence*; Gretton, *Inhibition and Adjudication*; Maher and Cusine, *Diligence*.

[13] See McBryde, *Bankruptcy*, pp. 102–106.

[14] See Anton, *Private International Law*, pp. 597–601.

[15] Memorandum No. 26, *Corporeal Moveables: Some Problems of Classification*, para. 32. See also Gordon, *Scottish Land Law*, para. 1.56: "If the distinction between heritable and moveable property is becoming increasingly irrelevant in the modern world, the distinction between immoveable and moveable property is becoming increasingly important."

This proposal seems to be justifiable; in the modern context the designation "heritable" is something of an anachronism because its basis, in a once important distinction in succession, has largely disappeared in modern law.[16] Moreover, because the distinction between land and its accessories and moveable property is important in a number of different areas it does seem that the neutral umbrella phrase "immovable property" is more appropriate.

Corporeal and incorporeal property

The distinction between immoveable and moveable property is **1.04** primarily a matter of a policy-based justification for the recognition of obvious differences of form between two types of thing. The other major division—between corporeal things and incorporeals—is, however, based upon a more fundamental distinction.

The corporeal/incorporeal dichotomy reflects an incontrovertible difference in character: on the one hand, a corporeal thing having a physical existence which is the essence of the thing as an item of property; on the other hand, an incorporeal in which the property itself has no material existence although it may relate to a corporeal thing and it may be evidenced by some material form, typically a document.

In the case of *Burghead Harbour Co.* v. *George*[17] Lord Kinnear saw the distinction as one between things.

> "*Res corporales* are according to the legal definition physical things which can be touched; and *res incorporales* are things which do not admit of being handled, but consist *in jure*, and so are more properly rights than subjects . . . All rights, therefore, are incorporeal; and the distinction really is not between two kinds of right, but between things which are objects of right and the legal conception of the right itself."

The corporeal/incorporeal distinction also tends to produce a divergence in the form of rules applicable to legal acts; thus, the assignment

---

[16] In any event, the appropriateness of a classification of the law of succession being applied to property is open to question. The danger of this can be seen in the possibility of rights being heritable or moveable by destination—in the sense of by reference to the express or implied intention of the owner—for the purposes of succession. (See Erskine, II.ii.14; Bell, *Prin.*, § 1491; *Baird* v. *Watson* (1880) 8 R. 233; see below, para. 1.08.) For the purposes of property, the question of heritable or moveable must be an essentially objective issue and, given the possible legitimate interests of third parties, there can hardly be room for reference to the intention of a party, regarding the appropriate destination of a thing, as a basis for determining whether the item concerned is heritable or moveable. Scots law recognises this (see Erskine, II.ii.14), and the position seems to underline that it is potentially misleading to apply the categories of succession to property.

[17] (1906) 8 F. 982 at p. 996. See also Erskine, II.ii.1.

of an obligation requires a deed of transfer and intimation to the debtor because one is dealing with a right rather than a thing and there can be no actual delivery of possession.[18]

On the basis of the two major distinctions between, in the first place, heritable and moveable property and, secondly, corporeal and incorporeal property, the category of corporeal moveables emerges as a separate division, justifying independent treatment.[19]

Scope of corporeal moveables; heritable or moveable?

1.05   The basis and importance of the heritable/moveable distinction has been referred to already[20] but, for the purpose of establishing the scope of the subject, it is necessary to examine the division more closely.

As an aid to the problem of allocating borderline subjects as heritable or moveable, some authorities distinguish the basis of classification depending upon whether it is by reference to the nature of the thing, or by reason of the fact that the thing is linked with another thing, or through the application of the concept of destination. Bell[21] explains this in a well known text:

> "The character of any subject or fund, as, in these important respects, heritable or moveable, may be either,—1. by its Nature, as being *immoveable*, like land or houses; or as moveable, like furniture or cattle: or, 2. by Connection or Accession to some subject which has by nature the character of moveable or immoveable: or, 3. by Destination of the owner, either as in connection with something else, or in regard to succession."

The three criteria of nature, connection or accession, and destination have been relevant in the development of the law and each may be looked at in greater detail.

Heritable or moveable by nature

1.06   Reduced to basics land is, by nature, heritable while things which have the capacity to move or be moved are, by nature, moveable.[22] The fact that part of a given unit of land may be moved does not mean that the entity is moveable; quarried stone is moveable by nature just as the unbroken stone is heritable by nature. A river or spring is not

---

[18] Bell, *Prin.*, § 1459.

[19] Bell, *Prin.*, §§ 1284–1285, recognises the category of corporeal moveables. The Scottish Law Commission in seven memoranda published in 1976 considered various relevant matters under the heading "Corporeal Moveables." See Memorandum No. 24, *Corporeal Moveables*: *General Introduction and Summary of Provisional Proposals*, para. 3.

[20] See above, paras. 1.01–1.02.

[21] *Prin.* § 1470.

[22] See Stair, II.i.2; Bell, *Prin.*, § 1472.

moveable because the water moves and can be moved. A diverted watercourse remains by nature heritable. The removal of a quantity of water produces a natural moveable but then, of course, one can no longer speak of removed water as a "river" or "spring." The topsoil covering a parcel of arable land may be susceptible to removal but, regardless of this fact, the proprietary entity is by nature heritable; on the other hand, a quantity of topsoil removed and bagged for sale is a thing by nature moveable.

These instances of the recognition of things as heritable or moveable demonstrate the importance of an accurate identification of the proprietary entity concerned. Once the thing is correctly identified it may well be clear that it is by nature heritable or moveable, as the case may be.

Heritable or moveable by connection or annexation

Where one is concerned with two or more possibly separate entities **1.07** the second criterion, looking to connection or annexation, may be applicable. Though there may be no doubt that a free-standing cabinet is a separate entity of moveable property, even though made up of different parts, the issue could be complicated by its being affixed to a wall. In this case one cannot resolve the problem by the simple touchstone "heritable or moveable by nature" because it is not possible definitely to identify the proprietary entity concerned.

The concept of connection or annexation—or *accessio*—may determine or confirm the character of a thing as heritable or moveable when the identity of an accessory item is subsumed under that of the principal thing.[23] Accession is a mode of acquisition of ownership[24]; but for present purposes it is enough to note its rôle in determining the character of a thing as heritable or moveable.

Heritable or moveable by destination

The nature of a thing and its relationship with another thing may **1.08** determine its classification as heritable or moveable. By destination a key to the door of a building is heritable; its *raison d'être* is the door and the significance of the relationship outweighs the fact that, as a thing, a key has all the characteristics of a moveable. This concept is closely related to the doctrine of accession or connection; destination, however, does not turn on a physical link but, rather, on the incontrovertible conclusion that one thing is auxiliary or subsidiary to another: hence the label "constructive annexation."[25]

---

[23] See Erskine, II.i.14: "in two things which have an intimate connection with or dependence upon one another, the property of the principal thing draws after it that of its accessory."

[24] See below, para. 3.01.

[25] See below, para. 3.21.

For the purposes of succession—seemingly, to facilitate giving effect to the will of the deceased—the law recognises that property may be heritable or moveable by destination.[26] In an early case[27] the majority of the court treated as heritable building components placed adjacent to a house under construction, the intention of the deceased as to the destiny of the items concerned being accepted in the circumstances. *Animus* inferred in this way may be appropriate to determine the rights of succession deriving from an act of will; however, it would be contrary to principle for this doctrine of destination to apply to the law of property in general.[28] In cases of original acquisition proprietary consequences follow, first and foremost, as a matter of objective conclusion from the circumstances, with the will factor having a possible rôle only where the circumstances are, in any event, consistent with acquisition. In principle, the annexor's intention that a moveable should vest in the owner of a heritable, to which it is affixed, can only be relevant if the physical circumstances are consistent with this result.[29]

Right of ownership

1.09   Scots law follows Roman law in the theory of an absolute right of ownership.[30] Proof of a right of ownership prevails over other claims not derived from the owner's right.[31] An owner who can show that he lost possession involuntarily[32] can, in principle, recover the thing from even an innocent onerous possessor. Both in terms of nature and scope ownership is the quintessential right; Erskine[33] describes it as the "sovereign or primary real right." Where it has not been limited it gives the fullest possible right in and to the thing itself, encompassing the constituent elements of the rights to use and fruits and the power of disposal.[34]

Although in theory ownership is an absolute right in actual fact it is often no more than a collection of residual rights, to the extent that one tends to think of the meaningful criterion of ownership as an intact right of disposal.[35] There are two aspects to the diminution of the scope of ownership: as Erskine[36] notes, an owner may be restrained "by law or paction."

---

[26] Bell, *Prin.*, § 1475, refers to the concept of destination operating through "a manifest purpose" serving to "characterize the thing as heritable" in a text which contrasts this form of destination with the recognition of an owner's intention as to "destination in point of succession."

[27] *Johnston* v. *Dobie* (1783) Mor. 5443.

[28] See above, n. 16.

[29] See below, para. 3.15.

[30] See Erskine, II.i.1.

[31] See below, para. 10.03.

[32] Stair, III.ii.7.

[33] II.i.1.

[34] Stair, II.i.Pr.; Bell, *Prin.*, § 1284.

[35] See Stair, II.i.Pr.: the "power of disposal of things in their substance, fruits, or use."

[36] II.i.1.

First, the owner's rights are invariably limited by external controls.[37] Particular moveables, or classes of moveables, are frequently affected. Types of moveable property with potential for causing harm—for example, animals and motor vehicles—are subject to controls which curtail the right of use. Secondly, as a matter of the exercise of the right of ownership, an owner may choose to relinquish part of his right. This may be seen as an internal diminution and is distinguishable from the external control type in being a voluntary, and often temporary, limitation of the right. Such a curtailment of the right may take the form of either a personal or a real right. In the former case the owner does no more than bind himself by contract to allow another party to have the use or fruits of the thing. In the latter the owner actually makes over a part or aspect of his right of ownership. In respect of moveable property, while there is considerable scope for the former the potential rôle of the latter is limited. This is because in principle the creation of a real right in moveable property requires a transfer of possession and it is only relatively infrequently that an owner would want to part with the possession of a moveable while retaining ownership.

Divisibility of ownership

Although Scots law received the Romanist theory of a right of **1.10** ownership made up of constituent rights of *usus, fructus* and *abusus*[38] the system, in its development, did not take this to be the only possible basis upon which the right could be dealt with. The law also reflects feudal influences. While the Roman system is predicated upon a unitary right of ownership, with lesser rights recognised only in accordance with the tripartite breakdown, feudal law accepts what, in effect, amounts to degrees of ownership. As Stair[39] points out, the respective characterisation of the rights of feudal superior and feudal vassal as *dominium directum* and *dominium utile* reflects the truth that "it can hardly be determined, whether the right of property is in the superior or vassal alone."

In the case of moveable property the feudal conception of a hierarchy of ownership has not been a dominating influence but it has added a dimension, and a measure of flexibility, to Scots law. The institution of trusts—applicable, of course, to moveable as well as heritable property—demonstrates this. It is well known that systems which adhere to the dogma of ownership divisible only in terms of use, fruits and disposal find it difficult to conceive of trustee and beneficiary as contemporaneous owners, their respective rights differing in nature, or scope, rather than type.[40] But, as Professor Sir Thomas Smith[41] has

---

[37] See Erskine, II.i.2.
[38] Stair, II.i.Pr.
[39] Stair, II.iii.7.
[40] See, *e.g.* David and Brierley, *Major Legal Systems* (3rd ed., 1985), para. 312; Bolgár, "Why no trusts in the Civil law?" (1953) 2 Am.J.C.L. 204.
[41] *Short Commentary*, pp. 460–461.

shown, the influences of feudal law have provided increased scope for the fragmentation of ownership, although primarily in the areas of trusts and succession and, in consequence, with probably greater impact upon heritable property.

Formal requirements of ownership

1.11   The modes of acquisition of ownership are dealt with in Chapters 2–9. In general, there is no requirement of a written or formal title to moveable property. In some instances documents relating to the carriage or storage of goods are the means by which ownership, or lessor rights, are transferred or created—the most important example is a bill of lading in respect of goods in shipment—but once the transferee has obtained possession such documents have no rôle in relation to title.[42] There are only two classes of moveable property in respect of which a document of title is required by law: ships and aircraft.

In respect of ships the Merchant Shipping Act 1894 requires that every British ship—excluding river boats or coasters of not more than 15 tons' carrying capacity—be registered in the register of shipping.[43] Title is as *per* the register[44] regardless of the facts as to possession.[45]

The Department of Trade maintains a register of aircraft. Given that the purpose of this register is to limit the right of ownership to certain categories of qualified persons it follows that the register must be definitive on a question of ownership.[46]

Proof of ownership

1.12   Subject to the limited exceptions mentioned above, the right of ownership in moveable property does not require any special title or document. The acquisition and transmission of rights is generally free from requirements of form: as Stair[47] put it, "neither needs the title, constitution, or transmission, of property in moveables, be instructed by writ." In a market economy the interests of commerce preclude onerous requirements of form which might inhibit the free flow of goods.[48] It follows that proof of ownership may be by a variety of means, with inference from the circumstances under which the thing is held having a possible rôle.

---

[42] See below, para. 8.27.

[43] ss.2(1) and 3(1).

[44] It may be noted that the register records the ownership position based upon the 64 shares into which the ownership of a ship may be divided—s.5. In respect of fishing boats the number of shares is 16: see the Sea Fishing Boats (Scotland) Act 1886, s.3.

[45] See *Hooper* v. *Gumm* (1867) L.R. 2 Ch. 282.

[46] See Air Navigation Order 1970 (S.I. 1970 No. 954), art. 4.

[47] II.i.42.

[48] See Erskine, II.i.24: "And, indeed, commerce could not have a free course if it behoved the possessors of moveables, which often pass from hand to hand without either witnesses or writing, to prove the titles of their possession."

Given the absence of a document of title, proof of ownership will normally involve reference to the means by which the right was acquired. To this end the evidence of a predecessor in title might be required. Documentary evidence, such as a bill of sale or receipt, could be put forward in support of the transaction on the basis of which ownership is claimed. Particular facts may go some way towards proof of title. A name written in a book, initials branded on livestock, a telephone number in a capsule attached to the collar of a dog are examples. In relation to motor vehicles, although the registration book is not conclusive as to ownership it is evidence of title.[49]

The Institutional writers acknowledge the importance of possession when title to moveables is at issue. As Stair[50] points out, the absence of formalities in relation to the acquisition and transmission of the right of ownership limits the means of direct proof, with the consequence that the *status quo* as to possession becomes important. Erskine[51] also recognised the link:

"Such is the natural connection between property and possession, that in moveables, even when they have a former owner, the law presumes the property to be in the possessor; so that till positive evidence be brought that he is not the right owner, he will be accounted such by the bare effect of his possession."

There is a negative aspect of this presumption in favour of a possessor. Where the *status quo* as to possession is against the claimant, the common law requires not only proof of ownership but proof of the circumstances in which possession was lost: "but he must instruct the manner how his possession ceased, as being either taken from him by violence, or by stealth, or having strayed, and being lost or the like."[52]

Although one finds, in the case law, recognition of the importance of possession to the question of ownership,[53] it seems that the law has moved away from any doctrinal equating of possession and ownership. As Lord Cockburn noted in *Anderson* v. *Buchanan*[54]: "This is a presumption liable to be rebutted, and perhaps liable to be rebutted easily."

The very fact that the claimant asserts a title to a thing held by another must, necessarily, involve a burden of proof. However, this

---

[49] See *Central Newbury Car Auctions Ltd.* v. *Unity Finance Ltd.* [1957] 1 Q.B. 371.
[50] II.i.42.
[51] II.i.24.
[52] Stair, II.i.42. See also Erskine, II.i.24; Bell, *Prin.*, § 1314.
[53] See, *e.g. Macdougal* v. *Whitelaw* (1840) 2 D. 500 *per* Lord Gillies at p. 505: "But if the house was hers, then I think the common rule holds that possession presumes property, and the furniture of the house must be presumed to be hers, in the absence of any proof to the contrary."
[54] (1848) 11 D. 270 at p. 284.

said, the particular circumstances between the parties are all important. For example, in the case of goods sold remaining in the custody of
the seller the presumption of a simulated transaction,[55] based upon the
doctrine of possession presuming ownership, "will be stronger or
weaker according to circumstances; and if the good faith of the
transaction is clearly proved, will altogether disappear."[56]

Deriving from the doctrine that possession demonstrates title is the
concept of reputed ownership. This applies "where the true owner
allows another to assume publicly the appearance of ownership, . . .
and to deceive and mislead creditors by raising a false ground of
credit."[57] But in a number of dicta, the courts have emphasised the
limited scope of this device[58] and, by necessary implication, these
statements detract from the efficacy of the parent doctrine. One may
note, especially, the comments of Lord President Cooper in *George
Hopkinson Ltd.* v. *Napier & Son*[59] to the effect that "the doctrine of
reputed ownership arising from possession of moveables . . . is a
doctrine which may very easily be pushed much too far."[60] In this case
the learned Lord President did not regard it as an overstatement to say
that in modern law,

> "any creditor proposing to poind the furniture in an average
> working-class dwelling is put on his inquiry as to whether the
> furniture is the property of his debtor or is only held by him on
> some limited title of possession. The possession of the furniture
> *per se* only goes a short distance towards establishing a presump-
> tion of ownership."[61]

As the court pointed out, a true owner may be personally barred from
proving his ownership, but "if the circumstances do not raise the plea
of bar . . . the possession of the moveables can create no more than a
presumption of fact, more or less strong according to the circumstances, but capable of being redargued."[62]

---

[55] See below, para. 12.04.

[56] *Orr's Tr.* v. *Tullis* (1870) 8 M. 936 *per* Lord Justice-Clerk Moncreiff at p. 947. See also *Mitchell* v. *Heys & Sons* (1894) 21 R. 600 at pp. 610–611.

[57] *Marston* v. *Kerr's Tr.* (1879) 6 R. 898 *per* Lord Gifford at p. 901.

[58] See, *e.g. Robertsons* v. *McIntyre* (1882) 9 R. 772 *per* Lord Justice-Clerk Moncreiff at p. 778: "The doctrine of reputed ownership . . . has been paid little attention to of late years, and is no longer of much importance." See also *Lamonby* v. *Foulds Ltd.*, 1928 S.C. 89 at p. 96.

[59] 1953 S.C. 139 at p. 147.

[60] But *cf. Prangnell-O'Neill* v. *Lady Skiffington*, 1984 S.L.T. 282 *per* Lord Hunter at p. 284.

[61] 1953 S.C. 139 at p. 147.

[62] *Ibid.*; citing Gloag and Irvine, *Rights in Security*, pp. 236 ff. Of course, where the possessor is a *bona fide* onerous acquirer his position will be relatively strong; see Stair, III.ii.7. As the Scottish Law Commission, Memorandum No. 27, *Corporeal Moveables: Protection of the Onerous Bona Fide Acquirer of Another's Property*, para. 12, has noted: "Since at common law a buyer acquired a real right only when possession was transferred to him, this presumption was normally efficacious, and favoured by the law in the interests of commerce." See below, para. 10.16.

In modern law, it seems to be recognised that because ownership in moveable property is not subject to any requirements of formal title, proof of the right cannot be subject to fixed prescriptions or limitations. Given the importance of the physical possession of moveable property it follows that inferences may be drawn from the apparent circumstances under which the thing is held. It would appear, however, that the law has moved away from any generalised approach to proof by inference because the particular circumstances are of primary importance. That this approach is justified is supported by the simple example of A holding B's moveable thing under contract. Proof of the contractual relationship would confirm B's ownership and would displace any possible inference arising from A's physical possession.

Possession

The recognition, in Scots law, of an ultimate and distinct right of **1.13** ownership means that lesser rights cannot equal the right of an owner. Scots law does not know the degrees of possession of English law.[63] As shown,[64] the fact of possession may be important to the determination of ownership in moveables but, in principle, it is clear that this is more a matter of proof than the recognition of a competing right. Unless and until possession becomes ownership it remains an inferior right, and this is so regardless of the fact that all the beneficial elements of ownership—use, fruits and *de facto* control—may reside in the possessor. The nature of possession as no more than a right bearing the potential of ownership is aptly put in Stair's identification of it as: "the way to property" which "in some cases doth fully accomplish it" but, hence, amounts to no more than "a distinct lesser right than property."[65]

But, unless the use of the word is limited to possession proper, not all forms of possession have a concomitant potential to translate into ownership. In this regard the context of the holding is all-important in that it determines the nature of the right loosely described as "possession" but, possibly, meaning no more than the physical holding of a thing.[66] This is not to say that Scots law recognises different degrees of possession; the different forms are conceptually distinct. In the interests of clarity one can distinguish the general forms possession may take; in doing so one does not concede that a wide usage is acceptable,

---

[63] Stair, II.i.10 speaks of "degrees," but this is clearly not intended to mean degrees of possession in the English law sense of equating ownership with a better right to possession than the defendant has. See Buckland and McNair, *Roman Law and Common Law*, p. 67.

[64] See above, para. 1.12.

[65] II.i.8. See below, para. 1.16, regarding possession leading to ownership.

[66] The statement that a party "has possession" normally implies the right of possession, whereas to say that someone is "in possession" may mean no more than that the party concerned is holder of the thing.

but merely that it may occur. First, possession may be no more than a *de facto* condition not even protected against self-help at the instance of the party actually entitled to possession, for example, a holding obtained by force or clandestinely or, it is submitted, in some other manner against the will of the owner.[67] Secondly, it may be the precarious holding of a thing subject to the owner's will.[68] Thirdly, it may be a state protected by a contractual right available only against the owner: mere *detentio* or custody,[69] not a proprietary condition but an obligation with no standing against the holders of real rights other than the owner.[70] Fourthly, the strongest form—and possession proper—occurs where the thing is held in circumstances which support "an *animus* or design in the detainer of holding it as his own property."[71]

As shown, provided physical possession is maintained, the right is to some extent protected by the presumption of ownership.[72] Moreover, possession proper is protected against unlawful deprivation by the remedy of spuilzie.[73]

Natural and civil possession

1.14   The hallmark of possession proper is the possessor's state of mind in holding the thing as his own property: "an act of the mind, which is the inclination or affection to make use of the thing detained."[74] This requisite state of mind does not necessarily demand actual physical control, provided the circumstances are consistent with an intention to hold as owner. Scots law, accordingly, distinguishes natural and civil possession: the former applying to the case of actual physical control; the latter to possession through the physical control of another, for

---

[67] The limited authority for a remedy of self-help suggests that it is only available to one entitled to possession against an unlawful dispossessor. See Walker, *Civil Remedies*, p. 262; Scot. Law Com., Memo. No. 31, *Corporeaal Moveables*; *Remedies*, paras. 3–5.

[68] See Erskine, II.i.23.

[69] As Bell, *Prin.*, § 1311, puts it: "a conditional and limited possession, held not for the custodier, but for another." See *Sim* v. *Grant* (1862) 24 D. 1033 at pp. 1038–1040, regarding the distinction between mere custody and the right of possession providing for use and enjoyment.

[70] Erskine, II.i.20, notes that this is not possession proper: "Yet detention is not sufficient by itself; the possessor must also hold it as his own right."

[71] *Ibid.* One may contrast the state of a precarious holding which does not have "the essential character of proper possession, because a precarious possessor does not hold the subject *tanquam dominus*, or in his own name": Erskine, II.i.23.

[72] See above, para. 1.12.

[73] See below, para. 10.23.

[74] Stair, II.i.17. The requisite state of mind is usually labelled *animus possidendi* (Smith, *Short Commentary*, p. 461; Walker, *Principles*, III, p. 370). Strictly this would admit possession obtained against the owner's will, because a *mala fide* party can maintain an intention to hold the thing against others; but of course possession proper refers to the case of a holder who believes, and has grounds for believing, that he is owner (see Stair, II.i.24; below, para. 1.15) and the tag *animus domini* would surely be more appropriate.

example a party holding under a contract with the possessor.[75] Accordingly, one party may have natural possession while another is civil possessor. The actual holder may have the thing in his possession on the basis of a contractual right or his possession may be incidental to a limited real right[76]—for example, a right of security based upon pledge—while the civil possessor's position is that of owner.[77]

Civil possession, involving the holding of the thing by another, is a somewhat precarious state in that its existence is dependent upon proof of a legal relationship which overcomes the inference normally following from the physical control of moveables.[78] While, in principle, it is perfectly acceptable that a possessor should be free to part with the thing concerned for some limited purpose, the courts are wary of arrangements whereby one party has physical control while another seeks to retain or acquire the right of possession. One of many enunciations of this attitude is the dictum of Lord Neaves in *Moore* v. *Gledden*[79]:

> "Possession cannot be constituted by mere paction. It is a matter of fact, though there also enters into it the existence of an *animus possessendi* in addition to an overt act of corporeal possession or apprehension. But the outward or visible fact of possession cannot be supplied by mere paction or by anything committed to paper merely."

Bona fide and mala fide possession

The potential importance of possession, for various purposes, justi- **1.15** fies a distinction based upon the *animus* of the holder. Where the possessor holds as owner he may do so in an honest belief in his right of ownersship or, on the other hand, he may be asserting a right of ownership which he knows he is not entitled to. Erskine[80] defines the two states of mind:

> "A *bona fide* possessor is one who, though he be not truly proprietor of the subject which he possesses, yet believes himself

---

[75] See Erskine, II.i.22; Bell, *Prin.*, § 1312. Stair, II.i.10, notes that there are degrees of civil possession "as it cometh nearer to the natural possession." The point here is that possession through the holding of an agent or servant is closer to natural possession than possession through the physical control of an extraneous party who holds under a contract, *e.g.* a lessee. In the latter case possession is maintained entirely on the basis of the intention to hold the thing as owner, and arguably there can be no stronger manifestation of a right of ownership than the granting, to another, of a contractual right in the thing. This, perhaps, gives a clue to the designation "civil possession" as a derivative of *possessio civilis* applying to one who held as owner.

[76] See, *e.g. Mitchell's Trs.* v. *Gladstone* (1894) 21 R. 586 at pp. 592–593.

[77] See Erskine, II.i.22.

[78] See above, para. 1.12.

[79] (1869) 7 M. 1016 at p. 1020. See further above, para. 11.03.

[80] II.i.25.

proprietor upon probable grounds, and with good conscience . . .
as in the case of one who purchases a subject which he has reason
to think was the property of the seller, but which in truth
belonged to a third party. A *mala fide* possessor possesses a
subject not his own, and knows at the same time, or, which comes
to the same account, may upon the smallest reflection know that
he is not the rightful owner."

This distinction is important in various ways. The *mala fide* holding of
a thing does not give a title to possession,[81] nor does such a holder have
any right to the fruits of the thing.[82] A *mala fide* act of disposition may
be a basis for liability.[83]

Possession leading to ownership

1.16   An important aspect of possession is its rôle in giving a right of
ownership. This may occur, in a variety of ways, in the context of the
derivative transfer of ownership. At common law the transfer of the
right of ownership in corporeal moveables is effected by delivery—the
actual or constructive giving of possession to the transferee; as
Erskine[84] put it: "the delivery of the possession of a subject by the
proprietor, with an intention to transfer the property of it to the
receiver." The critical rôle of a transfer of possession as a prerequisite
to the creation of the real right of ownership in the transferee was
noted by Lord President Inglis in *Clark* v. *West Calder Oil Co.*[85]: "A
mere assignation of corporeal moveables *retenta possessione* is nothing
whatever but a personal obligation." The various modes of delivery—
including the type in which physical control is retained by the
transferor—all necessarily involve a transfer of possession.[86] But, it
should be noted, the sphere of operation of the common law requirement of a transfer of possession to pass ownership in moveable things
was much reduced with the provision in the Sale of Goods Act, 1893
for the passing of property pursuant to the conclusion of a contract of
sale.[87]

   As a matter of original acquisition the taking of possession gives a
right of ownership. Things not previously owned may be acquired on
the principle of natural law referred to by Stair[88]: "Property is
introduced by possession of things, which are yet simply void and
belong to none, and that without limitation."

---

[81] See *Louson* v. *Craik* (1842) 4 D. 1452 at p. 1458.
[82] See Stair, II.i.24: "This right is only competent to possessors *bona fide*, who do truly
think that which they possess to be their own, and know not the right of any other." See
below para. 6.04.
[83] See below, para. 10.07.
[84] II.i.18.
[85] (1882) 9 R. 1017 at p. 1024.
[86] See below, paras. 8.15 and 8.20.
[87] See below, para. 9.01.
[88] II.i.33. See below, para. 2.01.

Despite the Civilian influence upon the law relating to moveables, Scots law does not have a developed system of the acquisition of ownership by a possessor on the basis of positive prescription or *usucapio*.[89] The purpose of *usucapio*—to promote certainty by reducing the possibility of a claim against one who has maintained possession in a manner consistent with the right of ownership—is not achieved by the presumption of ownership which operates in favour of the possessor of a moveable. But, this said, there is probably not a strong case for a system of acquisitive prescription in respect of moveables.[90] Both as a matter of policy and on the basis of frequency of occurrence, the most important case of possession justifying a preference over the right of a claimant owner is that of the *bona fide* purchaser. But here also, Scots law tends to prefer the claimant able to establish his right of ownership.[91] This manifestation of the protection of possession will be dealt with as an exception to the owner's right to recover property in the hands of another.[92]

Distinction between original and derivative acquisition

The designation "original acquisition" applies to those circumstances **1.17** in which a title comes into being *de novo*, independent of any act of will on the part of the previous owner—if, indeed, the thing was subject to prior ownership. "Derivative acquisition," on the other hand, refers to the very familiar situation of the transmission of a right in a thing from a prior owner to the acquirer, occurring on the basis of an active concordance between the parties concerned. Given the obvious fact that proprietary rights are protected, it is to be expected that original acquisition is a limited concept: essentially restricted to the taking of unowned things and to certain exceptional cases in which the circumstances demand the recognition of a change of ownership.[93] An example of the latter is accession, whereby a subordinate, or accessory, and a principal item are joined to form a single proprietary

---

[89] Stair, II.xii.3 refers to the institutions of *usucapio* in respect of moveables and prescription in relation to immoveables of Roman law but, in a subsequent text (II.xii.11), states that "we have not these differences which we have shown were in the civil law." In fact the position as to the acquisitive prescription of moveables is inconclusive. See, generally, Scot. Law Com., Memo. No. 30, *Corporeal Moveables: Usucapion, or Acquisitive Prescription*, and below, paras. 7.02–7.03.

[90] See below, para. 7.01.

[91] See generally, Scot. Law Com. Memo. No. 27, *Corporeal Moveables: Protection of the Onerous Bona Fide Acquirer of Another's Property*.

[92] See below, paras. 10.15–10.22.

[93] Walker, *Principles*, III, p. 357, limits the concept to the case of "a moveable object not previously owned by another, as distinct from derivative acquisition from a previous owner." But the better view is that the distinction turns on whether or not ownership passes on the basis of an act of will of the prior owner. Ownership in an owned thing may pass to another through accession, and this is an instance of original rather than derivative acquisition because the new title arises from the circumstances of accession rather than by derivation from the prior owner.

unit with the logical consequence that the owner of the principal thing acquires what has been joined.[94]

Erskine[95] speaks of *occupatio*, or the taking of an unowned thing, as "the original method of acquiring property" but this is a reference to the historical evolution of systems of property rather than to the designation "original" as the antithesis of "derivative." In the same text, however, Erskine states the important distinction between acquisition through the proprietary circumstances and that following upon an act of will, at the same time distinguishing acquisitive prescription.

> "Occupation arises from a fact of the acquirer: accession, from the dependence or natural connection that the thing belonging to us hath with other things: and tradition, from the will of the former owner, joined with our acceptance of the thing delivered by him to us. By positive law, property may be transferred by prescription; but this last being also a way of losing property, falls to be explained under a separate title."[96]

Bell[97] uses the original/derivative distinction but sees original acquisition as either "the first effectual apprehension of a subject having no owner" or as "a natural, accidental, or intentional change, by which a new subject of property is produced." The notion of a new thing is usually applied to the case of *specificatio* where there must be a reallocation of rights because a new entity has come into being through the combination of previously separate items owned by different parties.[98] Where acquisition is on the basis of a subordinate thing merging with a principal item, there is not strictly a new thing because the identity of the principal item does not change.[99] This said, the essential point of the need for an adjustment of proprietary rights on account of a change that cannot otherwise be accommodated does emerge from Bell's definition.

Importance of the distinction

1.18   The original/derivative distinction is an aid to clarifying questions concerning the passing of ownership. Clearly, it may be of importance to determine whether ownership in a given item of property has passed. The rights of creditors may turn on this question. Moreover, the point in time at which ownership passed may be material: for

---

[94] See below, para. 3.01.
[95] II.i.9.
[96] *Ibid.*
[97] *Prin.*, § 1286.
[98] See below, para. 4.01.
[99] See below, para. 3.01.

example, in relation to the issue of risk. In questions of this nature it can only aid the inquiry if there is a clear understanding of the different bases upon which ownership passes. This point may be illustrated by an example. A receives B's solid fuel stove on the understanding that he will inform B within a week if he decides to buy. B does not hear from A within the time and proceeds to sell to C. When B takes steps to arrange for delivery to C it transpires that A has installed the stove in his kitchen. Has A become owner by accession— on the view that the stove is a "fixture"—regardless of the fact that A and B could probably not be said to have arrived at an agreement that ownership should pass? A problem such as this turns on the difference between acquisition by original means and the more usual derivative form.

CHAPTER 2

OCCUPATION

The concept of occupation

2.01 *Occupatio* is the taking of a thing, which is open to acquisition, with the intention to become owner of it. As Stair[1] points out, the recognition of a right acquired in this way may be contended for on the basis of natural law.

> "Property is introduced by possession of things, which are yet void and belong to none, and that without limitation. This is acknowledged by the law of nations, and their common consent, whence is that principle, *Quod nullius est, fit primi occupantis.*"

While the outward act is simply one of an assumption of physical control, the critical essentials are the availability of the thing for acquisition and the occupier's intention to make himself owner. Bell[2] gives a succinct definition: "Occupancy is the act of apprehending, with a purpose of appropriation, things which have no owner." Given that availability for acquisition must necessarily be a matter of ascertainable state the issue will most frequently centre on the physical and mental aspects of the claimant's taking of the thing. More specifically, whether the occupier obtained possession[3]—meaning, in this context, the requisite physical control by one who has the intention to hold the thing as owner.[4]

Occupation not applicable to previously-owned things

2.02 Scots law does not admit the full logic of *occupatio* in terms of a right to acquire any class of unowned thing by reduction to possession. Feudal concepts—the dominating source in respect of land law—have had some influence in relation to moveables,[5] in particular with regard

---

[1] II.i.33.

[2] *Prin.*, § 1287.

[3] As Erskine (II.i.9) notes, "by apprehending . . . or seizing . . . possession."

[4] See above, para. 1.13, n. 71.

[5] See Erskine, II.i.11. But the better view is that the sovereign's right to things normally owned but found ownerless does not follow from any narrow feudal rule based upon the notion of universal landlord, but rather upon the right of royal prerogative which justifies resort to the maxim *quod nullius est fit domini regis*. On this see the opinion of Lord Hunter in *L.A.* v. *University of Aberdeen and Budge*, 1963 S.C. 533 at pp. 542–545. For general observations on rights *inter regalia* in the context of the history of the feudal system, see *L.A.* v. *Balfour*, 1907 S.C. 1360.

18

to the limitation of the scope of acquisition by occupation to unowned things never previously subject to a right of ownership.[6] This result follows because the right to a thing vests in the Crown upon termination of the existing right in circumstances which would otherwise, in principle, leave it unowned and so open to acquisition.[7] The position is explained by Bell[8]:

"Things already appropriated, but lost, forgotton, or abandoned, fall under a different rule from that which regulates things that have never been appropriated. The rule is, '*quod nullius est fit domini regis.*' The principle on which this rests is public expediency, to avoid fraud, contests, and litigation, together with some slight purpose of adding to the public revenue."[9]

This rule has no application in respect of animals, birds or fish which are naturally wild. A wild creature returned to it natural free state cannot be distinguished from others of the same species never previously owned.[10] The primary purpose of the rule under consideration is to protect an owner's possibly extant right of ownership where the circumstances suggest that the thing concerned has been abandoned. It would be unworkable to give effect to this policy in relation to a wild animal which has regained its natural freedom and so terminated an existing right of ownership.

Bell, it should be noted, acknowledges the possibility of an element of compromise in the application of the rule favouring the Crown. In a passage concerned with the distinction between things never previously owned and things once subject to the right of ownership, he notes that in Scotland property is acquired by *occupatio* only in the former case:

---

[6] It seems that Erskine (II.i.12) recognised a distinction between valuable moveable property and other, not especially valuable things, from the point of view of the *rationale* for preferring the Crown. The former escheat on the same public benefit justification as applies to land; the latter, on the other hand, vest in the Crown on the basis of the wholly different justification of protecting the owner's right to recover.

[7] Bell, *Prin.*, § 1287, sees the choice as an equal one, but the better view is that it is only as a matter of policy that the Crown is preferred in the case of previously-owned things. Grotius' argument that the *fiscus* should be preferred in the case of treasure trove (*De Jure Belli ac Pacis*, II.viii.7) seems analogous.

[8] *Prin.*, § 1291.

[9] See McMillan, *Bona Vacantia*, p. 12: "In the case of *bona vacantia* the test of the public interest appears to be the commercial value of the thing. It is not in the public interest that all ownerless things should be taken into the possession of the Crown, irrespective of their value. If the thing is commercially valuable to the community the right will be exercised."

[10] See below, para. 2.05. One may also identify this difference in terms of the distinction between feudal and Roman law; see Smith, "The law relating to the treasure" in *St. Ninian's Isle and its Treasure* (1973), I, at p. 163: "The brocard *quod nullius est fit domini regis* represents the feudal outlook (in The broad sense of feudal), contrasting with the rule of the Civil or Roman law, *quod nullius est fit occupantis*, which latter certainly still applies in Scotland to the appropriation of wild animals."

"in the latter, the right goes to the Crown, and is generally given as a donation either to the finder or to another."[11] As the Scottish Law Commission noted, this statement only emphasises the Crown's entitlement in that another party acquires "not as a matter of right" but through donation.[12] The better view is that this should be seen from the point of view of the protection of an owner's interest in lost property. Modern statute law reflects this rationale in requiring the finder of lost property to deposit it with the police authority, who usually have a discretion to award the property to the finder if it is not claimed within a specified period.[13]

In respect of previously owned things it seems that Scots law does not readily infer an intention to abandon on the part of the owner from the circumstances in which a thing is left. But, this said, one must bear in mind that the law tends to favour the possessor of a moveable.[14]

Erskine[15] finds persuasive what he notes to be an English law distinction between strayed animals and inanimate things. Whereas, in the case of lost animals the owner's right terminated after a year[16]: "if the thing lost be inanimate, and so may be kept from perishing, with little or no inconvenience to the possessor, the property continues, by that law, with the owner, during all the years of prescription."

A reluctance to recognise the loss of the right of ownership through inference from the circumstances also emerges from the case of *Sands* v. *Bell and Balfour*,[17] where it was held that the Crown had no right to a parcel of flax which had lain in a public warehouse unclaimed for a period of 10 years. "It is quite clear that property cannot be lost by our law, in any shorter time than that of the negative prescription of 40 years; and till that time has expired, the natural and legal presumption is, that the owner will appear and claim them." One interpretation of this decision is that in the circumstances of the contract of deposit there is no need to question the continuation of an owner's interest.[18]

What authority there is on this question would appear to support McMillan's[19] statement that the Crown's prerogative right "in any particular case emerges as soon as it is apparent that an owner will not come forward."

---

[11] *Prin.*, § 1287.
[12] See Memo. No. 29, *Corporeal Moveables: Lost and Abandoned Property*, para. 3.
[13] See below, para. 2.08.
[14] See above, para. 1.12.
[15] II.i.12.
[16] Erskine notes that there is Scottish authority for this in *Quoniam Attachiamenta*, 48.14; see also Bankton, I.viii.4. As to the modern position concerning lost animals see below, para. 2.08.
[17] 22 May 1810, F.C.
[18] See McMillan, *Bona Vacantia*, p. 13, n. 2.
[19] *Idem*, p. 13.

Occupation applied to things not previously owned

Acquisition through taking, applied to things not previously owned, **2.03** is a concept of considerable scope, both from the point of view of the range of moveables covered and on the negative basis that the doctrine is subject to few limitations. In a passage from Erskine[20] both these points emerge:

"The doctrine of occupancy is also agreeable to the law of Scotland, in such moveable subjects—as have continued in their original state, and are presumed never to have had an owner,—whether animate or inanimate. Thus, pearls inclosed in shells, or pebbles cast on the shore, belong to the finder. Thus also we acquire the property of all wild beasts, fowls or fishes, as soon as we kill or apprehend them, whether upon our own grounds, or even those of another; for they can belong to no person, wherever they may be, while they retain their natural liberty; and consequently, must become the property of him who first seizes them."

The most usual application of *occupatio* is in relation to what may be termed wild-life; as Stair[21] notes, it applies to "all free creatures appropriated, as fowls of the air, wild beasts of the earth, fish of the sea." Given that the issue of ownership is likely to arise only in respect of things of worth or value to man, one can see that a primary field of acquisition by *occupatio* would be through hunting or fishing. It should be noted that the category of "wild-life" for the purposes of *occupatio* is, of course, limited to things which exist as independent entities of property. Wild fruits, flowers, trees and so on have no separate existence independent of the land on which they grow. By the principle of accession the right of ownership in such things falls to the heritable proprietor concerned.[22] In principle, when fruits or parts of growing things are detached they become, for the first time, independent items of property, as such not previously owned; but they remain accessory and so are not open to acquisition by *occupatio*. As Stair[23] puts it: "even the dung . . . followeth the property of that whereunto it is accessory."

Provided the essential requirements of the requisite taking of a thing open to acquisition are present, ownership passes to the occupier even though the activity concerned—usually hunting or fishing—is unlawful

---

[20] II.I.10.

[21] II.i.33. In *Livingstone* v. *E. Breadalbane* (1791) 3 Pat. 221 the House of Lord pronounced the following *obiter dictum* in upholding the argument of the respondent: "The animals which come under the description of game, being *ferae naturae*, are held in the law of Scotland, as in the Roman law, to be *res nullius*, and to belong to the occupier."

[22] See below, para. 3.04.

[23] II.i.34.

in the circumstances. *Occupatio* is applicable as a proprietary concept, and the taker's intention to make himself owner of a thing open to acquisition is effective regardless of the fact that the taking can be achieved only through an unlawful activity. Because "the right to take game is normally an incident of the ownership of land"[24] and because "game" is widely defined[25] the point is far from being a merely academic one. A poacher who has taken game in this way is entitled to legal restitution upon unauthorised seizure.[26] The Institutional writers are clear on the taker's entitlements; Erskine[27] for example:

> "The right of hunting, fowling, and fishing, is indeed restrained in many cases . . . But all game, though it should be caught in breach of these acts, or within another man's property, belongs, by the necessity of law, to him who hath seized it. The prohibition, therefore, in those statutes, can have no other effect than to inflict a fine on the trespasser, unless where the confiscation of what is caught makes a part of the statutory penalty."

Clearly, of course, a special statutory provision may override the common law, as Stair[28] notes, usually on the basis that the "positive law may make a part of the punishment to be the loss of what he hath taken." The need for such a provision only demonstrates the effectiveness of *occupatio*."[29]

An unowned wild animal, bird or fish in its natural state remains unowned, and so open to acquisition by the taker, even though conserved on private land. Although a landowner has the exclusive right to take game on his land[30] he only becomes owner of a particular item of game by specific appropriation—by reducing the animal, bird or fish to his possession. This said, a landowner may be able to make a general appropriation through some sufficient act of confinement of game within an area. But there can be no question of a charge of the

---

[24] Gordon, *Scottish Land Law*, para. 9.01.

[25] See *Colquhoun's Trs.* v. *Lee*, 1957 S.L.T.(Sh.Ct.) 50; Gordon, *Scottish Land Law*, paras. 9.02 and 9.03.

[26] See *Scott* v. *Everitt* (1853) 15 D. 288; see below, para. 10.12, n. 44. The landowner can of course protect his right by interdict; see, *e.g. Arthur* v. *Aird*, 1907 S.C. 1170.

[27] II.i.10. The point has been recognised in modern case law; see *Valentine* v. *Kennedy*, 1985 S.C.C.R. 89 *per* Sheriff Younger at p. 90: "a poacher accordingly owns his unlawful haul."

[28] II.i.33.

[29] Provision for the forfeiture of game unlawfully taken is to be found in various statutes dealing with poaching; *e.g.* the Poaching Prevention Act 1862, s.2. See generally, Gordon, *Criminal Law*, Chap. 52.

[30] See Erskine, II.vi.6: "the right of hunting, fowling, and fishing within one's own ground—naturally arises from one's property in the lands." Salmon fishing, however, is an exception, for at common law the right to fish for salmon was *inter regalia*—part of the feudal lord's right—and, as such, potentially property separate from the heritable subject concerned; see Stair, II.iii.69.

"theft" of a wild animal, bird or fish without specification as to the creature concerned having been first acquired by the complainant. This point is made by Lord Justice-Clerk Moncreiff in *Wilson* v. *Dykes*[31]: " '*Fit occupantis*,' is the brocard of the common law, and therefore an animal *ferae naturae* may be appropriated. But without specific appropriation a wild animal, although protected and preserved on private land, is not the property of any one."

In *Leith* v. *Leith*[32] Lord Curriehill explained that wild animals are neither part of the land (*partes soli*) nor accessories to it but—given their migratory habits—are, of necessity, *res nullius*. The learned judge went on to state—incorrectly, it is submitted—that as a consequence of this a landowner does not have an exclusive right to kill or capture wild animals. The true position, as indicated above, is that he does; but this point does not affect the conclusion, correctly stated by Lord Curriehill, that a wild animal is acquired by the taker: "The rule of law is *res nullius cedit occupanti*."[33]

Owned wild-life excluded

A wild creature already taken and reduced to sufficient physical **2.04** control is an owned thing and no longer open to acquisition by *occupatio* even though it remains wild. "The creatures are understood to be free while they are not within the power of any; but fishes within ponds are proper,[34] and fowls, though never so wild, while they are in custody."[35]

But the maintenance of active control is not necessary in relation to tamed wild-life in respect of which the taker's right of ownership remains intact provided the creature concerned does not revert to its natural wildness: "if they be tamed, contrary to their nature, are so long proper as their tameness remains."[36] Moreover, certain wild creatures, even though neither tamed nor confined by the taker, are retained on the basis that their instinct is to return to the taker's premises or property. The tendency to return—known as the *animus revertendi*—is a behavioural characteristic of certain species, notably bees and pigeons.[37]

---

[31] (1872) 10 M. 444 at p. 445. Of course, farmed deer or fish are owned and not open to acquisition. In a case concerned with rainbow trout it was noted that the principle involved is the same; see *Valentine* v. *Kennedy*, 1985 S.C.C.R. 89 *per* Sheriff Younger at p. 91: "There seems to me to be no difference in principle between an enclosure for wild animals such as deer and a water enclosure such as a stank for wild animals such as trout."

[32] (1862) 24 D. 1059.

[33] at p. 1077.

[34] See *Valentine* v. *Kennedy*, above at pp. 90–91.

[35] Stair, II.i.33; see also Erskine, II.i.10.

[36] *Ibid.*

[37] Stair, II.i.33.

Essentials of occupation

2.05   Assuming that the thing concerned is open to acquisition—in being
neither previously nor presently subject to the right of ownership—the
taker, intending to make himself owner, acquires on the basis of an act
giving him sufficient physical control in the circumstances. The *animus*
to acquire will normally be recognised as a matter of inference, but
more or less strongly depending upon the nature of the acts directed
towards obtaining physical control.

Decisions concerned with whale fishing are relevant to the problem
of the degree of physical control necessary. In the case of competing
claims to a whale the first harpooner was held to acquire provided that
he retained his hold of the fish until it was captured "although the
actual capture and killing of the whale may be accomplished by the
assistance of other persons."[38] The distinction is between an effective—
although not necessarily a final—act of seizure and a mere attempt to
bring the thing under physical control. Stair[39] explains:

> "So likewise, it is the first seizure that introduceth property, and
> not the first attempt and prosecution; as he who pursueth or
> woundeth a wild beast, a fowl or fish, is not thereby proprietor,
> unless he had brought it within his power, as if he had killed or
> wounded it to death, or otherwise given the effectual cause
> whereby it cannot use its native freedom."

Bell[40] contends for what must be the minimal sufficient physical
element, to constitute appropriation, in the taking and control of a
wild animal: "if one without wounding it, have an animal in pursuit,
and not beyond reach, another coming in and taking the animal does
not deprive the first of his right—the first being deemed the lawful
occupant." There must be some basis for a conclusion that the *corpus*
element is satisfied. Failing this one would be recognising acquisition
on the basis of the would-be taker's intention alone. In Bell's scenario
the active pursuit of a wild animal which is within reach is probably
just sufficient by way of a physical element.

Treasure

2.06   Scots law does not regulate rights to a find of treasure as a matter
distinguishable from lost or abandoned property in general.[41] Nor,
indeed, would this be logical: for if the law does not infer an intention

---

[38] *Aberdeen Arctic Co.* v. *Sutter* (1862) 4 Macq. 355, *per* Lord Chancellor Westbury at
p. 357.

[39] I.ii.33.

[40] *Prin.*, § 1289. *Cf.* Gordon, *Scottish Land Law*, para. 9.06.

[41] A distinction may be justified in systems which allow the finder of apparently
unowned property to acquire by *occupatio* where the circumstances support the
inference of an intention to abandon; in the case of concealed treasure such an intention
cannot be inferred.

to abandon in relation to property normally owned but found in circumstances consistent with abandonment,[42] it could hardly do so in respect of concealed treasure where the primary inference would be an intention to preserve rights.[43] Accordingly, the Institutional authorities are clear that the brocard *quod nullius fit domini regis* applies to a find of treasure. "So with us, treasures hid in the earth, whose proper owners cannot be known, are not his in whose ground they are found, nor the finder's, but belong to the King."[44] Erskine[45] draws attention to the difference between Scots and Roman law: "Hence, by our law, treasures hid under ground belong neither to the finder nor to the owner of the ground, as they did by the Roman . . . but to the king as escheat."

In the leading case of *Lord Advocate* v. *University of Aberdeen and Budge*[46] the Lord Ordinary, Lord Hunter, identified the right to treasure as "a right belonging to the sovereign by virtue of his royal prerogative and as head of a national community rather than by virtue of his position as universal landlord." In the Inner House Lord Mackintosh's opinion is to like effect:

> "This claim is based on the Crown's right as sovereign and like the Crown's right of *ultimus haeres* has nothing to do with the overlordship of the land . . . the law of treasure is concerned with moveable property and is not an incident of land tenure but is just a specialised instance of the rule *quod nullius est fit domini regis*."[47]

The identification of the Crown's entitlement as a matter of prerogative rather than an incident of feudal overlordship was important because the University of Aberdeen, as finder of valuable antiquities on St. Ninian's Isle in Shetland, claimed that the maxim *quod nullius*

---

[42] See Erskine, II.i.12: "The above rule for the Crown is also received . . . in that sort of moveable subjects which are presumed to have once had a proprietor, who is now unknown." See also above, para. 2.03.

[43] Hence, as Stair (III.iii.27) puts it: "treasures in the ground, whose owner appeareth not, are confiscated as caduciary, whereby the owners are presumed to relinquish, or lose the same." In *L.A.* v. *University of Aberdeen and Budge*, 1963 S.C. 533 at pp. 559–560, Lord Mackintosh rejected any contention that "in order to be treasure, the articles must have been deliberately hidden." Rather, in Lord Mackintosh's view, the epithet "hidden" referring to treasure, "means no more than 'concealed' and refers to the state or condition in which the goods or articles are found by the finder and does not refer back to the intention which the owner of the goods may have had in hiding them in the ground or putting them away in some other place."

[44] Stair, II.i.5. See also Bankton, I.iii.14–16; I.viii.9; II.i.8.

[45] II.i.12. See also *Cleghorn & Bryce* v. *Baird* (1696) Mor. 13522, where the court declined to apply the Civilian rule of equal division between finder and landowner: "But with us, treasure and all such things which are *nullius, non cedant occupanti*, but are the King's, and belong to the Fisk."

[46] 1963 S.C. 533 at p. 543.

[47] at p. 561.

est fit domini regis—a principle of feudal law—did not apply given that the lands in question were udal.[48]

The now trite position is that the principle *quod nullius est fit domini regis* applies to treasure as well as to any other moveables, apparently unowned but necessarily owned at some stage in the past. Given this, there would seem to be little point in the identification of treasure trove as a separate head of acquisition of ownership and, of course, this means that there is hardly any point in defining treasure as precious items found concealed in the ground or in the fabric of buildings.[49] Lord Hunter seems to have recognised this in his opinion as Lord Ordinary in the leading case.[50]

Lost and abandoned property under the common law

2.07　As shown[51] there is no possibility in Scots common law of acquisition by the finder of apparently unowned property on the basis of an inferred intention to abandon attributed to the owner. Given the presumption that the possessor of a moveable is owner[52] one can see that the law could not readily allow the assumption of possession by a finder, chance or otherwise.[53] The position of the Crown as residual owner may be seen to protect against this[54] and, as a matter of policy, it would seem to be preferable to give emphasis to the protection of the interest of an owner of lost property.

But it is academic to look at the common law in isolation, because the problem of lost and abandoned property is dealt with in legislation.[55] Superseding most prior statutes, the matter is now dealt with in the Civic Government (Scotland) Act 1982, Pt. VI—hereafter "the Act."[56]

Lost and abandoned property under the Act

2.08　Section 73 of the Act adopts the common law exclusion of acquisition by a finder:

---

[48] See generally, Small, Thomas and Wilson, *St. Ninian's Isle and its Treasure* (2 Vols., 1973), and esp. Smith, "The law relating to the treasure" (II, 149).

[49] See *Cleghorn & Bryce* v. *Baird* (1696) Mor. 13522, where it was held that recent coin is not treasure.

[50] *L.A.* v. *University of Aberdeen and Budge*, 1963 S.C. 533 at pp. 549–550.

[51] Above, para. 2.02.

[52] See above, para. 1.12.

[53] In so far as a finder cannot claim to be owner, his possession would be protected only against an immediate unlawful dispossessor; see below, para. 10.25.

[54] See above, para. 2.02.

[55] Scot. Law Com. Memo. No. 29, *Corporeal Moveables: Lost and Abandoned Property*, para. 5, has pointed out that statutory provisions have not been harmonised with the common law. But the notion of the Crown's interest being abrogated by legislation providing for the possible award of lost property to its finder—urged in para. 5—is open to question if the Crown's rôle is seen as being primarily to provide interim protection to the owner.

[56] In *Fleming* v. *Chief Constable of Strathclyde*, 1987 S.C.L.R. 303 at p. 307, Sheriff Principal Gillies held that Pt. VI of the 1982 Act applied only to "lost and found property" and did not cover "property taken by the police in the course of a criminal investigation."

"No person who—

(*a*) finds any property appearing to have been lost or abandoned;

(*b*) is the employer of a finder of such property; or

(*c*) owns or occupies the land or premises on which such property is found,

shall by reason only of the finding of that property have any right to claim ownership of it."

The meaning of "finder" is given in section 67[57] as: "any person taking possession of any property without the authority of the owner in circumstances which make it reasonable to infer that the property has been lost or abandoned." It is significant that the finder does not acquire even if the circumstances are consistent with abandonment. This, of course, is in keeping with the common law and necessary in terms of the object of the legislation to provide comprehensive regulation of the legal consequences of a find of owned or previously owned property.

Some exclusions from the system of the Act are provided for in section 67(2) on the basis of the retention of other provisions, governing either certain types of property or property found in particular places. The former category includes abandoned motor vehicles "whose removal is provided for by or under any enactment other than this Act"[58] and stray dogs which continue to be provided for by sections 3 and 4 of the Dogs Act 1906.[59] The latter category includes property found on British Railways Board premises, vehicles, trains or vessels,[60] and items found on any other public transport service premises or means of conveyance if provision is made for lost or abandoned property in any enactment other than the Act.[61]

Section 67 provides that the finder of apparently lost or abandoned property must "take reasonable care of it" and "without unreasonable delay deliver the property or report the fact that he has taken possession of it" to a constable, or to any of various specified persons,[62]

---

[57] s.79, the interpretation section, states that the meaning of "finder" is that given by s.67.

[58] s.67(2)(*c*). See s.14 of the Airports Authority Act 1975 and s.3 of the Refuse Disposal (Amenity) Act 1978.

[59] s.67(2)(*d*). Note that s.75 amends ss.3 and 4 of the Dogs Act 1906. See also the Animals (Scotland) Act 1987, s.3(1) and (2) and the Roads (Scotland) Act 1984, s.98, regarding the power of a road authority or constable to detain any animal straying on the road.

[60] s.67(2)(*b*).

[61] s.67(2)(*a*).

[62] s.67(3) refers to: "(*a*) the owner of the property; (*b*) the person having right to possession of it; (*c*) if the property has been found on land or premises, the owner or occupier thereof; (*d*) any person apparently having the authority to act on behalf of any of those persons." This subsection should be read with s.67(4) which provides for the duty of a person who takes possession of property or receives a report about its finding. The basic obligation is to restore the owner or the party with a right to possession, or report the matter to the police.

giving "a description of the property and information as to where it was found."[63]

Section 68 sets out the procedure to be followed by a chief constable[64] where property has been delivered, or a find reported, to the police, or in the case of property found by a constable.[65] First, he must "make such arrangements as he considers appropriate for the care and custody of the property."[66] Secondly, he must take reasonable steps to ascertain the identity of the owner, or the person entitled to possession.[67] After the expiry of two months from the date of delivery or reporting, the chief constable may, "having regard to the whole circumstances including the nature and value of the property and the actings of the finder"[68] offer the property to the finder[69] or sell it. If, in the opinion of the chief constable, it is deemed inappropriate to offer the property to the finder and impracticable to sell it, he may "dispose of it or make arrangements for its disposal otherwise as he thinks fit."[70] Subject to one exception, within the two-month period the chief constable may only act by returning the property to the owner or the person entitled to possession.[71] The only situation in which earlier disposal is allowed is where "the property cannot, in the opinion of the chief constable, be safely or conveniently kept"[72] for the two-month period.

The consequences, in terms of property rights, arising from the disposal of an item under sections 68 or 70 of the Act are provided for in section 71. The basic position is that disposal in terms of the Act, to a person taking in good faith, shall "vest the ownership of the property in that person."[73] But where property is disposed of otherwise than for value—i.e. given to the finder[74]: "any person who was immediately before the disposal the owner . . . shall be entitled within the period of one year after the date of the disposal to recover possession of the property as owner."[75]

---

[63] s.67(1).

[64] Defined in s.79 as "the chief constable for the police area in which the lost or abandoned property is found and includes a constable acting under his direction."

[65] It seems that the legislature intended a find of apparently lost or abandoned property by the police to be regulated under the system of the Act, but on this see the comment of "M.C." on the case of *Fleming* v. *Chief Constable of Strathclyde*, 1987 S.C.L.R. 303 at pp. 308–309.

[66] s.68(2).

[67] s.68(3).

[68] s.68(4).

[69] The chief constable is specifically empowered to do this in terms of s.70(1)(*b*).

[70] s.68(4).

[71] The functions of the chief constable in respect of claims by the owner or person entitled to possession are provided for in s.69.

[72] s.68(5).

[73] s.71(1); s.76 makes provision for appeals to the sheriff by a claimant to ownership (s.69), a finder (s.70) or a prior owner (s.72) against any decision of the chief constable.

[74] s.70(1)(*b*).

[75] s.71(2). The finality of this is indicated by s.72 providing for a previous owner's (limited) right to claim compensation.

Section 74 makes special provision for the acquisition of "any living creature"—other than a stray dog[76] or livestock.[77] Where the finder, at his request, has been given care and custody,[78] and the creature has continued to be in his care and custody unclaimed for a period of two months, he "shall at the end of that period become the owner of that creature."

---

[76] See above, n. 59.

[77] Livestock is defined in s.129 as "cattle, horses, asses, mules, hinnies, sheep, pigs, goats and poultry (which means the domestic varieties of fowls, turkeys, geese, ducks, guinea fowls, pigeons and quails), deer not in a wild state and while in captivity, pheasants, partridges and grouse."

[78] Under s.68(2).

CHAPTER 3

ACCESSION

GENERAL MATTERS

The concept of accession

3.01   Stair,[1] in a title concerned with ownership and possession, treats accession as one of a number of disparate forms of acquisition based upon natural law. As he shows,[2] the concept of the "accretion of parts" is applicable to a variety of circumstances involving a connecting factor sufficient to justify proprietary consequences. Stair is primarily concerned with the nature, and place in the scheme of things, of accession as an original mode of acquisition—an instance of "the law of rational nature."[3] Erskine,[4] paying more attention to what accession involves, defines the concept with close precision:

> "Property may be acquired not only by occupancy, but accession; by which, in two things which have an intimate connection with or dependence upon one another, the property of the principal thing draws after it that of its accessory; for whatever proceeds or ariseth from what is mine is also mine as being part of my property."

Erskine[5] puts accession and occupation together as forms of natural acquisition, by implication "original" in that, in principle, neither depends upon "the dispositive will of the owner,"[6] the essential feature

---

[1] II.i.34.

[2] *Ibid.*

[3] Stair, III.ii.3. That accession operates as a matter of consequence from the circumstances—in principle regardless of the will of the annexor—makes it an original mode of acquisition. Stair (III.i.39), states that a picture painted on a wall "doth necessarily cede to the ground": the word "necessarily" showing that the proprietary consequence is not open to control. (See below, para. 3.21.) The same point has been made in modern case law. See *Scottish Discount Co. Ltd.* v. *Blin*, 1985 S.C. 216, *per* Lord Cameron at p. 240: "parties by private agreement cannot change the legal character of what the law regards and holds to be heritable"; see also *Shetland Islands Council* v. *B.P. Petroleum Development*, 1990 S.L.T. 82, *per* Lord Cullen at p. 94: "a contractual arrangement between owner and occupier is ineffective to prevent what is annexed to heritage being treated as such." See also Gretton and Reid, "Romalpa clauses: the current position," 1985 S.L.T. (News) 329 at p. 333; Carey Miller, "Logical Consistency in Property," 1990 S.L.T. (News) 197 at p. 198.

[4] II.i.14.

[5] II. i. 9.

[6] Stair, III.ii.3.

of acquisition on a derivative basis.[7] But the important notion recognised in Erskine's definition is the proprietary consequence of the right of ownership in the accessory thing following that of the principal item, either on the basis of connection or dependence. Bell[8] refers to the same core feature: "the rule is '*accessorium sequitur principale*'; *i.e.* of two things having intimate connection, the property of the principal draws after it that of the accessory."

The reverse process of the separation of connected elements may also have proprietary consequences, if not through the very act of separation—as in certain instances of the acquisition of fruits[9]—then at least by making the removed part open to acquisition as an independent item of property.[10]

Instances of accession as a wide notion

The writers distinguish natural and industrial or artificial accession: **3.02** the former covers "that increase or augmentation which proceeds from the production of fruits, natural or industrial; or from the propagation of animals"[11]; the latter is concerned with various forms involving human activity in a primary rôle.[12] While these generalisations may be conceptually valid they are predicated upon a wide notion of accession—one which can be reduced to a number of distinguishable concepts.

First, one may distinguish accession concerned with animal or vegetable fruits from that involving the coming together of two things with the result that, from the point of view of property, the accessory item is subsumed under the identity of the principal element. In the case of fruits the parent and the fruit or progeny elements must eventually be separated and then become distinct items of property open to ownership by different parties. Although the accessory and principal factor is present in respect of fruits, and may be relevant to the rules governing the determination of rights, the case is clearly distinct from the notion of the owner of a principal item acquiring a right over an attached or dependent accessory. On this basis "fruits" will be dealt with separately in Chapter 6—a departure from the traditional approach of Scots law but, it would seem, justifiable in terms of both dogmatics and presentation. This said, there are some troublesome borderline instances involving the accessory/principal relationship; for example, the problem of mussel-scalps, the mussel being a virtually immobile mollusc which attaches itself to the sea-

[7] See above, para. 1.17.
[8] *Prin.*, § 1298.
[9] See below para. 6.01.
[10] See, *e.g. Bruce* v. *Erskine* (1707) Mor. 14092, concerning the difference between "stones lying in the craig unwroght" and those "separated from the bowels of the earth."
[11] Bell, *Prin.*, § 1297.
[12] Erskine, II.i.15; Bell, *Prin.*, § 1298.

shore with such "peculiar tenacity"[13] as to be regarded as *partes soli* on an analogy to plants.[14] In this case the issue is whether entitlement should be based upon the notion of accessory fruits or occupation.[15]

With regard to the so-called category of industrial fruits certain of the forms referred to by the authorities may each be justified on a more appropriate basis than accession. Although the bringing together of two or more elements is often involved the essential feature of accessory and principal is not always present. Specification[16] is concerned with the coming into being of a new entity of property to which the maker may be entitled regardless of the position as to proprietary rights in the constituents. The irreversible mixing of different substances belonging to two or more parties—*confusio* in the case of liquids, *commixtio* applied to solids[17]—necessitates a reallocation of rights and the principle of accession is only applicable where the constitutents can be identified as accessory and principal elements. Although there may be borderline overlap between accession, specification and *confusio/commixtio* it is often possible to recognise the distinct rôle of a particular concept[18] and, of course, this may give a distinct result.[19]

Subjects to be dealt with under accession

3.03   Limited to the circumstances of an accessory item falling to the owner of a principal thing to which it is annexed or attached with sufficient finality, or on the basis of its natural destination, one may identify a number of distinct instances of accession. The Institutional writers[20] mention *alluvio* and *avulsio*—involving the action of water upon land—but these are cases of the "addition of land to land from natural causes"[21] and are essentially concerned with heritable property.

As indicated above, the natural produce of the land, the progeny of animals, and interest on capital, all fall to be dealt with as "fruits" in so far as one is concerned with the rights to an item of property

---

[13] *Duchess of Sutherland* v. *Watson* (1868) 6 M. 199, *per* Lord Neaves at p. 213.

[14] *Lindsay* v. *Robertson* (1867) 5 M. 864 at p. 868; *Duchess of Sutherland* v. *Watson* (1868) 6 M. 199 at p. 213. But see *Parker* v. *Lord Advocate* (1902) 4 F. 698 at pp. 710–711, where the contention that mussels are *partes soli* was questioned by Lord President Kinross who preferred the view mussel-fishings constitute a separate feudal estate. In the House of Lords, [1904] A.C. 364, this issue was not taken any further.

[15] On the relationship between accession and fruits see also below, para. 6.01; regarding occupation see above, paras. 2.02–2.03.

[16] Stair, II.i.41; Erskine, II.i.16; Bell, *Prin.*, § 1298. See below, para. 4.01.

[17] Stair, II.i.36, 37; Erskine, II.i.17; Bell, *Prin.*, § 1298. See below, para. 5.01.

[18] See, *e.g.* *Bruce* v. *Erskine* (1707) Mor. 14092, where a distinction was recognised between the coming into being of a moveable in the quarrying of stone and the possible creation of a wholly new entity (specification) through work on the stone to make it suitable for ashlar masonry.

[19] For a possible example of this see Carey Miller, "Logical consistency in property," 1990 S.L.T. (News) 197 at pp. 198–199.

[20] Stair, II.i.35; Erskine, II.i.14.

[21] Rankine, *Landownership*, p. 112.

separated from its parent entity. But this said, the process of acquisition by a heritable proprietor of all which grows on his land is a matter of accession.[22] The authorities[23] also refer to the rule that heritable structures and things, which through affixation or destination attach to such structures,[24] are all accessory to the land. This form of accession—to which the label "fixtures" may be applied[25]—concerns heritable property from the point of view of what a given parcel of land includes.[26] But, of course, from another point of view these are instances of the acquisition of a moveable by the owner of land, and on this basis they fall to be dealt with in the present chapter. Finally, there is the wide category of the accession of one moveable thing to another, principal, moveable item.

Accordingly, accession will be dealt with under three main headings: growing things; fixtures and accession to moveables.

GROWING THINGS

Basis of accession in case of growing things

Growing things are, in principle, accessory to the land: "trees and all **3.04** plants, as the birth of the earth, are carried therewith."[27] One may justify this conclusion on the basis of the first criterion of accession recognised by Bell[28]: "of two substances, one of which can exist separately, the other not, the former is the principal." Both a seed and a potted plant are things with exist as independent items of property.[29] But, in either case, planting out will normally lead to accession to the soil in that neither seedling nor plant can exist independent of the soil. In this case the requirement of connection or dependence is unquestionably present in that the survival of the plant as a growing thing is dependent upon its continuing relationship with the soil.

Subject to an important limitation[30] the law recognises that growing things are *partes soli*: "Trees, shrubs, and all fruits whatever, which spring from the earth, belong to the owner of the field which produced them."[31]

---

[22] Stair, II.i.34; Erskine, II.i.14.
[23] Stair, II.i.40; Erskine, II.i.15.
[24] See Stair, II.i.38.
[25] See the definition of Lord Chelmsford in *Brand's Trs.* v. *Brand's Trs.* (1876) 3 R.(H.L.) 16 at p. 23. See Reid, "The Lord Chancellor's fixtures: *Brand's Trs.* v. *Brand's Trs.* re-examined" (1983) 28 J.L.S. 49.
[26] Hence the treatment of the topic in works such as Rankine, *Landownership*, pp. 116–133; Halliday, *Conveyancing*, II, pp. 23–26 and Gordon, *Scottish Land Law*, paras. 5.01–5.44.
[27] Stair, II.i.34.
[28] *Prin.*, § 1298.
[29] Stair, II.i.34: "if separated or contained in moveable boxes, they are not so carried with the ground."
[30] See below, para. 3.05.
[31] Erskine, II.i.14.

Annual cultivated crops excepted

3.05   A far-reaching restriction upon the consequences of the accession of growing things to land is recognised in the Institutional writings. While the principle applies to "the natural fruits of the ground,"[32] Stair qualifies his statement by pointing out that it does not extend to cultivated crops. "But by our custom, corns and industrial fruits are esteemed as distinct moveables, even before they are separated or ripe."[33] This is the basis of the maxim *messis sementem sequitur*—the harvest goes to the sower. More accurately, "if the crop was sown in *bona fide*, then the general rule *messis sementem sequitur* applies."[34]

Erskine[35] explains:

> "This rule, if understood without limitation, would comprehend all the fruits of the earth not yet separated from the ground (called by the Romans *pendentes*), because they continue *partes soli* until separation; but it is, by our usage, restricted to such of that kind as grow annually, for a tract of years together, without repeated culture or industry, as natural grass not yet cut, or fruits not yet plucked from the tree. For those annual fruits which require yearly seed and industry, as wheat, barley, etc., are accounted moveable even before separation, from the moment they are sown or planted . . . because the seed, and labour in preparing the ground, cannot be said to be employed on the lands for their perpetual use, but for the immediate profit of the possessor."

The justification for distinguishing annual cultivated crops as moveables is plausible: an exception to the principle of accession is seen as appropriate in the case of a claim by one who has put money and effort into the land for the purpose of a short-term benefit.[36] In the case of annual crops the dominating factor is the use of the land for a temporary purpose rather than any notion of permanent or long-term improvement. This distinction emerges from a dictum of Lord Medwyn in *Paul* v. *Cuthbertson*[37]: "It is an exception from this fundamental rule, that industrial fruits which are intended for the immediate profit of the proprietor, and not for the use of the ground, are accounted moveable even before separation."

---

[32] Stair, II.i.34. See also II.i.2.

[33] *Ibid.*

[34] *Swanson* v. *Grieve* (1891) 18 R. 371, *per* Lord Adam at p. 375. Regarding the general basis of a *bona fide* possessor's right to fruits see below, para. 6.04.

[35] II.ii.4.

[36] See Bell, *Prin.*, § 1473: "These go with the property of the seed and labour, as manufactures, in which the productive powers of the soil are employed." See also Gordon, *Scottish Land Law*, para. 5.38: "because they are a product of cultivation as well as of the land, and only temporarily in place in the soil."

[37] (1840) 2 D. 1286 at p. 1314.

Of course, the question of entitlement to the harvest may depend upon the relationship between the planter and the heritable proprietor, but in treating crops as moveables the law does not limit the right of the former pending separation. What is significant is that the *bona fide* producer is favoured as owner regardless of his actual standing in relation to the land. This is shown in a case[38] in which a tenant, disputing a claim to land under the Crofters Holdings (Scotland) Act 1886, sowed crops but had not yet reaped them when a decree of ejection was obtained against him; on the disputed question of entitlement to the harvest Lord President Inglis observed:

> "The Lord Ordinary has accordingly held, and I think rightly, that the crop raised during the interval caused by the litigation . . . cannot belong to the crofters. They did not sow it, nor did they labour the ground, and they had no concern with any part of the work necessary to produce the crop."

The better view is that, in modern law, a hay crop is an industrial fruit: but this would extend only to the first season's cut[39]; thereafter the annual crop of grass from the initial sowing would be a natural fruit—acceding to the soil—with a party other than the heritable proprietor only capable of acquiring the harvested crop. There is, however, authority supporting the extension of moveable status to the second summer after sowing in certain special circumstances. This applies where grass is sown with an annual crop, the intention being to harvest the "white" crop, in the normal way, in the year of sowing, and to cut the undersown grass the following summer.[40]

Trees distinguishable

In *Paul* v. *Cuthbertson*[41] the court distinguished trees from the **3.06** special case of cultivated crops.[42] Trees "while attached to and unseparated from the ground are reckoned *partes soli*" and, "like every thing else connected with and attached to the ground, belong to the proprietor of the ground as an accessory."[43]

Nursery trees, however, intended for planting out, are an exception; the better view is that in any question between the cultivating tenant

---

[38] *Swanson* v. *Grieve* (1891) 18 R. 371 at p. 375.

[39] *Marquis of Tweeddale* v. *Somner*, 19 Nov. 1816, F.C., *per* Lord Balgray: "Previous to 1730, hay was natural grass; therefore, if not cut, it passed to the landlord, like the apples on the trees. But now it is an industrial crop; although, if you let the seeds remain in the ground, it becomes again a natural crop." See also *Keith* v. *Logie's Heirs* (1825) 4 S. 267, *per* Lord Alloway at p. 270: "The first crop of hay from sown grass is as much an industrial crop as oats or barley."

[40] See *Lyall* v. *Cooper* (1832) 11 S. 96 at p. 102.

[41] (1840) 2 D. 1286.

[42] See above, para. 3.05, n. 37.

[43] *per* Lord Medwyn at p. 1314.

and the landowner nursery trees should be considered moveable as "truly part of the nurseryman's stock-in-trade."[44] But the case law makes clear that this exception is limited to the circumstances of the occupier of land operating a nursery business—the situation of "plants grown for sale in a nursery garden."[45] A dictum of Lord Deas in *Syme* v. *Harvey*[46] reflects this:

> "Such plants and trees could not be removed by the tenant of subjects occupied as a private mansion house and garden, although he had originally planted them himself. This shows that there is a marked and important distinction between the case of a tenant following out his trade, and the case of a tenant occupying with no such object."

The exception in respect of nursery stock should not be regarded as analogous to annual crops; this would be neither factually accurate[47] nor would it reflect the true rationale for the exception. Annual crops must be harvested in the short term and are properly thought of as the property of the party in occupation regardless of the question of ownership of the land. Nursery stock, while intended for removal at some stage, may be destined for planting out elsewhere in the same heritable unit and would, on this basis, be heritable *destinatione*.[48] But in the limited context of a nursery business the nursery stock remains moveable because it is intended for eventual removal elsewhere.

Given that it may not be apparent from the nature of the plants that nursery stock is intended for removal, it is important that the exception be limited to the context of an operative nursery business. If not restricted to the objectively apparent condition of a trading nursery the exception could be unfair to one acquiring an interest in the heritage and relying upon the inclusion of young trees and shrubs which would, in usual circumstances, be heritable by accession.[49]

Law as stated not put into question by contrary dicta

3.07   In the case of *Chalmer's Tr.* v. *Dick's Tr.*[50] the Lord Ordinary (Johnston), in an *obiter dictum*, confirmed by the Second Division, gave a somewhat different version of the law from the established one.

---

[44] Nicholson's note (b) to Erskine, II.ii.4.

[45] Gordon, *Scottish Land Law*, para. 5.39.

[46] (1861) 24 D. 202 at p. 214.

[47] As Lord Deas pointed out in *Syme* v. *Harvey* (1861) 24 D. 202 at p. 214, although nursery stock may be said to be the tenant's crop "they are certainly not an annual, not even a biennial crop. Young fruit-trees do not become saleable in a season; and the most valuable evergreens and ornamental trees and shrubs are those which have been in the nursery for several years."

[48] See *Gordon* v. *Gordon*, Dec. 2, 1806, Hume 188 at p. 189.

[49] See, *e.g. Begbie* v. *Boyd* (1837) 16 S. 232.

[50] 1909 S.C. 761.

While accepting the general rule that one who sows a crop is entitled to reap it, the view taken was that Erskine,[51] correctly interpreted, did not lay down that a crop is moveable pending separation but, rather, that it is *pars soli* "but the law recognises the right of the tenant who has sown it, to separate it from the soil, unless he contracted not to do so."[52] On this basis the heritable proprietor, and those claiming through him, would be primarily entitled with the sower of the crop having to establish his right to reap in the circumstances. Clearly, where a dispute arises pending harvest of the crop this interpretation favours the creditors of a bankrupt proprietor on the basis that the crop accedes to the land and vests in the bankrupt's trustee.

In *Morison* v. *A. & D. F. Lockhart*[53] Lord Kinnear, not mentioning the above, confirmed the law as stated in *Paul* v. *Cuthbertson*[54]:

> "that while ordinary industrial crops which are sold and consumed from year to year are moveable before separation, trees which are intended to be parts of the ground for generations, and part of the soil, cannot be conveyed so long as they are still growing, excepting as part of the land, however effectively they may be sold and delivered when they are cut down and turned into corporeal moveables."

In *McKinley* v. *Hutchison's Tr.*[55] Lord Hunter pointed out that the statements in *Chalmer's Tr.*[56] were *obiter*: "With reference to these expressions of opinion I do not desire to say anything one way or the other; certainly I am not to be held as concurring with these views."[57] The better view would appear to be that a growing crop is moveable and, of course, this has implications going far beyond a tenant's right to reap.[58]

Consequences of recognition of growing things as moveable or heritable

The recognition of a right to a certain category of growing things as **3.08** moveables means, of course, that one party may own the land and another the standing crop. This facilitates any dealing with the crop as an item separate from the land, and severance is not a prerequisite to the transfer of property to a purchaser,[59] whether at common law[60] or

---

[51] II.ii.4.

[52] *Chalmer's Tr.* v. *Dick's Tr.* 1909 S.C. 761 *per* Lord Low at p. 769.

[53] 1912 S.C. 1017 at p. 1028.

[54] (1840) 2 D. 1286.

[55] 1935 S.L.T. 62 at p. 64.

[56] 1909 S.C. 761.

[57] Cf. *Trinity House of Leith* v. *Mitchell & Rae Ltd.*, 1957 S.L.T. (Sh.Ct.) 38 at p. 40, preferring the approach in *Chalmer's Tr.* v. *Dick's Tr.*, 1909 S.C. 761.

[58] See below, para. 3.08. See generally Gordon, *Scottish Land Law*, para. 5.39.

[59] See *Kennedy's Tr.* v. *Hamilton & Manson* (1897) 25 R. 252, *per* Lord Trayner at p. 259: "I think it proved that the contract between the defenders and Kennedy was a contract of sale of Kennedy's crop of hay; that it was the intention of parties that the property should pass on the contract being completed, and that therefore the property in the hay was in the defenders at the time they removed it from Kennedy's premises."

[60] See below, para. 8.17.

under the Sale of Goods Act 1979.[61] Moreover, the owner of the crop will not be affected by claims against the land which might otherwise be prejudicial to his position. The recognition of a cultivated annual crop as moveable property protects the position of one with a limited or temporary interest in the land concerned—typically a tenant. Clearly, this is especially justifiable when the interest includes the right to cultivate the land. Indeed, it is arguably correct that it should be open to one who cultivated on the basis of no more than an honest belief in his right to the land to claim the crop as moveable property.[62] Were it not for the exception a party growing an annual crop would be subject to the consequences of accession which probably means that improvements through horticulture vest in the landowner, as in *Burns* v. *Fleming*[63] where the court denied a tenant, vacating the subjects let, the right to remove shrubs and turf which he had planted.

Because of the ensuing potential for the recognition of a right of property in a party other than the heritable proprietor important consequences can follow from the designation of a standing crop as moveable. As corporeal moveable property which can be sold by auction for behoof of a creditor,[64] a growing crop is subject to the diligence of personal poinding.[65] Moreover, a heritable creditor will not have a preferential claim against the trustee of a sequestrated crop producer—typically a tenant of the land.[66] A testamentary trustee must yield to the trustee in bankruptcy of the tenant in respect of the proceeds of a crop cultivated by the tenant.[67]

---

[61] See below, para. 9.07.

[62] See *Trinity House of Leith* v. *Mitchell & Rae Ltd.*, 1957 S.L.T. (Sh.Ct.) 38 *per* Sheriff-Substitute Walker at p. 39: "Lord Trayner in his *Latin Maxims* gives as an example of the working of the maxim [*messis sementem sequitur*] the case of a man who mistakenly, but with good reason, believes himself to be the owner of land on which he sows a crop. His *bona fides* saves him. But I do not think a man who sows on ground which he knows has been claimed by his creditor is in the same position."

[63] (1880) 8 R. 226.

[64] See Gloag and Henderson, para. 48.16.

[65] See Erskine, III.vi.22: "Growing corns may be poinded; for they are truly moveable: and their prices and quantities are as capable of being fixed before their separation from the ground as after it." In *Elders* v. *Allen* 1833 11 S. 902 at pp. 905–906 the competence of poinding a crop was not in doubt but the issue was whether this could be done when the crop was in braird—*i.e.* when only the first shoots had appeared. It was held that there could be no poinding at this early stage because "goods can only be poinded when we can lay hold of the *ipsa corpora* to be sold" (*per* Lord Meadowbank at p. 905) and subject it to valuation. Lord Justice-Clerk Boyle observed (at p. 905) *obiter*, that poinding of wheat would probably be competent in June when "an estimation of the value might have been made pretty near." Of course, poinding by a tenant's creditor is only competent when the tenant is owner of the (moveable) crop; see *Dun* v. *Johnston* (1818) Hume 451 at p. 452 where the question of ownership was in dispute. See also Maher and Cusine, *Diligence*, para. 7.28.

[66] See *Lovett's Trs.* v. *Wilson* (1896) 3 S.L.T. 224; 275, *per* Lord Stormonth Darling (at p. 224): "It seems clear that the growing crops as well as other moveable effects on the farm, passed to the trustee at the date of sequestration, and that the pursuers [heritable creditors] have not averred any lawful possession which could compete with his." See also *Hart* v. *Baird* (1897) 5 S.L.T. 172 *per* Lord Kincairney at p. 173: "I think it cannot be doubted that the crop . . . formed part of the tenant's estate."

[67] See *Murray's Tr.* v. *Graham* (1889) 26 S.L.R. 762 at p. 764.

FIXTURES

Accession to land dominating concept

Stair[68] refers to the constitution of property "by necessary conjunc- **3.09**
tion in construction . . . whereby a beam or any other material built
into a house, becomes proper to the owner of the house or building."
But the accession of a component to a building means accession to the
land on which the building stands for, as Stair[69] notes: "It is a rule in
the Roman law, which we follow, *inaedificatum solo cedit solo*; for
thereby all buildings of houses, walls, wells, dykes etc. and generally,
all things fixed to the ground or walls, are accounted as parts of the
ground."

As Erskine[70] shows, the principle is the same whether one is
concerned with the accession to land of a building or other structure,
made from moveable parts or components, or with the annexation of
things to an existing building so that these also accede to the principal
element—the land. "Things, by their own nature moveable, might
become immoveable, by their being fixed or united to an immoveable
subject for its perpetual use, as stone, marble, wood, used either in
building any edifice, or for additional ornaments to it after it is built."

The extent to which the recognition of this form of accession—and
the resolution of problems of heritable or moveable—tend to be
dominated by the abstract issue of the relationship of accessory to
principal, rather than primarily by reference to the physical means or
degree of attachment, is apparent from a passage in Bell.[71] "Things,
though in themselves by nature moveable, may become heritable by
accession. So, what has been by art so annexed to land (although not
built in or fixed to it) that it cannot be removed without destruction, or
change of nature, or of use, in the one or in the other subject, is
heritable by accession."

The notion of heritable *destinatione* shows the overriding importance
of the relationship in that this may mean that a thing readily moveable
in the physical sense—for example, the key to a door—is in fact
heritable,[72] *a fortiori* a part of heritable subjects disannexed for a
temporary purpose remains heritable.[73]

---

[68] II.i.38.

[69] II.i.40.

[70] II.ii.2. Regarding Erskine's formulation see Reid, "The Lord Chancellor's fixtures:
Brand's Trs. v. *Brand's Trs.* re-examined" (1983) 28 J.L.S. 49: "For Erskine, then, two
requirements had to be met before a moveable article was considered a fixture. First, the
article must be to some extent 'fixed or united'; and, second, this attachment must be for
the heritage's 'perpetual use,' that is, the article must be clearly accessory to the heritage
and the attachment permanent."

[71] *Prin.*, § 1473.

[72] See below, para. 3.17.

[73] See Erskine, II.i.14.

The term "fixtures"

3.10   The term "fixtures" is a label of convenience, adopted from English practice,[74] referring to the law applicable to the problem of determining the status of a thing as moveable or heritable where the question of accession is at issue in the context of building.[75]

A "fixture" is something which has lost its independent moveable status through accession to a heritable subject. Lord Chelmsford, in the leading case of *Brand's Trs.* v. *Brand's Trs.*,[76] having noted that the law as to fixtures "is the same in Scotland as in England," went on to define the term. "The meaning of the word is anything annexed to the freehold, that is, fastened to or connected with it, not in mere juxtaposition with the soil. Whatever is so annexed becomes part of the realty, and the person who was the owner of it when it was a chattel loses his property in it, which immediately vests in the owner of the soil." In short, the common and well-recognised occurrence of the accession of a moveable item to the land—*inaedificatum solo, solo cedit.*[77]

Attention should be drawn to a specialised English law usage whereby the term "fixture" refers to the case of a moveable which, though attached to land, is open to disannexure by someone other than the heritable proprietor, on the basis of a limited right to the subjects concerned. Scots law knows this situation but does not apply the label "fixture" to it.[78]

Relationship between parties not central to issue of accession

3.11   The better view is that the question whether a moveable has acceded to a heritable subject is a proprietary issue and, as such, primarily a matter of the relationship between the thing and the land.[79] Given,

---

[74] See, *e.g.*, the dictum of Lord Ellenborough C.J. in *Elwes* v. *Maw* [1802] 3 East 38, referred to by Rankine, *Landownership*, at pp. 117–118.

[75] It is beyond the scope of this work to consider the meaning of "fixture" for valuation purposes. (On this see Armour, *Valuation for Rating*, Chap. 9; see also *Stair Memorial Encyclopaedia*, Vol. 24, para. 44.) Although valuation cases frequently address the issues which arise, and apply the criteria developed, in the common law context (see Gordon, *Scottish Land Law*, paras. 5.43 and 5.44) this normally occurs in the process of interpretation of statutory provisions—see, *e.g.* s.42 of the Lands Valuation (Scotland) Act 1854. In *Scottish Discount Co. Ltd.* v. *Blin*, 1985 S.C. 216 at p. 235, Lord President Emslie noted that he derived no assistance from decisions of the Lands Valuation Appeal Court in valuation cases dealing with machinery, "since that court is not concerned with any question as to a right of property and is concerned only to apply statutory provisions."

[76] (1876) 3 R.(H.L.) 16 at p. 23. But *cf. Dixon* v. *Fisher* (1843) 5 D. 775 *per* Lord Cockburn at p. 794: "We are not so rich in cases as our southern neighbours are . . . apparently because the legal rule has either been more clear, or more steadily adhered to." See also Gordon, *Scottish Land Law*, para. 5.02; Reid, "The Lord Chancellor's Fixtures: *Brand's Trs.* v. *Brand's Trs.* re-examined" (1983) 28 J.L.S. 49 at p. 50.

[77] The report in *Brand's Trs.* v. *Brand's Trs.* (1876) 3 R.(H.L.) 16 at p. 23 mistakenly gives the counterpart maxim *plantatur solo, solo cedit* which, of course, refers to the accession of growing things rather than buildings.

[78] See Rankine, *Landownership*, p. 117. Regarding the right of disannexure see below, para. 3.16.

[79] See below, para. 3.14.

however, the fact of accession the issue of a right to disannex and restore the prior position not infrequently arises but, logically, only on the premise that ownership in the annexed thing has passed to the heritable proprietor.[80] Failing this the question of a right of disannexure should not arise because it is, in principle, always open to an owner to recover possession.[81] Where this subsequent question[82] of a right of removal arises, the relationship between annexor and landowner becomes relevant. In determining the right of a given annexor to disannex one is also dealing with a proprietary issue; however, the balance in favour of the annexor as against parties with an interest in the heritable *status quo* can only be assessed by giving consideration to the nature of the annexor's relationship with the landowner.

In *Brand's Trs.* v. *Brand's Trs.*[83] Lord Chancellor Cairns demonstrated the logic of the separate treatment of the question of accession and a possible right of removal, the latter only arising on the issue of accession being satisfied.[84]

> "Looking at it in that way, I would remind your Lordships that there are with regard to matters of this kind, which are included under the comprehensive term of 'fixtures,' two general rules, a correct appreciation of which will, as it seems to me, go far to solve the whole difficulty in this case. My Lords, one of those rules is the general well-known rule that whatever is fixed to the freehold of land becomes part of the freehold or the inheritance. The other is quite a different and separate rule. Whatever once becomes part of the inheritance cannot be severed by a limited owner . . . Those, my Lords, are two rules—not one by way of exception to the other, but two rules standing consistently together. My Lords, an exception indeed, and a very important exception, has been made not to the first of these rules, but to the second . . . Under that exception a tenant who has fixed to the inheritance things for the purpose of trade has a certain power of severance and removal during the tenancy."

This statement of the law has been seen as a departure from the approach of prevailing Scottish case law in favour of the English rules

---

[80] See below, para. 3.16.

[81] See below, para. 10.03.

[82] See Gordon, *Scottish Land Law*, para. 5.03: "There are two issues. One is whether the alleged fixture has ever been made part of the land and has ceased to be moveable. The other is whether, if so, it can be removed and reclaimed by its former owner."

[83] (1876) 3 R.(H.L.) 16 at p. 20.

[84] As Professor Sir Thomas Smith pointed out (*Short Commentary*, p. 501), some cases seem to blur the issues of annexation and a right of removal by taking the position that moveable status is not lost in respect of things to which a right of removal applies. See the dictum of Lord Justice-Clerk Moncreiff in *Dowall* v. *Miln* (1874) 1 R. 1180 at pp. 1182–1183. See also *Syme* v. *Harvey* (1861) 24 D. 202 at p. 211; *Christie* v. *Smith's Exrx.*, 1949 S.C. 572 at pp. 583–584.

of trade fixtures,[85] but the recent interpretation of *Brand's Trs.* by a court of seven judges of the Court of Session makes the decision compatible with Scots law prior to it.[86]

Bases upon which issue of accession is determined

3.12   The considerations applicable to the question whether a moveable thing has become heritable by accession to land fall into three type classes. First, there are the purely physical features of the relationship; how the thing is annexed, affixed or connected to heritable property. Secondly, it may be relevant to look at the circumstances of the relationship from the more abstract point of view of its purpose, function, or design. Given the nature of the thing, what does its relationship with the heritable setting tell us? Here the emphasis is upon the wider context of the rôle of the thing within its environment. Thirdly, the intention behind the act of placing a moveable in a certain position in relation to heritable property may be material to the issue of accession.

Regarding intention, two forms are distinguishable. The inferred intention behind the act of annexation is determined objectively by reference to the features of the relationship—actual or abstract. The usual issue here is whether the circumstances demonstrate an intention that the relationship should be permanent. The rôle of "intention" from this point of view is to provide confirmation of what tends to be demonstrated by consideration of the first two factors. To this extent the issue of the objective intention of the annexor is hardly separable from the physical facts and the circumstances of the relationship. The second form of intention is the actual subjective intent of the party or parties responsible for making the annexation—the annexor's *ipse dixit*. Clearly, intention in this form is a wholly different matter from the other considerations which are all objective in point of view. Subjective intention has a limited rôle because the problem of accession is primarily a matter of the circumstances and nature of the relationship between moveable and heritable. To allow subjective intention a dominant rôle would, of course, mean that the issue of accession could be determined by contractual arrangement but this would be unacceptable, at any rate in so far as the result arrived at differed from what would follow applying criteria of the law of property.[87]

There is no formula to determine the weight to be attached to factors distinguishable in terms of the different approaches to the

---

[85] See Reid, "The Lord Chancellor's Fixtures: *Brand's Trs.* v. *Brand's Trs.* re-examined" (1983) 28 J.L.S. 49 at pp. 51–52. See also Gordon, *Scottish Land Law*, para. 5.03.
[86] *Scottish Discount Co. Ltd.* v. *Blin*, 1985 S.C. 216 at pp. 229–232. See below, para. 3.12.
[87] On this see below, para. 3.21, n. 3.

accession of moveables to land. Each case must be looked at on its own facts. As Lord McLaren put it in *Howie's Trs.* v. *McLay*[88]: "in the question whether an article in its nature moveable is attached to the heritable estate, the law can only, I think, establish presumptions. The actual decision must depend upon the facts of the case." Accordingly, there is probably no "first test" or fundamental requirement and as Lord Justice-Clerk Thompson put it in *Christie* v. *Smith's Exrx.*[89]: "it is as a general rule only by a consideration of the whole circumstance surrounding the history, object and function of the structure that it is possible to decide whether it is heritable or moveable."

Given, however, that objective considerations dominate in the issue whether annexation has occurred, it is usual to look first to the actual physical circumstances before considering other factors. But one would go no further than this in giving primacy to the physical circumstances. *Cliffplant Ltd.* v. *Kinnaird*[90], an Extra Division decision, has been interpreted to the effect[91] that *Brand's Trs.* v. *Brand's Trs.*[92] was an innovatory decision in effect laying down that the only relevant consideration was that of physical attachment to the land. But in *Scottish Discount Co. Ltd.* v. *Blin*[93] a seven-judge court overruled *Cliffplant Ltd.* "in so far as it may be thought to declare that whatever is physically attached to the soil is a 'fixture' in the sense of the law." Lord President Emslie—approving Professor Gloag's conclusion that, in view of the number of considerations, "it is impossible to lay down any very exact rules as to what consitutes a fixture"[94]—observed: "It is clear . . . that the question in all cases is a question of fact, that the list of considerations mentioned is not exhaustive, and that each case must depend greatly upon its own circumstances."[95]

In what follows the different tests are considered under the headings of physical circumstances; rôle factors; and intention.

Physical circumstances

As indicated[96] in *Brand's Trs.* v. *Brand's Trs.*, fixtures were defined **3.13** with emphasis upon the physical circumstances as "anything annexed to the freehold, that is, fastened to or connected with it, not in mere juxtaposition with the soil."[97]

In the modern case of *Christie* v. *Smith's Exrx.*[98] Lord Justice-Clerk Thompson emphasised the importance of the physical facts of annexa-

---

[88] (1902) 5 F. 214 at p. 220.
[89] 1949 S.C. 572 at p. 579.
[90] 1981 S.C. 9.
[91] See *Scottish Discount Co. Ltd.* v. *Blin*, 1985 S.C. 216 at p. 230.
[92] (1876) 3 R.(H.L.) 16.
[93] 1985 S.C. 216, *per* Lord President Emslie at p. 232.
[94] *Green's Encyclopaedia of the Law of Scotland*, Vol. VII, s.2, para. 363.
[95] *Scottish Discount Co. Ltd.* v. *Blin*, 1985 S.C. 216 at p. 233.
[96] Above, para. 3.10, n. 76.
[97] *Brand's Trs.* v. *Brand's Trs.* (1876) 3 R.(H.L.) 16 *per* Lord Chelmsford at p. 23.
[98] 1949 S.C. 572 at p. 578.

tion in a decision concerning the status of a summerhouse as moveable or heritable. "No doubt the element of annexation to the soil is of importance, and on occasion it may be conclusive, as the annexation may be of such a character as to imply the presence of the other main elements pointing to the structure's being heritable."

The courts sometimes measure the sufficiency of the physical circumstances by reference to the positive criterion of permanence. In *Syme* v. *Harvey*,[99] a case primarily concerned with the question of a right of removal, Lord Curriehill noted the general recognition of the factor of permanence "as the element of chief importance in considering the effect of annextion in a question between the heir and executor of the owner."[1] In *Howie's Trs.* v. *McLay*,[2] Lord President Kinross, in a statement of the various relevant criteria, also alluded to the question of permanence:

> "The first question, then, in such a case, is whether the thing has become a fixture, and this may depend upon, *inter alia*, the character and degree of its attachment to the soil or building, upon whether the attachment is of a permanent or *quasi*-permanent character, upon whether the building to which it is attached is specially adapted for it, or it is specially adapted for the building; the intention of the person who attached it, and how far the soil or building would be affected by its removal."

Of course, the notion of permanence can be applied to the entire circumstances of the relationship between the entity or element concerned and the heritable subjects, but it is especially apposite as a means of testing the finality of the actual physical link.

Another test, sometimes applied to the question of the finality of the relationship, is that of disannexure without injury.[3] "When that property, which is in its nature moveable, becomes so attached physically to a heritable subject that it cannot be disjointed therefrom without injury to itself, or that to which it is attached, it becomes a proper accessory, and is heritable by accession."[4]

Rankine[5] refers, with apparent approval, to the test of removal without injury but, as Lord Cockburn noted in *Dixon* v. *Fisher*,[6] this

---

[99] (1861) 24 D. 202 at p. 212.

[1] This dictum proceeds upon the misconceived basis that the relationship between the parties is directly material to the issue whether annexation has occurred, but nonetheless the point is well made that a primary question is whether one can conclude from the circumstances that the erection was made for permanent use.

[2] (1902) 5 F. 214 at p. 216.

[3] Sometimes labelled the "removeability test" and applied as an issue in the wider question of incorporation. (See, *e.g. Christie* v. *Smith's Exrx.*, 1949 S.C. 572 at p. 578).

[4] *Dowall* v. *Miln* (1874) 1 R. 1180 *per* Lord Justice-Clerk Moncreiff at p. 1182.

[5] *Landownership*, p. 120. Rankine refers to *Hellawell* v. *Eastwood* (1851) 6 Exch. 295 at p. 312 where Parke B. applied the test of removal *integre salve et commode*.

[6] (1843) 5 D. 775 at p. 795.

criterion tends to give too much emphasis to the physical form of fixing. "All that is wanted, is to get them fixed to the land—not fixed indissolubly, but in such a manner as to denote that they were meant to be connected with, and to serve the uses of, the property."

While the test of ready removal without serious damage is a useful measure of the extent of the physical connection,[7] its utility has probably diminished in modern times. Less elaborate methods of construction or connection, and simplified means of disannexure, tend towards providing for the possibility of change without damage. In the modern context permanence may well be more conclusively demonstrated by the abstract relationship between thing and land.

A tendency to give emphasis to the physical attachment factor to the exclusion of other considerations may lead to unjustifiable results; for example, the conclusion that fire-grates were not part of the heritable subjects sold because they could be removed without damage to the structure.[8]

Rôle factors

A variety of considerations, other than the form and extent of **3.14** physical annexation, may give insight into the relationship between the disputed element and the heritage concerned. While the test of physical circumstances is concerned with the actual means of annexation or connection, one is here looking to relevant associating factors. Considerations of purpose, function or design may well be important in a question of accession to heritage, especially where the physical circumstances are inconclusive.

In *Dowall* v. *Miln*[9] Lord Justice-Clerk Moncreiff recognised that non-physical factors could have a rôle in the determination of accession, where removal without damage was possible but where "a certain amount of fixture coincided with" one of the following situations:

> "(1) Where the article is essential or material to the enjoyment of the fruits or the use of the heritable subject; or (2) If there is a special adaptation in the construction of the article itself to the uses or improvement of the heritable property to which it is attached which it would not possess if placed elsewhere; or (3)

---

[7] See Rankine, *Landownership*, p. 120: "[the] element of removeability *salva rei substantia* will be found to run through all the cases in which the decision has turned mainly on physical conditions." Rankine refers to the case of *Niven* v. *Pitcairn* (1823) 2 S. 270, concerned with lead vessels held down by their own weight. In modern law, it is submitted, the inference of permanence, deriving from the circumstances, would be more important than any question of the ease of removal, given that modern technology would probably make removal possible without damage.

[8] *Nisbet* v. *Mitchell-Innes* (1880) 7 R. 575 at p. 579. In this case a remit was made to a man of skill—a builder—to report *inter alia* on the degree and manner of attachment.

[9] (1874) 1 R. 1180 at p. 1182.

Express declaration by the owner of an intention that the articles should be annexed to the real estate."

We are here concerned with the first two categories in this dictum—the third is dealt with below.[10] In the first grouping, the basis for inclusion is the particular rôle of the thing in the context in which it is found. By way of elaboration Lord Moncreiff referred[11] to a dictum of Lord Cockburn[12] concerned with the accession of mining apparatus and equipment to the heritable subjects on which workings were situate.

> "I conceive that this rule not only assigns to the heir the larger and the fixed machines, but such smaller articles as, though not physically attached to these greater machines, or capable from their use of being so, form parts of the general apparatus; provided they be so fitted and constructed as to belong specially to this particular machinery, and not to be equally suited for any other."

The latter part of this statement limits the category by requiring the thing to have something approaching a rôle exclusive to the context concerned. This does not, it is submitted, mean that the thing must be incapable of being adapted to other circumstances because this fact should be irrelevant where the thing has an essential function or utility within the heritable context. There is a close analogy to items heritable by destination[13]—for example, the cover of a well; it would be irrelevant that a well-cover could be used to cover a well elsewhere.

In respect of the second category in Lord Justice-Clerk Moncreiff's statement[14]—where there has been some special adaptation of the thing to its environment—the court went on to distinguish two cases. First, "adjuncts of fixed machinery" which though "capable of being easily enough removed of themselves" are necessary for the particular use to which the heritable property has been put. This, it was held, included "all those adjuncts of fixed machinery which are devoted to the due cultivation of land, or the working of mines, quarries, clayfields or other heritable subjects yielding profit."[15] Secondly, there are "ornamental objects, made for and expressly adapted to the decoration or enjoyment of the real estate."[16] This distinction reflects the respective

---

[10] See para. 3.15.
[11] (1874) 1 R. 1180 at p. 1183.
[12] *Dixon* v. *Fisher* (1843) 5 D. 775 at p. 801.
[13] See below, para. 3.17.
[14] As quoted above, n. 9.
[15] (1874) 1 R. 1180 at p. 1183.
[16] *Ibid*.

fact situations of *Dixon* v. *Fisher*[17] and the English case of *D'Eyncourt* v. *Gregory*,[18] considered in some detail by Rankine.[19]

In the case of things having an essential rôle in some process or industry, carried on in works which are part of the land, the necessary link on the basis of function or purpose should be clear. But in relation to things which are associated with the heritable structure in a merely decorative rôle the function or purpose test will only be satisfied if there has been specific adaptation to the environment. Arguably, this is simply a matter of the sufficiency of the function or purpose requirement which all cases of this general type must satisfy. The function and purpose criterion may be satisfied in different ways and the sufficiency of a particular form is always a relative question to be considered against the impression conveyed if the thing is seen removed from its environment. This said, one can see that the argument of function and purpose is bound to be more convincing in relation to things which have some active essential rôle as opposed to those which only serve an optional passive function.

In the more difficult passive function category certain tests have been laid down by the courts as aids to assessing the importance of the rôle function of a thing measured against its potential divorced from the environment concerned. In *Howie's Tr.* v. *McLay*,[20] Lord McLaren commented as follows:

> "In the case of residential property the presumption is, as I gather from the decisions, that articles which have a value independent of the value of the heritable estate are not considered to be fixtures if the attachment is only for support and is of such a character that the article can be displaced without injury to the building."

One may contrast, for example, a mantelpiece mirror unit designed and made to be fixed to a wall and a picture or tapestry, of intrinsic value, which happens to be fixed to a wall for its support and presentation in the environment concerned.

This distinction seems to have been recognised in *Cochrane* v. *Stevenson*[21] regarding pictures which had been let into the panelling of a room. One may note the remarks of Lord Adam: "it does not appear to me that that sort of attachment is such as to render a presumably moveable subject like a picture part of the heritable subject, with the

---

[17] (1843) 5 D. 775. The issue in this case was whether mining machinery erected by a deceased mine-owner was heritable or moveable for the purposes of succession.

[18] (1866) L.R. 3 Eq. 382. This case was concerned with the question whether decorative and artistic items acceded to a house and were so subject to the terms of the will of a liferenter.

[19] *Landownership*, pp. 123–124.

[20] (1902) 5 F. 214 at p. 219.

[21] (1891) 18 R. 1208.

result that it goes with it."[22] Commenting on this decision, Lord McLaren, in *Howie's Trs.*[23] noted: "I may here observe that the decision would not necessarily be the same if the pictures had been merely decorative; but in this case the pictures had a certain artistic and historical value which was independent of their position in the mansion-house."

In the same decision[24] Lord McLaren refers to the case of machinery in an industrial setting as a potentially more obvious instance of accession based upon rôle within environment.

> "the machine is affixed by being adapted to its environment, and I cannot see that it is of the least importance whether the adaptation consists in building up or in levelling down, in steadying by bolts and nuts, or in making use of the weight of the machine itself, where weight is sufficient to secure the requisite stability."

The process taking place in a given heritable context may require the deployment of things which, in a different setting, might be considered moveable items. Arguably, the stronger or more obvious the rôle function the more tenuous a physical connection will suffice. The strongest case is most likely to be an environment purpose-designed and equipped. The purchase of heritable subjects comprising a bottling plant would be likely to include—on the basis of accession—attached but physically moveable items essential to the operation concerned, as well as things not physically attached but by destination part of the unit. Given the concept of constructive annexation,[25] the better view is that the link in terms of rôle within context or environment may be so obvious that no actual physical attachment is necessary. But to what extent the thing—removed from its context—could function as an independent entity, would have to be taken into consideration.

A greater emphasis upon rôle function would seem to be appropriate in modern circumstances where the means of construction and methods of disannexure may facilitate removal without damage. Lord Justice-Clerk Thompson noted this in *Christie* v. *Smith's Exrx.*[26]

> "But the degree of annexation may vary tremendously, particularly in view of modern methods. This variation may arise from the mode of annexation and the extent of it. So too the element of removability varies from case to case, and here again modern methods make removable things which would formerly have hardly been so regarded."

---

[22] *Ibid.* at p. 1214.
[23] (1902) 5 F. 214 at p. 219.
[24] *Idem* at p. 220.
[25] See below para. 3.17.
[26] 1949 S.C. 572 at p. 578.

Although, regarding the summerhouse in this case, the court went on
to take the view that there were factors in its construction and erection
which did point to permanence, nonetheless the abstract factors were
also considered to be important: "But there are other elements of
importance and it is as a general rule only by a consideration of the
whole circumstances surrounding the history, object and function of
the structure that it is possible to decide whether it is heritable or
moveable."[27]

Annexor's intention

The possible relevance of intention when an owner erects a structure **3.15**
on his property was noted in *Syme* v. *Harvey*.[28] "In cases of that kind,
the solution of the question does not depend merely upon the nature
and completeness of the physical annexation, but also upon the
intention with which that annexation was made." Lord Curriehill went
on to state that the issue of permanence is the "element of chief
importance" and the opinion goes on to speak of the annexor's
purpose in a way which indicates that the issue was seen as whether the
annexor intended the thing to be attached to the heritable subject on a
permanent basis.

It seems that "intention" in this form is derived by inference from
the circumstances and, as such, does not have a primary function but
merely a confirmatory rôle. One might equally ask: "Do the circumstances indicate finality or permanence?" The issue does not change if
the question is put in the form: "Do the circumstances indicate that the
annexor intended finality or permanence?" In so far as the basis upon
which the question of permanence is determined is by an objective
consideration of the circumstances—by assessment of the actual form,
nature and degree of annexation and the abstract rôle factors of
purpose, function and design—it is immaterial what shorthand formula
is applied to describe the inquiry.

Even though reference to the annexor's inferred intention—as a
derivative of objective criteria—is no more than a neutral consideration, to refer to it may tend towards the conclusion that actual or
expressed intention has a primary rôle. But, of course, this cannot be
correct if accession occurs as a matter of consequence from the
circumstances in which an accessory item is in some way brought into
union with a principal object. In *Scottish Discount Co. Ltd.* v. *Blin*[29]
Lord President Emslie quoted a dictum of Lord Cockburn in *Dixon* v.
Fisher[30] to the effect that the annexor's opinion of the result in law is
immaterial, "for no man can make his property real or personal by

---

[27] *Idem* at p. 579.
[28] (1861) 24 D. 202 *per* Lord Curriehill at p. 212.
[29] 1985 S.C. 216 at p. 235.
[30] (1843) 5 D. 775 at p. 793.

merely thinking it so." The point was also recognised by two judges in
Christie v. *Smith's Exrx.*,[31] in which it arose as a pertinent issue
because there was evidence that Mr Smith had explained his decision
to erect the summerhouse some distance removed from the farmhouse
on the basis that "I might lift it at any time."[32]

Lord MacKay ruled out reference to the annexor's *ipse dixit* but left
the matter open concerning any question of a tenant's right of
removal: "I would therefore completely exclude as between (a) heir
and executor, (b) buyer and seller, all that which may be called
'original intention.' We must look at the structure as it stood, as a
whole, for many years past."[33] Lord Jamieson makes the same point
without any reservation: "the question whether an article or building
was intended to become part of heritable subjects to which it has been
annexed or on which it has been placed is not to be determined by
extrinsic evidence, but by circumstances patent for all to see, such as
its nature, position and the degree and object of annexation."[34]

But is it possible for evidence of actual intention to have a rôle as a
decisive factor when the objective facts are equivocal? Could evidence
of the annexor's actual intention tilt the balance in a borderline case?
Only, it is suggested, if the circumstances are, in any event, consistent
with such a result. It would seem that, at most, evidence of the
annexor's actual intention can have a confirmatory rôle. Where, for
example, circumstances point to the possibility of the thing concerned
having a particular rôle in the heritable context, evidence that the
annexor intended this purpose must tend to confirm that the thing has
that rôle.

The possibility of intention cast in such a rôle was considered in
Scottish Discount Co. Ltd. v. *Blin*,[35] the leading decision in modern
Scots law. The issue of fact before the court in this case was whether
two massive pairs of scrap shears had acceded to a scrap-merchant's
heritable premises. The question of intention was material because the
shears were subject to a hire-purchase agreement which, so it was
contended, led to the inference that final annexation had not been
intended as this would have been incompatible with the circumstances.
Lord President Emslie—referring to the opinion of Lord Cockburn in
Dixon v. *Fisher*[36]—declined to recognise any blanket exclusion of the
consideration of intention.

> "I am not persuaded, however, that in asking the question
> whether an article has become a fixture it will never be permissible

---

[31] 1949 S.C. 572.
[32] *Idem* at p. 577.
[33] *Idem* at p. 583.
[34] *Idem* at p. 587.
[35] 1985 S.C. 216.
[36] (1843) 5 D. 775 at p. 793: "In considering this subject, I entirely disregard the view said to have been formed upon it by the deceased himself. His opinion of the law is clearly immaterial; for no man can make his property real or personal by merely thinking it so."

to notice that it was acquired by the person who installed it on his land, under a hire purchase agreement. That circumstance, it seems to me, may, when the matter is otherwise in fine balance, be of some relevance in deciding whether the installation was or was not intended to be a permanent or quasi-permanent addition to the land."[37]

As an instance of the intention factor possibly tilting the balance, one may give the example of a wall-hanging of innate artistic character and value, fixed to a wall in a manner which would support permanence, but positioned to conceal an unsightly crack in the masonry. Arguably, it would be relevant to the issue of permanence that the owner had said that he affixed the wall-hanging to cover up the crack.

Also in the case of *Scottish Discount Co. Ltd.* v. *Blin*,[38] Lord Cameron noted the significance, from the point of view of the relevance of intention, of the fact that the item concerned was installed on the basis of an agreement reflecting the parties' intention as to the destiny of the thing. While the parties cannot, by private agreement, determine the legal character of a thing so as to affect the rights of third parties, and, as Lord Cameron noted, "while the tests to be applied are essentially objective and not subjective"—

"it does not necessarily or always follow, in my opinion, that the nature of the contract or agreement between the parties which was the legal instrument by which, *e.g.* a piece of machinery was moved and installed in a factory or yard may not be taken into account as itself an item of evidence relevant to an objective determination of the matter of intention."[39]

On this basis, in so far as the inquiry is primarily concerned with the circumstances of installation, it does seem appropriate that an objective assessment of the parties' intention, as reflected in their agreement, should not be excluded from consideration.

A dictum of Lord Grieve, in the same case, is specific in contending for the possible relevance of the terms of a hire-purchase agreement as evidence of intention material to the issue of permanence of annexation. "For instance, the agreement might be of a very short duration and thus indicative of an intention that the article in question was not to be regarded as even a quasi-permanent feature of the heritage to which it had been attached."[40] But, in the matter concerned, Lord Grieve did not regard the hire-purchase agreement as capable of

---

[37] 1985 S.C. 216 at p. 235.
[38] *Idem* at p. 132.
[39] *Ibid.*
[40] *Idem* at p. 135.

supporting any such argument; indeed, on the view taken no valid
argument pointing to an intention other than one of permanent
annexation could be derived from the contract because, on the basis of
it, the hire-purchaser did "precisely what he would have done had he
been able to purchase the shears outright."[41]

3.16 *Right to disannex*

3.16a General observations. As indicated,[42] where one is concerned with the
fait accompli of an accessory moveable having acceded to land there is,
in principle, no room for any variation on the basis of the relationship
in which the parties stand. From the point of view of proprietary
consequences there can be only one result to the case of A's bricks
built into a house under construction on B's land; whether A and B are
mutual strangers, or whether A has a limited right to B's land, the
result, from a proprietary point of view, must be the same. As Lord
Chancellor Cairns noted in the leading case of *Brand's Trs.* v. *Brand's
Trs.*,[43] to this rule there is "so far as I am aware, no exception
whatever."[44] The learned Lord Chancellor was at pains to emphasise
the distinction between the conclusion in appropriate circumstances,
that accession to heritage has occurred, and the consequence of this
fact, that whatever has acceded cannot be severed by a limited owner.[45]
The court went on to explain the exceptional cases in which a right of
severance exists. It may be noted that the opinions in the leading case
in modern law do not dissent from the essence of what was laid down
in *Brand's Trs.*[46]

Whether an item of moveable property has lost its identity through
accession to heritage is frequently an issue between parties contending
for and against such a result. Various contexts are possible. Entitlement to legal rights of succession is a right only to the deceased's
moveable estate and there is obvious scope for a dispute between those
entitled to legal rights and claimants to the heritage.[47] The buyer and
seller of heritage may dispute the identification of items as, on the one
hand, part of the land to which the buyer has a right, and, on the other

---

[41] *Ibid.*

[42] See above, para. 3.11.

[43] (1876) 3 R.(H.L.) 16 at p. 20.

[44] See *Scottish Discount Co. Ltd.* v. *Blin*, 1985 S.C. 216 at pp. 232 and 244 in
clarification of the point that in this dictum the Lord Chancellor was referring to the *fait
accompli* of acquisition by accession.

[45] *Idem* at p. 20.

[46] See *Scottish Discount Co. Ltd.* v. *Blin*, above. At p. 231 Lord President Emslie
rejects as a fallacy the view that things annexed remain moveable in so far as the
annexor has a right of severance. See also the dictum of Lord Grieve at pp. 243–244, in
essence recognising a continuing state of accession subject to a right of removal in favour
of a tenant upon termination of his lease.

[47] Prior to the Succession (Scotland) Act 1964, one may note, this issue could have
arisen between heir and executor; see, *e.g. Reid's Exrs.* v. *Reid* (1890) 17 R. 519. See
Gordon, *Scottish Land Law*, para. 5.19.

hand, as moveables which remain the property of the seller.[48] The practice, however, is for conveyancers "to deal expressly in the missives of sale with items over which there is likely to be difficulty."[49] A personal creditor, or a trustee on bankruptcy, may contend for continuing moveable status against the holder of a standard security who seeks to claim that by annexation the thing concerned has become heritable. Where an effective real right of security is granted the only issue is whether the disputed item "has been made heritable by being affixed in the legal sense of the term."[50]

In principle, in the above cases, the relationship between the parties has no relevance to the question whether accession has occurred; moreover, none of the above situations gives rise to a right of disannexation. But another possible relationship is between the owner and a party with a limited interest in the heritage concerned. The most important case of a tenant of leased property will be looked at, but liferent is also a possible context.[51]

Landlord and tenant. Other things being equal, in the context of lease **3.16b** the inference of intention to attach on a permanent basis is less strong than it would be when the annexation is made by the landowner. While, in the latter case, the presumption will normally be, "that what was done by the proprietor was meant to remain, and the heir will have the benefit, unless it appears to have been done for some obviously temporary purpose."[52] On the other hand, as between landlord and tenant—

> "the presumption of intention is the other way. The presumption is, that the improvement made by the tenant at his own expense,

---

[48] See, e.g. Nisbet v. Mitchell-Innes (1880) 7 R. 575. In Cochrane v. Stevenson (1891) 18 R. 1208 at p. 1210 the Lord Ordinary (Kyllachy), opined that the intention of the parties might have a greater rôle in the case of a dispute following the sale of heritable subjects; the better view, however, is that even inter partes this could only be true as a matter of contract rather than property. This distinction was explained by Lord Cullen in Shetland Islands Council v. B.P. Petroleum Development, 1990 S.L.T. 82 at p. 94, and although the context was lease the remarks of the learned Lord Ordinary are of general relevance. "It is no doubt true that reference is frequently made to the position of third parties when it is observed that a contractual arrangement between owner and occupier is ineffective to prevent what is annexed to the heritage being treated as such. However that is no more than is indicative of the universal significance of the right of property. It follows from that universality that no agreement between owner and occupier can affect the matter of ownership of heritable fixtures even as between them. It is, of course, an entirely different matter if the owner confers upon the occupier a specific contractual right with reference to the subjects, such as a right of removal or of alteration."
[49] Gordon, Scottish Land Law, para. 5.21. It is beyond the scope of the present work to deal with the problem of the disposition superseding the missives and the consequences of this from the point of view of what is included as part of the land. On this see Gordon, loc. cit.
[50] Howie's Trs. v. McLay (1902) 5 F. 214 per Lord McLaren at p. 220. See also Scottish Discount Co. Ltd. v. Blin, 1985 S.C. 216.
[51] See Fisher v. Dixon (1845) 4 Bell's App. 286 at p. 356.
[52] Syme v. Harvey (1861) 24 D. 202 per Lord Deas at p. 213.

on a subject which is not his property, was intended by him for his own benefit, and that, except in the case of a long lease, he did not intend to increase the permanent value of the subject by adding to it what could easily be taken away."[53]

Upon the death of the lessee, pending termination of the lease, the right of removal would pass to a successor to the lease[54] but, of course, this is no more than the normal consequence of the transmission of the lessee's right. Given that fixtures remain heritable pending removal, the right of a successor to a lease will prevail over that of the trustee of a deceased bankrupt tenant entitled to claim the moveable estate on behalf of creditors.[55]

Within the category of lease a distinction is drawn between, on the one hand, the case of a thing affixed by the tenant for the purpose of trade or business activity and, on the other hand, annexations made for the purpose of improving the amenity of the subject let.

In the case of *Syme* v. *Harvey*[56] Lord Deas came to the conclusion that there was "a marked and important distinction between the case of a tenant following out his trade, and the case of a tenant occupying with no such object." In this case the court allowed the removal of greenhouses and other substantial structures erected for the purposes of the nursery and florist's business conducted on the premises.[57]

While a tenant's right to remove trade fixtures has been most readily recognised in the development of the law,[58] it is also the case that the tenant of residential premises may remove things annexed for amenity but probably, it seems, on a more stringent test of what constitutes injury to the heritage concerned. In relation to trade fixtures there is a presumption of the tenant's right to disannex on termination of the

---

[53] *Ibid.* See also *Dowall* v. *Miln* (1874) 1 R. 1180 at p. 1183. It should be noted that there is no question of items annexed by a tenant to the subjects let remaining moveable. In *Brand's Trs.* v. *Brand's Trs.* (1876) 3 R.(H.L.) 16 at p. 22 Lord Chancellor Cairns specifically rejected the opinion of Lord Gifford to this effect, as expressed in the Court of Session hearing of the matter ((1874) 2 R. 258 at p. 269): "it does not remain a moveable *quoad omnia*; there does exist on the part of the tenant a right to remove that which has been thus fixed; but if he does not exercise that right it continues to be that which it became when it was first fixed,—namely, a part of the inheritance." This dictum, it may be noted, was quoted with approval by Lord President Emslie in *Scottish Discount Co. Ltd.* v. *Blin*, above, at p. 231. In *Miller* v. *Muirhead* (1894) 21 R. 658, the court was concerned with a tenant's assignment of his rights to things annexed, to his landlord as security. Lord Rutherfurd Clark held that this could only amount to a renunciation by the tenant of his right of removal: "So long as it is so attached it must belong to the owner of the soil, for he is necessarily owner of everything which is part of it. The tenant possesses it as part of the subject of the lease, but in no other character. He has a right to make it his own by severing it from the soil" (at p. 660).
[54] See *Brand's Trs.* v. *Brand's Trs.* (above) at p. 23. The relevant passage is explained by Lord President Inglis in *Reid's Exrs.* v. *Reid* (1890) 17 R. 519 at p. 522.
[55] See *Murray's Tr.* v. *Graham* (1889) 26 S.L.R. 762.
[56] (1861) 24 D. 202 at p. 214.
[57] The case of nursery plants is analogous; see above, para. 3.06.
[58] See, *e.g.* Lord Chancellor Cairns in *Brand's Trs.* v. *Brand's Trs.*, above, at p. 20: "a very important exception."

lease. In respect of things fixed to enhance the amenity of a residential property, removal by the tenant is probably only permissible if it can be achieved without serious damage to the land or building. The English case of *Spyer* v. *Phillipson*[59] would seem to reflect this approach.[60] In this case the executors of the long-term lessee of a flat were held entitled to remove items of value even though damage resulted but, significantly, disannexation did not affect the structure of the property and, of course, the damage was reparable by the lessee's executors.

Special position of agricultural tenants. In addition to the distinct **3.16c** classes of trade and amenity fixtures one may also distinguish the case of annexations to the land involving property owned by an agricultural tenant. At common law the right of removal of items annexed for agricultural purposes was less far-reaching than that applying in the case of trade fixtures.[61] The matter has, however, been provided for by statute.[62]

The legislation makes provision, first, for any engine, machine, fencing or other fixture affixed to an agricultural holding by a tenant, and, secondly, for any building—other than one in respect of which the tenant is entitled to compensation under the Act—erected by a tenant. In either case, provided the improvement was not made in pursuance of an obligation by the tenant or as a substitute for a fixture or building belonging to the landlord, the item concerned

> "shall be removable by the tenant at any time during the continuance of the tenancy or before the expiration of six months, or such longer period as may be agreed, from the termination of the tenancy and shall remain his property so long as he may remove it by virtue of this subsection."[63]

The Act provides that removal shall be effected without avoidable damage but, in any event, that the tenant is, immediately upon removal, liable to compensate the landlord for all damage occasioned by the act of removal.[64] The right of removal is conditional upon the

---

[59] [1931] 2 Ch. 183.

[60] One may note that this decision is referred to as illustrative by Smith, *Short Commentary*, p. 506. In *Brand's Trs.* v. *Brand's Trs.*, above, at p. 23 Lord Chelmsford stated that "[t]he law as to fixtures is the same in Scotland as in England." In relation to the particular issue concerned this not infrequent theme of the era was probably accurate, but the difficulty with the statement in *Brand's Trs.* is its generality; see Reid, "The Lord Chancellor's Fixtures: *Brand's Trs.* v. *Brand's Trs.* re-examined" (1983) 28 J.L.S. 49 at p. 50.

[61] "That exception has been established in favour of the fixtures which have been attached to the inheritance for the purpose of trade, and perhaps to a minor degree for the purpose of agriculture" *per* Lord Chancellor Cairns in *Brand's Trs.* v. *Brand's Trs.* (1876) 3 R.(H.L.) 16 at p. 20.

[62] Agricultural Holdings (Scotland) Act. See Gill, *The Law of Agricultural Holdings in Scotland*, Chap. 7.

[63] s.14(1).

[64] s.14(4).

tenant's having paid all rent due and "satisfied all his other obligations to the landlord in respect of the holding."[65] More importantly, the legislation provides for the retention by the landlord of a right to purchase, from the tenant, the improvement concerned. To this effect the tenant must—at least one month prior to both the intended date of the exercise of the right of removal and, where applicable, the date of termination of the tenancy—give to the landlord written notice of his intention to remove a fixture or building.[66] The landlord may then exercise his overriding right by giving, prior to the expiry of the tenant's notice, written counter-notice of his intention to purchase the item concerned; whereupon the landlord will be liable to pay to the tenant the fair value, to an incoming tenant of the holding, of the fixture or building concerned.[67]

Constructive annexation

3.17   Certain things which are physically moveable may be heritable on the basis of their being accessory to heritable subjects. What might be called "rôle destination" may be conclusive on the issue whether, from a property point of view, a particular thing exists as an independent item or whether it is part of some principal entity. Bell[68] applies the heading "destination." This is an apt label for the concept of constructive annexation, because the essence of the notion is the rôle destiny of an accessory thing linking it to some principal subject to which it is not physically connected in any final sense. But the term "destination" has a specialised application in the law of succession and it is important to distinguish this.[69]

A standard example of constructive annexation is the key of a door; the seller of a house must deliver to the purchaser the keys of the property concerned. This may have a symbolic significance but, as a matter of property, the buyer is entitled to the keys as items accessory to the premises purchased.[70] On this basis keys are heritable and as Lord President Clyde put it, "the principle of constructive annexation . . . affords the only basis of the heir's right to the keys of the house to which he succeeds."[71]

The examples of keys, well-covers, and removable chimney cowls are instances of what Bell[72] sees as heritable by destination on the basis

---

[65] s.14(2)(*a*).

[66] s.14(2)(*b*).

[67] s.14(3).

[68] *Prin.*, § 1475.

[69] See below, para. 3.18. In Gloag and Henderson, things part of a principal subject though not physically attached are treated as "constructive fixtures" (para. 36.5), while the concept of destination is stated to be applicable "in questions of succession" (para. 36.6).

[70] See *Dixon* v. *Fisher* (1843) 5 D. 775 *per* Lord Cockburn at p. 801: "The key of a door . . . though moveable *sua natura*, is a fixture, because it alone is fitted for the use of the particular lock."

[71] *Fairlie's Trs.* v. *Fairlie's C.B.*, 1932 S.C. 216 at pp. 221–222.

[72] *Prin.*, § 1475.

of "a manifest purpose of such an annexation or connection as would by accession characterise the thing as heritable." The essential but detachable parts of a machine are subject to the same principle; if the machine is heritable, through its annexation to land, the detachable parts will also be heritable. Lord Cottenham noted this in the House of Lords decision in *Fisher* v. *Dixon*[73]: "if the *corpus* of the machinery is to be held to belong to the heir, it is hardly necessary to say that we must hold that all that belongs to that machinery, although more or less capable of being detached from it . . . must necessarily follow the principal and remain attached to the freehold."

While most instances of constructive annexation can be justified on the basis of rôle destination, some applications of the concept seem to involve a legal fiction.[74] The classification of title deeds as heritable by destination[75] would seem to be more a matter of convenience than destination in any philosophically rational sense.

Destination for the purposes of succession

The label "destination" is probably best known in the law of succession in the context of the common law distinction between heritable and moveable property. Bell[76] recognised the concept in this rôle as something distinct from accession in the proprietary sense: "Destination . . . may operate either where there is a manifest purpose[77] . . . or where there is a destination in point of succession to the heir or executor." **3.18**

From the point of view of property, it is submitted, one would not be concerned with destination which is wholly a matter of succession in the sense of the destiny of a moveable determined as heritable purely on the basis of an act of will—as in the case of "heirship moveables."[78] But in so far as the basis is destination in the sense of constructive

---

[73] (1845) 4 Bell's App. 286 at p. 357.

[74] See Gordon, *Scottish Land Law*, para. 5.11.

[75] See *Christie* v. *Ruxton* (1862) 24 D. 1182 *per* Lord Benholme at p. 1185: "Their only value is relative to, or as adjuncts of and accessory to, separate rights, whether of property or of obligation." Arguably, the doctrine of title deeds as heritable by destination applies only to the deeds necessary to establish title to the land concerned; see *Porteous* v. *Henderson* (1898) 25 R. 563 *per* Lord Justice-Clerk MacDonald at p. 567: "The pursuer here has got the writs necessary to give him a complete and good title. That was what he had a right to demand."

[76] *Prin.*, § 1475.

[77] See text to n. 72 above.

[78] Erskine, II.ii.14, recognised this to be a matter of an act of will: "the right of settling any part of his estate in whatever manner he pleases"—*i.e.* as heritable or moveable. One may note the comment of Lord President Clyde in *Fairlie's Trs.* v. *Fairlie's C.B.*, 1932 S.C. 216 at p. 221: "Even heirship moveables are spoken of in the law of Scotland as heritable by 'implied destination.' " See also Reid, "The Lord Chancellor's Fixtures: *Brand's Trs.* v. *Brand's Trs.* re-examined" (1983) 28 J.L.S. 49 at p. 50: "In questions between heir and executor articles otherwise moveable could sometimes be regarded as heritable *for the purposes of succession only*."

annexation, the instances of moveables deemed heritable—for the purpose of succession—are relevant to the law of property.[79]

Destination in the context of succession was of some importance prior to the removal, by the Succession (Scotland) Act 1964, of the distinction between the right of the heir to the heritable estate and the right of the executor to moveables.[80] A not insignificant case law is evidence of this. A number of decisions deal with the "heritable by destination" character of building materials intended for use in a building under construction but not yet completed upon the death of the landowner.[81] Lord President Clyde saw the basis of these cases as potentially proprietary: "it seems little more than an accident that the heir's right in these cases was not attributed to the principle of constructive annexation."[82] But is this valid? If, of course, the setting aside of specific items for incorporation in a building under construction has immediate proprietary effect, then there could no longer be any possibility of diligence involving the items concerned. The better view, it seems, is that, pending actual annexation, there is no proprietary effect; unless of course a change of ownership occurs, on the basis of succession, following the death of the landowner.

It would seem that the concept of destination—on the basis of which moveable things are deemed heritable for the purposes of succession—involves not only a natural link between the thing and the land but also an act of will, at any rate implied, on the part of the deceased. This point was recognised by Lord President Inglis in a dictum distinguishing the cases—both labelled "destination"—of a deceased tenant farmer's dung and items set aside for inclusion in a building, the construction of which was overtaken by the death of the landowner.[83]

"Accordingly, although the dung is moveable *sua natura*, it became heritable by being dedicated to the land, as much as the parts of a building which are brought to the ground for the purpose of being added to the building, but are not yet added. Indeed, the case of the dung is the clearer of the two, because the owner of the building may take away the materials during his lifetime, and use them for a different purpose, or even sell them, and supply their place with other material, whereas a tenant in the case of the dung has no such liberty."

---

[79] See Smith, *Short Commentary*, pp. 506–507; Gordon, *Scottish Land Law*, para. 1.37.

[80] Since the Succession (Scotland) Act 1964 the question may still arise concerning legal rights which, of course, only apply in respect of a deceased's moveable estate. See Meston, *The Succession (Scotland) Act 1964*, pp. 13–14; MacDonald, *Succession*, paras. 4.2 and 4.12.

[81] See, *e.g. Johnston* v. *Dobie* (1783) Mor. 5443; *Malloch* v. *Maclean* (1867) 5 M. 335.

[82] *Fairlie's Trs.* v. *Fairlie's C.B.*, 1932 S.C. 216 at pp. 221–222.

[83] *Reid's Exrs.* v. *Reid* (1890) 17 R. 519 at pp. 522–523.

Arguably, farm dung is accessory to the land as a matter of property even though it has a distinct identity and could be sold and delivered as an independent commodity. Applying objective criteria, the destiny of a heap of dung as something to be ploughed back into the land would appear to be almost conclusive. The proprietary character manifests itself in the conclusion that farm dung would not be open to diligence unless, of course, it was not produced on the farm but had been brought in.[84] This, it is submitted, would be so whether the question arose before or after the death of the farmer and regardless of whether the land was farmed by the owner or by a tenant. *Per contra*, the better view is that the components set aside for inclusion in a building in the course of erection would be subject to diligence, at any rate pending the death of the landowner. Bell[85] recognised this point concerning destination as a matter of succession: "The character thus accidentally impressed on subjects by destination, although it has ruled questions of succession, is not admitted, to change them in respect of diligence." It is suggested that Bell's reference to this is consistent with the recognition of a fundamental difference between destination as a matter of property *per se* and the possibility that, in appropriate circumstances in terms of a link between moveable and heritable, a party may, by act of will, determine the future character of moveable property as heritable.

ACCESSION TO MOVEABLES

Identification of principal element

The accession of a moveable thing to a principal entity which is also **3.19** moveable has less frequent incidence than the case of accession to heritable subjects: but, where it does occur, the inquiry tends to proceed on a different basis. In the latter situation the land is invariably seen as the principal element, and the issue is usually whether annexation has occurred. In the case involving only moveables, one may well have first to determine whether the rôles of accessory and principal exist and, if so, how the elements are cast. As Bell[86] noted: "of two things having intimate connection, the property of the principal draws after it that of the accessory; the only difficulty is to fix which is principal."

Stair,[87] recognising the problem, argued that one should identify principal and accessory elements from the point of view of "the design

---

[84] See *Murray's Tr. v. Graham* (1889) 26 S.L.R. 762 at pp. 763 and 764. *Cf.* the case of growing annual crops, above, para. 3.08, n. 65.

[85] *Prin.*, § 1475.

[86] *Ibid.*, § 1298.

[87] II.i.39.

of the artifact." This, it seems, comes down to saying that one should establish the accessory and principal parts by looking, in the first instance, to the nature and rôle of the things as items of property, regardless of the ulterior factor of value. Accordingly, on this basis, materials woven into cloth, "though much more precious than the cloth, are accessory thereto, and the property of the whole befalleth not to the owner of the materials, but to the owner of the cloth."[88] Where a precious stone is set in a gold ring it becomes accessory, "though more precious than the gold."[89] Conceptually, the ring continues to be the dominating proprietary entity. On this basis, one may contrast the case of a gem merely set into a precious metal which does not, itself, have any rôle as an item of property; in this case the gold setting becomes accessory to the jewel.[90]

Bell,[91] in an analysis aimed at practical application, reduces various criteria to their essence and prescribes a systematic order of inquiry:

> "1. That of two substances, one of which can exist separately, the other not, the former is the principal.
>
> 2. That where both can exist separately, the principal is that which the other is taken to adorn or complete.
>
> 3. That in the absence of these indications bulk prevails; next value."

The first test would only be applicable to the most obvious instances of accession; for example, paint applied to a table and so no longer capable of a separate existence as an identifiable thing. Bell's second criterion—in effect the primary test applicable to the less obvious but more difficult case—is essentially concerned with dominant rôle, and would thus appear to be consistent with Stair. Regarding the third basis of distinction, the better view is that value should be considered before bulk. Value, after all, is a fundamental measure applicable to all property, whereas bulk has no universal relevance.

On the basis of dominating rôle it is arguably not an exception that a picture is principal and the canvas or paper is accessory.[92] Looking at the nature of the thing as an item of property it is clear that the painting, drawing or other form dominates to the exclusion of the material having any identity[93]; arguably, in fact, the material loses any

---

[88] *Idem.*

[89] *Idem.*

[90] *Quaere*: would the result be otherwise if the setting was made to form a brooch?

[91] *Prin.*, § 1298.

[92] In respect of a mural, however, the land upon which the building is situate would be principal and, as in the case of a fixture, the landowner would acquire. See Stair, II.i.39; Erskine, II.i.16.

[93] Stair, II.i.39. Erskine, II.i.15, puts forward the view that it may be preferable to think in terms of *specificatio* (see below, para. 4.01)—the coming into being of a new thing—"for a piece of canvas, paper or parchment, after it is painted or written upon, is no longer looked upon as so much paper, but as a picture, a bond or a disposition."

relevant identity in the sense that its utility and purpose is consumed by use.[94]

Both Stair[95] and Erskine[96] treat writing and printing in the same way as painting, but this ignores the critical point that the actual form and manner of recording of a written composition do not have any bearing upon its intrinsic nature although, of course, presentation may have aesthetic significance. In prose, poetry or any form of communication by writing the essential feature is the particular use of words, and the better view is that a literary composition has a proprietary existence independent of the fact of its recording. On this basis one distinguishes a bookowner's right over the physical entity of a particular volume from the author's copyright over the text concerned. Accordingly, the better view would appear to be that the written or printed characters do accede to the paper but without giving any right to the composition. The decision in *Rollo* v. *Thomson*[97] would appear to support the proposition that, in the situation in which the owner of the copyright claims from the owner of the paper, the former should prevail. In this case a draftsman, formerly employed by an engineering firm, was held not to be entitled to drawings of machines made in furtherance of the business of his former employers—including some made on his own paper.

Criterion of annexation

The rôles of principal and accessory having been identified, it may **3.20** also be an issue whether annexation has occurred. Stair,[98] referring with apparent approval to Roman law, speaks of the accessory thing being acquiring by the owner of the principal artifact, "if without destruction thereof, or considerable detriment thereto, such materials could not be separated therefrom." The question of a change of ownership only arises when the union is permanent in some sense and a practical criterion is whether separation is possible without damage. Detriment, in the sense of the mere diminution of the principal thing following the removal of the accessory, is not an appropriate test because a change of ownership is only justified if separation cannot be achieved without damage. By way of example: A takes his car to the XY garage for a service; B's car is in to have a sunroof and new tyres fitted. Acting in error the garage staff service B's car and fit a sunroof

---

[94] Stair, II.i.39.

[95] *Idem.*

[96] II.i.15.

[97] (1857) 19 D. 994 *per* Lord Deas at p. 996: "The working drawings were all either prepared under the direction of the advocators or revised by them . . . [they] . . . were intended exclusively for the purposes of the advocators' works, and I do not doubt that they are their property. I am not moved by the fact that the respondent paid the stationer for the books."

[98] II.i.39.

and new tyres to A's vehicle. Both sunroof and tyres are accessory to the car, but whereas the sunroof cannot be removed without damage the tyres are easily removable. From the point of view of proprietary consequences the permanently-fitted sunroof must inevitably accede to the car but there is no change of ownership of the tyres.[99]

Proprietary consequences not open to control

3.21   Accession takes place regardless of the state of mind of the party making the annexation. Given that the identity of the accessory thing is lost, it is an unavoidable consequence of the proprietary facts that the owner of the principal entity acquires. As Stair[1] points out, Roman law recognised that it made no difference "whether these materials were made use of *bona* or *mala fide*; nor did the inherent *labes* of materials stolen, hinder the accession and appropriation thereof by contexture." The issue of good or bad faith could, of course, be relevant to the separate issue of an obligation to make compensation.

As a matter of original rather than derivative acquisition,[2] accession is not open to control through contract. In so far as the parties seek to depart from the consequences of accession as determined by the law of property, what they do will have only contractual effect.[3]

Constructive annexation to moveables

3.22   The concept of constructive annexation, as the basis of the recognition of what is included in a particular proprietary right, is not restricted to the circumstances of accession to heritable property.[4] A moveable item may, by destination, accede to another moveable, and this could be relevant from the point of view of what the purchaser of the principal entity is entitled to. The jack supplied with a motor vehicle, for example, goes with the car and the normal position would be that—unless the parties have agreed otherwise—a buyer of the vehicle would be entitled to it as part of the subject purchased. But other unattached motor accessories would not necessarily "go with the

---

[99] This approach may cause hardship to an innocent purchaser of the car who, understandably enough, would assume that the tyres go with the vehicle. The solution to this, however, should be on the basis of the policy-based protection of an innocent purchaser rather than through a distortion of the principles of property law.

[1] II.i.39.

[2] See above, paras. 1.17 and 3.01.

[3] See *Shetland Islands Council* v. *B.P. Petroleum Development* 1990 S.L.T. 82 *per* Lord Cullen at p. 94, as quoted above (para. 3.16a, n. 48). See also Gretton and Reid "Romalpa clauses: the current position," 1985 S.L.T. (News) 329 at p. 333: "It seems clear that a Romalpa clause cannot be used to prevent the operation of accession, for it is a settled principle that parties cannot contract out of such rules of the law of property as it does not suit them to observe. Accession operates mechanically in accordance with certain well-known rules." See also Carey Miller, "Logical consistency in property," 1990 S.L.T.(News) 197 at p. 198. Regarding Romalpa clauses and accession see below, para. 12.14.

[4] See above, para. 3.17.

car" on the basis of constructive annexation. Loose floor mats, for example, are distinguishable from a jack from the point of view of essential rôle.

CHAPTER 4

SPECIFICATION

The concept of specification

4.01   The making of a new entity of property raises the issue of a possible
reallocation of rights where the maker used another's materials. Both
Stair[1] and Erskine[2] note the essential factors of the production of a new
species from materials belonging to another.[3] The issue of a possible
change of ownership only arises where another's materials are used in
the production of a new thing with the consequence that vindication is
no longer possible.[4]

Specificatio is a concept distinguishable from *accessio*, although both
are original modes of acquisition involving the coming into being of a
single entity from two or more constituent elements. That the concepts
are distinct is borne out by the fact that they may be in virtual
competition, as in the case of a painting or drawing on another's
canvas or paper.[5] In principle, however, where this occurs accession
takes precedence; as Erskine[6] notes, a house built on another's land is
a new subject but the issue of the allocation of the right of ownership
does not arise because the house accedes to the land and, in fact, has
no separate existence as an entity of property distinct from the land.
Put another way, accession takes precedence over specification in so
far as the presence of a principal item may preclude the coming into
being of a new thing: accordingly, a mural belongs not to the painter
but to the owner of the house.[7]

---

[1] II.i.41.

[2] II.i.16.

[3] Case law has followed the Institutional writings which adopted the solution of
Justinian's Roman law. See the dictum of Lord Dundas in *International Banking
Corporation* v. *Ferguson, Shaw, & Sons*, 1910 S.C. 182 at p. 194: "In this state of
matters it seems to me that the case is a pure type for the application of the Roman
doctrine of *specificatio* . . . The doctrine of *specificatio* is undoubtedly part of the law of
Scotland. It is so recognised by all our Institutional writers." See also Lord Ardmillan in
Wylie and Lochhead v. *Mitchell* (1870) 8 M. 552 at p. 561: "the celebrated controversy
between the Proculians and the Sabinians—suppressed, yet scarcely settled, by what is
called the *media sententia* of Justinian."

[4] See *International Banking Corporation* v. *Ferguson, Shaw, & Sons, cit. supra* at pp.
191–192. Here Lord Low noted that where goods are dealt with "in such a way that they
no longer exist as separate or separable goods of a particular kind . . . there is a change
in the property of the goods, which may become in their new form either wholly the
property of the possessor, or the joint property of him and the true owner."

[5] See above para. 3.19.

[6] II.i.16.

[7] *Ibid.*

What is the basis of specification? In a modern case Lord President Clyde identified the doctrine as an equitable one,[8] but in a subsequent decision the correctness of this has been questioned.[9] The issue is important because the essential scope of the doctrine is necessarily determined—as a matter of logical conclusion—by its rationale; thus, the basis of specification is material to the question whether a maker in bad faith should acquire.[10]

The Institutional writers deal with specification as a form of accession.[11] Stair[12] states that the "materials cede to the workmanship," but in the same section notes that positive law is free to opt for any of a number of possible solutions. This seems to suggest that Stair did not regard the accession theory as conclusive. Given, however, that *specificatio* is concerned with the coming into being of a new thing, and the allocation of the right of ownership therein, its basis would appear to be a theory of logical entitlement. Whether the maker's right is explained as analogous to accession or occupation—in the sense of the first possessor of a new thing[13]—the rationale would seem to be a matter of the best claim to property where certain facts are present. More specifically, that reason dictates that the maker of a new—and, by definition, unowned—thing should acquire where there has been no prior determination of the right of ownership.[14] Stair's[15] reference to the freedom of positive law, in the case of the coming into being of a new thing, to opt for any of a number of possible alternatives, envisages solutions other than acquisition by the maker. This is consistent with the view that the creation of a new thing does not inevitably lead to a certain property consequence in the way that accession does. An important consequence of this is that specification is open to control on a derivative basis through agreement. In *Black* v. *Incorporation of Bakers, Glasgow*[16] Lord President Inglis noted that specification is "in certain circumstances a mode of transferring or acquiring property." In this case wheat was in the hands of a miller. On the basis of a delivery order relating to certain milled products,

---

[8] *McDonald* v. *Provan (of Scotland Street) Ltd.*, 1960 S.L.T. 231 at p. 232. See also the "natural equity" dictum of Lord President Inglis in *Wylie and Lochhead* v. *Mitchell* (1870) 8 M. 552 at p. 558 cited by Lord President Clyde.

[9] See *North-West Securities Ltd.* v. *Barrhead Coachworks Ltd.*, 1976 S.C. 68 *per* Lord McDonald at p. 72. See also Scot. Law Com., Memo. No. 28, *Corporeal Moveables: Mixing, Union and Creation*, paras. 15–20.

[10] See below, para. 4.04.

[11] Erskine, II.i.16; Bell, *Prin.*, § 1298. See above, para. 3.02.

[12] II.i.41.

[13] In *Oliver & Boyd* v. *The Marr Typefounding Co. Ltd.* (1901) 9 S.L.T. 170 at p. 171, Lord Stormonth Darling, in the Outer House, rejected the contention that the conversion of an article into another shape had the effect of terminating possession, but the dictum would not appear to exclude a theory of occupation.

[14] See Carey Miller, "Logical consistency in property," 1990 S.L.T. (News) 197 at pp. 198–199.

[15] II.i.41.

[16] (1867) 6 M. 136 at p. 141.

these were held to pass to a buyer as and when they came into existence. In principle, of course, this is an instance of derivative acquisition on the basis of *traditio* rather than original acquisition involving *specificatio*. But the important point is that, in respect of the making of a new thing, the parties concerned have greater scope for control of the proprietary consequences than is the case in respect of accession.[17]

Requirement of a new entity

4.02   The essential precondition to the application of *specificatio* is that a "new species or subject"[18] has come into being.[19] If there is no new thing—in the required sense—rights in the composite entity must be determined by reference to the interests of the owners of the constituent elements, unless of course *accessio* applies.[20] The allocation of rights in a corporate entity derived from subjects owned by different parties is dealt with in Chapter 5.

By what test is the question whether a new thing has come into being determined? Bell[21] applies the criterion of "a change being produced on the substance," and he goes on to give the examples of "flour from corn and wine from grapes." Stair[22] gives examples of the products of labour which do and do not constitute a change of species for the purpose of *specificatio*:

> "as wine of other men's grapes, malt of other men's bear, cloth of other men's wool, and even a ship of other men's timber; but not by the malting of barley, or dying of cloth, or the like, which change not the species."

The essential requirement, it would seem, is that a thing which has an identity distinct from its constituents has come into being. A simple criterion is that it goes by a different name; for example, a gate made from uniform wooden planks cut and nailed together—as distinct, it is suggested, from a nondescript item made from lengths of the same planks joined in a random manner. A change in the applicable

---

[17]; See the (unsuccessful) argument in *Re Peachdart Ltd.* [1984] 1 Ch. 131 at p. 142 noted below, para. 12.15.

[18] Erskine, II.i.16.

[19] See *North-West Securities Ltd.* v. *Barrhead Coachworks Ltd.*, 1976 S.C. 68 *per* Lord McDonald at p. 72: "It is of the essence of *specificatio* that the original article disappears . . . the creation of a new species . . . is fundamental to *specificatio*." Hence in *Armour* v. *Thyssen Edelstahlwerke A.G.*, 1989 S.L.T. 182 *per* Lord McDonald at p. 190, the pursuers argued that work carried out on the steel in effect "converted it into a different article."

[20] See above, para. 4.01.

[21] *Prin.*, § 1289.

[22] II.i.41.

commercial category would normally support the claim that a new thing has come into being.

Requirement of reducibility

Where a new species has come into being the issue of reducibility **4.03** arises. In *International Banking Corporation* v. *Ferguson, Shaw, & Sons*[23] Lord Justice-Clerk MacDonald noted the two essential factors in relation to the use of oil to make a lard compound: "This created a new species, and in such form that separation was no longer possible."

Accepting that questions of property consequence and possible compensation should be kept separate, it seems that the issue should be whether the new thing itself is reducible without damage.[24] The law, however, tends towards the criterion whether the constituent elements can be restored intact. Erskine's[25] treatment shows this:

> "where the new species can be again reduced to the mass or matter of which it was made, the law considers the former subject as still existing; wherefore the new species continues to belong to the proprietor of that former subject, which still exists, though under another form; as in the case of plate made of bullion."

The emphasis upon reducibility, as the primary criterion, is also found in the case law. One may note the approach of Lord Dundas in the *International Banking Corporation* case[26]: "a new species had been created . . . but of which the component parts could not after the creation be again resolved into their original elements."

Given that the law's solution is that "if the product can easily be reduced to the first matter, the owners of the matter remain proprietors of the whole,"[27] it does appear that the issue of reducibility is the dominating consideration. This, of course, means that if the thing can be restored to its component parts the question whether it is a new thing can be avoided.

---

[23] 1910 S.C. 182 at p. 193.

[24] Where the existence of a new thing is recognised, the question of its reducibility should arguably take account of possible detriment to the new product. Whether or not a new thing has come into being is an issue separate from the question whether it is reducible. The issue with which *specificatio* is concerned arises because a new thing has been produced and this is a condition of fact with which the law must deal. Arguably, it begs the question whether a new thing has in fact come into being to go directly to the issue of reducibility. As indicated, the difference that this makes is the extent to which the question of detriment to the new thing itself has any relevance in the determination of rights.

[25] II.i.16.

[26] 1910 S.C. 182 at p. 194.

[27] Stair, II.i.41.

Requirement of good faith

4.04   Bell[28] required good faith on the part of the maker of a new thing: "if the materials, as a separate existence, be destroyed in bona fide, the property is with the workman; the owner of the materials having a personal claim for a like quantity and quality, or for the price of the materials."

Although he does not deal directly with the issue, Stair[29] points out that whatever basis is applied to the problem of determining the ownership of a new thing the deprived party is always entitled to reparation "unless the presumption be strong enough to infer, that the workmanship was performed *animo donandi*, by him who knew the materials belonged to another." If the normal rule precluded acquisition by a *mala fide* maker there would be no logical need for this exception.[30] Stair's treatment of acquisition on the basis of contexture is relevant by way of analogy. Apparently adopting the Roman law approach, Stair[31] notes that where thread or other material was worked into cloth, or some other dominant thing, with the result that separation was impossible without destruction or considerable detriment, ownership passed to the owner of the dominant item regardless of whether the annexation was made in good or bad faith—"nor did the inherent *labes* of materials stolen, hinder the accession and appropriation thereof by contexture."[32] If in this case the question of ownership is determined on the basis of the proprietary circumstances and regardless of the annexor's *animus* then, as a matter of consistency, one would expect the same approach in the case of *specificatio*. Whether an owner is deprived of his interest through accession, or because a new thing has come into being, the question of rights in the new entity should be distinct from the issue of possible compensation. While the state of mind of the annexor or maker should be relevant to the issue of compensation, it is open to question whether it should be a consideration in respect of the proprietary consequences.

In *McDonald* v. *Provan (of Scotland Street) Ltd.*[33] Lord President Clyde regarded good faith on the part of the maker as a prerequisite to the doctrine of *specificatio*—"the doctrine can only be invoked where there is complete bona fides on the part of the manufacturer." In the

---

[28] *Prin.*, § 1298.

[29] II.i.41.

[30] This approach seems consistent with Stair's (II.i.41) definition as "that appropriation which is by specification, whereby, of materials belonging to other owners, a new species is produced."

[31] II.i.39.

[32] *Ibid.* As Scot. Law Com., Memo. No. 28, *Corporeal Moveables: Mixing, Union and Creation*, para. 8 noted: "It does not matter, in a question of ownership, if the materials were used *bona fide* or *mala fide*, nor even if they were stolen. The *labes realis* which normally attaches to stolen goods does not prevent their appropriation by this form of industrial accession."

[33] 1960 S.L.T. 231 at p. 232.

matter in hand the learned Lord President regarded the absence of good faith as a fatal defect:

> "In the present case the manufacturer was not constructing his new vehicle in *bona fide*. On the contrary a substantial portion of it was stolen by him from its rightful owner. This in itself excludes the doctrine of *specificatio* and introduces the other well-established principle of Scots law whereby the true owner of stolen property is entitled to follow and to recover his property into whoever's hands it may have gone."

The utility of Lord President Clyde's insistence on good faith is that it puts the law in a position to deny that the *mala fide* maker—possibly the thief of a constituent item—acquires a proprietary right in the new thing.

In addition to the direct authority of Bell[34] that good faith is required of the maker, Lord President Clyde cited the case of *Wylie and Lochhead* v. *Mitchell*[35] in support of his conclusion that *specificatio* "is an equitable doctrine, not a strict rule of law."[36] The better view, however, is that although the decision does not support the conclusion of an equitable doctrine it does raise the possibility of a solution based on equity. The decision would appear to be to the effect that the doctrine of *specificatio* is a rule of the law of property which may be contrasted with the equitable conclusion that entitlement should be shared according to the contributions of labour and materials.[37]

The opinion of Lord President Inglis[38] in *Wylie and Lochhead* v. *Mitchell* supports the conclusion that the possibility of a decision based

---

[34] *Prin.*, § 1298.

[35] (1870) 8 M. 552.

[36] *McDonald* v. *Provan (of Scotland Street) Ltd.*, 1960 S.L.T. 231 at p. 232. See also *Zahnrad Fabrik Passau GmbH* v. *Terex Ltd.*, 1986 S.L.T. 84 *per* Lord Davidson at p. 87: "The opinion of Lord President Inglis in *Wylie and Lochhead* supported the view that equitable considerations carried weight in this branch of the law. That case was authority for the general principle of equity that when the materials, skill and labour of two or more persons are voluntarily and inseparably combined in the production of an indivisible corporeal subject, the same belongs to the contributors jointly, the interest of each being in proportion to the value of his contribution."

[37] The distinctive feature of the facts in *Wylie and Lochhead* v. *Mitchell* (1870) 8 M. 552 was that the parties had contracted to create a new thing by both contributing materials and workmanship. Lord President Inglis expressly excluded *specificatio*; only in the circumstances of the inapplicability of any rule of the law of property did the court invoke "natural equity." (See at pp. 556–557.) A correct reading of the Lord President's opinion would, therefore, appear to be that *specificatio* applies as a rule of law rather than as a result derived from equity, and one may read into the opinion the conclusion (supported by Grotius, *De Jure Belli ac Pacis*, 2.8.19.2) that a resolution based upon equity leads to the conclusion that ownership in the new thing should be shared.

[38] At p. 558: "We are not entitled to follow this philosophical doctrine [the equitable basis of shared interests in the product as contended for by Grotius, *loc. cit.*] to all its just results, and to hold that the same rights of common property will arise from *specificatio* as from *confusio*, because we are restrained by the rules of law fixed as applicable to these particular categories."

upon principles of equity can only arise where the recognised rules of property are inapplicable.[39] It seems that the better view is that the proprietary consequences of the making of a new thing follows regardless of the state of mind of the maker.[40]

---

[39] *Ibid.*: "But when we are called upon to adjudicate in a case which cannot be brought within any ordinary and known category, we are, I apprehend, at liberty to adopt that principle of equity which will be most just in its results, without inquiring too curiously or balancing too nicely to which of several categories the new case has most general resemblance."

[40] Erskine (II.i.16) would appear to be consistent with this; while reduction to constituents is possible the former subjects are taken still to exist, but "where the new species cannot be so reduced, there is no room for that *fictio juris*; as in wine, which, because it cannot be again turned into the grapes of which it was made, becomes the property, not of the owner of the grapes but of the maker of the wine." The implication of this statement is that the effect of specification is for ownership to pass to the maker as a matter of proprietary consequence.

CHAPTER 5

CONFUSION/COMMIXTION

Change of ownership through mixing

The law of property must provide for a reallocation of rights of **5.01**
ownership when a single proprietary entity is constituted by the
merging of separate elements belonging to different parties. Stair
treats separately the cases of *confusio*[1] and *commixtio*[2]; the former a
merger of substances which gives a single entity, absolutely irreducible
to constituents, and the latter a mixture in respect of which, in theory,
separation is possible but, in practice, it is not.

Given that the property of two or more parties has been consoli-
dated to the extent that the *status quo ante* cannot be restored, it
follows that there must be a reallocation of rights. As Lord Shaw put
it, the solution secures "the extrication of the rights of parties by
applying [a] rule of distribution amongst co-owners."[3] Where a reallocation of rights occurs on the basis of *confusio* or *commixtio*, the
result is a instance of the acquisition of ownership in so far as what is
owned after the merger must necessarily differ from what was previously owned.

Rights in compound proportionate to value of constituents

In the case of the mixing of liquids—*confusio*—because there can be **5.02**
no separation of the constituents a change of proprietary rights occurs,
as Stair[4] puts it, to the extent

> "that what before belonged to several owners severally, becometh
> now to belong to the same owners *pro indiviso*, according to the
> proportion of the value of their shares."

Stair[5] notes that the same result follows in the case of *commixtio*
involving

> "grain or other arid bodies, belonging to diverse owners, which
> cannot be easily separated, or of any materials in one mass, work
> or artifice, if they be not separable,"

---

[1] II.i.36.
[2] II.i.37.
[3] *Tyzack & Branfoot Steamship Co. Ltd.* v. *Sandeman & Sons*, 1913 S.C. (H.L.) 84 at
p. 91.
[4] II.i.36.
[5] II.i.37.

71

even though

> "all the ingredients remain without alteration of their substance, so that in subtility, the property of each part might be considered as remaining with the former owner."[6]

Limited significance of liquid/solids distinction

5.03   The traditional distinction between liquids and solids is valid from the point of view of the actual consequences of mixing but, this said, the criterion of the separability of constituents is an overriding consideration. As Stair[7] shows, the commixture of flocks of sheep is only a distinguishable case "where each individual is discernible and separable, as having the several marks of their distinct owners." But even this case may produce the result of *commixtio* when, for example:

> "different flocks of unmarked lambs should in any way fall to come together, so that the owners, or the servants, could not distinguish their own, there was no remedy but to divide according to the number belonging to the several owners, and till that division were made, every owner had a proportionable interest in every individual, seeing none of them could say or instruct this or that to be properly his own."[8]

Change of ownership occurs regardless

5.04   Because the necessity for an adjustment of rights arises from the condition of an irreducible compound—a state which is the same regardless of the *animus* of the mixer—it follows that the circumstances under which the mixing occurred are not relevant to the allocation of rights although, of course, the mixer's act may give rise to a delictual claim.[9] Stair[10] is clear on the point that the proprietary consequences of *confusio* follow regardless of the motivating factor:

> "neither is there any difference, whether the confusion be made by the consent of parties, by accident, or by mistake, or fault, the

---

[6] See Scot. Law Com., Memo. No. 28, *Corporeal Moveables: Mixing, Union and Creation*, para. 6.

[7] II.i.37.

[8] *Ibid.*

[9] An example would be the culpable mixing of an exceptional single malt whisky with a supermarket blend; the solution given by Erskine (II.i.17) that "the owner of the high-priced wine has a right to demand that a larger share be allotted to him by the judge" would not meet the loss in this case. On the problem of possible liability for wrongful mixing see *Indian Oil Corp.* v. *Greenstone Shipping S.A.* [1988] 3 All E.R. 893, commented on in Carey Miller, "Does *confusio* need to confuse?" 1988 S.L.T. (News) 270 at p. 272.

[10] II.i.36.

effect being the same in all: for, because the parts are undiscernible and inseparable so as to give every owner the individual body he had before; therefore he can only receive by equivalence, the like value by division."

Although Stair[11] is here addressing the case of *confusio*, it is submitted that his statement applies equally to *commixtio* which is based "[u]pon the same ground"[12] and, in respect of which, it would be impossible to justify a different conclusion. The approach, one may note, is consistent with Stair's observation that in the case of contexture ownership passes regardless of whether the act was done in good or bad faith.[13]

The case in which substances are mixed, on the basis of an agreement—express or implied—providing for the allocation of rights in the resulting mixture is an exception to the rule that, on the mixing of substances, proprietary rights are determined regardless of intention. However, this would not be an instance of original acquisition through *confusio* or *commixtio*, but rather a case of derivative transfer with the process of mixing a form of delivery. If, in this situation, the agreement does not provide for the shares each party will have in the compound entity, the consent of the parties "makes the whole a common property, according to the shares that each owner had formerly in the several subjects."[14]

Subject to accession and specification

Where one can identify the distinct rôles of principal and accessory, **5.05** or where a new thing has come into being, the concepts of *accessio* or *specificatio* may apply to the exclusion of rules applicable because there has been a mixing. In so far as either of these concepts is applicable, the result must override the incidental fact that substances have been mixed. *Commixtio/confusio* is concerned with the necessary reallocation of the rights of owners of the constituent elements in a compound mixture. *Accessio* and *specificatio*, on the other hand, are based upon positive entitlement and the intrinsically superior right of one owner against another or others; in the former case the claim of the owner of the principal item, in the latter, the claim of the maker of a new thing.[15]

Erskine[16] notes that *specificatio* defeats *confusio*, and the mixer "whether he be one of the proprietors or a third party" acquires where

---

[11] *Ibid.*

[12] II.i.37.

[13] II.i.39. See above, para. 4.04.

[14] Erskine, II.i.17.

[15] But see the argument for a distinction between accession and specification; below, para. 12.15.

[16] II.i.17. See also Bell, *Prin.* § 1298(2): "If the union be of substances different, so as to create a *tertium quid*, the property is . . . with the owner of the materials, or with the manufacturer, according to the possibility or impossibility of restoring the original substances."

"a new species is formed, which cannot be again brought back to the first condition of those substances."

While it can be seen that a lesser substance might well, on mixing, accede to a principal one—for example, soda-water added to whisky— it is open to question whether *specificatio* has a rôle in the context of the mixing of different substances. It would seem somewhat arbitrary to identify as *specificatio* those instances of mere mixing which— without further processing or refinement—are seen to produce a new species because the mixture concerned happens to be labelled as a distinct substance. Should the maker of a quantity of "punch" have an overriding claim against the owners of the constituent liquids on the basis that it is a new thing? Arguably not.

CHAPTER 6

ACQUISITION OF FRUITS

GENERAL MATTERS

Exception to principle of accession

As indicated,[1] although the notion of "fruits" is in one sense a **6.01**
matter of accession it is also a distinct issue needing separate treatment. While accession applies as long as the fruit or progeny is
physically joined or connected by necessity to the parent thing,[2] upon
separation it becomes a distinct item of property—at any rate to the
extent that it is capable of independent existence.[3] But this said, the
connection between the fruit or progeny and the parent thing—
whether animal or vegetable—means that separation notwithstanding,
ownership in the fruit continues to vest in the owner of the parent
entity. The present section is concerned with an exception to this—the
case in which ownership in a fruit vests, upon separation, in a party
other than the owner of the parent thing.[4] The law recognises that both
the *bona fide* possessor and the liferenter are, in principle, entitled to
the fruits of property held.

Acquisition of fruits in the sense contemplated is an original mode of
acquiring property, at any rate to the extent that it does not involve
any act of will on the part of the owner of the fruit-yielding thing. This
may be contrasted with the derivative acquisition of fruits: typically the
situation of a party holding the parent property on the basis of a
contractual right which includes entitlement to fruits. In this situation
acquisition is derivative, with delivery to the party entitled upon
separation.

Usual instance possession of heritage

The most usual situation in which possession gives a right to fruits is **6.02**
in respect of land.[5] Obviously enough, the ownership and possession of
land are frequently separated and, of course, land may well have the

---

[1] Above, para. 3.02.
[2] See Erskine, II.i.14: "in two things which have an intimate connection with or
dependence upon one another, the property of the principal thing draws after it that of
its accessory; for whatever proceeds or arises from what is mine is also mine as being
part of my property."
[3] This makes possible the recognition of a right to fruits as a distinct aspect of the right
of possession. Scots law follows the civilian tradition in breaking down the right of
ownership into its constituent elements (see above, para. 1.10), one of which is the right
to fruits; see Stair, II.i.12.
[4] Erskine, II.i.14: "the owner holds them no longer as accessories of the field from
which they are disjoined, but as separate subjects; and therefore, if he shall after that
period sell the field, those trees or fruits which are thus disunited from the ground
continue his own."
[5] See Gordon, *Scottish Land Law*, para. 14.49.

capacity to produce fruits, whether natural or civil.[6]

Different classes of fruits

6.03   Scots law subdivides "fruits" in the wide and general sense into the
categories of natural, industrial and civil. The distinction between
natural and civil relates to the form of fruit, whereas the label
industrial applies to natural fruits produced by the industry of the
holder of the land concerned—essentially cultivated periodical crops.[7]
The primary relevance of the distinction between natural and industrial
is that, as against the owner, a holder of the fruit-bearing property may
have a more extensive right to fruits produced by his own industry.[8]
But the category of industrial fruits would appear to be of greater
importance in respect of fruits acquired on a derivative basis: most
usually by a party who holds the fruit-yielding entity not as owner but
by way of a limited right which acknowledges the owner's position; the
case of a leasehold tenant who grows an annual crop would be the
most usual instance of the acquisition of industrial fruits.[9] From the
point of view of the acquisition of fruits by the *bona fide* possessor and
the liferenter the distinction is of lesser importance[10] because, in both
these cases, there is general entitlement to fruits.[11]

The various stages, from coming into being to consumption, are
reflected in certain terms of art which are used in the context of the
acquisition of rights in fruits. Fruits are *pendentes* when, "not yet
separated from the subject which produced them," they "continue part
of it."[12] In an appropriate case fruits are acquired *perceptione* or by
reaping; including, in the case of civil fruits, the receipt of rents, dues
or interest. As Rankine[13] notes, the fact that by separation fruits cease
to be part of the subject which produced them and become independent things means that the notions of *fructus pendentes* and *fructus
percepti* are truly contrary.[14] Clearly enough, any reaped or received

---

[6] Scots law recognises this basic civilian distinction between the actual production of
the land and rents or profits deriving from landed property; see Erskine, II.i.26. See
further, below, para. 6.03 on the distinction between types of fruits.

[7] See Erskine, II.i.26.

[8] *Ibid.*

[9] The basis of the tenant's right to industrial fruits as one derived from the owner,
whose position is acknowledged in the very nature of the parties' relationship, emerges
from a description of the general purposes of agricultural leases given by Bell, *Prin.*, §
1179.

[10] See Rankine, *Landownership*, p. 84.

[11] Although, in principle, it is true that whereas natural fruits are only acquired by the
bona fide possessor or liferenter on separation, industrial or cultivated crops—through a
policy-based exception to the principle of *accessio* (see above, para. 3.05)—are not
considered the property of the landowner despite their connection with the land. This, of
course, may have implications from the point of view of diligence. See above, para. 3.08.

[12] Erskine, II.i.26.

[13] *Landownership*, pp. 83–84.

[14] See also Hume III, p. 241: "either *percepti* such as wool shorn from a sheep, crops
of corn in the barnyard, rents actually levied from the tenants; or . . . *fructus pendentes*,
that is in the opposite situations."

fruits may be consumed or retained. One view of the law takes this to be relevant to the final determination of rights: hence the category *fructus consumpti*.[15]

BONA FIDE POSSESSOR'S RIGHT TO FRUITS

Basis of bona fide possessor's right

A *bona fide* party is one who has an honest belief in his right of property in the land or moveable possessed and, on this basis, he **6.04** acquires fruits which are separated and so open to acquisition. The right to fruits is a benefit transient in nature, and it is appropriate that a party in the position of owner should enjoy the fruits as well as the use of the subject.

In *Houldsworth* v. *Brand's Trs.*[16] Lord Gifford noted that the *bona fide* possessor's right to fruits arises "[f]rom considerations of equity." The Institutional writers consider the basis underlying the doctrine and it appears that justification may be found in both considerations of equity and of justice and from a point of view of legal principle.

Stair[17] has no difficulty in justifying acquisition on the basis of consumption:

> "because they who enjoy that which they think their own, do consume the fruits thereof without expectation of repetition[18] or accompt, else they are presumed to reserve them, or employ them profitably for restitution; and if it were otherwise, there could be no quiet or security to men's minds, who could call nothing securely their own, if the event of a dubious right might make them restore what they had consumed *bona fide*."

The rationale is from the negative point of view that because the restitution of fruits consumed by a *bona fide* possessor cannot be permitted[19] one may say that there is acquisition through consumption.

Stair's justification does no more than support the view that consumed fruits are acquired. Erskine, on the other hand, contends for acquisition regardless of consumption[20] and this, of course, requires a more positive justification. Erskine[21] argues that the *bona fide* possessor's entitlement is based upon his essential contribution to the production of fruits.

---

[15] See Stair, I.vii.12; see below, para. 6.07.
[16] (1876) 3 R. 304 at p. 316.
[17] II.i.23.
[18] See below, para. 10.03, n. 24.
[19] See Stair, I.vii.12.
[20] See below, para. 6.07.
[21] II.i.25.

"This doctrine has been introduced, that the minds of men would bestow their pains and money on what they believe their own, and who afterwards enjoy the profits thereof, may be secured from the continual apprehensions under which they might labour, if the event of a doubtful right should lay them under a necessity of accounting for what they had thus possssed *bona fide*."[22]

A rationale derived from legal principle without overt policy justification is put forward by Rankine[23]; the argument is simply that the *bona fide* possessor's right is derived from the principle "that property in moveables is presumed from possession." Fruits are taken, so Rankine argues,

"as never having been, in their character of independent subjects, the property of the true owner of the land; but, on the contrary, as belonging to the person who, being in possession of the principal subject for the time being, also possesses its fruits as soon as they come to have an independent existence in the eye of the law."

The *bona fide* possessor's right, according to Rankine, is in fact more correctly seen to be warranted as a corollary of the accepted position that a possessor's *mala fides* would justify the restoration of the subject possessed with all that had been derived from it.[24]

There is no definitive answer or justification to explain the *bona fide* possessor's right to fruits. It does seem, however, that there are a number of acceptable reasons for the rule that separated fruits vest in the possessor—*a fortiori*, for Stair's more restricted variant that consumed fruits are acquired.[25]

When is possession bona fide?

6.05   Stair[26] gives a succinct characterisation of possessors in good faith as those "who do truly think that which they possess to be their own, and know not the right of any others." Erskine[27] introduces an objective element in the requirement of a reasonable basis for the belief:

"A *bona fide* possessor is one who, though he be not truly proprietor of the subject which he possesses, yet believes himself proprietor upon probable grounds, and with a good conscience."

---

[22] Complementary to this one may note the "most material consideration of any," mentioned by Hume (III, p. 241): "that though the defender have saved and profited, yet still his plan of life and expence must have been calculated, upon the whole, on the footing of the revenue which he truly believed himself to have right to."

[23] *Landownership*, p. 76.

[24] *Idem*, pp. 76–77.

[25] See below, para. 6.07.

[26] II.i.24.

[27] II.i.25.

Although, in principle, *bona fides* is a subjective condition—a matter of the possessor's belief in his right to the thing—a claim to this state of mind must at least be consistent with the circumstances. Where a party is in possession of land under a lease from the owner he can hardly be heard to assert a belief in the acquisition of a right of ownership. Given that the condition of subjective good faith must necessarily follow on from a commencement of possession consistent with a belief in the acquisition of a right of ownership, one can see that, for practical purposes, the basis upon which possession was acquired is of central importance. As Lord President Inglis stated in *Huntly's Trs.* v. *Hallyburton's Trs.*[28] "[t]he doctrine of *bona fide* consumption, I think, applies only to the case of a person who has possessed on an apparently good title, which is afterwards found to be invalid": the classic instance, of course, being "the case of one who purchases a subject which he had reason to think was the property of the seller, but which in truth belonged to a third party."[29]

The circumstances may be such that, on an objective assessment, the presence of subjective good faith can be taken for granted. A dictum of Lord Cowan in *Menzies* v. *Menzies*[30] illustrates this.

> "But, in the first place, the defender possessed the whole locality lands by virtue of the deed of locality; and, in the second place, to me it does seem impossible to doubt that she did so in perfect good faith and in justifiable reliance upon her unchallengeable title."

Looking at the possessor's position from a negative point of view, a *mala fide* possessor is one who "possesses a subject not his own, and knows at the same time, or, which comes to the same account, may upon the smallest reflection know that he is not the rightful owner."[31] Stair[32] refers to "private knowledge"—as opposed to knowledge intimated through legal process—and notes that "at least unless the private knowledge be certain, it is not regarded, nor doth constitute the knower in *mala fides*." These touchstones may appear to reflect different points of view but, arguably, there is no difference in the substance of what is said. Erskine's criterion of a possessor's knowledge that he is not owner carries the necessary implication that the party concerned is certain about his position. The test is simply whether there is knowledge of the true facts, which "upon the smallest reflection"[33] would cause the possessor to realise that he is not owner.

---

[28] (1880) 8 R. 50 at pp. 59–60.
[29] Erskine, II.i.25.
[30] (1863) 1 M. 1025 at p. 1034.
[31] Erskine, II.i.25.
[32] II.i.24.
[33] Erskine, II.i.25.

The aspect of realisation of the true position must necessarily be determined objectively and it is submitted that, given proof of knowledge of the facts, it would not be open to the possessor to contend that he had not reflected upon their implications.

The issue of *mala fides* may arise through the denial of a claim that the fruit-bearing thing was acquired *bona fide*; alternatively, it may arise in relation to the question when possession in good faith came to an end.[34]

Certain circumstances are incompatible with a claim to *bona fide* possession. Erskine[35] excludes possession "attained by stealth, fraud or violence" and one can see that proof of such circumstances could hardly leave room for the recognition of a claim by the owner that he honestly believed he had acquired a right of property.

Somewhat more difficult to justify is the exclusion of possession based upon a mistake of law. Stair[36] is clear that there can be no claim to *bona fide* possession in this case: "yet when by a common or known law, the title is void materially, in this case the possessor is not esteemed to possess *bona fide*, it being so evident, *nam ignorantia juris non excusat*." Erskine,[37] to like effect, states that possession cannot be styled *bona fide* "where the title of it is void by the obvious and universally known rules of law."

This exclusion would appear to be a matter of policy; a legal bar to acquisition must prevail regardless of the fact of the possessor's honest belief in his right.[38]

The fact that the right to possession is in dispute does not necessarily mean that a continuation of possession is *mala fide*. Unless a party can be said to be *mala fide* in contesting the issue of a right to possession it does not necessarily follow that his continuing possession is in bad faith. In such a case the matter must be looked at from a wholly objective position. In *Swanson* v. *Grieve*[39] Lord President Inglis could not say that the claimants' case was so clear that the tenant in possession was "*in mala fide* in litigating" the matter.

Right to fruits not limited to case of competing titles

6.06   The issue of a *bona fide* possessor's right to fruits most usually arises in the circumstances of competing claims to ownership in the fruit-yielding property. However, it is submitted that it may also arise where

---

[34] See below, para. 6.08.

[35] II.i.27.

[36] II.i.24.

[37] II.i.27.

[38] The example given by Erskine (II.i.27) of a minor's contracts illustrates the difference between a mistake of law and one of fact: "one cannot possess *bona fide* upon a right granted by a minor having curators, without their consent. But a right granted by a minor who has no curators, though it be set aside afterwards on the head of minority and lesion, is a sufficient foundation for a *bona fide* possession; and consequently has the effect to make all the intermediate fruits, received prior to the reduction, to belong to the possessor."

[39] (1891) 18 R. 371 at p. 374. See below, para. 6.08.

title is not in dispute but the possessor has consumed fruits on the basis of an honest belief in a right subsequently contested by the owner. The case of *Morrison* v. *School Board of St. Andrews*[40] illustrates, but does not decide the point. Heritable subjects were acquired by a trust for educational purposes, but to be held for the truster's successors on any discontinuation of a particular educational system. When this occurred the school was transferred to a school board in terms of applicable legislation and the income—the fruits—of the trust was applied to maintaining the school. A claim by the truster's successors to remit rents received by the defenders was met by the defence of *bona fide* consumption, but the point was raised that the concept had no application because there were not two competing titles involved. A majority of the Court of Session held that although the board possessed under a colourable title it did so in the honest belief in a right to fruits. This approach avoided the issue of the absence of competing titles which Lord Salvesen, dissenting, regarded as fatal to the claim to fruits.[41]

The better view would appear to be that the majority ruling is correct; an honest belief, on the part of the school board, in its rights to possession and fruits—without seeing itself as owner—was sufficient from the point of view of the acquisition of fruits.[42]

Are unconsumed fruits acquired?

Stair is clear in restricting the acquisition of fruits by a *bona fide* **6.07** possessor to items actually consumed. The limitation is mentioned first in the context of restitution[43] and its application to things and "their natural birth and fruits extant, not *bona fide* consumed."[44] The point is made again in the property context that, one of the two rights deriving from possession is "the right of appropriation of the fruits consumed *bona fide*."[45]

Erskine,[46] on the other hand, is expressly to the effect that the *bona fide* possessor's right extends to extant fruits even though unconsumed:

---

[40] 1918 S.C. 51.

[41] *Idem*, p. 64. On this issue see Gordon, *Scottish Land Law*, para. 14.51.

[42] The right of ownership comprises the constituent rights of possession, use, fruits and the right to part with or destroy the thing concerned. (See Hume, III, 201, where the right of property is defined in terms of powers: the power to use and enjoy the thing; the power to recover it when lost or removed, and the power of alienation or disposal. Hume's definition, although wider than mine in that the protection of ownership is included, is essentially the same with regard to what may be said to be the rights of enjoyment of property.) Given that the right of ownership may be broken down between different parties on the basis of the *usus, fructus, abusus* division, it follows that, for the purpose of the acquisition of fruits, it is not necessary for the possessor to believe that he is owner in the sense of having the power of disposal.

[43] I.vii.10.

[44] See also I.vii.12: "whereby what fruits he, who hath possessed *bona fide*, hath consumed, though he have profited, and been enriched thereby, he is not obliged to restore the same."

[45] Stair, II.i.22.

[46] II.i.25.

"it is universally agreed that, by our customs, perception of the fruits is by itself sufficient for acquiring their property; so that if the fruits have been *percepti* by the possessor, he may retain them as his own, though they should be still extant."[47]

Hume,[48] recognising that Erskine did not agree, prefers Stair on the basis that it is appropriate to regard unconsumed fruits as accessories of the principal thing.[49] Rankine,[50] however, quotes Erskine with approval and goes on to say that: "[i]t is not necessary that they should be consumed—including, in that term, alienated or immixed beyond recognition." Given that the considerations supporting the acquisition of fruits tend generally to recognise the entitlement of the *bona fide* possessor by reason of his relationship with the fruit-bearing property, it does seem appropriate that the "property in the fruits passes to the *bona fide* possessor of the principal subject by their mere separation."[51]

Case law does not resolve this issue. In *Duke of Roxburghe* v. *Wauchope*[52] Lord Gifford appears to accept that Scots law departed from a requirement of consumption.[53] In *Menzies* v. *Menzies*,[54] however, although the question was not in issue, all three opinions make reference to the defence of *bona fide* perception and consumption in a manner which suggests that the court took for granted that both elements were necessary.[55] Moreover, in the subsequent case of *Huntly's Trs.* v. *Hallyburton's Trs.*[56] Lord President Inglis speaks of "[t]he doctrine of *bona fide* consumption."

Two leading modern text-writers consider that Scots law does not accept the requirement of consumption of later Roman law. Professor

---

[47] In *Duke of Roxburghe* v. *Wauchope* (1825) 1 W. & S. 41 at p. 56, Lord Gifford indicates a tentative preference for Erskine, "who states the more modern law upon the subject, and more at large than Lord Stair, though Lord Stair is of the highest authority in the law of Scotland."

[48] III, p. 242: "Yet, I confess, I do not well see how we are to get over what Lord Stair says, that these fruits while extant are accessories of the principal thing; and the subjects therefore of a *rei vindicatio* at his instance."

[49] See also Bankton, I.viii.12, 18.

[50] *Landownership*, p. 83.

[51] *Ibid.*

[52] (1825) 1 W. & S. 41 at p. 58: "if a party is *bona fide* in possession, he is entitled to the rents which have become due during that time, even although he may not have received the rents till after that period . . . The question of consumption cannot, therefore, come into the consideration of the Court. But, generally speaking, the question is, whether they had been received *bona fide* during the time of a *bona fide* possession." See also *Cleghorn* v. *Eliott* (1842) 4 D. 1389 at pp. 1391–1392.

[53] Gordon, *Scottish Land Law*, para. 14.48, notes that on the principle *messis sementem sequitur* the harvest goes to the *bona fide* sower (see above para. 3.05) and it does appear that a general prerequisite of consumption would be inconsistent with this.

[54] (1863) 1 M. 1025.

[55] See Lord Neaves at p. 1037; Lord Justice-Clerk Inglis at p. 1038. See also the *obiter dictum* of Lord Young in *Liqr. of West Lothian Oil Co. Ltd.* v. *Mair* (1892) 20 R. 64 at p. 70: "*fruges bona fide perceptae et consumptae* are held to be the property of the party who is ultimately found not to have the title."

[56] (1880) 8 R. 50 at pp. 59–60.

Sir Thomas Smith[57] maintains that Scots law departed from the maxim *"Bona fide possessor facit fructus perceptos et consumptos suos,"* and that "[p]erception or ingathering of the fruits gives good title in them to the *bona fide* possessor." Professor Gordon[58] states that the Roman maxim "understates" Scots law in that "the *bona fide* possessor is entitled to all fruits separated, not gathered, during his *bona fides*, even if the fruits have not been consumed."

The better view, on the authorities, would appear to be that consumption is not a prerequisite. It is submitted that this is also supported on the basis of principle. As Rankine[59] notes, the rule of later Roman law—requiring consumption—followed by Stair[60] is questionable from a dogmatic point of view through its "taking back with one hand what it gave with the other." This is valid in the sense that control of the right of consumption is synonymous with ownership and, indeed, inconsistent with any lesser right. Separated fruits are open to acquisition as independent items of property; to contend that such fruits, while unconsumed, remain accessory to the parent entity is incompatible with the premise which gives the right of consumption— *i.e.* that ownership in the separated fruits vests in the *bona fide* possessor.

Termination of bona fide possessor's right

Where possession is in good faith, on what basis is this state of mind **6.08** taken to change to one of bad faith with the consequence that the right to fruits is terminated? Knowledge that the fruit-yielding thing is in fact the property of another—*conscientia rei alienae*—is the critical requirement. But, just as the state of *bona fides* is largely inferred, equally there must be some event which can be taken to justify the inference of a changed state of mind on the part of the possessor.

Erskine[61] comments that a *bona fide* state of mind must necessarily come to an end "when the possessor can have no longer a probable opinion that the subject is his own; for it is in that opinion that the essence of *bona fides* consisteth." Following on from this, Erskine[62] considers the circumstances in which a change in the possessor's state of mind can be inferred: "*Mala fides* is therefore induced by *conscientia rei alienae*, though such consciousness should not proceed from legal interpellation, but barely from private knowledge; for private knowledge necessarily implies consciousness." Rankine[63] has difficulty in interpreting this statement because, as he sees it, "[t]he change

---

[57] *Short Commentary*, p. 296.
[58] *Scottish Land Law*, para. 14.48.
[59] *Landownership*, p. 83.
[60] See I.vii.10, 12; II.i.22, 23.
[61] II.i.28.
[62] *Ibid.*
[63] *Landownership*, p. 81.

cannot be effected otherwise than in the course of judicial proceedings." This is the position taken by Stair.[64] "But private knowledge upon information, without legal diligence, or other solemnity allowed in law, at least unless that private knowledge be certain, it is not regarded, nor doth constitute the knower in *mala fide*."

The apparent difference between Erskine and Stair can probably be explained by the likelihood that the two writers are commenting from different points of view. The former—concerned with the possessor's actual state of mind—would appear to be supporting the proposition that the commencement of legal proceedings will not necessarily shake a possessor's honest belief in his right to the subject concerned. Stair, on the other hand, would seem to be looking at the question of the continuing existence of a possessor's good faith from the point of view of the need for some external event on the basis of which a changed state of mind may be inferred. One can see the emphasis upon inferential findings in Stair's[65] statement that where the possessor has no probable title "a citation and production of any other evidently preferable right is sufficient," whereas, in the case of competition between two titles "*mala fides* is only induced by litiscontestation, or sentence." What will be regarded as a sufficient event from which to infer a changed state of mind must, necessarily, depend upon the strength of the inference of good faith deriving from the claimed basis of the right to possession.[66]

Taken to its logical conclusion, this approach means that the issue of the termination of the right to fruits may be litigated down to its final appeal.[67] One may note, as an illustration of this, a comment of Lord Ormidale in *Houldsworth* v. *Brand's Tr.,*[68] in which he referred to the decision in the earlier case of *Carnegy* v. *Scott*[69] as a case: "of such great difficulty that it was only ultimately determined against the tenant in the House of Lords, where a previous judgment in his favour by the Court of Session was reversed, and therefore he was subjected in violent profits[70] only from the date of the reversal."

In *Menzies* v. *Menzies*[71] Lord Cowan regarded "the period at which the defence of *bona fides* should be held to cease" as the "only

---

[64] II.i.24.

[65] *Ibid.*

[66] Hence, as Rankine, *Landownership*, p. 82 puts it, in so far as "*bona fides* is founded on some grounds which it is only reasonable to defend at law . . . it is only brought to an end by a judgment of a competent Court." See, *e.g. Swanson* v. *Grieve* (1891) 18 R. 371 at p. 374.

[67] See Stair II.i.24; Erskine, II.i.29.

[68] (1876) 3 R. 304 at p. 314.

[69] (1830) 4 W. & S. 431.

[70] See Stair, II.ix.44; Erskine, II.vi.54; Rankine, *Landownership*, p. 23: the pursuer's right to damages on the basis of the greatest profit he could have made out of the property unlawfully possessed—in the case of certain urban properties computed as a fixed multiple of the applicable rent. It should be noted that this is a doctrine of the law of lease and, as such, of limited relevance to the question of the right of a *bona fide* possessor to fruits.

[71] (1863) 1 M. 1025 at p. 1035.

question attended with any difficulty." Here, "having regard to the fact that the whole questions at issue between the parties were brought under appeal," the court took the view that the defence of *bona fides* should "be maintained down to the date of judgment of the House of Lords."[72] In this case, although pending any litigation the defender's state of mind was considered to be *optima fide*, it was eventually decided that she did not have a right to the fruits in question.

Arguably, it is inappropriate to allow a *bona fide* possessor's right to fruits to continue beyond the point at which the very question of the right becomes an issue in litigation. That the defender continues to maintain an honest and justifiable belief in his right—clearly, perfectly possible from a subjective point of view—should not prevail against the principle that the right to the fruits and benefits of property, the subject of litigation, should be suspended pending the outcome of judicial proceedings. As a matter of fairness to both parties, it is submitted, the question of the possessor's continuing *bona fides* should not arise beyond that stage in the proceedings at which it has become a final issue in the litigation concerned.[73]

LIFERENTER'S RIGHT TO FRUITS

Basis of liferenter's right

Liferent is essentially the counterpart of the civil law personal **6.09** servitude of usufruct[74] which constituted "the power of disposal of the use and fruits, saving the substance of the thing."[75] Given the break-down of the right of ownership on the basis of the constituent rights of *usus, fructus* and *abusus,*[76] it follows that an interest, for a limited timespan, which leaves the substance of the thing intact, must be restricted to the rights of use and fruits. Hence the identification by Rankine[77] of the rights of a liferenter to "make every use of the subject liferented, and ingather and appropriate its fruits, natural, industrial, and civil, with the sole limitation that he shall not thereby waste or destroy its substance (*salva rei substantia*)."

---

[72] *Ibid.*

[73] It should be noted that the case law does recognise certain limits to the extent to which a party in possession is permitted to retain a right to fruits despite the fact of legal proceedings. In *Jute Industries Ltd.* v. *Wilson & Graham Ltd.*, 1955 S.L.T.(Sh. Ct.) 46, it was held that a "without prejudice" consent not to enforce a decree of removal prior to a stated date did not mean that the party in occupation would be *bona fide* until that date.

[74] Erskine, II.ix.39, notes that the Roman personal servitudes of usufruct, use and habitation could all "be called liferent rights; for they all fell on the death of him who had the right to them."

[75] Stair, II.vi.1.

[76] The rights to the use and the fruits and "*abusus*"—the ultimate power to do as one pleases with the thing.

[77] *Landownership*, p. 722.

Limitation to property not subject to wasting

6.10   The essential nature of liferent as a right to the available benefits of the use and fruits of a thing "without wasting its substance"[78] limits the class of thing to which the concept may be applied.[79] But, of course, from the point of view of the acquisition of fruits the limiting factor is the capacity of a thing to yield fruits. The bearing of fruits does not, in principle, diminish the substance of a thing, and the question whether liferent is competent will tend to devolve upon the issue whether the use of the thing has this effect.[80]

Traditionally the "wasting factor" limited the application of liferent to heritable subjects and to money.[81] In modern practice, however, a common form of liferent is over a *universitas* of mixed heritable and moveable property—typically an ongoing farm. In such a case the law looks to the overall position with regard to the requirement that the substance be maintained. As Lord President Inglis[82] put it, "we are not to weigh in too nice scales, whether the stocking which is left is exactly the same as was received, but, unless there is a palpable difference, we are just to set the one against the other." But, in any event, the limitation of liferent to land and money seems unduly restrictive. In principle there would appear to be no possible objection to a liferent over a herd of cattle or a flock of sheep with the liferenter entitled to the fruits, whether in the form of produce—milk or wool—or excess progeny, and subject only to an obligation to maintain the numbers at substantially the original level.

The liferenter's right to fruits may be subject to his use of the fruit-bearing thing in a particular manner. Arguably, for example, in the case of the liferent of an ongoing farm as a *universitas* it would not be open to the liferenter to remove a certain herd of stock and establish it on another farm.[83] If this was done it would seem that there would be no right to fruits produced by the herd because this right would be available only through the *universitas* as an intact entity.

Liferenter's right to fruits may be regulated by trust

6.11   Although a treatment of the means by which liferents are con-stituted[84] is beyond the scope of this book, it is necessary to draw attention to the fact that the precise scope of a liferenter's right to

---

[78] Erskine, II.ix.40. See also Stair, II.vi.4.

[79] As Erskine (II.ix.40) notes: "A usufruct, therefore, cannot be constituted on corns, wine, or other fungibles which perish in the use, *quorum usus consistit in abusa*."

[80] What may well arise, assuming that liferent is competent, is the issue whether certain "produce of the land"—such as trees and minerals—may be removed by the liferenter as fruits without diminishing the substance of the property. See below, para. 6.12.

[81] See Erskine, II.ix.40: "But the word liferent is, by the usage of Scotland, applied only to heritable subjects, or to money."

[82] *Rogers* v. *Scott* (1867) 5 M. 1078 at p. 1084.

[83] *Cf. Cochran* v. *Cochran* (1755) Mor. 8280, where it was held that, in the case of the liferent of a house and certain furniture, the furniture could not be removed from the house and used elsewhere.

[84] See Gordon, *Scottish Land Law*, paras. 17.05–17.35.

fruits may be determined by reference to the manner in which the right is created. The traditional mode of creation was to vest the property concerned directly in the liferenter. In the case of "liferents by constitution"[85] this was achieved either by the owner granting a liferent to another or through the transmission of the liferent to one party and the fee to another. In an alternative form—"liferent by reservation"[86]—the owner conveyed the fee to another while reserving to himself the liferent. In modern practice, however, a form of constitution interposing a trust is usually resorted to. Whether the liferent follows from a settlement *inter vivos* or one *mortis causa*, it is customary to convey the property concerned to trustees "in trust for the beneficiary liferenter, and on the expiry of the liferent, in trust to convey the legal estate to the fiar or fiars."[87]

The significance of this is that the trust deed may provide for the right to fruits. In the case of liferent constituted by trust the liferenter has a beneficial interest which—depending upon an interpretation of the terms of the trust[88]—may be a greater or lesser right than would have applied in the case of a directly-constituted liferent. However, the trust-based form may provide for liferent *simpliciter*—without any attempt to state the scope of the interest—and, in this situation, it has been held that the liferenter's position is the same as it would have been had the interest been created directly.[89]

Difficulties in determining what constitutes fruits   **6.12**

General observations. Natural fruits[90]—the produce of land, the progeny of animals—are not difficult to identify, although in some instances it may be debatable whether growing things are available as fruits or are in fact part of the *corpus* of the heritage.[91] The identification of civil fruits,[92] on the other hand, may be less straightforward. Because civil fruits—payments from interest or other earnings generated by capital—are not innately distinguishable from payments from capital itself, it may well be necessary to examine the particular circumstances to identify the source of the payment as capital or income.   **6.12a**

In a case[93] in which the liferentrix was entitled to the "free income of the trust-estate" the question arose whether duplicands of feuduty[94] amounted to income. Lord MacLaren applied a test based upon the question whether the capital remained intact.

---

[85] See Bell, *Prin.*, § 1041.
[86] See Bell, *Prin.*, § 1040.
[87] Smith, *Short Commentary*, p. 487.
[88] See, *e.g.* Montgomerie-Fleming's Tr. v. Montgomerie-Fleming (1901) 3 F. 591.
[89] See *Johnstone* v. *Mackenzie's Trs.* 1912 S.C.(H.L.) 106 at p. 109.
[90] See Bell, *Prin.*, § 1045.
[91] See above, para. 3.06; below, para. 6.126.
[92] See Bell, *Prin.*, § 1047.
[93] *Ross's Trs.* v. *Nicoll* (1902) 5 F. 146.
[94] Payments, additional to the usual annual payments, due in terms of the feu contract—in this case at fixed intervals of 25 years or, in one instance, 22 years.

"In general, I should be disposed to hold that every payment to be made from a trust-estate, which does not involve a diminution of capital, ought to be regarded as a payment out of income, whether that payment is made yearly or half-yearly, or periodically at longer intervals. All such payments when made to the trust-estate are to be regarded as part of the profits as distinguished from the *corpus* of the estate, and therefore fall to be made over from the estate to the person who is beneficially entitled to the income."[95]

In arriving at the amount due to a liferenter as income, the sum deducted as expenditure may well be in issue. In this regard one may note the distinction drawn by Lord President Dunedin in *Vallambrosa Rubber Co. Ltd.* v. *Inland Revenue*[96]:

"Now, I do not say that this consideration is absolutely final or determinative, but in a rough way I think it is not a bad criterion of what is capital expenditure—as against what is income expenditure—to say that capital expenditure is a thing that is going to be spent once and for all, and income expenditure is a thing that is going to recur every year."

In *Davidson's Trs.* v. *Ogilvie*[97] the Second Division was concerned with a liferentrix's entitlement arising from the publication of her late husband's literary works. It was held that royalties and profits paid after the testator's death in respect of works published during his lifetime was income; the proceeds of works published by the trustees after his death, however, were held to be capital.[98] A better view would seem to be that while the outright value of a manuscript or published work is a matter of capital—being indistinguishable from the capital value of any other asset—income generated by the work is a fruit to which the holder of a liferent should, in principle, be entitled.[99]

---

[95] at p. 149; see also the opinion of Lord President Kinross at p. 148: "these duplicands of feu-duty . . . do not come out of capital, and they leave the capital of the estate untouched. Accordingly they are, *prima facie*, payable to the person who has the right to the enjoyment of the income of the estate."

[96] 1910 S.C. 519 at p. 525.

[97] 1910 S.C. 294.

[98] Lord Ardwall (at p. 298) recognised an analogy with the circumstances of minerals: in particular the distinction drawn between, on the one hand, the proceeds of workings which were income prior to the testator's death and, on the other hand, an interest in mineral wealth which, at that time, had not yet begun to be exploited. See below, para. 6.12c.

[99] In the case of what may termed a "copyright asset"—whether a literary work, a computer program, an invention or some other creation which the author is entitled to—it would seem that the distinction should be between, on the one hand, an outright sale of the composition or idea—a sale of the copyright or patent—and, on the other hand, what is earned through the sale of copies of the publication or product. Applying the test of *Ross's Trs.* v. *Nicoll* (1902) 5 F. 146, the appropriate conclusion would appear to be that, in the case of a literary work, all royalties should be regarded as fruits because, in principle, the capital value of the work remains undiminished.

The particular areas of timber, minerals and payments to company shareholders involve some difficulty in the determination of what constitutes fruits.

Right to timber. The common law recognised that, in principle, timber, **6.12b** in so far as it was not renascent, was part of the *corpus* of the estate vesting in the fiar. From the point of view of the entitlement of a liferenter, the principle that the right must be exercised *salva rerum substantia*—without diminishing the substance of the property—means that woods and orchards must be retained essentially as they were when the property was received.[1] "Growing timber, when it is of that kind that does not shoot up from the root after cutting, *e.g.* firs, is justly accounted part of the lands, and not a fruit; and so cannot fall under liferent."[2] A right to cut timber could, of course, be granted to the liferenter,[3] but this would be an instance of acquisition on a derivative basis.[4]

In the case of a wood divided up for periodical cutting, a liferenter may continue with the intended scheme,[5] but the practice of periodical cutting of a part must be present.[6]

Although the liferenter is entitled to the normal incidence of fallen timber[7] he does not obtain a right to trees blown down in an "extraordinary storm," because these remain part of the total *corpus* vesting in the fiar even though physically disannexed from the land.[8]

There has long been authority for the proposition that a liferenter is entitled to cut timber for the purpose of effecting repairs to the

---

[1] See Stair, II.vi.4.

[2] Erskine, II.ix.58; see *Tait* v. *Maitland* (1825) 4 S. 247 *per* Lord Craigie at p. 251: "She herself has no right to cut the woods; and if she were attempting to do so, the fiar would be entitled to interfere, and there can be no doubt that he might name a factor to protect his interest."

[3] See, *e.g. Dingwall* v. *Duff* (1833) 12 S. 216 at p. 218, where the court intervened, at the instance of the fiar, to curtail the abuse of such a right which the liferenter was required to exercise "without injury to my estate."

[4] See above, para. 6.01.

[5] "Where it has been divided into different hags, one of which has been annually cut by the proprietor, the liferenter may continue the course of the former yearly cuttings; because these are understood to be the constant annual fruits which the proprietor intended the subject should yield to him": Erskine II.ix.58. See also Stair, II.iii.74; *Dickson* v. *Dickson* (1823) 2 S. 152 at p. 153; *Paul* v. *Cuthbertson* (1840) 2 D. 1286 at p. 1298.

[6] "The liferenter is not to cut the copse when he likes; but if he happen to be in possession when the time for cutting comes, he has a right to do so according to usage": *Macalister's Trs.* v. *Macalister* (1851) 13 D. 1239 *per* Lord President Boyle at p. 1242. See also Erskine, II.ix.58: "though it should arrive at the proper maturity during the liferent; because such wood does not appear to have been intended for yearly profit."

[7] Erskine, II.ix.58.

[8] See *Macalister's Trs.* v *Macalister* (1851) 13 D. 1239 *per* Lord Probationer Cowan at pp. 1241–1242: "I think the principle applicable to trees thus blown down is quite different from that of the case of ordinary windfalls. It is admitted that the wood on the estate belongs to the fiar; and the question is, whether, when, in consequence of an extraordinary storm a large portion of the wood is blown down, that can be held to have passed in property from the fiar, whose it was, to the liferenter. I should say certainly not."

liferented property,[9] although in later case law the right appears to have been limited to the case of a liferenter enjoying a specific entitlement to cut timber.[10] In *Macalister's Trs.* v. *Macalister*[11] the Lord Ordinary saw a liferenter's entitlement as follows:

> "to cut at the sight of the fiars such grown timber as is required for repairing fences, and other purposes of the estate, and is entitled to apply to such purposes, as far as required, any trees that may have been blown down."[12]

6.12c Right to minerals. Minerals, being finite, are "even more obviously than standing timber"[13] part of the *corpus* of the land, and therefore, in principle, not open to acquisition as fruits.[14]

But, although the principle of minerals as *partes soli* has not been departed from, modern law recognises the liferenter's right to the profits of existing mines.[15] Lord Watson in *Campbell* v. *Wardlaw*,[16] while accepting that minerals are not fruits as such, explained this development in the law:

> "But there has been introduced into the law this provision, that if the owner of the soil, the fiar, creates a mineral estate bearing fruits, by working or letting a particular seam of minerals, he thereby brings it within the right of usufruct."

In the subsequent case of *Ranken's Trs.* v. *Ranken*[17] Lord Low interpreted this dictum as establishing

> "that where a testator leaves the income or liferent of his estate to certain persons, the income to which the beneficiaries are entitled includes the produce of any minerals which were worked during the lifetime of the testator, but does not include the produce of mines which were opened after his death."[18]

---

[9] See *Stanfield* v. *Wilson* (1680) Mor. 8244.

[10] See *Lang and Cross* v. *Duke of Douglas* (1752) Mor. 8246; Erskine, II.ix.58.

[11] (1851) 13 D. 1239 at p. 1240.

[12] The decision of the First Division, while upholding the Lord Ordinary, contains no comment upon this *obiter dictum*. In any event, however, in so far as the right derives from the implied consent of the fiar it would not be instance of the original acquisition of fruits. See above, para. 6.01.

[13] Rankine, *Landownership*, p. 730.

[14] "Whatever is *pars soli*, part of the fee itself, cannot fall under the right of liferent. Coal, freestone, limestone, minerals of all kinds . . . are indubitably *partes soli* . . . no liferenter, therefore, has a right to those, insomuch that though a colliery has been opened by the proprietor previously to the commencement of the liferent, the liferenter cannot continue it without an express right": Erskine, II.ix.57. But *cf.* Stair, II.iii.74.

[15] One may note that there would appear to be authority for this in Stair, II.iii.74.

[16] (1883) 10 R.(H.L.) 65 at p. 68.

[17] 1908 S.C. 3 at p. 6.

[18] See also *Naismith's Trs.* v. *Naismith*, 1909 S.C. 1380 at p. 1386 where, on the question of rents and lordships deriving from mineral rights, the court regarded the cases of *Campbell* (1883) 10 R.(H.L.) 65 and *Ranken's Trs.*, 1908 S.C. 3 as "the ruling authorities."

In *Nugent* v. *Nugent's Trs.*[19] the House of Lords declined to place a restriction upon the concept of an "opened mine" by requiring that mines be actually operating at the time of commencement of the liferent.[20]

Of course, a trust deed may provide for a more extensive right in favour of a liferenter than entitlement restricted to opened mines[21]: however, the basis of acquisition would then be derivative rather than a matter of entitlement to fruits as original acquisition.[22]

Payments to company shareholders. By obvious analogy to the simple **6.12d** case of civil fruits in the form of interest on capital, dividends on shares fall to a liferenter[23] entitled at the time the benefit is declared.[24] But some payments from interests in the form of stocks or shares may raise the issue of an inroad into capital; moreover, the general touchstone laid down in *Ross's Trs.* v. *Nicoll*[25]—any payment not involving a diminution of capital is *prima facie* a payment from income[26]—may be unhelpful with regard to possibly complex financial adjustments under company law.

The first principle regarding a liferenter's entitlement to share income, as a matter of fruits, is that the determinative option rests with the company. In *Re Bouch: Sproule* v. *Bouch*,[27] Fry L.J. explained the position in a dictum which was adopted by the House of Lords[28] and applied in Scots law[29]:

---

[19] (1899) 2 F.(H.L.) 21.

[20] See the dictum of Lord Shand at p. 24: "these mines, although in a sense dormant mines—by which I mean mines the working of which had been for a time suspended, it may be because of a diminished price to be got for the mineral, or some other temporary cause—must be regarded as opened mines in the sense which the law has always attached to these words in questions like the present."

[21] See the *obiter dictum* of Lord Low in *Ranken's Trs.* v. *Ranken*, 1908 S.C. 3 at p. 6: "No doubt there may be a modification of this rule if the special terms of the trust deed require it, and shew that it was the intention of the testator to include minerals that might be worked in future."

[22] See above, para. 6.01.

[23] Of course the liferenter is only entitled to income from the trust after the truster's death. "What would have been income of the truster had he lived became, when paid to the trustees after his death, an asset of his trust": *Manclark* v. *Thomson's Trs.*, 1958 S.C. 147 *per* Lord President Clyde at p. 160.

[24] If shares are sold by trustees prior to the declaration of a dividend the liferenter should, in principle, be entitled to a portion of the proceeds in lieu of income by way of dividend: see *Donaldson* v. *Donaldson's Trs.* (1851) 14 D. 165; *McLeod's Trs.* v. *McLeod*, 1916 S.C. 604. In *Cameron's Factor* v. *Cameron* (1873) 1 R. 21, it was held that the proceeds of shares sold prior to the declaration of a dividend fell to be apportioned as between capital and income on the basis of the dividend anticipated at the date of sale rather than the dividend ultimately paid. The Apportionment Act 1870 provides, in s.2, that dividends, and other periodical payments in the nature of income, "shall, like interest on money lent, be considered as accruing from day to day, and shall be apportionable in respect of time accordingly."

[25] (1902) 5 F. 146.

[26] See above, para. 6.12a, n. 95.

[27] (1885) 29 Ch.D. 635 at p. 653.

[28] (1887) 12 App.Cas. 385 at p. 397.

[29] See *Blyth's Trs.* v. *Milne* (1905) 7 F. 799 at p. 805; *Howard's Trs.* v. *Howard*, 1907 S.C. 1274 at pp. 1278–1279.

"Where a testator or settlor directs or permits the subject of his
disposition to remain as shares or stock in a company which has
the power either of distributing its profits as dividends, or of
converting them into capital, and the company validly exercises
this power, such exercise of its power is binding on all persons
interested under him . . . and consequently what is paid by the
company as dividend goes to the tenant for life[30] and what is paid
by the company to the shareholder as capital, or appropriated as
an increase of the capital stock in the concern, enures to the
benefit of all who are interested in the capital."

To similar effect one may note the dictum of Lord President Normand
in *Forgie's Trs.* v. *Forgie*[31] regarding the choice between the transfer of
assets to a new company—leaving the proceeds available for distribution among shareholders upon the liquidation of the original company—or, alternatively, the distribution of accumulated profits before
liquidation and the subsequent transfer of the residue only to the new
company. "Probably the choice between these two courses depended
upon practical considerations which are not before us. But the choice
was made, and it was that act of choice which determines the character
of the payment."[32]

It seems, however, that one must qualify any notion of an open
discretion giving a company the power to declare that payments to
shareholders amount to either capital or income. The critical consideration is not what the payment is called by the company but the basis
under which it is made—in short what, in fact, the company has opted
to do. This, of course, may raise the question of the courses of action
actually open to a company. The issue of the means available to a
company to distribute funds was emphasised by Lord Russell in
delivering the opinion of the Privy Council in *Hill* v. *Permanent
Trustee Company of New South Wales*[33]:

"A limited company not in liquidation can make no payment by
way of return of capital to its shareholders except as a step in an
authorised reduction of capital. Any other payment made by it by
means of which it parts with moneys to its shareholders must and
can only be made by way of dividing profits. Whether the payment

---

[30] *i.e.* the liferenter.

[31] 1941 S.C. 188 at pp. 194–195.

[32] The strength of the principle that the determining option lies with the company is
illustrated by the situation of the application of accumulated profits to capital purposes
by a company without the formal power to increase its capital. In such a case any
distribution of the funds concerned would be a payment of capital which a liferenter
would not be entitled to. See *Irving* v. *Houstoun* (1803) 4 Pat. 521.

[33] [1930] A.C. 720 at p. 731.

is called 'dividend' or 'bonus,' or any other name, it still must remain a payment on division of profits."[34]

Although, given changes in company legislation, the application of this dictum has been questioned from the point of view of its accuracy,[35] it is submitted that its basis remains valid in that a company decision as to whether a payment to shareholders is to be debited to capital or income accounts is controlled by ruling company law. Although the Court of Appeal[36] agreed that the substance of Lord Russell's observations were out-of-date, it reiterated that the "mechanics" of the distribution of funds by a company are "an essential factor in determining the character as between capital and income of the sum distributed."[37] The judgment proceeds as follows:

"A company . . . can . . . make a distribution amongst its members . . . in one of two ways—but only one of two ways: that is by a distribution of divisible profits, that is, by way of dividend: and by way of a return of capital pursuant to an order of the court upon a petition for reduction of capital in accordance with the Act. The question whether a given distribution lawfully made by a company is of the former or the latter description may thus justly be determined by reference to the method or mechanics of distribution, permitted or enjoined by the Act, which the company has adopted in regard to it: and the answer to the question must prima facie also determine the question whether the distribution is capital or income as between tenant for life and remainder-man of a settled shareholding."[38]

That the critical issue is not how the distribution is designated, but rather what it amounts to from the point of view of company law, emerges from the decision of the First Division in *Thomson's Trs.* v. *Thomson*.[39] One may note the opinion of Lord President Clyde:

"a limited company which is not in liquidation can make no payment by way of return of capital to its shareholders except as a

---

[34] See also *Thomson's Trs.* v. *Thomson*, 1955 S.C. 476 *per* Lord Russell at p. 484: "In accordance with well-established legal principles it is clear that that distribution was in its nature a division of profits by a company and would, if and when received by the trustees in respect of the trust holding of company shares, have belonged to the person beneficially entitled to the income of the trust estate . . . That conclusion, which must prevail even against the company's expressed intention to distribute the stock as capital, is so clearly vouched by the authorities referred to that it was not and could not reasonably be challenged by counsel representing the fiars' interest."
[35] See *Duff's Settlements: Re National Provincial Bank Ltd.* v. *Gregson* [1951] 1 Ch. 721 at p. 727.
[36] [1951] 1 Ch. 923 at p. 928.
[37] at p. 930.
[38] *per* Jenkins L.J., reading the judgment of the court, at pp. 930–931.
[39] 1955 S.C. 476 at pp. 481–482.

step in an authorised reduction of capital, and merely to call the payment capital will not make it so."[40]

---

[40] See also *Manclark* v. *Thomson's Trs.*, 1958 S.C. 147 at pp. 166–167. In this case the First Division applied this principle and so curtailed the effect of a decision by trustees intended to move the benefit of a distribution of stock from liferenters to fiars.

CHAPTER 7

PRESCRIPTION

Limited rôle in relation to moveables

An important issue concerning moveables is whether a *bona fide* **7.01**
onerous acquirer can obtain a good title regardless of a defect arising
from the fact that a predecessor was not in a position to pass
ownership. The law deals with this problem in two ways: first,
specifically, through various exceptions to the principle that the true
owner can vindicate[1]; and, secondly, by tending to protect generally
the *status quo* of possession.[2] These measures protect the immediate
position of *bona fide* possession which, of course, may well be of
primary importance in respect of moveable property. For present
purposes the point is that in so far as the *status quo* of innocent
onerous possession is protected, there is correspondingly less scope for
acquisitive prescription.[3]

Institutional writers at variance

Stair[4] contends for a common law rule of positive (or acquisitive) **7.02**
prescription based upon 40 years' continuous possession applying to
moveables as well as to heritable property.[5] Given the long period,

---

[1] See below, paras. 10.15–10.22.
[2] See above, para. 1.12.
[3] See Scot. Law Com., Memo. No. 30, *Corporeal Moveables: Usucapion or Acquisitive Prescription*, para. 4: "In legal systems which give immediate protection to the title of the acquirer or purchaser of moveables in good faith, the need for usucapion to fortify defective title is relegated to a subordinate role; while in those which hold that the acquirer or purchaser has no better title than his author, the need for prescription to fortify title is most apparent. Scots law until the 19th century was little troubled with problems of title to moveables. The common law attitude, except in the case of stolen property, was generally favourable to commerce and to a presumption or reputation of ownership based on possession. The role of usucapion was, therefore, subordinate." Arguably the rôle, or potential rôle, of acquisitive prescription in relation to moveables remains a matter of secondary importance in modern law. It would seem that this is so because the primary problem concerns the immediate choice between a *bona fide* onerous acquirer and the true owner: the fundamental issue being the policy question whether the former should be protected against the latter.
[4] II.xii.11.
[5] Kames, *Elucidations*, 259, applies the label *usucapio* to the process of acquisition based on 40 years' continuous possession. It seems that some writers considered that the early legislation provided a basis for the acquisition of moveable property by prescription, even if only by analogy to heritable property; see, *e.g.* Bankton, II.xii.1. Napier, *Prescription*, p. 39, n. 1, comments that Stair, IV.xl.20, "seems to blend all the operations of Prescription under the act 1617." It should be noted, however, that the Prescription and Limitation (Scotland) Act 1973 repeals the old legislation (see Sched. 5, Pt. I) and, in modern law, the question can only be whether a right of positive (acquisitive) prescription of moveables exists at common law.

Stair's view is that possession need not be in good faith.[6] This could, in any event, be contended for on the view that the fundamental basis of acquisitive prescription is an assertion of title, not necessarily supported by an honest belief in the right to possession.

Erskine[7] refers to the elapse of 40 years as a matter of negative prescription on the basis of which a proprietor's right to recover an item of moveable property is extinguished. According to Erskine, the rule follows from the presumption that a possessor is owner:

> "There is no statute establishing a positive prescription in moveable rights or subjects, nor indeed was one necessary; for since the property of moveables is presumed from possession alone, without any title in writing, the proprietor's neglecting for forty years together to claim them, by which he is cut off from all right of action for recovering their property, effectually secures the possessor."

Stair and Erskine apparently differ as to the commom law position[8]; while Stair maintains that the rule of positive prescription based upon 40 years' possession applies equally to heritable and moveable property, Erskine reasons that, given the protection accorded a possessor of moveables, the logical position is that an owner's right to recover is finally barred following 40 years' non-action.

Hume,[9] it may be noted, supports the view that an owner's right to recover his moveable property "is limited by the doctrines of positive prescription . . . in virtue of which the possessor gains a right—an absolute and unimpeachable right, in virtue of his 40 years possession of the thing as his own." He[10] goes on to refer to the presumption of possession applying to moveables as another limitation upon the owner's right of vindication.

Napier,[11] in a monograph on prescription, rejects any rule of positive prescription of moveables by 40 years' possession, and endorses the position contended for by Erskine.[12]

---

[6] II.xii.11: "because our prescription is so long, there is little question with us, *de bona fide.*"

[7] III.vii.7.

[8] But see Napier, *Prescription*, pp. 38–39, where the author argues that Stair (II.xii.13) did not treat the case of *Parishioners of Aberscherder* v. *Parish of Gemrie* (1633) Mor. 10972 as a matter of acquisitive prescription because he only commences to deal with the Act of 1617, giving effect to this, in a subsequent text (II.xii.15). Napier (p. 39) rationalises Stair's treatment of the problem on the basis "that the case of the possession of a moveable is sufficiently protected *negative*, by the operation of the statute of obligations [1469 c. 28 and 1474 c. 54], it not being requisite, in such a case to found *positive* upon the production of a written title, as in the case of an heritable subject." Be this as it may, Stair's text (II.xii.11) on the common law position would appear to be concerned with positive prescription in so far as it speaks of "continual possession free from interruption" without any need for good faith on the part of the possessor.

[9] III, p. 228.

[10] *Ibid.*

[11] *Prescription*, pp. 76–77.

[12] III.vii.7.

From a point of view of Institutional authority, the question of the common law as to the prescription of moveable property is inconclusive with the two most important writers giving contrary views.

Inconclusive case law

Stair[13] refers to the case of *Parishioners of Aberscherder* v. *Parish of* **7.03** *Gemrie*[14] in support of a common law rule that 40 years' possession of a moveable thing gives title. In this case a church bell was loaned by one congregation to another; over 40 years later the lending congregation failed in its attempt to recover the bell.

According to one point of view, there is some doubt as to whether the basis of this decision was negative or positive prescription.[15] However, in Morison's *Dictionary* the section heading and rubric refer to positive prescription, and the report would appear to support this in that the decision against the pursuers was based upon the defender's "40 years possession bypast, uninterrupted." Had the basis been negative prescription, extinguishing the pursuer's right to recover possession, one would have expected the fact of their non-action for 40 years to have been the ratio.

But the real difficulty with this case is that its apparent basis in positive prescription is incompatible with the circumstances of loan. The foundation rationale behind positive prescription is that the claimant possessor has held the thing as if he were owner for the requisite period, during which time the legal owner has failed to assert his right. As More explained in the notes to his edition of Stair,[16] the necessary condition for positive prescription is a title to ownership in some shape or form. "But prescription can never run without a title, direct or presumed . . . The title must be appropriate to the subject, relative to which the prescriptive right is claimed; and hence, no prescriptive title to lands can be pleaded where there is no seisin."

In relation to moveables, given that no formal title is required as a prerequisite to the acquisition of ownership, the basis of the claimant's title will be his *animus domini*—the intention to hold the thing as owner—but of course this must be compatible with the circumstances under which the thing is held. While there may be acquisition in the circumstances of purchase from a non-owner, prescription could not run in the case of a thing held on loan because the basis under which the item was held would preclude the assertion of a right of ownership by the claimant.[17]

---

[13] II.xii.13.

[14] (1633) Mor. 10972.

[15] See above, n. 8. See also Scot. Law Com., Memo. No. 30, *Corporeal Moveables: Usucapion or Acquisitive Prescription*, Appendix, para. 2.

[16] (5th ed., 1832), I, AA, cclxxvii.

[17] Clearly, one is concerned with the actual circumstances under which the thing is held rather than the holder's *animus* in any subjective sense; prescription would not run in the case of a unilateral assumption of rights over something held on the basis of a contract or precariously in circumstances which acknowledged the title of the true owner.

In view of this the case of the kirk bell must necessarily be construed—against an *ex facie* reading of it—as a decision in fact based upon negative prescription[18]: the claimant's right to recover the bell loaned to the defenders being extinguished through failure to resort to it for a period in excess of 40 years. This, however, leaves open the question of the existence of a concept of acquisitive—or positive—prescription based upon the claimant's holding the thing concerned as owner for a continuous period of 40 years.

In *Ramsay* v. *Wilson*[19] the Lords, dealing with a case involving the possession of jewellery—apparently for a period of 10 or 12 years—held that "there is no usucapion in moveables in Scotland, by possession, in less than 40 years, but only a presumptive title." More[20] cites this decision as authority for his proposition that "a right to moveables, even against the true owner, may be acquired by prescription."

In *Sands* v. *Bell & Balfour*[21] it was held that the Crown had no claim to property which had lain for 10 years in a public warehouse unclaimed by the owners. The court upheld the defender's position which included the argument that a right to property cannot be lost by any shorter period of negative prescription than 40 years. Because the Crown had not asserted any right of ownership over the property there could, in any event, be no question of positive prescription.

The case law applicable to a rule of acquisitive prescription based upon 40 years' continuous possession of a moveable thing is hardly conclusive. At most it supports the possibility of such a rule—possibly to a sufficient degree to enable a modern court to recognise the rule if it was felt appropriate to do so. However, this said, the limited potential rôle of a rule of this type is such that there must be doubt over the likelihood of its recognition in modern law.[22]

---

[18] That this was the true basis of the decision seems to be accepted in the case of *Presbytery of Edinburgh* v. *University of Edinburgh* (1890) 28 S.L.R. 567 at p. 574.

[19] (1666) Mor. 9113.

[20] *Op. cit.*, AA, cclxxvi.

[21] May 22, 1810, F.C.

[22] See above, n. 3. It may be noted that Scot. Law Com., Memo. No. 30, *Corporeal Moveables: Usucapion or Acquisitive Prescription*, para. 4, saw the rôle of acquisitive prescription of moveables as follows: "Today the potential value of usucapion . . . would be to fortify the defective title of *bona fide* gratuitous acquirers from transferors who had no right or only a qualified right to transfer; to fortify the defective title of *bona fide* onerous acquirers of moveables infected with a *vitium reale*; and generally to permit the eventual acquisition of unchallengeable ownership by an acquirer on ostensibly valid title by transfer *inter vivos* or *mortis causa*." It is suggested that this does not indicate a major rôle. First, the incidence of gratuitous acquisition is limited. Secondly, the possession of a moveable on the basis of good faith onerous acquisition is, in any event, protected by various devices applicable in different circumstances. (See below, paras. 10.15–10.22.) Thirdly, the general protection contemplated by the Scottish Law Commission was by way of a long period of *usucapio*, but this could only have meaningful application to the limited class of moveables which appreciate in value.

Relationship between positive and negative prescription

Napier[23] is critical of texts in Erskine[24] which seem to be based upon **7.04** the assumption that negative and positive prescription operate in conjunction in a certain sense. The contention is that the same end-result follows whether the acquisition of the right of ownership is recognised, on the basis of positive or acquisitive prescription, or whether the claim to recover the thing is barred by negative prescription.

While it is true that the possessor's position is secured by a denial—through lapse of time—of the owner's right to claim the thing, the absence of a complementary rule of positive prescription means that the matter cannot be finally determined pending a claim by the owner.[25] This point illustrates the fact that the rôles of positive and negative prescription are distinct: on the one hand, a substantive basis for the assertion of a right of ownership; on the other, the more limited device of a defence available against a party asserting a title.

From the point of view of the position as between possessor and owner, it does appear that positive and negative prescription are "two sides of a coin."[26] However, with regard to implications beyond the immediate parties, it is significant that positive prescription has active proprietary effect leading to a real right available "against the whole world," whereas, in terms of direct effect, negative prescription does not go beyond the issue between the claimant to ownership and the possessor.

It is probably true, however, that the distinction is of limited importance in relation to moveable property, because possession without title carries with it the same benefits which the owner in possession would enjoy. Moreover, the question of title will generally only be in issue where the pursuer claims ownership—either against the possessor himself, his trustee in bankruptcy or a poinding creditor; in such circumstances negative prescription will, in effect, determine the issue of title.

Negative prescription under the Prescription and Limitation (Scotland) Act 1973

Although it is doubtful if there is a common law rule providing for **7.05** the acquisition of moveable property by prescription, there is a relevant rule of negative prescription in modern law.

---

[23] *Prescription*, pp. 77–80; Napier's discussion of the problem relates to heritable property but, in principle, the question as to the interrelation of positive and negative prescription arises equally in respect of moveable property.

[24] *e.g.* III.vii.8.

[25] "Merely to cut off a remedy without fortifying a right of ownership in anyone would be to create a vacuum and uncertainty as to title—a result which a sound law of prescription or usucapion should avoid": Scot. Law Com., Memo. No. 30, *Corporeal Moveables: Usucapion or Acquisitive Prescription*, para. 3.

[26] Scot. Law Com., *loc. cit.*

Section 8 of the Prescription and Limitation (Scotland Act) 1973[27] provides that if an exercisable or enforceable right relating to heritable or moveable property subsists for a continuous period of 20 years unexercised or unenforced, and without any relevant claim in relation to it having been made, then, upon the expiry of that period, the right is extinguished. It is clear from Schedule 3, listing imprescriptible rights, that the reference to rights in section 8(2) covers the right of ownership in moveable property.[28] The right to recover stolen property "from the person by whom it was stolen or from any person privy to the stealing thereof"[29] is excluded. For the purposes of the legislation theft does not produce a *vitium reale*. Accordingly a subsequent party, innocent of the theft, may in appropriate circumstances resort to section 8 and defeat the claim of an owner originally deprived by theft. This special provision regulating the application of negative prescription in respect of the right to recover stolen goods shows conclusively that section 8 makes the owner's right to recover possession of an item of moveable property potentially subject to negative prescription.

It should be noted that under section 6 of the Prescription and Limitation (Scotland) Act 1973 an obligation of restitution is subject to a five-year period of negative prescription.[30] It has been suggested that the effect of this is that an owner's right to claim delivery of moveables is subject to the five-year period of negative prescription.[31] This issue is dealt with in the context of the owner's vindicatory right,[32] but for present purposes it may be noted that the better view is that the owner's real right to recover is subject only to the 20-year period of negative prescription provided for in section 8.[33]

---

[27] See generally, Walker, *The Law of Prescription and Limitation of Actions in Scotland*.

[28] Sched. 3(a) lists "any real right of ownership in land" as imprescriptible leaving a real right of ownership in moveable property covered by s.8.

[29] Sched. 3(g).

[30] Sched. 1, Pt. 1(b) provides for the application of the five-year period of extinctive prescription under s.6 "to any obligation based on redress of unjustified enrichment, including without prejudice to that generality any obligation of restitution, repetition or recompense."

[31] Scot. Law Com., *op. cit.*, para. 3: "the obligation of restitution, which in practice justifies a conclusion for delivery of corporeal moveables, now prescribes in five years instead of in 20 as formerly."

[32] See above para. 10.13.

[33] But it seems that a case can be made for a much-reduced period of negative prescription; see Carey Miller, "Moveables: do we need acquisitive prescription?" 1989 S.L.T.(News) 285 at pp. 288–289.

CHAPTER 8

DERIVATIVE ACQUISITION AT COMMON LAW

GENERAL MATTERS

Basis of derivative acquisition

As indicated,[1] the most usual and important[2] mode of acquisition is **8.01** derivative, where title is passed from disposer to acquirer. In this form of acquisition title is transmitted or, put another way, one may say that the transferee derives his title from the transferor. As Stair[3] notes, what is special about an act of disposition is that it achieves the transmission, or conveyance of real rights from the disponer to his singular successor."

The possibility of the transfer of title by derivative means follows from the nature of the right of ownership including, as it does, the *jus disponendi* or power of disposal. Hume[4] recognised this: "The power of disposal *inter vivos* is plainly founded on the owner's natural power and command over the subject."

Passing of ownership in case of sale regulated by statute

In the case of sale—by far the most common form of transaction **8.02** antecedent to the act of transmission of title—the common law was, on January 1, 1894, displaced by the Sale of Goods Act 1893. This Act "introduced into the law of sale of corporeal moveables the English rule that property passes in accordance with the intention of the parties"[5] and, as such, it constituted "a statutory exception to the general law of Scotland regarding transfer of property in moveables."[6] The transfer of ownership pursuant to the Act is dealt with in Chapter 9.

Essential elements of derivative acquisition

Stair[7] urges that, in principle, title may be transferred by "the **8.03** dispositive will of the owner alone." In so far as possession may be retained by act of will, without any necessary corporeal act, it follows,

---

[1] Above, para. 1.18.
[2] See Bell, *Prin.*, § 1286: "transference from one who has already acquired . . . is in the present day the most frequent and important mode of acquiring property." See also Erskine, II.i.18.
[3] III.ii.3.
[4] III, p. 243.
[5] Gordon, *Studies in the Transfer of Property by Traditio*, p. 214.
[6] Smith, *Short Commentary*, p. 540.
[7] III.ii.4.

according to Stair's argument,[8] that the right may be relinquished on the same basis:

"therefore, the act of the will alone, as it retaineth, so may it relinquish that right or possession, whereby it ceaseth to be the former owner's; and therefore, if the will be not simply to relinquish but to remit or transmit the right to any other, *hoc ipso* that other doth become *dominus*; dominium being the power of disposal."

But while natural law requires no more than the mental act of motivation to transfer ownership:

"for utility's sake . . . almost all nations require some kind of possession, to accomplish real rights, that thereby the will of the owner may sensibly touch the thing disponed, and thereby be more manifest and sure; so the law saith, *Traditionibus et usucapionibus, non nudis pactis, dominia rerum transferuntur*, with which our custom accordeth."[9]

Other writers simply refer to the two basic essentials for acquisition of the right of ownership on a derivative basis. Thus Erskine[10]:

"Two things are therefore required to the conveyance of property in this manner: *First*, The intention or consent of the former owner to transfer it upon some just or proper title of alienation, as sale, gift, exchange, etc.: *secondly*, The actual delivery of it, in pursuance of that intention. The first is called *causa*, the other the *modus, transferendi dominii*."

That, as far as the common law is concerned, delivery is required to transfer a real right in moveable property is fully accepted in modern law; one may note, for example, the dictum of Lord President Inglis in *Clark* v. *West Calder Oil Co.*[11]: "[a] mere assignation of corporeal moveables *retenta possessione* is nothing whatever but a personal obligation." Moreover, it is equally clear that the transfer of a right of property is driven by the parties' intention. As Lord Rutherfurd Clark put it in *Hogarth* v. *Smart's Tr.*[12]: "[p]roperty cannot pass by mere possession contrary to the wish of both giver and receiver."

---

[8] *Ibid.*
[9] Stair, III.ii.5.
[10] II.i.18.
[11] (1882) 9 R. 1017 at p. 1024.
[12] (1882) 9 R. 964 at p. 969.

The two requirements—an act of will and actual delivery[13]—for the derivative passing of ownership are stated upon the assumption that the transferor is owner or is acting on the authority of the owner. Scots law recognises the general principle, that "no one can convey a better or more ample right to another, than he has in his own person."[14] This is the principle of the well-known brocard *nemo dat quod non habet*,[15] and although it is subject to exceptions,[16] certainly, in so far as one is stating the basis under which property passes, the assumption would be that the transferor is owner or authorised to represent the owner. Moreover, in addition to the requirement of the transferor's title to pass ownership, the parties must be legally competent to give and receive ownership or, put in the negative, there must be no legal disability, in either party, which would prevent the passing of ownership.

The essentials of derivative acquisition, which will be examined in some detail in this chapter, are accordingly (1) the parties must be in a position to pass and acquire ownership; (2) the parties must intend the passing of ownership; and (3) there must be delivery according to a recognised method. These aspects of the matter will be dealt with under the respective headings of "title and competence," "intention" and "delivery."

TITLE AND COMPETENCE

The transferor's title

In principle no one can transfer a more extensive right than he has; **8.04** Hume[17] states the position in relation to one who purports to transfer the right of ownership in a thing to which he does not have title: "if he had not the property, as little can any of the after acquirers, how fair and onerous soever they be: since no one can convey a better or more ample right to another, than he has in his own person."

This principle is not gainsaid by the presumption of ownership arising from possession.[18] While the law may lean towards the protec-

---

[13] See also Hume, III, p. 235: "only two things are naturally requisite to the transference of Property—the will of the owner to convey the thing in property, and the actual delivery in pursuance of a bargain to that effect." Bell, *Prin.*, § 1299, refers to "the conventional will to convey" and "the overt act by which the real right is transferred." Modern writers are to like effect; see Reid and Gretton, "All Sums Retention of Title," 1989 S.L.T. (News) 185 at p. 187: "At common law two things are required to transfer ownership, namely intention (*animus transferendi*) and delivery (*traditio*)." Regarding the acceptance of and justifications for the *traditio* principle in Scots law, see Gordon, *Studies in the Transfer of Property by Traditio*, pp. 210–214.

[14] Hume, III, p. 232.

[15] Gow, *Mercantile Law*, p. 118, n. 5, regards the Romanist maxim *nemo plus juris ad alium transferre potest quam ipse habet* as the "analogous Scots brocard."

[16] See below, paras. 10.15–10.22.

[17] III, p. 232.

[18] See above, para. 1.12.

tion of an onerous *bona fide* acquirer, the relevant point, for present purposes, is that it remains competent for an owner to attack an alleged transfer of title in a moveable thing on the basis that it was an unauthorised act. That this is the residual position is supported by the First Division case of *Morrisson* v. *Robertson*,[19] where Lord Kinnear adopted certain parts of the speech of Lord Chancellor Cairns in the well-known English case of *Cundy* v. *Lindsay*[20]:

> "His Lordship says:—'By the law of our country the purchaser of a chattel'—or, as we should say, corporeal moveable—'takes the chattel as a general rule subject to what may turn out to be certain infirmities in the title . . . If it turns out that the chattel has been found by the person who professed to sell it, the purchaser will not obtain a title good as against the real owner. If it turns out that the chattel has been stolen by the person who has professed to sell it, the purchaser will not obtain a title.''

There are exceptions to the general principle that a transferee acquires no better title than his transferor was capable of passing; these, however, are more appropriately dealt with as exceptions to the owner's right of vindication, because it is primarily in the context of an attempt to assert a right of ownership that such matters arise.[21]

Competence to give and receive ownership

8.05   In that the transfer of ownership is a legal act, involving the coincidence of intention to give and intention to receive, it follows that the question of capacity may be relevant. If either party is subject to any disability affecting capacity, a legally effective transfer can only be achieved if the incapacity is made good in the manner required by law. Whether the disability is one of age,[22] mental capacity, intoxication or disease, the position regarding capacity to transmit and receive property—and what is required from the point of view of a legally effective transfer—is analogous to the position in respect of contractual capacity in general.[23]

Accordingly, for example, the transfer of moveable property by a pupil will be ineffective to pass ownership to the transferee; an

---

[19] 1908 S.C. 332 at pp. 337–338.

[20] 1878 L.R. 3 App.Cas. 459.

[21] See below, paras. 10.15–10.22.

[22] The last vestige of the disability of a married woman—the minor wife being subject to her husband's curatorship, or that of her father if the husband was also a minor—has disappeared. See s.3 of the Law Reform (Husband and Wife) (Scotland) Act 1984 and s.24 of the Family Law (Scotland) Act 1985. On the married woman's disability in earlier law see Clive, *Husband and Wife*, pp. 260–265.

[23] See McBryde, *Contract*, paras. 8.01–8.54.

effective act of disposition will only be achieved by the act of a tutor.[24] By like token pupillary incapacity means that there can be no act of acceptance on the part of a pupil transferee,[25] although he is a proper transferee in the sense of "the person in whose name alone the titles of his property can be made up."[26] However, although a pupil, being in a state of legal incapacity, cannot accept delivery, it is perfectly competent for the legal tutor of the party concerned to accept transfer on behalf of the pupil.[27] Both in respect of receiving and transmitting, in particular circumstances there may be an argument on the basis of the possible qualification that the obligation is enforceable by the pupil in so far as it is beneficial to him.[28]

A minor, at any rate, has contractual capacity in respect of the purchase of "necessaries" at a reasonable price.[29] It follows that a minor has the capacity to accept delivery of a necessary item, intending to acquire it, and on this basis a transfer of ownership can take place.

Competence to give and receive ownership may also be in issue arising from a question of the capacity of a legal person to be bound by an act of acquisition or disposal. The question of powers and the *ultra vires* doctrine are relevant and one could be concerned with a company, a partnership or, indeed, any juristic person capable of ownership.[30] Most of the case law in point relates to heritable property, but the decisions are nonetheless apposite to illustrate the requirement of powers which, clearly, applies in the same way in relation to the acquisition or disposal of moveables by a juristic person.[31]

The consequence of incapacity is that ownership does not pass. As Bell[32] puts it: "[r]estitution will therefore be given, not only against the

---

[24] See, *e.g.*, Bell, *Prin.*, § 2067: "No act done by the pupil . . . has any effect without the imposition of a guardian." See also *Hill* v. *City of Glasgow Bank* (1879) 7 R. 68 *per* Lord President Inglis at p. 74: "A pupil is under incapacity, and no act done by a pupil can have any effect whatever." It may be noted that the tutors of pupils and the curators of minors have extensive power to dispose of moveable property in the course of their administration of the property of the person lacking capacity. See Erskine, I.vii.17: "But frequent instances occur in our practice of tutors and curators disposing of the most valuable and durable moveables belonging to the minor, by their own authority."

[25] But see *Linton* v. *Inland Revenue,* 1928 S.C. 209 at p. 213, where Lord President Clyde—referring to the proposition that a pupil, being in a state of legal incapacity, could not legally accept—commented: "No authority was quoted to us for that extreme proposition."

[26] *Drummond's Trs.* v. *Peel's Trs.*, 1929 S.C. 484 *per* Lord President Clyde at p. 493.

[27] See *Linton* v. *Inland Revenue*, 1928 S.C. 209 at p. 213.

[28] See *Drummond's Trs.* v. *Peel's Trs.*, 1929 S.C. 484 at p. 493.

[29] See s.3(2) of the Sale of Goods Act 1979, commented on below, para. 9.04. On the question whether the section applies to pupils, see Scot. Law Com., Consultative Memo. No. 65, *Legal Capacity and Responsibility of Minors and Pupils* (1985), para. 2.18.

[30] The question could also arise in relation to a voluntary association, because even though ownership would vest in the collective membership the issue of powers would arise in relation to acts of acquisition or disposal.

[31] *e.g.* in *Kidd* v. *Paton's Trs.*, 1912 (2) S.L.T. 363 at p. 365, it was held, *per* Lord Hunter, that a conveyance by trustees to a company was void "as an act *ultra vires* of them."

[32] *Comm.*, I, 261.

buyer, but even against purchasers from him, where the seller is incapable of full and legal consent."

THE INTENTION REQUIREMENT

The causal/abstract distinction

8.06   While it is trite that the common law requires delivery to pass property in corporeal moveables,[33] it is not clear whether the intention to deliver, and its counterpart the intention to receive, fall to be established by reference to the antecedent contract or on the theory of a separate and self-contained agreement as to the passing of ownership. In so far as delivery is an independent legal act it must include a motivating *animus* element. There can be no separate requirement of physical delivery without concomitant *animus*, because a requirement of delivery which stands or falls by the motivating force of its underlying contract is not a distinct requirement. But the mental element of delivery may be derived or transposed from the antecedent agreement, and the issue is whether this is the correct analysis or whether it must be sought independently as a concomitant of the act of transfer itself. To apply the technical labels, the issue is whether the law follows a causal or an abstract theory concerning the passing of ownership by *traditio*.[34] Put another way, the question is—"What is the appropriate analysis of the requirement of *justa causa traditionis*; must there be a causal basis for delivery in the sense of a valid underlying transaction or does it suffice if the intention to pass and receive ownership can be inferred from the circumstances of the handing over of the thing regardless of the validity—or even the existence—of any underlying transaction?"

Authorities inconclusive on theory of transfer of title

8.07   There is a paucity of authority relevant to the analysis of the basis of derivative acquisition in Scots law.[35] In a memorandum concerned with the problems of the passing of risk and ownership in corporeal

---

[33] The maxim *traditionibus et usucapionibus, non nudis pactis, dominia rerum trans-feruntur* is accepted by the Institutional writers: see Stair, III.ii.5; Erskine, II.i.18. Gordon, *Studies in the Transfer of Property by Traditio*, pp. 210–211, points out that the earliest Institutional writer, Sir Thomas Craig, (*Jus Feudale*, 2.vii.1), "accepts the Roman rule without discussion and his acceptance is readily understandable when one considers the sources of Scots law as he sets them out."

[34] On the different approaches see Scot. Law Com., Memo. No. 25, *Corporeal Moveables: Passing of Risk and Ownership*, para. 12; see also Carey Miller, *The Acquisition and Protection of Ownership*, pp. 124–134. See further, below para. 10.17, n. 94.

[35] But in so far as this matter is an issue in Scots law it is the same problem as that debated in the literature of Roman law. See Evans-Jones and MacCormack, "*Iusta causa traditionis*" and Gordon, "The importance of the *iusta causa* of *traditio*," both in *New Perspectives in the Roman Law of Property* (ed. Birks), pp. 99–109, 123–135.

moveables the Scottish Law Commission commented: "We know of no express decision on the application of the abstract theory of *justa causa traditionis* in Scots law."[36]

The relative absence of judicial or juristic analysis on this important question may, possibly, be explained by the fact that the contract of sale—by far the most likely context in which the issue would arise—was in 1893 made subject to statutory regulation in the Sale of Goods Act, now replaced by the consolidating Sale of Goods Act 1979.[37] This fundamentally English law derived codification[38] deals, *inter alia*, with the transfer of title on sale and, not surprisingly, the legislation has been of greater importance than the common law on questions concerning the passing of ownership in moveable property.[39] The common law remains applicable to the passing of ownership in the context of the contracts of gift, exchange and loan for consumption but, of course, the incidence of these contracts is relatively small compared to sale.[40]

Support for abstract theory of acquisition in Institutional writings

Stair and Erskine state the law on the passing of property in moveables in terms which are open to construction as representing the abstract theory. **8.08**

Dealing with derivative acquisition *inter vivos*, Stair[41] sees "the law of rational nature" as requiring an act of will as the basis of the exercise of a power of disposal: "it must needs be an act of will, for by it, rights are both acquired, relinquished, and alienated." But, Stair notes, a transferor's will may be determined from different points of view: "a resolution to dispose, a paction, contract or obligation to dispose, and a present will or consent that that which is the disponer's be the acquirer's."[42] The bare preliminary intention to dispose of property "may be dissolved by contrary resolution."[43] More importantly, "paction does only constitute or transmit a personal right or obligation, whereby the person obliged may be compelled to transmit

---

[36] Scot. Law Com., Memo. No. 25, *Corporeal Moveables: Passing of Risk and Ownership*, para. 12.

[37] Although, it should be noted, one does not find treatment of the problem in the active 19th-century case law prior to 1893.

[38] See Professor Sir Thomas Smith's comments, in his Tagore Law Lectures, in *Property Problems in Sale*, pp. 14–15.

[39] See Gordon, *Studies in the Transfer of Property by Traditio*, pp. 214–215.

[40] It is somewhat surprising that the circumstances of a defective sale—to which the Sale of Goods Act would not apply—has not produced any thorough judicial analysis of the common law basis under which ownership in corporeal moveable property passes. On this, see Scot. Law Com., Memo. No. 25, *Corporeal Moveables: Passing of Risk and Ownership*, para. 15.

[41] III.ii.3.

[42] *Ibid.*

[43] *Ibid.*

the real right,"[44] and, given this, it "must needs then be the present dispositive will of the owner, which conveyeth the right to the other."[45]

Erskine,[46] introducing *traditio* as the principal mode of transferring property, defined it as "the delivery of the possession of a subject by the proprietor, with an intention to transfer the property of it to the receiver." In the same section Erskine goes on to explain the essentials of conveyance. The treatment could be taken to be stating a causal theory in identifying the requirement of *causa* as the transferor's intention to transfer "upon some just or proper title of alienation, as sale, gift, exchange, etc."[47] But in the final part of the section Erskine emphasises the importance of the *animus* element, urging that the requirement of a public act of delivery is primarily required as earnest of the intention to convey, "so that he who gets the last conveyance with the first tradition, is preferred to the property, according to the rule *Traditionibus et usucapionibus, non nudis pactis, transferuntur rerum dominia.*"

The priority accorded to the acquirer receiving the "first tradition" may be interpreted to indicate that Erskine's theory of delivery is abstract. Provided the owner intended to transfer ownership in the thing in the first instance, a subsequent party—the transferee by the last conveyance—acquires a real right. This result is predicated upon the passing of ownership by the "first tradition" and, following Erskine's own definition, would be achieved by the owner giving delivery of the thing with the intention to transfer the right of ownership. A causal approach, which determined the issue of the passing of ownership following the "last conveyance" by reference to the question whether the underlying contract—on the basis of which the owner made the "first tradition"—had been set aside or not, would be incompatible with Erskine's analysis.

Hume's lectures contain material which is compatible with an abstract approach to the passing of ownership. Where an owner delivers a moveable "upon a title *habile ad transferendum dominium*" but on the basis of a fraudulent underlying bargain, he may recover from the immediate acquirer[48]; "yet he cannot at all recover it from anyone who has afterwards purchased the thing *bona fide* from that person, and has got delivery in pursuance of his bargain."[49] This, Hume goes on to show, follows from the recognition of the two essentials of the transfer of title in the will of the owner to convey and

---

[44] *Ibid.*

[45] *Ibid.*

[46] II.i.18.

[47] *Ibid.*

[48] Not, according to Hume, on the basis of a proprietary right, but by a personal claim because a fraudulent acquirer—as distinguished from a thief who obtains possession against the will of the owner—"has all the right of the real owner transferred to him and the property is fully vested in him." See Hume, III, p. 235, n. 198.

[49] *Idem*, at p. 235. See below, para. 10.17.

actual delivery: "[w]hen these two circumstances concur in any case, the party receiver has the real right in him for the time; how unjustifiable soever the means he has employed for procuring the owner's consent to convey."[50]

Hume goes on to distinguish the case of a transferor prevailed upon by force and fear—"concussed to convey" on the basis of "nominal" consent—as opposed to one who although deceived does actually consent. While in the former case property does not pass, in the latter "the property passes to the buyer in the mean-time, how blameable soever his conduct may be."[51]

Hume's treatment identifies a cardinal feature of the abstract approach to the passing of ownership. The essence of the abstract theory is that, regardless of the validity of the underlying contract, ownership passes on the basis of delivery, given and received in the context of the parties' mutual intention that ownership should pass. But one can never wholly separate the parties' "agreement" to transfer ownership from the underlying contract which is normally the source of their motivation. The intention of transferor and transferee that ownership should pass usually follows as a matter of inference from the circumstances of delivery and, in most cases, the fact of at least a perceived contractual relationship which is consistent with this.

The "agreement" to transfer ownership is accordingly, in large measure, determined by reference to the relevant contractual basis: but, of course, the critical point of the abstract theory is that the basis need not be valid or even real. A putative basis may adequately demonstrate that the parties were in agreement that ownership should pass by delivery and no more is required of the underlying contract by the abstract theory. Hume's apparent recognition of "an agreement to convey" following on "a suitable contract" is open to interpretation as a statement of the abstract approach. A "suitable contract" is not necessarily one innately valid or even real but merely appropriate as a basis for "an agreement to convey" property.[52]

Support for the abstract theory in case law

The Scottish Law Commission, in a memorandum published in 1976, **8.09** find support for the tentative view that Scots law recognises an abstract system of passing of ownership in certain nineteenth-century cases.

---

[50] *Idem*, at pp. 235–236.

[51] *Idem*, at p. 236.

[52] It may be noted that Scot. Law Com., Memo. No. 25, *Corporeal Moveables: Passing of Risk and Ownership*, para. 13 refers to the fact that a passage from the Roman-Dutch writer Voet (*ad Pandectas*, 41.1.35), which can be taken to lend support to the abstract approach, is cited by Bell (*Prin.*, § 1299) and that this is a factor counting towards the contention that in Scots law the approach is abstract rather than causal. It is submitted, however, that the relevant passages in Bell and Voet are less convincing, from the point of view of lending support to the abstract theory, than the Scottish Institutional writings referred to above. On this, see further Carey Miller, "The owner's all-conquering right?: Scottish version," in *Essays in Honour of Ellison Kahn* (ed. Visser), pp. 87–107.

"We note that in such Scottish cases as *Stuart* v. *Kennedy*—which involved nullity because of *dissensus*—and *Cuthbertson* v. *Lowes*—which involved statutory nullity—there was no suggestion that the transferor could have claimed delivery of the property transferred either from the transferee or from a third party. Though the courts did not expressly apply the abstract theory of *iusta causa traditionis* (valid transfer despite putative cause) they possibly recognised it implicitly."[53]

The point made is that in these two cases—and in the earlier decision in *Wilson* v. *Marquis of Breadalbane,* cited in a footnote—ownership was taken to pass depite the absence of a legally acceptable underlying contract. But do these cases actually point in the direction of an abstract theory, or is there some other explanation for the conclusion that ownership passed despite the absence of an antecedent *causa*?

In *Wilson* v. *Marquis of Breadalbane*[54] the parties were not *ad idem* as to the price of cattle sold and delivered. In a claim by the seller for the balance due on the basis of the higher figure, the court accepted that both parties had laboured under a genuine mistake as to the price, in consequence of which, Lord Justice-Clerk Inglis reasoned, "[i]f the question had arisen *rebus integris*, there would have been no contract. The cattle would have belonged to the pursuer, the vendor; and the price to the defender, the vendee."[55] But the stock had been appropriated by the defender who insisted "on his right to the cattle as bought and paid for."[56] In these circumstances, the court took the view that the only apposite solution was that the defender must pay the market value. The reasoning which sees this decision as pointing to an abstract approach is simply that, if ownership passed despite the absence of a valid underlying *causa*, then it must have passed on the basis of the parties' mutual intention that it should pass by delivery—the abstract approach.[57] But an interpretation of the decision which is, arguably, more consistent with the actual reasoning in *Wilson* is that the court—recognising that restitution was not possible in the circumstances—sought to regularise the defective agreement by fixing a price on the basis of market value.[58]

---

[53] *Idem*, para. 14.

[54] (1859) 21 D. 957.

[55] *Idem*, at pp. 963–964.

[56] *Ibid*.

[57] A possible difficulty with this approach, it should be noted, is that an absence of *consensus* as to the price would not only be fatal to the contract but—on one view of the nature of the abstract approach—also to the parties' "agreement" as to the passing of ownership. Where, as in most cases, the intentions to pass and receive ownership are implied, it is strained and artificial wholly to dissociate intention as to the passing of ownership from its obvious source in the underlying contract.

[58] This interpretation is supported by Gloag, *The Law of Contract,* at p. 450: "it was held that there was no concluded contract, but that as the buyer did not offer to return the cattle he must pay the market price."

Stuart & Co v. *Kennedy*[59] also involved a misunderstanding as to the price. Again, the court took the view that although there was no contract it was too late for *restitutio in integrum*.[60] As in the earlier case the *ratio* was not the passing of ownership on the basis of the abstract theory—although the decision was also open to this construction—but, apparently, the necessity to shore up the defective consent by retrospective judicial determination of the price on the basis of market value.

In *Cuthbertson* v. *Lowes*[61] potatoes were sold and delivered on the basis of a contract which was illegal and unenforceable for non-compliance with the weights and measures legislation. Although the court took the view that the seller could not, in the circumstances, recover the price by implementation of the contract the remedy of recovery of market value was allowed.

In none of these cases does the court actually recognise the passing of ownership despite the absence of antecedent cause. The decisions are, however, open to argument—at any rate by extrapolation—that ownership must have passed in accordance with the abstract theory, given the absence of a sufficient relationship to provide a contractual basis.

Case law concerned with the perpetual problem of two innocent claimants—an owner deprived by theft or fraud and a subsequent honest purchaser—is also relevant to the identification of the system of transfer of ownership in Scots law. In *Morrisson* v. *Robertson*[62] one Telford falsely represented that he was the son of a dairyman Wilson to whom the pursuer Morrisson had sold stock in the past. Believing that Telford was buying as agent for Wilson, the pursuer entered into a credit sale and delivered two cows to Telford who, in turn, sold on to Robertson, the defender, an innocent party. Given that the pursuer had believed the transaction to be with Wilson, as principal, the court proceeded on the premise that there had been no contract and, accordingly, the common law, rather than the Sale of Goods Act, applied. The conclusion was that there could have been no acquisition by the defender because the facts as between the pursuer and Telford precluded the passing of title to the latter. This broad *ratio* is uninstructive on the abstract/causal issue because the conclusion that ownership did not pass to Telford is consistent with either theory. On an abstract approach one would say that, regardless of the question of underlying *causa*, there was no intention on the part of pursuer Morrisson to pass ownership to Telford by delivery of the cows. From

---

[59] (1885) 13 R. 221.

[60] "But if something has followed, if the contract is partly or wholly performed, you cannot then undo the contract and hold both parties free": *per* Lord President Inglis at p. 223.

[61] (1870) 8 M. 1073.

[62] 1908 S.C. 332.

a causal point of view, the absence of an antecedent contractual basis would have prevented the passing of ownership. In the result the decision is inconclusive on the question of the basis upon which ownership passes.[63]

In *Macleod* v. *Kerr*[64] the parties both claimed ownership in a car which the original owner Kerr had delivered to one Galloway, a fraudulent party who gave a false name and a bad cheque. The vehicle was sold by Galloway to Gibson—the other claimant—who purchased in good faith. The court contrasted the facts with those in *Morrisson* on the interpretation that "there was a complete contract of sale of the car by Mr Kerr to Galloway for there was no dubiety in the present case as to the identity of the purchaser, namely, the man who came in answer to the advertisement."[65] Distinguishing the circumstances of void and voidable contracts the court concluded that ownership passed to the innocent party. "The contract, having been induced by fraud, was voidable, not void. Therefore it conferred a title to the car on Galloway, who could transfer ownership of it to a purchaser in good faith until his title was avoided."[66] The focus on the underlying contract identifies the reasoning as causal. The fact that the same conclusion could have been arrived at by reference to Kerr's intention to transfer his right of ownership is neither here nor there: the court opted for a causal approach.[67]

A rare instance of judicial comment specifically relevant to the identification of the basis of delivery appears in the Second Division case of *Bell, Rannie & Co.* v. *White's Tr.*[68] Concerning the point that the parties knew that wine deposited in an hotel cellar remained the property of the wine merchants "until it should be removed from the bins for comsumption in the hotel," Lord Kinnear commented as follows: "It is said that delivery transfers property, but that is true only when delivery is made in execution of a contract to transfer property,

---

[63] See the opinions of Lords McLaren and Pearson at pp. 337 and 339–340 respectively. Lord Kinnear, at p. 338, however, does seem to recognise the possibility of ownership passing pursuant to the transferor's intention as an alternative to its passing on the basis of the underlying contract: "if such third parties have acquired their title through a person who himself did not acquire the goods by virtue of any contract with the true owner, *or to whom they were not intentionally transferred by the true owner upon any title* [my emphasis], then the pursuer can obtain no better title than the person from whom he acquired."

[64] 1965 S.C. 253.

[65] *per* Lord President Clyde at p. 256.

[66] *per* Lord Guthrie at p. 259.

[67] Professor Sir Thomas Smith noted this in a comment on the case: "In *MacLeod* v. *Kerr* in a sense it did not matter whether the *contract* was reducible on account of fraud or actually reduced—though the First Division considered the problem in those terms. Property and possession had been delivered, and the right *in rem* could have been revoked only by reduction and restitution or vindication from R ['R' for rogue—referring to Galloway] before he had parted with it to a purchaser in good faith": (1967) 12 J.L.S. 206 at pp. 207–208.

[68] (1885) 22 S.L.R. 597.

or else in circumstances which bar the true owner from denying that the property has been transferred."[69] Arguably, this dictum lends support to the abstract theory in that, while recognising that in practice delivery is usually pursuant to a contract, it accepts that the necessary mental element may be inferred from the circumstances.

In *Richmond* v. *Railton*[70] it was noted that property passed because nothing transpired between the parties "to induce delivery without the condition of payment." This suggests that one should look to the parties' intention concerning the passing of property as associated with the act of delivery—the abstract approach.

It may also be noted that that the device of reservation of title[71] is possible only because the transfer of ownership involves the distinct elements of delivery, actual or constructive, and the parties' mutual intention that ownership should pass. Clearly, there could be no reservation of title if the unavoidable effect of delivery was to convey property.[72]

Conclusion on theory of acquisition

It would appear that Scots law has not felt the need to clarify the **8.10** basis upon which derivative acquisition occurs from the point of view of an analysis of the *animus* aspect of delivery.[73] Where the issue of the transferor's intention to pass ownership has arisen, the tendency has been to refer back to the parties' contractual relationship. Given this, Professor W. W. McBryde questions the view that *justa causa traditionis* is part of Scots law.[74] The learned writer argues—with respect, correctly—that the cases of *Wilson*,[75] *Stuart*[76] and *Cuthbertson*,[77] referred to above,[78] are not authority for the abstract theory of the passing of ownership. Professor McBryde refers also to other cases—

---

[69] at p. 598.

[70] (1854) 16 D. 403 at p. 406.

[71] See below, para. 12.01.

[72] The dictum of Lord Young in *Clarke & Co.* v. *Miller & Son's Tr.* (1885) 12 R. 1035 at p. 1042 (quoted below, para. 12.02, n. 20) is unsound; see the better view as stated by Lord President Inglis in *Murdoch & Co. Ltd.* v. *Greig* (1889) 16 R. 396 at p. 402 (quoted below, para. 12.02, nn. 19, 21).

[73] Despite the potential of the Institutional writers, as a starting-point for the development of a theory of acquisition, Scots law offers relatively little by way of analysis. Modern juristic writing, with the notable exception of the works of Professor Sir Thomas Smith (see, *e.g. Short Commentary*, pp. 538–539) have tended to follow the case law without attempting to work out a theory of acquisition. Clearly the Sale of Goods Act has been a major factor inhibiting the development of the law, and unfortunately, in the few cases in which the dogmatic basis of the common law might have been explained, the decisions have been arrived at avoiding the need to do so. See, *e.g. Morrisson* v. *Robertson* 1908, S.C. 332 at pp. 338–339.

[74] See *The Law of Contract*, paras. 26.31–26.37.

[75] (1859) 21 D. 957.

[76] (1885) 13 R. 221.

[77] (1870) 8 M. 1073.

[78] para. 8.09.

concerned with capacity,[79] authority,[80] force and fear[81] and public policy[82]—and points out that the courts have determined questions relevant to the passing of property without necessary recourse to the notion of *justa causa traditionis*. This may be so, but the decisions in the cases concerned would, very probably, have produced an overall picture of greater mutual consistency had each been arrived at in answer to the same question: "Is there a real agreement to transfer ownership despite a defective underlying contract?" Moreover, it is submitted, Scots law recognises the notion of *justa causa traditionis* in the sense of an appropriate basis for the existence of an "agreement" to convey. For while, clearly, there can be no such agreement if the underlying *causa* is hire or loan there may be mutual consent to transfer ownership if the *causa*, albeit defective, is sale or gift. As Professor Gordon[83] has shown, on this basis "the *causa* of delivery is virtually to be equated with the intention to transfer ownership."

Arguably, however, the absence of authority is not as serious, from the point of view of the certainty of the law, as it might be in an area in which the undetermined solution was a question of policy preference or interpretation. This, it is suggested, is because the abstract approach to the passing of ownership may be contended for, as a matter of what is logically appropriate, in any system in which the transmission of property involves the requirement of a self-contained act of conveyance. It is trite that Scots law maintains a strict distinction between contract and conveyance as separate legal acts[84]: and, of course, this can only mean that the act of conveyance must be supported by *animus*. That the mental element must be independent—rather than determined by reference to the underlying contract—also follows, otherwise the act of delivery is reduced to a consequence of the underlying contract.[85]

The Delivery Requirement

General Matters

Relationship between intention and delivery

8.11   The requirement of delivery to pass ownership in moveable property is not wholly separate from, what some authorities[86] see as the primary essential, of the owner's intention to transfer ownership. The handing

---

[79] *e.g. Cardross v. Hamilton* (1708) Mor. 8951; *Gall v. Bird* (1855) 17 D. 1027.
[80] *e.g. Kidd v. Paton's Trs.*, 1912 (2) S.L.T. 363.
[81] *e.g. Cassie v. Fleming* (1632) Mor. 10279.
[82] *e.g. Trevalion & Co. v. Blanche & Co.*, 1919 S.C. 617.
[83] "The importance of the *iusta causa* of *traditio*," in *New Perspectives in the Roman Law of Property*, 123 at p. 125.
[84] See above, para. 8.06, n. 33.
[85] See Carey Miller, *The Acquisition and Protection of Ownership*, pp. 124–125.
[86] *e.g.* Stair, III.ii.4.

over of the possession of a thing carries with it the implication of an intention to convey. Moreover, the relationship between intent and delivery has both doctrinal and practical implications. From the former point of view, the physical handing over is required as a matter of giving effect to the foundation essential of dispositive intent[87]; as a matter of practicality, the inference attaching to the handing over of a moveable thing is of such strength that "the disposition is presumed without the necessity to prove the same."[88] Delivery is, at the same time, a mere consequence of the owner's act of will to convey the thing and, also, the primary touchstone of that intent.[89]

Other reasons supporting the delivery requirement

That delivery is both the natural culmination and the manifestation **8.12** of the transferor's intention to convey his right of ownership does not explain its significance beyond the importance of this act of will. But there are also sound policy reasons—concerned with interests outside the particular relationship—for the requirement. Given that the ownership of moveables cannot, in general, be a matter of record,[90] it follows that the protection of the interests of third parties has to be achieved through the notice implicit in a requirement of handing over. Bell[91] notes the importance of delivery from this point of view and, particularly, with regard to the interests of the creditors of the transferor in "preventing the appearance of possession . . . from continuing the credit of the property unduly."[92] On this basis "the question is not merely one of investing the acquirer, but of divesting the transferor."[93]

This said, it must be noted that the law tends to be a compromise reflecting a tension between two separate broad interests. On the one hand, the interest in the protection of third-party creditors which tends to call for the restriction of delivery—effective to transfer ownership— to an overt handing-over or allocation to the acquiring party, sufficient as notice that the transferor has been divested and the transferee

---

[87] Stair's analysis (III.ii.3–7) clearly demonstrates this reasoning; see esp. III.ii.7: "it doth . . . consummate the disposition."

[88] Stair, III.ii.7.

[89] For a survey of the Scottish juristic analysis of the *traditio* requirement see Gordon, *Studies in the Transfer of Property by Traditio*, pp. 210–213.

[90] Although certain particular moveables can be and are subject to a registration system; regarding ships and aircraft see above, para. 1.11.

[91] *Comm.*, I, 178.

[92] Gordon, *Studies in the Transfer of Property by Traditio*, pp. 213–214, draws attention to Pufendorf's *De iure naturae et gentiun*, IV.ix.5ff and the distinction made between ownership as a *qualitas moralis* and a *facultas physica*. The learned writer points out (p. 214) that "the *facultas physica* is almost inevitably treated to a greater or lesser extent as the badge of the *qualitas moralis*"—hence the relevance of delivery from the point of view of the protection of third parties with a legitimate interest in the proprietary position of the transferor.

[93] *Idem*, p. 214.

invested. On the other hand, and to some extent opposing this interest, one has the even wider general interest in the promotion of commercial activity tending to support the recognition of various forms of constructive delivery.[94]

Allocation of risk inappropriate criterion of effectiveness of delivery

8.13   Bell[95] considers the view that "if in any case it be doubtful whether the property be altered, the most correct decision is to assign the right to him who must bear the burden of the loss should the subject perish." But, as Bell goes on to show, this reasoning is flawed because the incidence of risk does not follow the right of ownership.[96] Moreover, the risk in sale, at common law, was determined from the point of view of obligations rather than property.[97]

Forms of delivery

8.14   Considering the significance of possession as a presumptive factor regarding the ownership of moveables,[98] it is not surprising that the law gives emphasis to the requirement of actual delivery to transfer title.[99] Moreover, the ease with which moveable property can be dealt with, and the variety of reasons for which custody may be transferred, call for a demonstrable act of conveyance.[1]

Accordingly, in the case of moveables, Erskine[2] notes that "the *ipsa corpora* . . . are put by tradition under the power of the acquirer." Hume[3] also emphasises the need for an act demonstrable of the

---

[94] See Bell, *Comm.*, I, 178: "an adherence to this plain and simple rule is utterly impossible amidst the complicated transactions of modern trade."

[95] *Comm.*, I, 180.

[96] At common law the risk passed to the purchaser in the case of a perfected sale even though ownership was only transferred by act of delivery. Stair, I.xiv.7, debates the matter, but since *Hutchieson* v. *McDonald* (1744) Elch., Sale, No. 5, it has been beyond doubt; see Bell, *Prin.*, § 87.

[97] Bell, *Comm.*, I, 180 explains the rule in terms of obligations: thus, while the seller's obligation to deliver may be extinguished by the loss of the thing without his fault, the buyer's obligation to pay the price stands. It is debatable whether this analysis is preferable to that which accords the risk to the buyer, on the reasoning that, of two innocent parties, the buyer has the beneficial interest in the thing from the point of view of any increase in market value or through fruits. However, either way, it is clear that the Roman law derived exception to the basic rule that risk follows ownership is a matter of obligations and, as such, has no relevance to the issue of delivery nor, in particular, to the determination of the basis upon which property should pass.

[98] See above, para. 1.12.

[99] See Stair, III.ii.6: "[p]ossession is requisite . . . to the conveyance of the property of moveable goods."

[1] See Stair, III.ii.7: "The passing of moveables from the proprietor must be so evidently instructed, that there may no probability remain of their being recovered, and thereafter alienated."

[2] II.i.19. Dealing with delivery in general, Erskine (*ibid.*) regards a symbolic form acceptable as an alternative to actual delivery only where, as in the case of heritable subjects, this "must of necessity be made use of where real delivery is impracticable."

[3] III, p. 246.

transferor's relinquishing and the transferee's assuming power over the thing: "the legal way of delivering a moveable subject is the same as the natural way; that is by actual transportation of the thing from under the owner's power and command, into that of the other party."

Though, however, the basic emphasis of the common law is to require actual delivery, the position is not as rigid as might appear from the above. First, there is considerable flexibility within the requirement of actual delivery. Hume[4] qualifies his above statement to allow for this. "All I mean to say is, that the thing must be brought into the same state of custody, safety, and command, with the other parts of the acquirer's property of that sort,—regard being always had to the nature and description of the subject in question and the sort of keeping it allows." Secondly, the authorities recognise a certain, if limited, rôle for symbolical delivery. Erskine[5]:

> "Though moveables are capable of real delivery, it is not always necessary that the *ipsa corpora* of moveables be delivered. If, for instance, the subjects to be conveyed be under lock and key, the delivery of the key to the purchaser is accounted a legal tradition of all that is contained in the repository."[6]

Thirdly, there is the possibility of what has come to be labelled constructive delivery, where the item concerned is in the custody of a third party who continues to hold but henceforth on behalf of the transferee.[7]

As Professor Gordon has shown,[8] the civilian forms alternative to actual delivery—*brevi manu*, *longa manu* and *constitutum possessorium*—can be identified in Scots law. But there is no general use of the Romanist concepts as categories of delivery; rather, Scots law has developed a distinctive classification based upon the categories of actual, symbolical and constructive.

A natural consequence of the historical emphasis upon the significance of possession as a criterion of ownership was not only a tendency to require actual delivery but also the development of an extended notion of the scope of actual delivery. Both the concepts of possession and delivery are to some extent open-ended notions, and the need to give effect to commercial interests by recognising a variety of forms of inferred delivery has led to an accommodation in which the possession requirement is satisfied by an extended category of actual delivery. A statement by Bell[9] speaks to this necessary adaptation:

---

[4] *Ibid.*
[5] II.i.19.
[6] See below, para. 8.16 on this being a questionable instance of symbolical delivery.
[7] See Stair, III.ii.5.
[8] *Studies in the Transfer of Property by Traditio*, pp. 215–222.
[9] *Comm.*, I, 181–182.

"although delivery of the commodity is necessary to the passing of property, it still is not indispensably required that it should be of that actual and unequivocal kind which places the thing sold within the grasp and in the personal apprehension of the buyer, or of his servants, clerks and others, whom the law identifies with him and considers as his hands; but that acts of possession less immediate and direct are by construction of law held sufficient, when actual tradition into the buyer's hands cannot be given."

A consequence of an extended notion of what amounts to actual delivery—including certain cases in which actual delivery may only be said to be inferred—is that there is correspondingly limited scope for separate categories of constructive or inferred delivery. One sees this in that the classes of symbolical and constructive delivery are both limited to somewhat narrow and specialised scope. But the nomenclature of actual, symbolical and constructive[10] delivery are only labels which any useful exposition must go behind to identify the range of circumstances covered.

Actual Delivery

Simple form of handing over to the transferee reflects essentials

8.15   Delivery "by the actual transportation of the thing from under the owner's power and command, into that of the other party"[11] takes its most straightforward form where the thing is handed over to and received by the acquiring party in person.[12] Actual delivery in the sense of from hand to hand is conclusive in that it provides a basis from which to infer the intentions to pass and receive title and, at the same time, satisfies the physical element of a demonstrable assumption of power and control by the transferee.[13] But, clearly, there are means other than actual delivery in this literal sense by which the essential mental and physical elements may be satisfied. In this regard one may note a dictum concurred in by five judges and expressed in a joint opinion in the case of *Gibson* v. *Forbes*[14]:

---

[10] In *Mathison* v. *Alison* (1854) 17 D. 274 at pp. 282–283 the phrase "constructive delivery" is used in the usual sense of the word "constructive" as any appropriate circumstances from which delivery may be inferred (see also the opinion of Lord Cockburn in *Boak* v. *Megget* (1844) 6 D. 662 at p. 675); as a term of art in relation to delivery in Scots law, however, the word has come to refer to the case of a thing held by a third party, formerly for the transferor but subsequently for the transferee.

[11] Hume, III, p. 246.

[12] Bell, *Comm.*, I, 183: "The simplest case of all is, where a person goes into a shop and buys and brings off with him an article there exposed for sale."

[13] Regarding the mental and physical elements in the transfer of possession of a moveable item see the dicta of Lord Neaves in *Moore* v. *Gledden* (1869) 7 M. 1016 at pp. 1020–1021.

[14] (1833) 11 S. 916 at p. 925.

"There was not only no ordinary delivery from hand to hand, but there was no delivery of any kind, no change of possession, or power over the subject held by the seller, into possession or power over the subject held by the buyer, in any mode or form whatever."

No numerus clausus of forms of actual delivery

There is no limit to the variety of circumstances which may amount **8.16** to actual delivery in the sense of the two essential aspects being satisfied, but some of the more common instances may be considered.

The delivery of keys, giving the transferee access to the subject concerned, may constitute delivery. Although Erskine[15] classifies this as symbolical delivery the correct position is probably that it is actual delivery, because the essential feature is the obtaining of power and control over the thing.[16] Accordingly, the handing over of a key for some limited purpose will be ineffective from the point of view of delivery.[17] In *West Lothian Oil Co. Ltd.* v. *Mair*[18] the transferee—for the purpose of the creation of a real right of security—was held to have acquired possession of a quantity of barrels where the same remained in the yard of the transferor but were enclosed within a fenced area, to which the transferee held the key.[19] *Gibson* v. *Forbes*[20] was an instance of the common case of a competition between a purchaser and the trustee in sequestration which, in principle, presents the same problem as an attempt to create a real security interest in favour of a particular creditor. The critical question in such cases is whether ownership—or a real right of security—has been acquired, through acts amounting to delivery, prior to the vesting of the insolvent estate in the trustee for

---

[15] II.i.19.

[16] See Bell, *Comm.*, I, 186: "Where goods are in a repository of the seller, from which the buyer does not wish them removed, but which he is willing to make the ultimate place of their destination for a time, the giving up of the key of that repository by the seller to the buyer is an act of real delivery. It differs from symbolical delivery in this, that a symbol is properly nothing more than the sign of the thing transferred—the image by which it is represented to the senses; whereas the delivery of the key gives the buyer access to the actual possession of the subject, and power over it, while the seller is excluded." See also Hume, III, p. 251 (as quoted below, para. 8.23, n. 84) and the comments of Gordon, *Studies in the Transfer of Property by Traditio*, pp. 216–217.

[17] Hume, III, p. 251, refers to the facts of the unreported case of *Dudgeon & Brodie* v. *John More* (July 3, 1801): "the delivery of the key must have been made however with the purpose of putting the goods absolutely and fully into the power of the vendee; for if the key, of a granary for instance, was given, explicitly and specially for some limited and single purpose, as for instance that the buyer's servants might turn and air the grain, or use means to kill the vermin in the granary,—the same virtue is not to be attached to it."

[18] (1892) 20 R. 64.

[19] "Now, I am of opinion, upon the evidence, that the setting of the goods apart in the yard by themselves, which was locked up, and the key delivered to the purchaser upon payment of the price, amounted to delivery at the common law": *per* Lord Young at p. 69.

[20] (1833) 11 S. 916.

the benefit of all creditors.[21] In *Gibson* wine bottled for a purchaser was set aside in special bins and the transferor's records were made to show the transferee as owner. A majority of the court decided the matter accepting that there had been delivery,[22] but arguably this conclusion is questionable, given the absence of any active assumption of control by the purchaser.[23]

The rationale of a transfer of control and power would exclude—at any rate as actual delivery—the handing over of a purely symbolic key, but it would not matter that the transferor himself retains access because this does not necessarily detract from the transferee having been placed in a position of control.[24] Nor does it matter that the transferor, having purported to give exclusive access, in fact retains a means of entry which would enable him to bar entry to the transferee.[25] Where the circumstances justify the inference of possession by the transferee, the mere possibility that the transferor may act in bad faith and prevent access does not negative delivery.

The marking of goods to indicate acquisition by the transferee[26] may, in some cases, be sufficient to transfer ownership even though the items concerned remain in the custody of the transferor. But, of course, the general circumstances must be consistent with this result.[27] Marking which is of an enduring nature—such as the branding of livestock—would very probably go far to satisfy the requirements of actual delivery; arguably, in such a case, both *animus* and *corpus* elements would be satisfied and the interests of third parties protected by the clear indication that someone other than the natural possessor was owner. In this regard one may note *obiter* remarks subscribed to by seven judges in a case in which the court of 14 was equally divided[28]:

> "Had the pursuer, indeed, before the cattle were so carried back to their pastures, put his mark upon them, there might have been

---

[21] See below, para. 11.02.

[22] Five members of the 13-judge court returned a joint opinion in which it was reasoned that delivery had occurred; three members of the court simply concluded that there had been no undue preference, however, although they did not consider the delivery aspect, their conclusion could only have been reached on the premise that property had passed.

[23] In *Boak* v. *Megget* (1844) 6 D. 662 a quantity of unmarked hides were set aside so as to be distinguishable from the seller's stock, but the Second Division held that there had been no delivery in the circumstances.

[24] As Bell, *Comm.*, I, 186 notes: "It will not prevent this kind of delivery from having effect, that the seller has a double or master key by which he may open the door, or that he may get access by some indirect and unusual means."

[25] Bell, *Comm.*, I, 186.

[26] In *Boak* v. *Megget* (1844) 6 D. 662 at p. 672 Lord Medwyn observed that no mark was put upon the hides by the buyers.

[27] See the note of the Lord Ordinary in *Orr's Tr.* v. *Tullis* (1870) 8 M. 936 at p. 944.

[28] To resolve this deadlock Lord Craigie agreed not to vote, and in the event the section of the court subscribing to the opinion quoted from in my text represented the majority.

some room for contending that this amounted to a taking of possession . . . the purpose of applying the buyer's mark in such a case, is not to distinguish the animal from others of the same kind, but to point out that it has become the buyer's. It produces its effects only as a symbolical taking of possession, and as indicating that if the article is allowed still to remain with the seller, it remains, not as his property, but as a deposit, or the subject of location."[29]

Although it may be possible to infer the mental and physical elements of a change of possession from the circumstances—and so conclude that ownership has passed by delivery—there must be a sufficient basis for this; where the item concerned remains in the custody of the transferor it is simply more difficult to justify the conclusion that delivery has occurred.[30] Arguably, the control factor is of greater importance than the act of delivery itself—frequently a matter primarily between the parties—especially where the circumstances are not potentially misleading to third parties.[31] One need hardly say that in determining the extent of control obtained by the transferee it is appropriate to consider how much potential control has been retained by the transferor.

Delivery of standing crops and trees

While grain and timber are subject to the general rules relating to delivery, special considerations apply to growing crops and trees whether standing or cut. **8.17**

Cultivated periodic crops are deemed moveable[32]—despite being attached to the land—and as such are open to delivery pending their harvesting. In *Grant* v. *Smith*[33] growing corn was sold and "delivered to the buyers by a sort of symbolical delivery," which was sustained by the Lords as an effective means of transfer. The circumstances of

---

[29] *Lang* v. *Bruce* (1832) 10 S. 777 at p. 790; see also Bell. *Comm.*, I, 187, n. 6.

[30] See *Broughton* v. *J. & A. Aitchison*, 15 Nov. 1809, F.C. In this case—where a delivery order was handed over but the goods remained on premises controlled by the seller's servant—the majority held that effective delivery had taken place, but the basis was minimal and the dissenting opinion of Lord President Blair is the most convincing judgment. Emphasising that this was not a case of constructive delivery, where the subject was in the hands of a consignee, depositary or third party (see below, para. 8.20), the Lord President opined (at p. 418) that the owners' possession, in their own lofts, remained "as clear, absolute, unequivocal, and actual possession, as could be had, without holding it themselves, or putting it in their pockets."

[31] But see *Pattison's Tr.* v. *Liston* (1893) 20 R. 806 which seems to give unwarranted emphasis to the act of delivery. In this case the court did not accept that the delivery of furniture had occurred on the basis of written intimation because the transferee already held the key in his capacity as letting agent for the transferor. Given the recognition of constructive delivery (see below, para. 8.20), it is difficult to see why the court regarded this as a critical failing. On this see also below, para. 11.06, n. 48.

[32] See above, para. 3.05.

[33] (1758) Mor. 9561.

periodical crop production make it desirable for delivery to be possible prior to harvesting,[34] and the notorious nature of this fact is sufficient to put third parties on their guard.

According to Bell[35] the marking of standing trees is "good constructive delivery."[36] However, Bell sees the decision in *Paul* v. *Cuthbertson*[37] as authority the other way. In this case the full court rejected "symbolical" delivery—taking the form of the handing over of several trees cut from the land concerned—applied to a stand of unfelled trees. The basis of the decision was that growing trees—as distinct from crops[38]—are heritable subjects not separable from the land until cut.[39] This would seem to justify the requirement of actual marking in the case of trees as against the mere handing over of a symbol in the case of a growing crop. In *Allan* v. *Millar*[40] it was held that raspberry bushes could be disposed of as moveable on the basis of being sold as part of a *universitas* preponderatingly moveable even though "*[p]rima facie*, no doubt, growing bushes are heritable, and are properly regarded as *partes soli*." A logical conclusion would be that symbolical delivery of the growing bushes would be competent. But the difficulty with the decision is that, in so far as a heritable element is involved, one would expect the law relating to the sale of heritage to dictate.

Assuming, however, that a stand of timber has been cut it would seem that delivery should be recognised on the basis of *traditio longa manu*—an extension of actual delivery, hence: "by the long hand."[41] Arguably, the physical and mental elements are satisfied by the transferee—or his agent or servant—felling the trees which he has a contractual right to, with a view to their removal in due course. Moreover, the interests of heritable creditors are protected provided the trees remain uncut; once cut, even though remaining on the land, one would expect recognition of the possibility of acquisition by another.

On the above basis the case of a cut stand of timber would be distinguishable from delivery following a contract for the purchase of a

---

[34] One may note the maxim *messis sementem sequitur*—the harvest goes to the sower. See above, para. 3.05.

[35] *Comm.*, I, 187.

[36] Bell is here using the word "constructive" in its usual sense; see above, para. 8.14, n. 10.

[37] (1840) 2 D. 1286 at p. 1312.

[38] See above, para. 3.06.

[39] This distinction leads to a debatable point concerning the definition of "goods" for the purposes of the Sale of Goods Act 1979. See below, para. 9.07, n. 63.

[40] 1932 S.C. 620, *per* Lord Justice-Clerk Alness at pp. 624–625.

[41] Although this label does not seem to be used in Scots law, Gordon (*Studies in the Transfer of Property by Traditio*, p. 216) contends that the concept is recognised and cites Bell, *Comm.*, I, 181 and n. 3. In the footnote Bell refers to the established civilian position in which *traditio longa manu* was well developed: however, some caution is necessary in imputing this to Scots common law given the system's general reluctance to admit delivery where the subject is retained on the premises of the transferor.

quantity of a commodity which required repeated acts of delivery. In the latter case ownership would only pass on a piecemeal basis as and when the separate deliveries were made.[42]

Rôle of trade custom in recognising an extended notion of actual delivery

In some cases one finds the argument that a particular arrangement **8.18** between the parties amounts to delivery in that, on the basis of a trade practice or custom, it is recognised as such. In *Grant* v. *Smith*,[43] for example, the successful defender contended that the sale of growing crops was a matter of "universal practice over the whole country" and that a decision ruling out this possibility would render ineffectual "a very common and necessary branch of commerce . . . to the great detriment of the public."

In *Boak* v. *Megget*[44] one finds recognition of the fact that exceptions to the rule requiring the actual transmission of possession to the transferee may be based upon the custom or usage of particular trades:

"cases where the possession of the party is not really looked to, in the usage and from the nature of the trade, as necessarily proving that the stock apparently on hand is his, and not considered as creating such a presumption in the actual business of that trade."

But the case law also contains statements indicating the desirability of general conformity with the common law regulation of delivery. In *Broughton* v. *J. & A. Aitchison*[45] Lord President Blair commented on the practice of bakers to pay for grain pending delivery from the grain merchant as a practice which "could not change the general law of the country, to which it is the business of creditors to accommodate their dealings." In *Anderson* v. *McCall*[46] Lord Neaves commented to similar effect: "But questions as to the constitution of real rights of property, and preferences in bankruptcy between competing creditors, depend upon principles of general law, which cannot be affected by local usage, or individual understanding."

From the point of view of possible prejudice to general creditors one can, perhaps, explain the apparently contradictory dicta in *Grant* and

---

[42] See *Collins* v. *Marquis' Creditors* (1804) Mor. 14223; Bell, *Comm.*, I, 183. *Cf.* *Broughton* v. *Aitchison*, 15 Nov. 1809, F.C.

[43] (1758) Mor. 9561.

[44] (1844) 6 D. 662, *per* Lord Justice-Clerk Hope at p. 669.

[45] 15 Nov. 1809, F.C. It should be noted that although there was considerable division of opinion in this case, the majority view seems to recognise the trade custom of bakers to make payment for grain but to leave it in the store of the supplier until there is space for it at the bakery premises.

[46] (1866) 4 M. 765 at p. 771.

Broughton. In the case of standing crops the economics of farming give rise to the probability that a buyer will have been found prior to the harvest; in the case of the grain merchant general creditors will be justified in the assumption that what the merchant holds in stock may be regarded as assets of his business.

In *Gibson* v. *Forbes*[47] what may be taken to be the majority opinion[48] has no bearing on the present question but Lord MacKenzie, in a dissenting opinion, took the view that proof of a general practice in the wine trade could not be taken as a basis for the recognition of the passing of property in wine left with the sellers—"it is too much to say that the law must bend to any difficulty of giving delivery in cases of this sort." All it showed, Lord Mackenzie observed, was that the risk from bankruptcy in the trade could not be felt to be too great.

The better view would appear to be that proof of an established trade custom—on the basis of which the passing of property is recognised although natural possession remains with the transferor—should neither be conclusive nor, necessarily, regarded as a consideration without weight. As Lord Justice-Clerk Hope urged in *Boak* v. *Megget*,[49] the issue of overriding importance is the question of potential prejudice to general creditors—the implication being that no alleged custom could be accepted if the court was not satisfied on this score.

> "In these cases,[50] I think the principle really at the foundation of the exceptions is what I have stated—*viz*. that the possession does not, in the particular and notorious facts of the trade, and in the opinion of the public, and of creditors who are to be protected, import that the goods or stock are really the property of the party in whose hands they are seen; and therefore, that to exclude proof of the actual fact, would give the public a benefit, which, in dealing with the party, they did not truly believe they had."

No active good faith requirement for delivery

8.19   The act of delivery must satisfy the requirements of the physical and mental elements. The fact that the parties honestly believe that the means adopted will be effective to transfer ownership does not take the matter any further.[51]

But good faith may be an issue in a negative sense. If the transaction is simulated—typically where the transferee is a creditor of the

---

[47] (1833) 11 S. 916 at pp. 925–926.
[48] See above, para. 8.16, n. 22.
[49] (1844) 6 D. 662 at p. 670.
[50] This is a reference to the instances given by Bell, *Comm.*, I, 187–188.
[51] See *Kinneil* v. *Menzies* (1790) Mor. 4973. From the terse report of this case it does appear that the defender honestly believed that he had acquired furniture purchased from but, for convenience, left in the possession of the seller who subsequently became bankrupt.

transferor and the primary intention is to put the transferee in a position of preference as against other creditors—it may well be questionable whether the parties intended ownership to pass, and to this extent, one may say that there is a requirement of good faith, at any rate in a negative sense.[52]

Constructive Delivery

Basis of constructive delivery

The notion of constructive delivery has been developed to accom-   **8.20** modate the case of an owner who does not have natural possession of a thing yet wishes to convey title in it. Stair[53] recognised that while actual delivery was the principal means of passing ownership on a derivative basis, as a matter of utility, "possession lawfully attained by virtue of the disposition, although not delivered by the disponer," could be regarded as the equivalent, for: "if the deponer were not in possession himself, and so cannot deliver it; yet the acquirer may recover it from the detainer."

Given the fact that goods destined for retail sale—whether as commodities or components in manufactured goods—are frequently stored in premises controlled by someone other than their owner, it is a matter of commercial necessity that a simple means be available for the owner to transfer his right to a purchaser who receives the goods direct.

The theoretical justification for this form of delivery is that the transferor gives to the transferee the possession and control, however indirect or circumscribed, which he had over the thing held by a third party. Lord President Blair explained the point in the case of *Broughton* v. *J. & A. Aitchison*[54] on the basis that what the law required by way of delivery of moveables was the transfer of possession or, more specifically, "that the same sort of posssion which was formerly in the seller was afterwards in the purchaser." In *Mathison* v. *Alison*,[55] subsequently regarded as the leading case on constructive delivery,[56] Lord Cowan, adopting the explanation of Lord President Blair, noted that: "the law requires, in cases of civil or constructive delivery, the same description and extent of possession which was formerly in the seller, to be after the sale vested in the purchaser."

From the point of view of the interests of commerce, the most important form of constructive delivery is that facilitating the transfer

---

[52] As Lord Neaves put it in *Orr's Trs.* v. *Tullis* (1870) 8 M. 936 at p. 951: "Indeed, even if an apparent delivery takes place, if it seems to be merely nominal, and is followed, or its effect undone, by an immediate restitution, the possession will not be held to have passed." See further, below, paras. 8.25, 12.05–12.06.

[53] III.ii.5.

[54] 15 Nov. 1809, F.C.

[55] (1854) 17 D. 274 at p. 284.

[56] See *Anderson* v. *McCall* (1866) 4 M. 765 at p. 770.

of ownership in goods held by a third party. However, a simpler form, but one also based upon the notion of vesting in the transferee the same residual right of possession as formerly vested in the transferor, is also recognised. This form, labelled *traditio brevi manu*, will be dealt with first.

Traditio brevi manu

8.21   A form of constructive delivery—justifiable on the basis of a transfer sufficient to change natural possession to civil possession[57]—is the case of acquisition by a transferee who already holds the thing but on some basis other than that of owner.

Stair[58] gives this instance of delivery as the companion form to the case involving a third party in custody: "or the acquirer might have been in possession before, by any other title, as by custody, conduction . . . in which case none require delivery."[59] Erskine notes that while this mode is sometimes regarded as fictitious delivery,[60] "the plain reason why tradition is not required in that case is, because there is no room for it; for no subject can be delivered to one who hath it already in his custody."[61] The important point, however, is that the fiction of delivery—dictated by convenience—in the case of *traditio brevi manu* has no potential for prejudice to third parties. The law is concerned to protect third parties—usually the creditors of the transferor—who are unlikely to be aware of circumstances which may mean that the proprietary *status quo* is other than as it appears to be. But in the case of *traditio brevi manu* the transferring owner's creditors should already be on their guard, given that the thing is in the natural possession of another.[62]

---

[57] See above, para. 1.14.

[58] III.ii.5.

[59] See also Erskine, II.i.19: "Notwithstanding the general rule, that property cannot be acquired but by tradition, yet where the possession or custody of a subject hath been before with the person to whom the property is to be transferred, *ex. gr.* if he who had been intrusted with the custody of a thing should purchase it from the owner, no tradition is necessary for perfecting the purchase, either real or symbolical."

[60] *Ibid.*: "It is commonly said, that in such cases there is a *ficta traditio*: the depositary is supposed to redeliver to the owner the thing deposited, and he again is supposed to give it back to the purchaser, upon the title of vendition, which is called by doctors, *fictio brevis manus.*"

[61] This seems rather to beg the question (see Gordon, *Studies in the Transfer of Property by Traditio*, p. 216), but Erskine may simply be saying that it would be unacceptably cumbersome to require the thing to be restored and then redelivered. As Scot. Law Com., Memo. No. 25, *Corporeal Moveables: Passing of Risk and Ownership*, para. 66, put it: "Only a primitive and formalistic system of law would require the goods to be restored to the owner so that he could thereafter retransfer possession by tradition."

[62] From a wider point of view the device is potentially beneficial to the transferee's creditors who may, in any event, be relying upon the apparent fact of possession by their debtor.

Traditio brevi manu has been accepted in Scottish case law from an early date.[63] Considering the emphasis upon possession, one can understand that there has been no difficulty in accommodating the device. This point comes across in the case of *Orr's Tr.* v. *Tullis*,[64] where Lord Justice-Clerk Moncreiff rejected an argument urging that "some ostensible corporeal act—some change in the actual local situation or custody of moveables sold, is necessary to pass the property." The learned Lord Justice-Clerk pointed out that this is only so where possession has not been attained by the transferee, but:

"It is manifestly not true when possession has been attained. The simplest illustration of this is the case in which the thing sold is at the time of the sale in the possession of the purchaser. If a man hire a horse or carriage, and purchase it while his contract of hire is current, the property has passed; for no delivery could make the possession more complete than it was before."[65]

Requirements of constructive delivery where the goods are held by a third party

In *Anderson* v. *McCall*[66] Lord Justice-Clerk Inglis answered the **8.22** question "what is constructive delivery, and how is it operated?" by prescribing the following requirements:

"In order to operate constructive delivery by means of a delivery-order, there must be three independent persons,—the vendor, the vendee, and the custodier of the goods, and if the custodier of the goods be identical with the vendor, there ceases to be a third independent person; and, therefore, constructive delivery cannot in that case be effected by a delivery-order."

In the same case, Lord Cowan[67] also emphasised the requirement of an independent third party: "Where the goods sold are in the custody of a third party, and lying in his warehouse, the legal principle is, that the independent custodier of the warehouse to whom the transfer has been duly intimated becomes the custodier of the purchaser."[68]

---

[63] Gordon, *Studies in the Transfer of Property by Traditio*, p. 216 cites Hope, *Major Practicks*, II.iv.3, where reference is made to the case of *Park* v. *Findlay* decided in 1621 to the effect that there was no need to deliver "quher the goods wer els in the buyer's possessione." See also *Arbuthnott* v. *Paterson* (1798) Mor. 14220.
[64] (1870) 8 M. 936 at pp. 945–946.
[65] *Ibid.*
[66] (1866) 4 M. 765 at p. 770.
[67] at p. 770.
[68] In both *Anderson* v. *McCall* (1866) 4 M. 765 and the subsequent case of *Dobell, Beckett & Co.* v. *Neilson* (1904) 7 F. 281, constructive delivery did not take place because the order was sent to a storekeeper employed by the transferor rather than having the rôle of an independent contractor. In *Melrose* v. *Hastie* (1850) 12 D. 665 at p. 671 Lord Mackenzie declined to recognise constructive delivery on the basis of an endorsement made on a delivery note handed to the seller's importing agent: "I have never heard of property being passed by intimation to an importing agent, who was not the actual custodier."

In *Pochin & Co.* v. *Robinows & Marjoribanks*,[69] Lord President
Inglis stated that two essentials are indispensable to constructive
delivery. First, on the authority of *Anderson* v. *McCall*[70] the learned
Lord President laid down the requirement that the custodier "hold an
independent position, and be neither the owner nor in any way
identified with the owner of the goods."[71] Secondly, the court held that
the goods had to be specific in the sense that "they be capable of
identification, either as one total undivided quantity stored in a
particular place, or at least a specified quantity, forming part of an
identified whole."[72] Where these two conditions are present the
intimation of the delivery order to the custodier effects delivery on a
constructive basis, "because the custodier from that time becomes in
law holder for the purchaser, just as before he was holder for the
seller."[73]

In *Mathison* v. *Alison*[74] the court rejected, as delivery, an entry,
reflecting the sale of a quantity of spirits, in the private warehouse-
book of the seller. In the view of Lord Deas[75] these circumstances
failed to satisfy the requirements of constructive delivery on two
counts. First: because the goods were in the distiller's own private
bonded warehouse the public would have no reason to suppose "but
that the goods are his own property." Secondly: because the public
had no right of access to the books in which the relevant entries were
made.

The transfer of ownership may be achieved by constructive delivery
even though it was not necessarily the intention of the parties that the
property should "permanently or ultimately"[76] remain with the transferee. Provided the parties intend that ownership should pass it does
not matter that their ultimate motivation is the creation of a security
interest which they may not intend to be of permanent duration. In
this case, because there is no special danger of the deception of general
creditors—given that the goods are in any event in the natural

---

[69] (1869) 7 M. 622 at pp. 628–629.

[70] (1866) 4 M. 765.

[71] In *Rhind's Tr.* v. *Robertson & Baxter* (1891) 18 R. 623 at pp. 628–629 Lord Trayner
declined to recognise constructive delivery where a delivery order was handed to an
excise officer: "He had a key of the warehouse where the goods were stored, but that
only for the purpose of enabling him to protect the interests of the excise. In these
circumstances . . . the goods . . . remained in the possession of the debtor."

[72] Clearly, the foundation requirement of an intention to convey and a corresponding
intention to receive (see above, para. 8.03) makes it essential that the subjects involved
are sufficiently identified.

[73] *Pochin & Co.* v. *Robinows & Marjoribanks* (1869) 7 M. 622 *per* Lord President
Inglis at p. 629.

[74] (1854) 17 D. 274.

[75] at p. 281.

[76] *per* Lord President McNeill in *Hamilton* v. *Western Bank of Scotland* (1856) 19 D.
152 at p. 160.

possession of a party other than the owner—there is no particular requirement of good faith.[77]

Standing of constitutum possessorium

What is the standing, from the point of view of acceptability as a **8.23** mode of delivery, of an undertaking by the present possessor that he will henceforth hold the thing not as owner but on some other basis: for example, as borrower or hirer?[78] As shown,[79] it is accepted that in the converse situation a party with natural possession, usually holding the thing on the basis of a contractual right, acquires by constructive delivery—designated *traditio brevi manu*—where he obtains civil possession following a change in the basis under which he holds the thing.[80] Moreover, the law also accepts delivery on the basis of an instruction given to a third party to hold the thing henceforth for the transferee, instead of for the transferor.[81]

Stair[82] notes that possession may be attained without the handing over of a symbol and without the interposition of a third party, but by mere "conjunction of interest"; however, it is not apparent that he is thinking beyond heritable property and the possibility, for example, of transferring the right of property while leaving the transferor with possession on the basis of a liferent. Hume[83] takes the matter further, albeit somewhat tentatively. After indicating that the usual and ordinary rule is that moveables are transferred by being handed over into the power of the transferee, he adds that he would not, however, go to the extent of saying "that a case may not be imagined, attended with such circumstances as to open the way for an exception though there be no removal of the thing." Hume[84] puts forward the case of the purchase of a horse from a livery stable where the circumstances are that:—

> "I find it convenient to let the horse remain at livery in the same stable; but that he is there tended exclusively and dressed and

---

[77] See at p. 162 where Lord Ivory rejected the contention that an outright transfer intended to provide a right of security was "against . . . good faith." *Cf.* the case of *constitutum possessorium* below para. 8.25.

[78] Some Romanist-based systems accept this as a possible form of delivery—usually identified as *constitutum possessorium*. See Scot. Law Com., Memo. No. 25, *Corporeal Moveables: Passing of Risk and Ownership*, para. 68.

[79] Above, para. 8.21.

[80] See above, para. 1.14.

[81] See above, para. 8.22. See Gordon, *Studies in the Transfer of Property by Traditio*, p. 217, where the learned author points out that the rationale behind this is that there is delivery in the intimation which puts the thing "out of the control of the present possessor and into the control of the acquirer."

[82] II.i.16.

[83] III, p. 251.

[84] *Ibid.*

taken out to exercise by my servant, that I pay for his keeping and shoeing, pay the farrier and sadler's bill, and that the horse cloths and other things are marked with my initials."

Hume[85] refers to the Second Division case of *Eadie* v. *Young*[86] involving the sale of two cart and horse combinations, the same being retained by the seller/transferor as hirer. Documents, testifying to the two contracts, had been signed by the parties and it was established that payments were made by the transferor in consideration for the hire of the horses and carts. After the reversal of an initial decision the transferee succeeded against a poinding creditor of the transferor, but the changed circumstances of possession appear not to be the only basis upon which delivery was accepted to have taken place.[87]

Bell[88] also supports the possibility of acquisition—despite the fact of natural possession remaining with the transferor—in certain cases of necessity "where goods are purchased from a manufacturer before some necessary operation of his art is completed." In *Orr's Tr.* v. *Tullis*[89] Lord Neaves recognised the instance of the acquisition of a ship built in the yard of the transferor[90]—the circumstances Bell[91] described as "a ship on the stocks."[92] As indicated,[93] the view taken by Lord Justice-Clerk Hope in *Boak* v. *Megget*,[94] was that cases of this sort were most appropriately explained, not as instances of any principle of constructive delivery[95] but, rather, as cases in which it was possible to adopt a convenient solution because there was no possibility of prejudice to creditors of the transferor given that the circumstances would be a matter of general knowledge.

Essential features of delivery by constitutum possessorium

8.24   The case law tends to show that *constitutum possessorium* is only admitted where the circumstances support and justify the conclusion that the transferor continues to hold the thing in some capacity other

---

[85] III, p. 252.

[86] (1815) Hume's Dec., 705.

[87] A form of symbolic handing over of the halters to the transferee and their return by him, followed by a verbal invocation by transferee to transferor to use the horses well, as well as the marking of the carts with plates bearing the name of the transferee, were other acts aimed at achieving the passing of ownership.

[88] *Comm.*, I, 187.

[89] (1870) 8 M. 936 at p. 950.

[90] "It would be contrary to common sense and shocking to common justice to hold that, because he furnishes the materials and builds in his own yard, the property does not pass till the ship is launched."

[91] *Comm.*, I, 187.

[92] See also *Simpson* v. *Creditors of Duncanson* (1786) Mor. 14204; *McBain* v. *Wallace & Co.* (1881) 8 R. 360; (1881) 8 R.(H.L.) 106.

[93] Above, para. 8.18.

[94] (1844) 6 D. 662 at pp. 669–671.

[95] 'But it is important to remember that constructive delivery, when possession remains with the seller, is in the general case wholly unavailing": at p. 669.

than that of owner. In *Eadie* v. *Young*[96] such circumstances were present in the marking of the carts with the transferee's name and the payment of rent by the transferor. *Gibson* v. *Forbes*[97] is not a true case of *constitutum possessorium*—nor, indeed, are any of the "warehouse" cases—because the emphasis was upon the wine being identified, set aside and held for the transferee rather than retained by the transferor for his own use or purpose, but on a basis other than that of owner.[98]

The difficulty with the true *constitutum possessorium* cases is that the transferor continues *de facto* to possess and use the thing as if he were owner. Given the emphasis of the law upon the reasonable inference a creditor may draw from the circumstances of natural possession, one can appreciate that the facts must necessarily demonstrate that the transferor no longer holds as owner but on some other footing. Professor Gordon[99] has explained the difficulty in a passage adopted by the Scottish Law Commission[1]:

> "The difficulty felt by Scottish judges over *constitutum possessorium* has been that there is a rule of law that in the case of corporeal moveables possession creates a presumption of ownership. Given this rule, delivery is of less importance than possession; the fact of possession is of more importance than the method by which it was acquired. Furthermore, the fact of possession is one readily accessible to the knowledge of third parties and one reason alleged for the rule requiring delivery in Scots law is that the transfer should be made apparent to third parties."

Anderson v. *Buchanan*[2] shows the reluctance of the courts to recognise delivery on the basis of an alleged, but unsubstantiated, change from civil to natural possession[3] by the transferor. In this case furniture was purchased, at appraisal value, from the trustee of a bankrupt estate by a party sympathetic to the bankrupt's plight, the latter being permitted to retain the use of the furniture. The issue before the court was whether ownership had passed to the purchaser who claimed the furniture against a subsequent poinding creditor. The majority of the court did not accept that there was any basis for recognising that delivery had taken place:

---

[96] (1815) Hume's Dec. 705.

[97] (1833) 11 S. 916; see above, para. 8.15, n. 13.

[98] This point was recognised in *Sim* v. *Grant* (1862) 24 D. 1033 at p. 1038, in which the alleged transferor of a horse retained not only custody but also use and the power of disposal. In contrasting the facts before the court with the typical situation of goods retained in the seller's warehouse Lord Justice-Clerk Inglis noted that in the latter situation possession by the seller "is the bare custody, which is nothing but a burden on him, because it occupies his warehouse, unless, indeed, he retains it in security."

[99] *Studies in the Transfer of Property by Traditio*, pp. 218–219.

[1] Memo. No. 25, *Corporeal Moveables: Passing of Risk and Ownership*, para. 71.

[2] (1848) 11 D. 270.

[3] See above, para. 1.14.

"On the contrary, it is admitted that the furniture, which had previously been in Gordon's house, was just allowed to remain with him, without the intervention of any circumstances to attest, or to imply, that the ownership had been transferred to the complainer."[4]

In *Anderson* there was no contractual relationship on the basis of which delivery could be inferred by recourse to the reasoning that the natural possessor's position was now incompatible with that of an owner. The subsequent case of *Orr's Tr.* v. *Tullis*[5] is distinguishable on this basis. Here the owner of premises let as a printing office bought his tenant's plant and equipment but, in a new lease, granted to the tenant the use of the moveables concerned. As Lord Justice-Clerk Moncreiff noted,[6] the circumstances differed from cases in which the seller "continued to possess on his title of ownership": "But there is a clear distinction between cases in which possession is simply continued by the seller and those in which a new title of possession, specific and determinate, with known rights and limits, is acquired by him."

A dictum of Lord Neaves in *Orr's Tr.*[7] illustrates how delivery may be achieved by contractual arrangements which produce a change in the title of possession; moreover, that this is legally competent is taken to be trite.

"A man is both a horse-dealer and a livery stabler. He sells me one of his horses, and I leave the horse in his custody on the distinct contract of livery. It may be that I ride it or that I am prevented from doing so by weather or accident. But I pay for the horse, and I pay punctually for its being kept at livery for months. It would, I think, be a gross caricature of the law of Scotland to say that this was not good delivery, by an open change of possession. That which the dealer formerly possessed as owner he now has merely the custody of in his livery stables, in a distinct and recognised capacity of a different kind."

Requirement of good faith in case of constitutum possessorium

8.25   In *Orr's Tr.* v. *Tullis*[8] Lord Neaves referred to the importance of good faith in any situation in which it was claimed that delivery had been effected by *constitutum possessorium*: "Now, in all such cases there is one requisite that is indispensable. The transaction must be *bona fide*. If there is any semblance or suspicion of collusion or simulation this will materially alter the case."

---

[4] *per* Lord Cockburn at p. 284. *Cf. Macdougall* v. *Whitelaw* (1840) 2 D. 500 at p. 505.
[5] (1870) 8 M. 936.
[6] at p. 946.
[7] at p. 951.
[8] (1870) 8 M. 936 at p. 951. See also *Robertsons* v. *McIntyre* (1882) 9 R. 772 at p. 778.

As indicated,[9] although the act of delivery will be ineffective if the parties intend something other than the transfer of ownership, good faith is not a general requirement of delivery.[10] Why then should it be a prerequisite in the case of constitutum possessorium? The reason is that delivery effected on a contractual basis—leaving the transferor in the position of owner—is open to abuse and potentially prejudicial to creditors. Moreover, because in most cases the transferee requires possession of the thing concerned, there is only a limited need for *constitutum possessorium*[11] and restricting its use will not be likely to inhibit commerce.

Not infrequently, however, *constitutum possessorium* has been used for the purpose of creating a security interest by giving the transferee/creditor ownership while leaving the transferor/debtor with the natural possession and use of the thing. Because the law looks differently at, on the one hand, the *causae* of outright sale, exchange or gift and, on the other hand, the *causa* of security,[12] it follows that it is necessary to distinguish the application of *constitutum possessorium* to an outright transfer of ownership from its use to create a real security interest. Provided the parties genuinely intended—in applying *constitutum possessorium* to the creation of a security interest—that the transferee should become owner, it does not matter that their motive is the creation of a security interest.[13] Where, however, the transaction is a simulated one in the sense that the parties do not, in good faith, intend that ownership should pass but, rather, seek merely to create a security interest on the pretext of some other transaction—usually sale—*constitutum possessorium* will be ineffective to pass ownership.[14]

Symbolical Delivery

Limited scope of symbolical delivery proper

As indicated[15] various forms, on the basis of which a change of possession may be inferred, are sometimes identified as symbolical delivery. But in most cases the inference is founded upon the transferee obtaining a measure of control over the thing[16]: a matter more of **8.26**

---

[9] Above, para. 8.19.

[10] In the case of actual delivery ownership will pass regardless of motive but creditors are protected, in the event of the transferor's insolvency, by the common law rules against fraudulent preferences and the provisions on unfair preferences under s.36 of the Bankruptcy (Scotland) Act 1985.

[11] A possible instance is the case of a horse purchased but left with the seller under a livery contract; see above, para. 8.24.

[12] See below, para. 11.11.

[13] See *Union Bank* v. *Mackenzie* (1865) 3 M. 765 at p. 772; *Robertsons* v. *McIntyre* (1882) 9 R. 772 at p. 777.

[14] See below, para. 12.05.

[15] Above, paras. 8.14, 8.16.

[16] But Stair, II.i.15 recognises both the form of the handing over of a part as "a symbol or token . . . when the thing to be possest is present" and a "merely supposititious" representative token, as in the case of "delivery . . . by a wisp of straw, which ordinarily is in the absence of the thing to be possessed."

actual than of symbolical delivery. A dictum of Lord Chancellor Brougham in *Maxwell and Co.* v. *Stevenson and Co.*[17] shows how what at first sight may be taken to be symbolical delivery is, in fact, more appropriately seen as an instance of actual delivery: "If I deliver the key of a warehouse, it is a symbolical delivery of the warehouse, but an actual delivery of the goods in the warehouse."[18]

It seems that the law only knows to a limited degree symbolical delivery in the literal sense of the handing over and receiving of something as a symbol of the parties' intention that ownership should pass.[19] But where no form of actual delivery is possible, yet the interests of commerce support the need for the recognition of a means of conveying ownership, out-and-out symbolical delivery may be recognised. The conveyance of a standing cultivated crop by the symbolical handing over of a few ears or leaves[20] is an instance of this.[21] It may be noted that the crop must be growing or standing because, just as there can be no actual delivery of a thing not yet in existence, there can be no symbolical delivery of a thing not yet extant.

Symbolical delivery in some shape or form is not infrequently combined with the marking of the items concerned[22] but, of course, any form of marking introduces an element of actual delivery through the inference that control has passed to someone other than the party in possession.

In principle symbolical delivery is no less effective than actual delivery.[23] However, the law's emphasis upon the inferences which may properly be drawn from the circumstances of natural possession[24] must

---

[17] (1831) 5 W. & S. 269 at p. 279.

[18] Hume, III, pp. 250–251 is most persuasive on the appropriate analysis of the handing over of the key to premises: "But this does not happen under the notion of a figurative or symbolical delivery, or, as if the key were given, or taken, as a token or representative of the goods. In truth, in the nature of things,—possession of the key is the essence of a genuine and real substantial delivery. It admits the buyer, and excludes the seller; it conveys the goods out of the natural power and command of the one party, and into that of the other, and this just as effectually and substantially, as if the goods were moved into the buyer's own warehouse, out of that of the seller." See also Gordon, *Studies in the Transfer of Property by Traditio*, pp. 216–217.

[19] Whether the emphasis is upon putting the transferee in actual control or upon symbolical delivery in the literal sense, there must be an intention to make the transferee owner; see the dictum of Lord Trayner in *Pattison's Tr.* v. *Liston* (1893) 20 R. 806 at p. 814: "there was no delivery of the keys to, or retention of the keys by, the defender, for the purpose or with the effect of thereby giving him delivery of the furniture in the bankrupt's house."

[20] See *Grant* v. *Smith* (1758) Mor. 9561; above, para. 8.17.

[21] The better view, it is submitted, is that an identified area of felled timber could also be transferred on the basis of the handing over and receiving of a felled tree—or part thereof—although this also could be seen as a kind of actual delivery in so far as the transferee obtains access to and control over an identified area of cut timber. In *Paul* v. *Cuthbertson* (1840) 21 D. 1286 it was held that there could be no delivery of standing timber as moveable property. See above, para. 8.17.

[22] See, *e.g. Eadie* v. *Young* (1815) Hume's Dec. 705; above, para. 8.23.

[23] As the successful party answered in *Gray* v. *Cowie* (1684) Mor. 9121.

[24] See above, para. 1.12.

necessarily limit the scope of symbolical delivery as it does that of constructive delivery.[25] The Bill Chamber decision in *Fraser* v. *Frisby*[26] illustrates this point. Here the court declined to recognise that the execution of a trust conveyance was effective in giving a real right in moveables where delivery was symbolic in merely going "through the form of taking possession, by making up inventories of the whole effects etc. in the house."[27]

Bills of lading

A bill of lading—the negotiable document of title to shipped **8.27** goods—is said to be the main and most obvious instance of symbolical delivery in modern law.[28] Certainly, it can be said that delivery of a bill of lading—with the transferor intending to pass and the transferee intending to receive ownership in the goods to which it relates—"has the same legal effect as delivery of the goods."[29] A bill of lading facilitates the transfer of possession and this has the potential to give a change of ownership[30] but, of course, subject to the usual requirements applying to derivative acquisition.[31]

The significance of a bill of lading as an instrument of property was recognised in an early case in which the majority opinion was that "proper possession of the goods was held, not by the shipmaster or owner, but through them, first by the shipper, and then by the indorsee to the bills of lading."[32] In *Hayman & Son* v. *McLintock*[33] Lord McLaren noted the quality of negotiability of a bill of lading which made possible the transfer of ownership in maritime cargo.

> "Bills of lading have been long in use, and as far back as we have any knowledge of their use they were held to be negotiable. Such

---

[25] See above, para. 8.24.

[26] (1830) 8 S. 982.

[27] at p. 982.

[28] See, *e.g.* Gloag and Henderson, para. 20.22; Gordon, *Studies in the Transfer of Property by Traditio*, p. 215; Smith, *Short Commentary*, p. 539.

[29] Smith, *loc. cit.* The rôle of a bill of lading as an instrument of property is acknowledged in the preamble to the Bills of Lading Act 1855, passed to provide for the passing of contractual rights concomitant with the passing of property. This result did not otherwise obtain in English law (although, in principle, it did in Scots law), because the doctrine of privity of contract prevented a third party from acquiring rights in a contract entered into by others. The relevant introductory part of the preamble reads: "Whereas by the custom of merchants, a bill of lading of goods being transferable by endorsement, the property in the goods may thereby pass to the endorsee."

[30] Rodger, "Pledge of bills of lading in Scots law," 1971 J.R. 193 at p. 202, commenting on *Hamilton* v. *Western Bank* (1856) 19 D. 152 makes this important point: "[T]he *Hamilton* decision implies that transfer of a bill of lading transfers ownership when really all it does is to transfer possession." See also Gretton, "Pledge, bills of lading, trusts and property law," 1990 J.R. 23 at pp. 28–29.

[31] See above, para. 8.03.

[32] *Bogle* v. *Dunmore & Co.* (1787) Mor. 14216 at 14218.

[33] 1907 S.C. 936 at p. 952.

bills, expressed to be for so many bags of flour or quarters of grain on board a particular ship, would pass by blank indorsation from hand to hand while the ship was at sea."

Earlier in his opinion the learned judge had noted that while the law may once have been that the transferability of a bill of lading was limited to the circumstances of goods on board a ship at sea:

"the later law has settled that the question as to the effect of a bill of lading does not depend upon the arrival, or even the unloading, of a ship, and that a bill of lading must be taken to be an effective document of title representing the goods until they have been actually delivered to the person in right of the bill."[34]

Accordingly, even when the goods are stored, subsequent to shipment, the relevant bill of lading remains the means by which the title is transferred.[35]

It was also noted in *Hayman & Son* v. *McLintock*[36] that the nature of a bill of lading is inconsistent with any rule requiring that the goods be specifically ascertained before ownership could pass by transfer of the bill. As Lord McLaren observed, the circumstances of the transferor and the transferee being separated from the goods being transferred precludes any requirement of specific ascertainment.

"How is it possible . . . that the goods could be specifically ascertained, or that the various persons who took such bills of lading could examine and verify the goods while the ship was in mid-ocean? We know that bills of lading are granted for portions of cargo in bulk which cannot, of course, be ascertained; and where bills of lading are granted in these circumstances they must operate as a transfer of an unascertained quantity of goods on board the ship, until delivery is made in terms of the obligation."[37]

---

[34] at p. 951. But see *Price & Pierce Ltd.* v. *Bank of Scotland*, 1910 S.C. 1095 *per* Lord Johnston at p. 1114: "A bill of lading may be a good symbol of possession while the cargo is subject to the bill of lading. But I am not prepared to admit that it continues so indefinitely, and after the cargo is discharged, at any rate unless active use has been made of it."

[35] On this basis a bill of lading is distinguishable from a mere delivery order which, of course, can only be effective as a means of transferring ownership in goods when presented to an independent party holding the goods on behalf of the transferor (see above, para. 8.22). Given this difference, the court in *Hayman & Son* v. *McLintock* (1907 S.C. 936 at p. 952) rejected any analogy between the two devices.

[36] 1907 S.C. 936.

[37] at p. 952.

On the basis of Lord McLaren's dictum the transfer—whether intended as an outright conveyance of ownership or as a pledge—of a bill of lading relating to an unascertained portion of a bulk shipment would create a real right. The transferee would obtain a real interest in the undifferentiated part in question. The special character of a bill of lading as a document of title relating to a specified quantity of goods in shipment would give this result. One might contrast the handing over of a mere delivery order which would be ineffective to create a real interest in an unascertained portion of bulk goods in store.[38]

It seems that the view taken by Lord McLaren was that while section 16 of the Sale of Goods Act 1893,[39] requiring specific ascertainment as a prerequisite to the passing of property, was applicable to the delivery order situation it had no rôle in relation to the passing of property under a bill of lading. Although the decision in *Hayman & Son* v. *McLintock*[40] remains the leading authority on this issue in Scots law, English decisions—including some recent ones—are to the effect that section 16 of the Sale of Goods Act 1979 must be complied with even where the transfer, or creation of security, is by way of the handing over of a bill of lading.[41] The Scottish Law Commission, in a discussion paper,[42] regard section 16 as applicable to the bill of lading situation.

From the manner in which a bill of lading operates, it would appear that the better view is that the transfer of ownership by bill of lading is not an instance of symbolical delivery properly speaking. A bill of lading is not handed over as a symbol of the goods, in the sense of the giving and receiving of a token representing the act of delivery and reflecting the parties' concordant intentions that ownership should pass.[43] Transfer by bill of lading is rather a *sui generis* device, providing as a matter of necessity for the transfer of ownership in goods, in the course of carriage by sea or in storage after shipment. It would seem to be more accurate to think of a bill of lading primarily as a negotiable

---

[38] See above, n. 35. See also below, para. 11.09.

[39] See below, para. 9.05, n. 32.

[40] 1907 S.C. 936.

[41] See, *e.g. Karlshamns Oljefabriker* v. *Eastport Navigation* [1982] 1 All E.R. 208 *per* Mustill J. at p. 213: "The absence of any ascertainment during the voyage would mean that s.16 prevented the property from passing, whatever the parties may have intended"; *The Aramis* [1989] 1 Lloyd's Rep. 213 *per* O'Connor L.J. at p. 230: "Section 16 of the Sale of Goods Act 1979 makes it clear that the property does not pass until the contract quantity is separated from the bulk. Normally this will happen at the time when delivery is made, be it from ship or silo, to the person presenting the bill of lading."

[42] "The dictum by Lord McLaren in *Hayman* v. *Mclintock*, 1907 S.C. 936 at p. 952, to the effect that property in the unascertained goods can pass if they are covered by a bill of lading which is transferred seems to be inconsistent with section 16": Scot. Law Com., D.P. No. 83, *Bulk Goods* (1989), para. 2.3, n. 1. See also paras. 2.7, 3.2.

[43] But there is a certain analogy between the case of a bill of lading and "symbolical" delivery in the form of the handing over of a key giving access to stored goods (see above, para. 8.26, esp. n. 18).

document of title,[44] rather than as a symbol of the goods concerned.[45] On this basis it would appear to be of questionable accuracy to say that a bill of lading "operates as a constructive transfer of possession of the goods."[46] If the holder of the bill of lading has possession then the transfer of the bill transfers possession, and it would appear to be inappropriate to speak of this as a constructive act because pending delivery of the goods it is the only means by which proprietary rights can be conveyed.

---

[44] A bill of lading gives a good title regardless of the fraud of the indorser: see *Price & Pierce Ltd.* v. *Bank of Scotland*, 1910 S.C. 1095; affd. 1912 S.C.(H.L.) 19.

[45] But "bills of lading are not negotiable instruments, ownership can only be transferred if there is an appropriate *causa* accompanying the *traditio*": Rodger, "Pledge of bills of lading in Scots law," 1971 J.R. 193 at p. 202. See also Gretton, "Pledge, bills of lading, trusts and property law," 1990 J.R. 23 at p. 27: "if the holder of a bill of lading transfers it, it is necessary to inquire *quo animo*."

[46] See Scot. Law Com., D.P. No. 83, *Bulk Goods* (1989), para. 3.2.

CHAPTER 9

DERIVATIVE ACQUISITION UNDER THE SALE OF GOODS ACT 1979

GENERAL MATTERS

Implications of legislation

From the point of view of property, the Sale of Goods Act 1893 **9.01** (now 1979) had radical effect in doing away with the requirement of delivery as a prerequisite to the passing of ownership.[1] The precursor of the Act, a statute of 1856,[2] had already moved in this direction in that, while it did not alter the law in respect of the transfer of title, it made adjustments—primarily from the point of view of the interests of creditors—to strengthen the position of purchasers and sub-purchasers who had not yet obtained delivery.

The Sale of Goods Act is essentially a codification of English law[3]; in particular, as Professor Sir Thomas Smith observed, the provisions which introduced "the doctrine that real rights may be transferred by agreement"—a doctrine revolutionary to Scots law—which "had long been accepted in English law."[4] Another modern authority, Professor J. M. Halliday, noted that the legislation: "altered the Scottish common law and substituted the English rules whereby the property in specific or ascertained goods passes when the parties to the contract of sale intend it to pass."[5]

The English-law inspired modification of Scots common law is limited to the circumstances of sale and is accordingly not an out-and-out abrogation of principles of property law. However, this said, given that sale is by far the most usual *causa* upon which the transfer of ownership will follow, the practical effect of the Sale of Goods Act is a virtual restatement of the law on derivative acquisition pertaining to moveables. Moreover, the displacement of the common law in respect of sale has probably retarded the development of any better understanding of the basis of derivative acquisition through case law and writing.[6]

---

[1] See above, para. 8.02.

[2] The Mercantile Law Amendment (Scotland) Act 1856; see esp. ss.1 and 2.

[3] Gow, *Mercantile Law*, p. 75 refers to the "avowed purpose" of the draftsman Sir Mackenzie Chalmers "to reproduce as accurately as possible the existing English law."

[4] *Property Problems in Sale*, p. 39.

[5] *Conveyancing*, I, p. 251.

[6] See above, para. 8.07.

Essentials of acquisition under the Sale of Goods Act 1979

9.02   At common law the essentials of derivative acquisition are (1) the
parties must be in a position to pass and acquire owership; (2) they
must intend the passing of ownership; and (3) there must be delivery
according to a recognised method.[7] The radical effect of the Sale of
Goods Act 1979[8] upon the passing of ownership pursuant to sale is its
abandoning of the essential of a separate act of delivery in favour of
the unitary basis of the parties' intention. Under the heading "Property passes when intended to pass," section 17 provides:

> "(1) Where there is a contract for the sale of specific or
> ascertained goods the property in them is transferred to the buyer
> at such time as the parties to the contract intend it to be
> transferred.
> (2) For the purposes of ascertaining the intention of the parties
> regard shall be had to the terms of the contract, the conduct of the
> parties and the circumstances of the case."[9]

As to the essential that the parties are in a position to pass and
acquire ownership—which may be seen to comprise the separate
elements of "title" and "competence"[10]—the Act merely supplements
the common law,[11] although with particularly important consequences
concerning "title" in the form of certain statutory exceptions to the
principle *nemo dat quod non habet*.[12]

The essentials of derivative acquisition, applying under the Act, are
simply (1) the parties must be in a position to pass and acquire
ownership; and (2) they must enter into a contract of sale "by which
the seller transfers or agrees to transfer the property in goods to the
buyer for a money consideration, called the price."[13] These aspects of
the matter will be dealt with under the headings of "title and
competence" and "sale encompassing transfer."

It may be noted that Part III of the Act dealing with "Effects of the
Contract" is divided up under two headings: "Transfer of property as
between seller and buyer"[14] and "Transfer of title."[15] This distinction
between the transfer of property and the transfer of title, although

---

[7] See above, para. 8.03.
[8] Subsequent references to legislation in the present chapter are, unless otherwise
stated, references to the Sale of Goods Act 1979.
[9] See *Scottish Transit Trust* v. *Scottish Land Cultivators*, 1955 S.C. 254 *per* Lord
Russell at p. 259.
[10] See above, para. 8.04.
[11] See below, para. 9.04.
[12] See below, paras. 10.20, 10.21.
[13] s.2(1).
[14] ss.16–20.
[15] ss.21–26.

possibly somewhat confusing from the point of view of an apparent distinction between "property" and "title,"[16] may be explained as follows. The former is concerned with what is necessary, assuming certain essential conditions are present, actually to transfer ownership pursuant to a contract of sale—from a Scottish point of view the counterpart of the delivery requirement of the common law. On the other hand, the sections under the heading "Transfer of title" are concerned with the principle *nemo dat quod non habet* and, more particularly, the exceptions to it.

This dichotomy is not illogical—although the labelling may not be wholly appropriate—because it is necessary to distinguish, on the one hand, the requirements, as between seller and buyer, on the basis of which ownership passes and, on the other hand, the essential precondition that the seller be owner and the exceptions to which this is subject.

TITLE AND COMPETENCE

The seller's title

The common law principle that no one can transfer a better right **9.03** than he has—*nemo dat quod non habet*[17]—continues to apply. The right may be one of part-ownership[18] for, clearly, it is competent to transfer title to a share.

As indicated,[19] the Act prescribes certain exceptions to the *nemo dat quod non habet* principle but these will be dealt with, together with those of the common law,[20] as exceptions to the owner's right to recover possession of his property.[21]

Competence

Capacity to contract is not fundamentally affected by the Act and **9.04** the basic position is that the common law continues to apply. The Act acknowledges this in section 3(1): "Capacity to buy and sell is regulated by the general law concerning capacity to contract and to transfer and acquire property."[22]

---

[16] See Atiyah, *Sale of Goods*, p. 281: "there is something rather curious about this terminology."

[17] See above, para. 8.04.

[18] The Act in s.2(2) provides that there "may be a contract of sale between one part owner and another." This provision was intended to obviate any possible problem arising from the English law doctrine that a party cannot contract with himself. See *Benjamin's Sale of Goods*, para. 119. Scots law has not experienced difficulty with a contract between one part-owner and another.

[19] Above, para. 9.02.

[20] See above, para. 8.04.

[21] See below, paras. 10.20, 10.21.

[22] See above, para. 8.05.

However, this said, the two subsections following the above deal with capacity:

> "(2) Where necessaries are sold and delivered to a minor or to a person who by reason of mental capacity or drunkeness is incompetent to contract, he must pay a reasonable price for them.
>
> (3) In subsection (2) above 'necessaries' means goods suitable to the condition in life of the minor or other person concerned and to his actual requirements at the time of the sale and delivery."[23]

In view of the savings clause in the Act[24] one might tend to assume that the provisions concerned are in derogation of the common law. However, at any rate in relation to minority, as far as Scots law is concerned, they are probably superfluous, certainly from the point of view of any direct application. The consensus of opinion of textbook writers is that section 3(2) does not impose upon a minor any liability which would not have been recognised at common law, in that a contract for necessaries has long been regarded as binding upon a minor.[25] Gloag,[26] however, suggests that the subsection may be applicable in the case of necessaries purchased "for the household by a minor living with his parent or other guardian." In *Hamilton* v. *Forrester*[27] a father was held to be liable in this situation but, as Gloag points out, in principle, under the Act, the minor would appear to be liable where the goods are sold and delivered to him.

Regarding mental incapacity[28] or drunkenness—in either case sufficient to render a person "incompetent to contract"—the Act qualifies the common law in providing that there may be liability for the purchase of necessary items.[29]

SALE ENCOMPASSING TRANSFER

General effect of legislation

9.05   The Act—intended to be comprehensive in its regulation of sale—deals with both contractual and proprietary matters. While one would not regard the aim of comprehensiveness as exceptional in the case of a codifying statute, the Act's modus in recasting sale to include proprietary effect is, from the point of view of Scots law, a fundamental and far-reaching change.[30]

---

[23] s.3.

[24] s.62(2).

[25] See Brown, *Sale of Goods*, p. 15; Gloag, *Contract* p. 83; Gloag and Henderson, para. 6.4; Gow, *Mercantile law*, p. 97.

[26] *Contract*, p. 83.

[27] (1825) 3 S. 572.

[28] Stair, I.x.13; Erskine, III.i.16.

[29] s.3(2).

[30] Gloag and Henderson, para. 17.3: "in this aspect the law has been altered so fundamentally."

A consequence of rolling into one contract and conveyance, with the latter in effect subsumed by the former, is that considerations which at common law were relevant primarily between the parties become important from a proprietary point of view. Most significantly, the rule of contract that the subject of the sale must be ascertained becomes a rule of property in section 16 of the Act.[31]

"Where there is a contract for the sale of unascertained goods no property in the goods is transferred to the buyer unless and until the goods are ascertained."[32]

The effects of the Act must accordingly be dealt with, depending upon whether the goods are specific or unascertained.

Specific or ascertained goods

Under the rubric "property passes when intended to pass," section **9.06** 17(1) provides that:

"Where there is a contract for the sale of specific or ascertained goods the property[33] in them is transferred to the buyer at such time as the parties to the contract intend it to be transferred."

"Specific goods" is defined[34] as "goods identified and agreed on at the time a contract of sale is made." "Ascertained" is not defined. Brown[35] takes it to refer to the situation of goods made specific by their being identified and agreed upon. Gow[36] interprets the word in similar fashion: "ascertained . . . goods which at the time the contract was made were not identified and agreed upon but which since its inception

---

[31] In principle, at common law, the goods had to be ascertained and specifically appropriated before there could be any intention to transfer ownership (see, *e.g.* above, para. 8.22, n. 72), but in the vast majority of cases the requirement could be satisfied by reference to the parties' underlying contract. In this sense the requirement that the goods be ascertained is more a matter of contract than property.

[32] See *Hayman & Son* v. *McLintock*, 1907 S.C. 936 *per* Lord President Dunedin at p. 951: "the 16th section of the Sale of Goods Act . . . specially provides that where there is a sale of unascertained goods the property shall not pass until the goods have been ascertained. Here nothing was done to ascertain the goods. These flour bags were not separately marked, and although, doubtless, if the buyer here had gone to the storekeeper and had got him to put aside the sacks or mark them, or put them into another room, that would have passed the property, yet, as he did none of these things the property, it seems to me, did not pass."

[33] The word "property" is defined in s.61(1) to mean "the general property in goods, and not merely a special property," but this is of no significance from the point of view of Scots law which does not know any notion of "special property." See Smith, *Property Problems in Sale*, p. 41.

[34] s.61(1).

[35] *Sale of Goods*, p. 113.

[36] *Mercantile Law*, p. 123.

have become so." This interpretation is consistent with the rule of section 16 that property cannot pass in unascertained goods—specifically, in the present context, generic goods—until the specific subject of the contract has been ascertained. In the scheme of the Act the question of the passing of property can only arise where there is a contract perfected in the sense of the subject-matter having been ascertained.[37]

The Act, in section 17(2), provides a guide as to how the parties' intention to transfer ownership pursuant to their contract is to be ascertained. As Lord Russell put it, "for the purpose of ascertaining the parties' intention, regard shall be had to three matters."[38] The three considerations specified in the subsection are "the terms of the contract, the conduct of the parties and the circumstances of the case."

Where the parties' contract provides for the passing of ownership this will very probably prevail in establishing the point in time raised by the clause "at such time as the parties to the contract intend it to be transferred."[39] Gow[40] refers to two cases concerned with shipbuilding contracts to illustrate the ascertaining of the parties' intention directly from the terms of their agreement. In *Carmichael, McLean & Co.'s Tr.* v. *Macbeth & Gray*[41] the court accepted that ownership passed as items were appropriated to the construction of a ship, because the parties had agreed that there would be piecemeal acquisition in this way. In *Laing* v. *Barclay, Curle & Co.*,[42] on the other hand, it was held that a term providing that the vessel should only be considered as delivered and finally accepted upon the satisfactory completion of a trial was determinative on the question of the transfer of title.

The emphasis upon the rôle of the parties in controlling the transfer of ownership through the medium of their agreement means that the law allows them "to settle the point for themselves by any intelligible expression of their intention."[43] Where, however, there is no evidence of express intention, the time of the passing of ownership must be established on an inferential basis. The potential difficulty of this is recognised in section 18 of the Act, which lays down five presumptive

---

[37] Gow, *Mercantile Law*, p. 124, one may note, contends that the classification of specific, ascertained and unascertained goods is inappropriate because the transfer of specific or ascertained goods can only be upon the premise that transfer is legally possible, in the sense of the transferor being owner. This criticism seems to be unfounded because the identification of the subject-matter, for the purposes of contract and conveyance, is a logically separate matter from the question of the transferor's title. S. 17, stating the general basis of conveyance through the parties' mutual intention, is in fact qualified by s.21 which prescribes the requirement that the seller has title.

[38] *Scottish Transit Trust* v. *Scottish Land Cultivators*, 1955 S.C. 254 at p. 259.

[39] s.17(1).

[40] *Mercantile Law*, p. 124.

[41] (1901) 4 F. 345, *per* Lord Trayner at p. 356: "I think the contract before us makes it very clear when the parties intended the property to pass."

[42] 1908 S.C.(H.L.) 1.

[43] *McEntire* v. *Crossley Brothers* [1895] A.C. 457, *per* Lord Watson at p. 467.

rules as an aid to establishing the intention of the parties. The first four
are applicable to the passing of title in specific goods. Each rule
provides for a distinct class of contractual circumstances—broadly
speaking, as follows: Rule 1—the straightforward case of the sale of a
specific item ready for delivery; Rule 2—the case in which the seller
must put the goods into a deliverable state; Rule 3—the case in which
the seller must do something for the purpose of ascertaining the price;
Rule 4—the case of goods delivered on approval or on a sale-or-return
basis.

The preamble to the setting out of these rules in section 18
commences with the words "Unless a different intention appears";
accordingly, the rules will only apply in the absence of proof of an
intention to the contrary. In this regard one may note the dictum of
Lord President Strathclyde in *Woodburn* v. *Andrew Motherwell Ltd.*,[44]
a case concerned with the sale of hay:

"The rules in section 18 are merely intended to be a guide in
ascertaining the intention of the parties. But, if the intention of
the parties is quite plain—as I think it is in this case—that the
property should pass at the time when the goods were placed at
the disposal of the buyer that he might convert them into bales,
then the rules of section 18 do not come into play at all."

Rule 1—sale of specific item ready for delivery

Rule 1 reads: **9.07**

"Where there is an unconditional contract for the sale of specific
goods in a deliverable state the property in the goods passes to the
buyer when the contract is made, and it is immaterial whether the
time of payment or the time of delivery, or both, be postponed."[45]

It is accepted that this rule is intended to cover the straightforward
instance of a contract for the sale, at a determined price, of a specific
item or specific goods.[46] However, the following aspects of the rule
require elucidation: "unconditional contract"; "specific goods"; "deliverable state" and the question of postponement of delivery or
payment.

"Unconditional contract" in section 18, rule 1, refers to a contract
not subject to any condition suspending the passing of ownership. The
phrase may simply be taken to confirm—what should in any event be
apparent—that, other things being equal, ownership will pass but only

[44] 1917 S.C. 533 at p. 538.
[45] s.18.
[46] See, *e.g.* Gloag and Henderson, para. 17.15.

if this is possible in the sense of the given contract not being subject to a condition suspending the passing of ownership.[47] In English law, however, an alternative interpretation was that "unconditional" referred to a contract containing no condition unfulfilled by the seller.[48] This strained interpretation was adopted because the original form of section 11(4)[49]—never applicable in Scotland—denied a buyer the right of repudiation for breach "where the contract is for specific goods, the property in which has passed to the buyer." This produced, in England, a reluctance to give "unconditional" in section 18, rule 1, its natural meaning because the effect of this would have been to deny, on a widespread basis, a right of rejection.[50] Scots law has not had this difficulty because the common law right of rejection was not affected by the Act.[51] Consequently, in Scots law, an "unconditional contract" is simply one not subject to a suspensive condition leading to the resulting position in which "the condition not having been fulfilled, the property did not pass."[52]

As stated,[53] "specific goods" is defined in section 61(1) as "goods identified and agreed on at the time a contract of sale is made," but, for the purpose of the passing of property the term may have a somewhat different meaning from that applicable in other contexts.[54] In the context of section 18, rule 1, the emphasis is upon specificity from the point of view of the efficacy of the passing of ownership. As Professor Gow[55] explains:

> "by *specific* is meant not merely goods which are identified and agreed upon at the time the contract is made but also in such relationship to the seller that if the parties so intend an immediate conveyance by the seller is legally possible."

Although the terms "specific goods" and "deliverable state" are open to analysis as independent concepts, the phrase "specific goods in a

---

[47] The Act lays down in s.2(3) that "[a] contract of sale may be absolute or conditional." Where the transfer of property is subject to a condition, the contract is called an "agreement to sell" (s.2(5)) and only becomes a "sale," in which property is transferred (s.2(4)), when the condition is fulfilled (s.2(6)).

[48] See, *e.g. Varley* v. *Whipp* [1900] 1 Q.B. 513 at p. 517.

[49] Then s.11(1)(c).

[50] On this and the reformed position in English law, see Atiyah, *Sale of Goods*, pp. 289–290.

[51] s.11(5) (s.11(2) in the original Act) specifies that in Scotland the option to repudiate for breach is open to the buyer. Case law, before and after the Act, reflects the common law basis of this; see *Couston Thomson & Co.* v. *Chapman* (1872) 10 M.(H.L.) 74; *Hansen* v. *Craig & Rose* (1859) 21 D. 432 at p. 441; *Kinnear* v. *Brodie* (1901) 3 F. 540 at p. 543. On the difference between English and Scots law see Gow, *Mercantile Law*, pp. 125–126.

[52] *Murdoch & Co. Ltd.* v. *Greig* (1889) 16 R. 396, *per* Lord President Inglis at p. 401.

[53] Above, para. 9.06.

[54] See Atiyah, *Sale of Goods*, p. 290.

[55] *Mercantile Law*, p. 124.

deliverable state" suggests that the appropriation of goods is for the purpose of their conveyance. Consequently, future goods—including "goods not yet in existence, and goods in existence but not yet acquired by the seller"[56]—probably, "can never be specific goods within the meaning of the Act."[57]

In principle, the requirement of "specific goods" is satisfied in the case of a sale *en blloc* or *per aversionem* where a quantity of some particular commodity is identified so as to avoid any need of measurement; as in the case of "all the grain in my steading" or "my crop of hay."[58] This issue arose in a well-known English case[59] concerning the sale of all the trees of a specified height in a designated Latvian forest, the buyer being allowed 15 years to remove the timber. The question whether ownership had passed on the basis of the Act came into issue when the Latvian state expropriated the forest land.[60] The Court of Appeal held that the timber was not "specific goods." This was decided on the construction of the buyer being entitled to fell those trees which attained the requisite height during the prescribed period—meaning, of course, that the quantity of timber sold depended upon the rate of growth of the trees. An *obiter* opinion[61] was that even if the contract was taken to mean trees of the requisite height at the time of agreement, it would still not be a sale of specific goods because the trees though identifiable were not "identified" at the time. But, on this basis, something more than specificity, in the sense of the subject being determined beyond any question, would seem to be required.[62]

It may be noted here that the definition of "goods" in the Act leads to a debatable issue in respect of the sale of uncut timber. Section 61(1), (the interpretation section) provides as follows:

> " 'goods' includes . . . in Scotland all corporeal moveables except money; and in particular 'goods' includes emblements, industrial growing crops, and things attached to or forming part of the land which are agreed to be severed before sale or under the contract of sale."

While there is no difficulty in respect of periodical crops which are, in any event, deemed moveable,[63] the definition raises the issue whether

---

[56] Atiyah, *Sale of Goods*, p. 53.
[57] *Ibid.*
[58] See *Kennedy's Tr.* v. *Hamilton & Manson* (1897) 25 R. 252, dicussed below, para. 9.10, n. 8.
[59] *Kursell* v. *Timber Operators and Contractors Ltd.* [1927] 1 K.B. 298.
[60] In Scots law the question of a sale of moveables could not have arisen pending the felling of the trees. See above, para. 3.06.
[61] at p. 314.
[62] Arguably, the case of "all the trees over three metres high in the XY forest" is no different from "all the round bales in my steading" when the steading contains both round and square bales.
[63] See *Kennedy's Tr.* v. *Hamilton & Manson* (1897) 25 R. 252 *per* Lord Trayner at p. 259 as quoted above, para. 3.08, n. 59. See above, paras. 3.05 and 8.17.

uncut timber—heritable for other purposes—is included as "goods" under the Act.[64] The better view would appear to be that the specific reference to "industrial growing crops" suggests that growing trees are excluded.[65] But, in any event, the relevant case law is to the effect that growing trees are not in a "deliverable state"[66] for the purposes of the transmission of property under the Act. In *Morison* v. *A. & D. F. Lockhart*[67] the following conclusion of Lord Johnston was accepted by Lord Kinnear[68]:

> "Till severed, growing trees are not in a 'deliverable state' within the meaning of the Act, for they are not (section 62(4)) 'in such a state that the buyer would, under the contract, be bound to take delivery of them,' for physically he could not do so. Hence a proprietor in a proper sale of timber may cut his growing trees and sell the felled timber, or he may sell his growing timber and agree to cut it for delivery, but there may come a time when supervening circumstances, and the law applicable to those circumstances, deprive him of the power to cut and so to render the timber deliverable."[69]

In section 61(5) the Act provides that: "Goods are in a deliverable state . . . when they are in such a state that the buyer would under the contract be bound to take delivery of them." From this it is apparent that there are two aspects to "deliverable state." The basic requirement is that the goods are in a deliverable state from a physical point of view; actual physical delivery must be possible in the circumstances.[70] Where this is the case the question arises whether the goods are "in that particular state which upon a proper construction of the contract the parties have chosen as 'deliverable.' "[71] That the terms of the contract may be relevant to the question whether the goods are in a "deliverable state" would seem to be clear from the wording of

---

[64] See Gow, "When are trees 'timber'?" 1962 S.L.T. (News) 13.

[65] But see *Morison* v. *A. & D. F. Lockhart*, 1912 S.C. 1017 *per* Lord Johnston at pp. 1022–1023: "Growing timber is admittedly attached to and in law forms part of the land, and is therefore 'goods' in the sense of the statute, and a contract of sale of growing timber to be cut is therefore a contract of sale of goods to which the provisions of the Act apply."

[66] See below.

[67] 1912 S.C. 1017 at p. 1023.

[68] at p. 1028.

[69] See also *Munro* v. *Liqr. of Balnagown Estate Co.*, 1949 S.C. 49 *per* Lord President Cooper at p. 55: "the property in the timber passes from seller to buyer on severance from the ground." This, in principle, would be the position in the case of a contract giving the buyer the right to cut.

[70] The English case of *Underwood Ltd.* v. *Burgh Castle Brick and Cement Syndicate* [1922] 1 K.B. 343 illustrates this. A 30-ton condensing engine was held not to be in a "deliverable state" until detached from its concrete base and disassembled.

[71] Gow, *Mercantile Law*, p. 127.

section 61(5): "in such a state that the buyer would *under the contract*[72] be bound to take delivery of them."[73] In this section 18, rule 1, is complimentary to rule 2 which provides that where something is required to be done to put the goods in a deliverable state, property does not pass until this requirement is satisfied.

It must be emphasised that the criterion of the buyer being bound to take the goods is limited to the state of the goods from the point of view of delivery in accordance with the terms of the contract. As Professor Atiyah points out,[74] section 61(5) cannot be interpreted to mean that if, in any circumstances, the buyer would not be bound to take delivery, then the goods are not in a "deliverable state." As the learned author points out, the fact that a buyer may not be bound to take delivery of defective goods does not necessarily mean that defective goods cannot be in a deliverable state for the purposes of the legislation.

The final part of rule 1 states that regardless of the postponement of the time for payment or the time for delivery, or both, property passes—given, of course, the presence of the circumstances referred to earlier in the rule. This part of the rule says no more than that a postponement of payment or delivery will not affect the conclusion that the parties intended property to pass but, of course, only if the circumstances do not indicate a different intention. Clearly, the postponement clause has no application where rule 1 is displaced because there is an express agreement that the passing of property is to be delayed. But, more significantly, as a matter of inference from the circumstances, it may appear that the parties intended to defer the passing of ownership and, in this situation, "the prima facie operation of rule 1 is displaced."[75] As Professor Atiyah points out, it may not be possible to ignore altogether the fact that there has been a postponement of the time for delivery or for payment or of both the times. An act of postponement "may be some indication of a contrary intention which excludes the operation of rule 1 altogether."[76] Accordingly, it appears that the rôle of the postponement clause in rule 1 is no more than to provide that where, for one reason or another, the time of payment or delivery is deferred, this will not necessarily detract from

---

[72] My emphasis. In the case of "industrial growing crops" one can see that the terms of the parties' contract would have the potential to determine the matter.

[73] The point was recognised by Bankes L.J. in *Underwood Ltd.* v. *Burgh Castle Brick and Cement Syndicate*, above, at p. 345: "A 'deliverable state' does not depend upon the mere completeness of the subject-matter in all its parts. It depends on the actual state of the goods at the date of the contract and the state in which they are to be delivered by the terms of the contract."

[74] *Sale of Goods*, p. 291.

[75] Atiyah, *Sale of Goods*, p. 292.

[76] *Idem*, p. 293. It would seem, however, that this would only be so where other circumstances supported a contrary intention because the object of the postponement clause is to exclude, from the fact of an act of postponement, the inference of an intention that ownership should not pass.

the conclusion that property passed upon the conclusion of the contract.

Providing for the contingency of the postponement of payment can only be on the assumption that the parties have agreed on the necessary details as to the means and time of payment. It would thus appear that in the statement that "property in the goods passes to the buyer when the contract is made" in rule 1, the Act contemplates the agreement of the parties as to the relevant details of the price.[77]

Given that one of the primary effects of the Act is to do away with delivery as a prerequisite to the passing of ownership, it follows that there must be scope for the postponement of the act of delivery without affecting the passing of property to the buyer. It would appear that in so far as there is a delivery requirement under the scheme of the Act, it is no more than that the goods be identified and put into a deliverable state.

Rule 1 displaced by contrary intention

9.08   As indicated,[78] rule 1 is predicated upon the assumption that the parties have reached agreement with regard to the necessary details of the price. In view of this, one can see the argument that in the case of the purchase of goods from a retail shop, ownership will not pass pending agreement as to the method of payment.[79]

As with other considerations relevant to the passing of ownership, the Act in section 17(2)—"regard shall be had to the terms of the contract, the conduct of the parties and the circumstances of the case"—leaves scope for the issue of the price to be a determining factor on the question of the parties' intention to pass property. In *Lacis* v. *Cashmarts*[80] Lord Parker C.J., taking section 18, rule 1 as the starting-point noted that: "The fundamental question . . . is: what is the intention of the parties" and, in this regard, the learned judge took section 17(2) as a basis for deciding the question of the passing of ownership according to his view of the circumstances of the case.

> "In my judgment when one is dealing with a case such as this, particularly a shop of the supermarket variety or the cash and

---

[77] The ascertainment of the price is not a prerequisite to the conclusion of a contract under the Act (see s.8) in the way that it was at common law (see, *e.g.* Bell, *Prin.*, § 92); however, arguably, it must necessarily be a prerequisite for the purposes of the operation of a presumption as to the intention of the parties that ownership should pass.

[78] *Idem.*

[79] See Atiyah, *Sale of Goods*, p. 293; *cf. Benjamin's Sale of Goods*, para. 288. Atiyah (p. 293) also contends that the rule that property passes upon the making of the contract "does not fit easily into the pattern of consumer sales"; moreover, he suggests that this may explain the fact that in modern times "very little is needed to rebut the inference that property passes on the making of the contract." (*R. V. Ward Ltd.* v. *Bignall* [1967] 1 Q.B. 534 *per* Diplock L.J. at p. 545). But apropos of the issue of price, these observations should be seen in the light of the conclusion that, without agreement as to all essential aspects of the price, there could not even be a rebuttable inference in terms of rule 1 that property had passed on the making of the contract.

[80] [1969] 2 Q.B. 400 at p. 407.

carry variety, as this was, the intention of the parties quite clearly as it seems to me is that the property shall not pass until the price is paid. That as it seems to me is in accordance with the reality and in accordance with commercial practice."

A number of other considerations may be relevant to the question whether the operation of rule 1 is displaced by proof of contrary intention.

Under the Act, "Risk prima facie passes with property,"[81] but the parties are free to depart from this by agreement.[82] Obviously enough, the incidence of risk determines liability to insure; however, from the point of view of applying facts concerning risk or insurance to the question whether property has passed, one must bear in mind that the liability to insure is a consequence of the passing of risk which is itself a consequence of the passing of property. The fact that the purchaser has taken out insurance does not in itself necessarily mean that the passing of ownership has transferred the risk. However, evidence of the purchaser's undertaking to insure may be a factor supporting the inference that the parties intended ownership to pass. But, indeed, such evidence may point the other way if a proper interpretation of the parties' agreement supports the conclusion that the intention was to transfer the risk to the buyer even though title remained with the seller. Given that section 20(1) allows the parties to depart from the normal position in which risk follows title, it is clear that there can be no assumption that the allocation of risk—even less the acceptance of liability to insure—is synonymous with the transfer of ownership. In the case of *Re Anchor Line (Henderson Brothers) Ltd.*[83] the Court of Appeal interpreted a contract for the purchase of a crane by deferred payment. The contract contained no specific provision concerning the passing of ownership, but a clause provided that the purchasers would have "entire charge of and responsibility for" the crane. Romer L.J., although at one stage inclined to consider the clause "inconsistent with the view that the vendors had retained the property in the crane,"[84] came to the conclusion that: "if the property had passed to the purchasers it is difficult to see why the clause should expressly refer to the fact that the responsibility for the crane was upon the purchasers. It would be natural to assume that it was, if the property had passed to them."

---

[81] s.20.
[82] s.20(1).
[83] [1937] Ch. 1.
[84] at p. 11.

Contractual terms concerning risk and insurance can only be interpreted in the context of all the relevant circumstances to determine the proper inference to be drawn.[85]

In the case of a contract to sell moveable and heritable property together, the normal inference would probably be that ownership of the moveables was intended to pass at the time of the conveyance of the heritage.[86] On this basis the presumption in section 18, rule 1, would very probably be rebutted. In the case of moveables sold under a contract providing for their installation or permanent fitting to heritage, the conclusion may well be that the intention was that property would only pass upon annexation.[87] Other things being equal a contract for the supply of a new central heating boiler with the seller undertaking to install would be likely to be construed in this way.

Rule 2—seller obliged to put goods into a deliverable state

9.09   Rule 2 reads:

> "Where there is a contract for the sale of specific goods and the seller is bound to do something to the goods for the purpose of putting them into a deliverable state, the property does not pass until the thing is done and the buyer has notice that it has been done."[88]

Professor Gow[89] points out that without the provision as to notice this rule has a close parallel in the common law rule that while a contractual duty remains a contract cannot be perfected with the result that the risk does not pass to the buyer. Moreover, this has been taken to extend to the situation of an obligation on the part of the seller "to do all that may be necessary to prepare the goods for delivery."[90]

As indicated, this rule is complementary to rule 1 which envisages the passing of property in goods "in a deliverable state."[91] For the

---

[85] See Atiyah, *Sale of Goods*, p. 294. Atiyah suggests certain factors which may be relevant in the process of determining the correct inference. A distinction may be drawn, the learned author suggests, between the case of mere advice to the buyer to insure and a stipulation requiring this. The former, Atiyah argues, may be consistent with transfer to the buyer whereas in the latter case, given that the seller has no apparent interest in the goods once property has passed, "the correct inference may well be that property and risk have not passed" (At p. 295). The difficulty with this distinction would appear to be that the parties may well intend that property should pass but nonetheless include in their contract a stipulation requiring the buyer to insure. Although, in principle, such a term would be unnecessary, it might be included to provide confirmation that the purchaser was aware of his obligation to insure.

[86] See *Commissioner of Stamps* v. *Queensland Meat Export Co. Ltd.* [1917] A.C. 624 at p. 628.

[87] See *Clark* v. *Bulmer* (1843) 11 M. & W. 243 at pp. 247–248.

[88] s.18.

[89] *Mercantile Law*, pp. 126–127.

[90] *Anderson & Crompton* v. *Walls* (1870) 9 M. 122 *per* Lord Cowan at p. 125.

[91] See above, para. 9.07.

purposes of rule 2 what is required to put the subject of the sale "into a deliverable state" corresponds with the state of goods "in a deliverable state" as required by rule 1. The goods must be deliverable both *ex sua natura*, in the sense of being physically open to or ready for delivery, and *ex conventione*, in the sense of being in the requisite condition as agreed by the parties.[92]

Rule 2 applies only to the seller being bound to act to achieve the required "deliverable state." The fact that the seller has undertaken to do acts after delivery—typically, to maintain the item sold in working order for a period of time—does not activate rule 2 to prevent ownership passing. An obligation upon the buyer to do something in relation to the subject can have no rôle in activating rule 2.[93] But an obligation upon the buyer could be taken to be a determining consideration with regard to the controlling factor of the parties' intention that property should pass.[94]

The requirement of notice gives effect to the view that it would be inequitable for the property—and the concomitant risk—to pass to a purchaser ignorant of determinative events subject to the control of the seller. Given that the Act requires that the buyer "has notice" that the necessary thing has been done to put the goods in a deliverable state, the correct interpretation would appear to be that notice implies knowledge on the part of the buyer.[95]

Rule 2 is intended to give effect to the concept of the transfer of ownership on the basis of the parties' intention and, of course, this must be capable of accommodating the passing of property prior to actual delivery. But it may not be easy to identify the point at which the transfer of ownership was intended; on one view the requirement that the goods be put into a deliverable state may be difficult to

---

[92] See Gow, *Mercantile Law*, p. 127. *Cf.* Atiyah, *Sale of Goods*, pp. 295–296 where the learned author places a more restricted meaning upon the wording "is bound to do something to the goods for the purpose of putting them in a deliverable state." On this construction the rule would not extend to the seller's contractual obligation unless he was bound to act to put the subject into a deliverable state in the physical sense. "Thus it seems that the Rule would not apply where the seller has agreed to repair the goods, for example, to overhaul a second-hand car." (p. 296). But in this situation "the court may simply fall back on Sect. 17 and hold that the property is not to pass until the repairs have been done as this is the presumed intention of the parties" (*Ibid.*).

[93] See Brown, *Sale of Goods*, p. 124.

[94] The proviso to s.18 would take the matter back to s.17. In the case, for example, of the buyer undertaking the removal of building rubble before a stipulated date although r. 2 would have no application it could be that the seller did not intend that ownership should pass pending removal because he wished to be in a position to deal otherwise with the rubble if the buyer failed to take it timeously.

[95] See *Benjamin's Sale of Goods*, para. 296. The learned authors contend that "[i]n accordance with the principle that there is in general no constructive notice in commercial transactions, constructive notice would be insufficient." The following English cases are given as authority: *Joseph* v. *Lyons* (1884) 15 Q.B.D. 280 at p. 287; *Manchester Trust* v. *Furness* [1895] 2 Q.B. 539 at p. 545; *Greer* v. *Downs Supply Co.* [1927] 2 K.B. 28 at pp. 36–37; *Worcester Works Finance Ltd.* v. *Cooden Engineering Co. Ltd.* [1972] 1 Q.B. 210 at p. 218.

distinguish from the initiation of the process of delivery.[96] In *Gowans v. Bowe & Sons* [97] the defenders, potato merchants, claimed a potato crop against the trustee of the bankrupt producing farmer. Sequestration occurred after the potatoes has been lifted and pitted on the farm and the issue was whether the right of ownership had passed to the buyers prior to the seller's sequestration. The parties' contract contained the usual provisions for transactions of this type. It was agreed that the mature crop would be lifted, stored in pits and covered with straw by the farmer. The buyer, when he required the crop, would clean, sort and bag the potatoes and the farmer would provide transport to the railhead or port as required where the buyer would arrange despatch. Lord Cullen took the view that the potatoes were put into a deliverable state by pitting:

> "Apart from the carting of the potatoes to station or harbour, the seller had nothing further to do, after pitting them, in the way of putting them in a deliverable state. He had cultivated them to maturity, lifted them from the earth and placed them in the pits, and it is not disputed that the buyers had notice of this."[98]

This case raises the question whether, in the event of the seller being subject to an obligation to deliver, or to commence the process of delivery, property in the goods could pass on the basis of rule 2: the argument being that, in these circumstances, something remains to be done to the goods "for the purpose of putting them into a deliverable state."[99] Gow,[1] it would appear, takes the view that this result would follow:

> "If it is the contractual duty of the seller that the goods shall be delivered at some specified place other than the place where the goods are at the time of the making of the contract they are not in such a state that the buyer is bound to take delivery of them until they reach that place."

But the better view would seem to be that an obligation to deliver, on the part of the seller, would altogether remove the case from rule 2 if a different intention from that of the passing of property upon the conclusion of the contract appeared to follow.[2]

The final requirement that the buyer has notice that the goods have been put into a deliverable state seems to confirm that rule 2 is

---

[96] See Gloag and Henderson, para. 17.15.
[97] 1910 2 S.L.T. 17.
[98] at p. 18.
[99] s.18, r. 2.
[1] *Mercantile Law*, p. 127.
[2] See the preamble to s.18.

concerned with a variation of the case of assumed intention that property should pass upon contract. The essential feature of the rule is that it applies where something remains to be done to put the goods into a deliverable state; without disregard for the language one can hardly say that an act, or partial act, of delivery could amount to putting the goods into a deliverable state. The parties may well intend that ownership should pass on the basis of their contract but yet provide for the manner or means of delivery. This, it seems, is how the court saw the parties' intention in *Gowans* v. *Bowe & Sons*[3]: the fact that the contract provided for the involvement of the seller in transporting the goods to the station or harbour did not gainsay the conclusion that the parties intended property in the potatoes to pass by their being "pitted" and so put into a deliverable state by the seller.[4]

Rule 3—necessary weighing, measuring or other acts

Rule 3 reads: **9.10**

> "Where there is a contract for the sale of specific goods in a deliverable state but the seller is bound to weigh, measure, test, or do some other act or thing with reference to the goods for the purpose of ascertaining the price, the property does not pass until the act or thing is done and the buyer has notice that it has been done."[5]

While rule 2 deals with the general category of contracts conditional by reason of the requirement that the goods be put into a deliverable state, rule 3 is concerned with the more particular case of a contract conditional by reason of a provision requiring the seller to weigh, measure or otherwise deal with the goods for the purpose of ascertaining the price.[6] The rule is only applicable if the act concerned is the duty of the seller.[7] In *Kennedy's Tr.* v. *Hamilton & Manson*[8] the

---

[3] 1910 (2) S.L.T. 17. See also *Woodburn* v. *Andrew Motherwell Ltd.*, 1917 S.C. 533 at p. 540 where the circumstances were taken to show that ownership had passed on contract regardless of the seller's obligation to deliver to the station.

[4] It is submitted that the fact that at common law "if a place be fixed for delivery the goods are held to be still the seller's till brought thither for delivery" (*Walker* v. *Langdales Chemical Co.* (1873) 11 M. 906 *per* Lord President Inglis at p. 909) does not have any bearing upon r. 2 which was drafted upon the premise of property passing on the basis of the parties' agreement—a notion foreign to the common law. But *cf.* Gow, *Mercantile Law*, p. 127.

[5] s.18.

[6] The condition must be a suspensive rather than a resolutive one; *i.e.* one which suspends the operation of the contract rather than one which has the potential to terminate an existing obligation. See *Jack* v. *Roberts & Gibson* (1865) 3 M. 554; *Hardy* v. *Sime*, 1938 S.L.T. 18.

[7] It seems that the limitation to the seller reflects the narrower English common law version of the rule that a contract for the sale of specific goods of unascertained extent, at a price based upon a given amount per unit, is only perfected when the price is ascertained by weighing or measuring. See *Turley* v. *Bates* (1863) 2 H. & C. 200 at p. 211; Gow, *Mercantile Law*, p. 128.

[8] (1897) 25 R. 252 at pp. 259–260.

court—finding that it had not been established that the contract was
conditional upon an act of weighing by the seller—held that property
in a hay crop sold at £2 10s per ton had passed upon the completion of
the contract.

Following rule 2 the purpose of rule 3 is also to provide for the
delaying of the passing of ownership in the case of a conditional
contract. But, of course, the circumstances must point to an intention
to suspend the passing of ownership pending the seller's act of
measurement, weighing or the like. Bearing in mind that the price
does not need to be ascertained for the purposes of the conclusion of
the contract[9]—nor, therefore, for the purpose of the passing of
ownership—it follows that one must consider the other possible
reasons for the term requiring an act of mensuration by the seller. A
dictum of Lord President Strathclyde in *Woodburn* v. *Andrew Motherwell Ltd.*[10] shows how this inquiry is controlled by its statutory setting.

> "No doubt what he did comes within the very letter of Rule 3 of
> section 18, because he did an act with reference to the goods
> which was necessary in order that the weight might be ascertained,
> and the price fixed. But that section is only an expansion of
> section 17. The rules in section 18 are merely intended to be a
> guide in ascertaining the intention of the parties. But, if the
> intention of the parties is quite plain—as I think it is in this case—
> that the property should pass at the time when the goods were
> placed at the disposal of the buyer . . . then the rules of section 18
> do not come into play at all."

Professor Gow[11] submits that "the party pleading the rule must
adduce circumstances showing an intention on the buyer not to concur
in the passing of property until ascertainment by act of the seller." The
circumstances of purchase at a slump price may tend to point the other
way; in such cases a term providing for mensuration by the seller has
been taken not to be intended to suspend the passing of ownership but
merely to provide for the possibility of a subsequent adjustment of the
price.[12]

Rule 4—goods on approval or "sale or return"

9.11   Rule 4 reads:

> "When goods are delivered to the buyer on approval or on sale
> or return or other similar terms the property in the goods passes
> to the buyer:

---

[9] s.8.
[10] 1917 S.C. 533 at p. 538.
[11] *Mercantile Law*, p. 128.
[12] See *Hansen* v. *Craig & Rose* (1859) 21 D. 432 *per* Lord Justice-Clerk Inglis at p.
441.

(*a*) when he signifies his approval or acceptance to the seller or does any other act adopting the transaction;

(*b*) if he does not signify his approval or acceptance to the seller but retains the goods without giving notice of rejection, then, if a time has been fixed for the return of the goods, on the expiration of that time, and, if no time has been fixed, on the expiration of a reasonable time."[13]

This rule applies to the various forms of conditional sale under which the contract itself[14]—and, therefore, of course, any proprietary implications it may have—is suspended[15] pending the buyer's acceptance of the goods, within a certain period, as agreed or determined on the basis of what is reasonable. Rule 4 is potentially applicable both to purchase by a consumer for his own use or consumption and to the case of goods supplied by a wholesaler to a retailer on a sale-or-return basis.[16] In *Cranston* v. *Mallow & Lien*[17] although a horse was delivered on a week's trial it was not a case of an unqualified option because the buyer could only return the animal if it did not meet the standard of a warranty. In these circumstances it was held that the contract was not one of sale on approval.[18]

The premise upon which rule 4 is constructed is that property in the goods concerned has not passed to the buyer prior to or upon delivery.[19] Where the parties have entered into a contract subject to a resolutive condition—providing for the possibility of termination within a period of approval—ownership would have passed to the buyer before or, at any rate, upon delivery, and rule 4 could, accordingly, have no application. As Professor Gow points out,[20] the distinction is between what is often labelled "sale or return,"[21] where

---

[13] s.18.

[14] See Bell, *Comm.*, I, 471: "If the sale is made in reference to the taste, or any other criterion, there is no sale or concluded bargain till that test has been applied, and expressly or tacitly the bargain bound by the seller's approbation."

[15] At common law there was some difficulty in deciding whether this sort of condition was suspensive or resolutive (see the conflicting authorities noted by Brown, *Sale of Goods*, pp. 128–129), but the assumption behind r. 4 is that the sale and the concomitant passing of ownership are suspended pending the occurence of the relevant event.

[16] "The contract of sale 'on approval' frequently, but not necessarily, applies to a transaction between retailer and consumer; the contract of sale 'on return' nearly always applies to a transaction between wholesaler and retailer": Gow, *Mercantile Law*, p. 236.

[17] 1912 S.C. 112.

[18] "It seems to me that the fair reading of the stipulation for a week's trial is that it was intended that the defenders should have that period for testing whether the horse conformed to the warranty or not" *per* Lord Cullen at p. 117.

[19] Although the introductory part of r. 4 reads as if the circumstances concerning delivery is the factor controlling the passing of property, one has to bear in mind the preamble to s.18 stating the general position of the various rules for ascertaining intention as applicable only if a different intention does not appear.

[20] *Mercantile Law*, p. 236.

[21] See *Macdonald* v. *Westren* (1888) 15 R. 988.

the very sale is suspended pending the buyer's approval, and, "sale and return,"[22] envisaging a completed contract of sale subject to a resolutive condition providing the right to reject the subject-matter and terminate the contract within a stated period.[23]

Where rule 4 is applicable because the goods have been delivered on a basis under which ownership was not intended to pass, property will pass—unless the circumstances point to a different intention—when the buyer "signifies his approval or acceptance to the seller." The case of express or actual acceptance—as envisaged in these words from rule 4—is straightforward; of greater potential difficulty is the alternative basis in rule 4 involving the buyer's inferred acceptance when he "does any other act adopting the transaction." The courts have tended towards the view that "any action by the buyer inconsistent with his free power to return the goods is an act adopting the transaction within the meaning of the Rule."[24]

What is the position, however, where the buyer asserts a right of ownership but, in doing so, acts contrary to the terms of the contract under which he holds the goods? Can one say, in this situation, that the buyer's conduct amounts to an "act adopting the transaction"? While it may be true that the buyer by his conduct has asserted a right of ownership incompatible with the return of the goods to the seller, it seems inappropriate to say that he has "adopted the transaction" when, in fact, such an inference is inconsistent with the terms of the

---

[22] See *Brown* v. *Marr, Barclay & Others* (1880) 7 R. 427.

[23] In the typical case in which this position arises the issue is between the original seller and, either an innocent third party acquirer from the original buyer, or a subsequent innocent party. Where the original sale was subject to a resolutive condition a *bona fide* third party may, clearly enough, acquire from the purchaser pending the operation of the condition. In the case of a suspensive sale, r. 4 may well be relevant because the third party will very probably argue that property passed to him because the buyer—the seller to the third party—in selling to him did an act "adopting the transaction." This, it should be noted, was the common law's answer to the problem of an act of disposition by a conditional purchaser. While the question whether property could have passed to the buyer pending the termination of his right to return the goods was a controversial one, the courts had no hesitation in recognising that an act of disposition satisfied the condition and so made possible the transmission of a right through the buyer. A dictum of Lord Justice-Clerk Moncreiff in the case of *Brown* v. *Marr, Barclay and Others*, above at p. 435, is in point. "But whenever the buyer exercises any right of property in the subject of the sale, as by selling, lending, hiring, or pledging the property, his option ceases, and he has no longer the right to return the goods, but becomes absolutely liable for the price. It follows, therefore, that even if this option, while unexercised, were suspensive of the sale, and prevented the property from passing from the original owner, the act which forfeits the right of return at the same time passes the property."

[24] Atiyah, *Sale of Goods*, p. 297. See *Brechin Auction Co. Ltd.* v. *Reid* (1895) 22 R. 711 *per* Lord President Robertson at pp. 714–715. In this case, decided on the basis of the common law, the court construed a contractual provision as giving a buyer "the power and option . . . at any time and without any antecedent notice, to convert himself into the owner of the cattle" and held that when the buyer "chose to realise the cattle by selling them to the defender he exercised that option." See also *Brown* v. *Marr, Barclay and Others* (1880) 7 R. 427 *per* Lord Moncreiff at p. 435 as quoted above, n. 23.

parties' contract. The facts in *Bryce* v. *Erhmann*[25] presented the court with this problem, but the Second Division did not accept that the result of a fraudulent disposition would be any different because the buyer had agreed that the goods would remain the property of the seller until invoiced by the latter to the former.[26] In the English case of *Weiner* v. *Gill*[27] a contract between manufacturing and retail jewellers provided that the goods were delivered on approbation, for cash sale or return, but included a term reserving ownership to the seller pending payment or the grant of credit—"goods held on approbation or sale or return remain the property of . . . until such goods are settled for or charged."[28] The Court of Appeal did not accept that section 18, rule 4, applied to determine the passing of ownership on the argument that the retailers had adopted the transaction in pawning the jewellery. On the contrary, the court took the view that the terms of the contract demonstrated that the parties' intention was to preclude the passing of ownership pending the buyer paying or the seller extending credit.

> "So that no means existed by which the buyer could exercise such an option as was indicated in r. 4. The only thing he could do was to pay cash for them or to get the plaintiff to debit him with the price."[29]

Where the contract of sale protects the seller's interest by reserving ownership pending some event it is difficult to see how one can construe a prior assertion of ownership by the buyer as an act "adopting the transaction." The better view would seem to be that an act "adopting the transaction" cannot be one contrary to its terms, because this would deny the dominant rôle of the parties' intention[30]— the guiding principle in sections 17 and 18.[31]

---

[25] (1904) 7 F. 5:

[26] "It seems to me that the only practical effect of that stipulation is that if . . . Anderson did not dispose of the goods by selling or pledging them, Ehrmann should be entitled to have them returned notwithstanding the bankruptcy of Anderson": *per* Lord Moncreiff at p. 17.

[27] [1906] 2 K.B. 574.

[28] at p. 579.

[29] *per* Sir Gorell Barnes, President, at p. 581.

[30] See Atiyah, *Sale of Goods*, p. 297: "An express stipulation that the property is not to pass until the goods are paid for is effective to protect the seller, because this is evidence of a contrary intention which overrides Rule 4."

[31] Gow, *Mercantile Law*, p. 237, comments on *Weiner* v. *Gill* [1906] 2 K.B. 574 as follows: "in principle the decision, and any English case following it, is unacceptable in Scots law if it means that where rule 4 is excluded by the contract a disposition by the possessor to a third party is necessarily inept." The point here is that a third party may be protected on some other basis despite the fact that s.18, r. 4 is inapplicable for the purposes of acquisition by the purchaser and transmission to the third party concerned. There are a number of bases under which the recognition of acquisition by a subsequent party may be contended for regardless of the circumstances between the owner and his immediate transferee. See below, paras. 10.15–10.22.

It should be noted here that the circumstances, possibly involving an act of the buyer, may cause ownership to vest in the buyer regardless of a reservation of title in favour of the seller. This may occur where acquisition on an original basis—typically through accession—has the effect of overriding the parties' intention.[32]

While section 18, rule 4(*a*) contemplates an acceptance, actual or inferred, rule 4(*b*) provides that notice of approval or acceptance be deemed to have been given on the expiration of the time for return of the goods, or, if no period or date has been fixed, upon the expiration of a reasonable time. Of course, even if a time limit is set the buyer may act as contemplated by rule 4(*a*) and either actually accept or, by his conduct, give a basis for inferring acceptance. The effect of sub-rule (*b*) is the same as a case of inferred acceptance under sub-rule (*a*), in that in both "the transaction may be completed without a communication of acceptance."[33] But rule 4(*b*) does not contemplate acceptance by the passage of a reasonable time regardless of the circumstances under which the goods were delivered. The opening words of rule 4, speaking of "delivery to the buyer on approval or on sale or return or other similar terms," contemplates, it is submitted, the potential buyer's agreement to accept on the trial basis offered. The delivery of unsolicited goods accompanied by an offer to sell them does not come within the rule.[34] Given this, it follows that the delivery of goods on sale or return cannot, for the purposes of section 18 rule 4(b), be on the basis of an option or offer by the "seller" without some form of acquiescence by the "buyer."

Rule 4(*b*) is probably only satisfied where the goods are retained by the buyer for the requisite period or for a reasonable period. The basis of the rule is the buyer's inferred acceptance based upon his failure to return the goods but the essential precondition of this conclusion is that he was in a position to effect return.[35]

Is rule 4 redundant?

9.12   Brown[36] argues that rule 4 is redundant because until the relationship—on the basis of which goods are handed over on approval or on sale or return—becomes a contract no property can pass but, at this point, rule 1 should apply given that delivery has taken place and the condition has been satisfied.

As a matter of logic there may be substance to Brown's point, but rule 4 does seem to serve a purpose in clarifying the basis upon which a

---

[32] See below, para. 12.14.

[33] Atiyah, *Sale of Goods*, p. 299.

[34] If it did, it could be contrary to the Unsolicited Goods and Services Act 1971, s.1.

[35] In *Re Ferrier* [1944] 1 Ch. 295 at pp. 296–297 goods were seized in execution two days after delivery to the buyer; on the question whether r. 4(*b*) could be applied, it was held that she had not retained the goods within the meaning of the rule.

[36] *Sale of Goods*, p. 130.

contract may be concluded in the circumstances concerned. The rules for ascertaining intention in section 18 aim to be comprehensive in providing bases for determining the point at which property passes—as a consequence of the conclusion of the parties' contract—in various distinct situations. What is important about rule 4 is that it provides a means of determining the point of transfer in the case of goods delivered on approval or on a sale-or-return basis; seeing that rule 1 is of no assistance on this issue it is difficult to accept that rule 4 is redundant.

Unascertained goods   **9.13**

Rule 5(1) reads:

> **General observations.** "Where there is a contract for the sale of **9.13a**
> unascertained or future goods by description, and goods of that
> description and in a deliverable state are unconditionally appropri-
> ated to the contract, either by the seller with the assent of the
> buyer or by the buyer with the assent of the seller, the property in
> the goods then passes to the buyer; and the assent may be express
> or implied, and may be given either before or after the appropria-
> tion is made."[37]

Under the common law the problem of a contract in respect of unascertained goods did not assume any proprietary dimension.[38] Delivery was necessary to pass property, and the ascertainment of the subject was a prerequisite to the act delivery.[39] The Act, however, in giving effect to the English law notion of the passing of property upon contract, had to deal with the problem of ascertainment because it is inconceivable that there could be any passing of ownership in goods agreed upon but not specifically ascertained.[40] Accordingly, section 16 provides that:

---

[37] s.18.

[38] Of course, the risk passed upon the perfection of a contract and, in the contract of sale, this involved the specific ascertainment of the subject. This, however, was a matter between the parties which did not detract from the importance of delivery where an issue concerned with the question of ownership arose. (See above, para. 8.13.) It may be noted that the common law rules relating to risk were applied by the First Division to the case of a contract of exchange; see *Widenmeyer* v. *Burn Stewart & Co.*, 1967 S.C. 85 and Scot. Law Com., Memo. No. 25, *Corporeal Moveables: Passing of Risk and Ownership*, paras. 2–5.

[39] On the forms of delivery in general, see above, para. 8.14.

[40] See Gow, *Mercantile Law*, p. 130: "The difficulty English law created for itself was that by accepting something less than delivery for a conveyance it had to find something other than the process whereby the goods identify themselves, in order to mark clearly and to the knowledge, actual or imputed, of the parties the point at which it could be said that the goods had become so individualised of consent that a conveyance of title is now possible."

"Where there is a contract for the sale of unascertained goods no property in the goods is transferred to the buyer unless and until the goods are ascertained."[41]

Ascertainment of the goods does not, of course, itself transfer ownership in them: section 17(1) provides that the property in specific or ascertained goods is transferred to the buyer "at such time as the parties to the contract intend it to be transferred."

The requirement that the goods must be ascertained may be taken to apply in three separate contexts. First, "future goods"—*i.e.*, goods not yet ascertained in the absolute sense of goods to be manufactured or acquired by the seller for the purpose of giving effect to the contract. Secondly, "generic goods"—*i.e.*, goods identified for the purpose of the contract by an accepted description of kind and quantity,[42] but where the particular items to be delivered have not yet been allocated to the contract. Thirdly, what may be described as "goods as a part"—*i.e.*, goods identified as a part or portion of an identified whole or unit, but where the particular items can only be ascertained on separation or severance from the whole.

In all three cases, rule 5 will apply, at any rate provided that it does not appear that the parties intended ownership to pass on some other basis than that provided for. The consequence of the passing of property provided for by rule 5 is subject to two essential requirements: (i) that particular goods as described are unconditionally appropriated to the contract; and (ii) that either party gives assent to the act of appropriation by the other.[43] The rule provides that assent, which may be express or implied, can be given either before or after the appropriation is made.[44] Rule 5(2), moreover, provides for a presumption of unconditional appropriation where the seller delivers goods to the buyer, or to a carrier

---

[41] See *Hayman & Son* v. *McLintock*, 1907 S.C. 936 *per* Lord President Dunedin at p. 951: "The trustee in the bankruptcy appeals simply to the 16th section of the Sale of Goods Act, which specially provides that where there is a sale of unascertained goods the property shall not pass until the goods have been ascertained."

[42] *e.g.* 50 cases of château bottled St Emelion claret 1985 vintage.

[43] Appropriation necessarily involves what may be seen to amount to physical and mental elements; the former in the actual appropriation of particular goods to the contract and the latter in the parties' agreement to this. To amount to a distinct requirement—albeit within the process of the passing of property—the act of appropriation must be supported by intention, hence the provision requiring assent. A dictum of Pearson J. in *Carlos Federspiel & Co. S.A.* v. *Charles Twigg & Co. Ltd.* [1957] 1 Lloyd's Rep. 240 at p. 255 is apposite: "A mere setting apart or selection of the seller of the goods which he expects to use in performance of the contract is not enough. If that is all, he can change his mind and use those goods in performance of some other contract and use some other goods in performance of this contract. To constitute an appropriation of the goods to the contract, the parties must have had, or be reasonably supposed to have had, an intention to attach the contract irrevocably to those goods, so that those goods and no others are the subject of the sale and become the property of the buyer."

[44] Put another way, one may say that there are no restrictions upon the basis by which the necessary assent may be arrived at.

for transmission to the buyer, without reservation by the seller of the buyer's right of disposal as contemplated in section 19.

The wording of rule 5 may be considered in closer detail by reference to the three categories of "future goods," "generic goods" and "goods as a part."

Future goods. Future goods in rule 5(1) are defined as goods "to be **9.13b** manufactured or acquired by the seller after the making of the contract of sale."[45] In the case of goods to be acquired by the seller, it would seem that "acquired" envisages the acquisition of a right of ownership by the seller; in that rule 5(1) contemplates the passing of ownership to the buyer on appropriation of the goods to the contract, it is plainly a prerequisite that the seller must himself be owner. In this context the word "approbation" applies to the situation in which the seller has acquired the goods, the buyer's agreement to take them is present and nothing remains to be done.[46]

In the case of manufactured goods the general rule is that the items concerned must be completed and ready for delivery, because only then does the issue arise as to whether the parties' mutual assent to the transmission of ownership is present. The question may well become a point of dispute in the context of the seller's insolvency, possibly where progress payments have been made by the buyer who, of course, will endeavour to establish that the property passed before the sequestration of the seller's estate. Assuming that the circumstances do not indicate some other intention,[47] ownership will pass when the goods have been completed and set aside for delivery in a manner—in terms of particular identification, finality and mutual agreement—sufficient to justify the objective conclusion that unconditional appropriation has occurred.[48]

---

[45] See s.61(1).

[46] See *Carlos Federspiel & Co. S.A.* v. *Charles Twigg & Co. Ltd.*, above, *per* Pearson J. at pp. 255–256—a case concerned with a buyer's order for bicycles to be manufactured by the seller: "usually, but not necessarily, the appropriating act is the last act to be performed by the seller. For instance, if delivery is to be taken by the buyer at the seller's premises and the seller has completed his part of the contract and has appropriated the goods when he has made the goods ready and has identified them and placed them in position to be taken by the buyer and has so informed the buyer, and if the buyer agrees to come and take them, that is the assent to the appropriation. But if there is a further act, an important and decisive act to be done by the seller, then there is *prima facie* evidence that probably the property does not pass until the final act is done." See also *Benjamin's Sale of Goods*, para. 331: "The act of appropriation must therefore so far identify the goods that the passing of property thereby becomes possible."

[47] If the contract provides for the passing of property a preparatory act of appropriation will not anticipate this, even if specifically assented to. This, of course, would be contrary to the overriding rôle of the parties' intention provided for in the preamble to s.18. See *Pollock & Son* v. *Robertson*, 1944 J.C. 98 at pp. 114–115.

[48] Gow, *Mercantile Law*, p. 133 refers to the case of *Atkinson* v. *Bell* (1828) 8 B. & C. 277, decided on the basis of the English common law, in support of the proposition that "mere completion of the article is not an act of appropriation." Although the machines ordered were produced and prepared for delivery to the satisfaction of the purchaser's

Regarding identification, the fact that the goods are stored with other similar things pending delivery will not bar the passing of ownership provided the seller can identify the particular items allocated to the buyer.[49] Professor Atiyah,[50] however, questions whether "this would be an acceptable rule where the only 'appropriation' is in the seller's mind, and there is no independent objective evidence of the 'appropriation,' for example, in the seller's books or records."

The overriding freedom of the parties to determine the basis upon which property passes means that there may be acquisition by the purchaser of the incomplete thing in the process of manufacture. A well-established custom in shipbuilding is for property to pass in a piecemeal fashion,[51] and the parties' intention that this should follow may well emerge from the terms of their contract.[52]

In *Wylie and Lochhead* v. *Mitchell*[53] Lord Ardmillan, in an *obiter dictum*, explained the basis of this approach in the practice that the first instalment of the contract price was normally payable upon the laying of the keel.

> "The keel of a ship is considered in law and in maritime and mercantile practice as figuratively denoting the whole ship. In short, the keel represents the ship, *navis sequitur carinam*. Therefore the act of laying the keel of a ship, as an act entitling to payment of part of the price, has the character of an *actus legitimus*, and it is naturally and properly considered as involving,

---

agent, ownership was held not to have passed prior to the seller's insolvency pending a reply to his letter to the buyers requesting instructions as to the means of delivery. But, on the other hand, where the contract provides for notice by the seller that the buyer should remove the completed goods, it would seem arguable that the parties contemplated the buyer's prior assent and that, in such a case, appropriation would take place upon receipt of notice by the buyer and regardless of the fact that he failed to respond to it.

[49] See Atiyah, *Sale of Goods*, p. 307; in *Hendy Lennox Ltd.* v. *Grahame Puttick Ltd.* [1984] 2 All E.R. 152 at p. 160 the particular generators sold were identified by their serial numbers recorded on delivery notes.

[50] *Ibid.* Atiyah refers to the New Zealand case of *Donaghy's Rope and Twine Co. Ltd.* v. *Wright, Stephenson & Co.* (1906) 25 N.Z.L.R. 641 where, it seems, appropriation was on the basis of the seller's unsupported claim to have identified the particular goods.

[51] See, *e.g. Simpson* v. *Creditors of Duncanson* (1786) Mor. 14204: "as the building proceeded, such an appropriation took place, as prevented his creditors from attaching the ship without refunding the sums advanced." See also *McBain* v. *Wallace & Co.* (1881) 8 R. 360 at pp. 369–370. See above, para. 8.23.

[52] In *Reid* v. *Macbeth & Gray* (1901) 4 F. 345 the relevant words were "shall, immediately as the same proceeds, become the property of the purchasers." One may note that the Second Division interpreted this as applying not only to materials actually used in construction but to all things destined for incorporation because, in the contract in question, the clause was stated to apply to materials "whether in the building-yard, workshop, river, or elsewhere." This decision was, however, reversed by the House of Lords, (1904) 6 F.(H.L.) 25, which followed its earlier decision in *Seath* v. *Moore* (1886) 13 R.(H.L.) 57.

[53] (1870) 8 M. 552 at p. 560.

when accompanied or followed by part payment, the constructive delivery of the ship itself."[54]

Regarding the keel as a symbol of the ship made room for the application of the doctrine of accession; on this basis the customer, as owner of the principal element, would acquire what was added in the course of the construction of the vessel. Moreover, it seems, these common law principles were influential in the form and interpretation of shipbuilding contracts.[55]

Ultimately, however, the question resolves itself upon the intention of the parties as expressed in their contract and, of course, this may deviate from what has become established as common practice.[56]

Generic goods. Given that the class of "goods to be acquired by the seller" is included in the category "future goods,"[57] it follows that the category "generic goods" is limited to goods held by the seller at the time of contract. This leaves, as the primary matters for consideration in respect of generic goods, the issues of on what basis goods are appropriated to the contract and in what circumstances assent may be inferred. Much of what has been said in relation to future goods is equally applicable to generic goods. Indeed, the formulation applied to manufactured goods, omitting the word "completed," seems to be apposite: thus—particular identification, finality and agreement.[58] The two essential questions are: first, have particular goods been designated to the contract with sufficient finality to enable property to pass? and, secondly, can the parties be said to have agreed, whether expressly or by inference, to the process or means of specification applied?[59]

9.13c

The first question will, in most cases, resolve itself upon a consideration of the steps taken by the seller to allocate specific goods to the contract. The second issue will usually be determined on an inferential

---

[54] *Cf.* the view that the shipbuilder is no more than a mandatory "employed to perform certain work and to furnish materials, and that he consequently never had any right of property in the thing called a ship"; on this view the materials "became the purchaser's, *specificatione*, from the moment of their being applied to the vessel": Brown, *Sale of Goods*, p. 132.

[55] See, *e.g. Reid* v. *Macbeth & Gray* (1904) 6 F.(H.L.) 25 *per* Lord Davey at p. 30: "according to the true construction of the clause it was only when the chattels in question were applied for the use of the ship, and became part of the structure of the ship, that it was intended that those words vesting the property should operate."

[56] See, *e.g. Laing* v. *Barclay, Curle & Co.*, 1908 S.C.(H.L.) 1 *per* Lord Robertson at p. 2: "In the pesent case I find the contract to require no aid or supplement from the statutory rules, for it seems to me to provide from the beginning to completion of this ship for the building of it by the shipbuilders with their materials, and transfers it to the purchasers only as a finished ship and at a stage not in fact yet reached."

[57] See s.61(1).

[58] See above under "future goods."

[59] The case of *National Coal Board* v. *Gamble* [1959] 1 Q.B. 11 at pp. 21–22 may be seen to illustrate the distinct elements. Here the loading of a lorry with coal ordered by the buyer could be taken to be an act of appropriation; but it was held that the property did not pass until the weighbridge ticket was accepted by the buyer, a ruling which could be seen to recognise the distinct requirement of assent.

basis from what the parties have agreed in respect of such matters as preparation for delivery, storage pending delivery and, of course, delivery itself[60]; but agreement may also be inferred—or a particular inference may be supported—by reference to the external factors of the parties' established prior conduct, or trade custom or practice. But the respective rôles of buyer and seller—and the juxtaposition of unconditional appropriation and assent—are open to variation and will very much depend upon the circumstances. A buyer of petrol from the usual self–service type filling station controls the act of appropriation— which could only be unconditional—by deciding when to stop the filling process, the seller's assent being implicit in the circumstances.[61]

9.13d Goods as a part. Where an anonymous part of a bulk is the subject of a contract there can be no appropriation and, therefore, no transfer of ownership until the particular subjects have been ascertained by separation or severance from the whole. In *Hayman & Son* v. *McLintock*[62] a flour merchant, in implementation of a contract, gave the purchaser delivery orders addressed to the keeper of a neutral store in which the seller's flour was kept. Although the storekeeper made appropriate book entries to indicate acquisition by the purchaser, he did nothing to separate the flour concerned from other flour in the store. It was held that ownership had not passed and that, upon the seller's bankruptcy, the entire quantity of sacks of flour passed to his trustee. As Lord President Dunedin observed:

> "These flour bags were not separately marked, and although, doubtless, if the buyer had gone to the storekeeper and had got him to put aside the sacks or mark them, or put them into another room, that would have passed the property, yet, as he did none of those things the property, it seems to me, did not pass. It is not enough merely to get an acknowledgment in general terms that so many of those bags belonging to the bankrupt are held for him."[63]

As Professor Gow[64] points out, there may be appropriation by "process of exhaustion" when the quantity contracted for remains after other orders have been removed.[65]

Appropriation deemed in case of delivery

9.14   Rule 5(2) reads:

---

[60] As Gow, *Mercantile Law*, p. 129 points out, appropriation is essentially the act of one party with agreement arrived at on the basis of prior or subsequent assent: "If both or all parties acting together individualise the goods, the problem of appropriation does not arise."

[61] See *Edwards* v. *Ddin* [1976] 1 W.L.R. 942 at pp. 944–945.

[62] 1907 S.C. 936; followed in *Laurie and Morewood* v. *Dudin & Sons* [1926] 1 K.B. 223 at pp. 235–236.

[63] at p. 951. (*cf.* n. 50 above). On the analogous common law position see *Anderson & Crompton* v. *Walls* (1870) 9 M. 122.

[64] *Mercantile law*, pp. 130–131.

[65] See *Wait & James* v. *Midland Bank* (1926) 31 Com.Cas. 172.

"Where, in pursuance of the contract, the seller delivers the goods to the buyer or to a carrier or other bailee or custodier (whether named by the buyer or not) for the purpose of transmission to the buyer, and does not reserve the right of disposal, he is to be taken to have unconditionally appropriated the goods to the contract."[66]

Section 18, rule 5(1) envisages the transfer of ownership upon the unconditional appropriation of the goods to the contract by one party provided the prior or subsequent assent of the other party can, at least, be inferred. As indicated, it is necessary to examine the circumstances of each distinct case to establish the coincidence of an unconditional act of appropriation and the assent of the other party thereto. However, where the seller, without reserving a right of disposal, has delivered the goods to the buyer, or to a carrier or some other party for transmission to the buyer, unconditional appropriation to the contract is presumed, subject, of course, to the general section 18 proviso that no contrary intention appears.

Delivery as contemplated in rule 5(2) "in pursuance of the contract" is on the assumption that the buyer intends to receive ownership upon delivery to him and, on this basis, the assent requirement would be satisfied. In the case of delivery to a carrier or agent there must needs be prior assent by the buyer to this because one would not necessarily infer assent to the passing of ownership pending receipt of the goods by the buyer, but, of course, this prior assent may be inferred from the parties' contract. In either case the seller's unconditional appropriation, being pursuant to the contract, will only be presumed if in accordance with the parties' agreement on such essential matters as the type and quantity of the goods[67] and the mode and timing of delivery.[68] Where delivery is to a carrier or agent for transmission to the buyer, the goods must needs be "the very goods which in due course he will surrender to the buyer."[69]

Clearly, there can be no appropriation, leading to the transmission of ownership, where a seller consigns a quantity of identical goods for delivery to more than one buyer. In this situation appropriation cannot occur until particular goods have been identified for delivery to individual purchasers.[70]

---

[66] s.18.

[67] See *Kwei Tek Chao* v. *British Traders and Shippers Ltd.* [1954] 2 Q.B. 459 at pp. 480–481.

[68] See *Re Sutro & Co. and Heilbut, Symons & Co.* [1917] 2 K.B. 348 at p. 357; *J. Aron & Co. (Inc.)* v. *Comptoir Wegimont* [1921] 3 K.B. 435 at p. 438.

[69] Gow, *Mercantile Law*, p. 131.

[70] See *Healy* v. *Howlett & Sons* [1917] 1 K.B. 337 *per* Avory J. at p. 345: "If it was impossible to determine which of the purchasers was bound to take the twenty bad boxes, it follows that no particular twenty boxes were the property of any particular purchaser at that time."

Seller's reservation of right of disposal

9.15   Section 19 provides for the reservation by a seller of goods of the right of disposal pending the fulfilment of one or more conditions. The general theme of the Act, of course, is that an unconditional contract of sale is a prerequisite to the passing of property pursuant thereto.[71] Section 19, arguably, does no more than state the positive side of this in the seller's right to protect himself by reservation of title pending payment.

Section 19(1) reads:

> "Where there is a contract for the sale of specific goods or where goods are subsequently appropriated to the contract, the seller may, by the terms of the contract or appropriation, reserve the right of disposal of the goods until certain conditions are fulfilled; and in such a case, notwithstanding the delivery of the goods to the buyer, or to a carrier or other bailee or custodier for the purpose of transmission to the buyer, the property in the goods does not pass to the buyer until the conditions imposed by the seller are fulfilled."

That the parties may contract on the basis that title will be reserved by the seller pending the fulfilment of certain conditions by the buyer is unexceptionable.[72] But the section goes further than this and allows the seller to reserve a right of disposal "where goods are subsequently appropriated to the contract." The effect of this is to give the seller the power to impose a condition suspending the passing of ownership at the stage of appropriation—when ownership would otherwise pass. From the property point of view section 19(1) assures the efficacy of such a unilateral reservation of title despite the fact that, as a matter of contract, what has been done by the seller may amount to breach of the terms agreed by the parties.[73] This said, given the Act's emphasis upon the rôle of the parties in determining the point at which ownership passes it must, necessarily, remain open to a seller to insert a controlling term, at any stage pending the event itself. Clearly, it would be open to the buyer to reject what the seller requires, in so far as he regards this as inconsistent with the agreement thus far. A disagreement of this type will raise a contractual problem but, obviously enough in the circumstances, there will be no question of

---

[71] See s.18, r. 1: "an unconditional contract for the sale of specific goods," see above, para. 9.07; see also s.18, r. 5: "unconditionally appropriated to the contract," see above, para. 9.13.

[72] Regarding the common law recognition of reservation of title, see below, para. 12.02.

[73] As *Benjamin's Sale of Goods*, para. 367 puts it: "A conditional appropriation of this nature will effectively prevent the property from passing, even though by reserving the right of disposal the seller is in breach of the terms of the contract of sale."

property passing. On the other hand, where the buyer allows matters to proceed without dissent from what the seller proposes, the inference will tend to be that the parties agreed the proposed basis for the passing of ownership.

The seller's reservation of the right of disposal of the goods may be express or implied. The presence of an express term, providing for payment within a stated period, may well support the inference that the parties intended that the passing of ownership should be reserved pending payment within the timescale provided for. In a leading English case[74] a specific parcel of wheat in a warehouse was sold on the terms: "payment cash within seven days against transfer order." Before delivery the wheat was requisitioned under wartime emergency powers; and in consequence the question arose whether the loss fell to the seller or to the buyer. The Court of Appeal held that the term as to payment amounted to a reservation in favour of the seller, because he was not bound to make over a delivery order until he had received payment. Given this, the court reasoned that property had not yet passed.

The second part of section 19(1) spells out that the seller's reservation of the right of disposal prevents the passing of property in the goods pending fulfilment of the conditions imposed, and that this is so notwithstanding the commencement, or indeed the completion of the process of delivery. The presumption in section 18, rule 5(2), it may be recalled, is that the commencement of the process of delivery—or *a fortiori* a completed act of delivery—amounts to an unconditional appropriation of goods to the contract which, as section 18, rule 5(1) provides, is, in the case of "unascertained or future goods by description," the essential requirement of the passing of property. But rule 5(2) anticipates section 19(1) in specifically excluding the case of a seller reserving the right of disposal.

It should be noted that while section 19(1) may be an effective protection to the seller—in vesting him with power to control the passing of ownership—his position is weakened if the buyer obtains possession. This is simply because under section 25(1) a buyer in possession, even though not owner, may pass a good title.[75] Accordingly, in the situation in which the buyer has obtained possession, while the seller will be protected against the buyer's insolvency, his protection will not necessarily extend to a right to recover from an onerous *bona fide* third party.

Section 19(2), concerned with goods sent by sea, reads:

"Where goods are shipped, and by the bill of lading the goods are deliverable to the order of the seller or his agent, the seller is prima facie to be taken to reserve the right of disposal."

---

[74] *Re Shipton Anderson & Co. and Harrison Bros. & Co.* [1915] 3 K.B. 676.
[75] See below, para. 10.21.

This subsection creates a rebuttable presumption that where goods are shipped, under a bill of lading in this form, the seller intended to retain his right to the goods. But the presumption may be rebutted by reference to the particular circumstances of the case. The conduct of the seller may give a basis from which another conclusion, as to his intention at the time of shipment, can be inferred.[76]

Section 19(3) provides specific protection in the case in which a bill of exchange is drawn upon the buyer and transmitted with a bill of lading for acceptance or payment. In this case—

> "the buyer is bound to return the bill of lading if he does not honour the bill of exchange, and if he wrongfully retains the bill of lading the property in the goods does not pass to him."

But, as with section 19(1), although section 19(3) protects a seller in the event of the buyer's bankruptcy the former is not protected in the event of the goods being sold on to a party in good faith who obtains possession or, more importantly in this case, the documents of title to the goods.[77]

---

[76] As, *e.g.* in the case of the subsequent transfer of the bill of lading to the purchaser otherwise than against payment. See *Van Casteel* v. *Booker* (1848) 2 Exch. 691 at p. 709.

[77] See s.25(1); see below, para. 10.21.

CHAPTER 10

PROTECTION OF RIGHT OF OWNERSHIP

GENERAL MATTERS

Range of applicable remedies

This chapter is concerned with substantive remedies which are **10.01** proprietary in the sense of deriving from the recognition of either the right of ownership or the right of possession. Remedies relevant to the protection of proprietary rights, but arising from some other basis, typically contractual or delictual, will not be dealt with.[1]

In the context of corporeal moveables the applicable remedies are primarily concerned with the right of possession—whether as an adjunct of the right of ownership or as an independent right.

Restitution is the owner's right to recover possession based upon the obligation to restore to which a holder, without right against the owner, is subject. Even if it is appropriate to classify restitution as a matter of obligation,[2] it remains essentially concerned with the protection of the right of ownership; a truism demonstrated by Stair's[3] description: "whereby that which is another's coming into our power . . . ought to be restored."

An issue which must be addressed at the outset concerns the use in the sources of the terms "vindication" and "restitution," and any implications this may have from the point of view of an exposition of the law.

Implications of terminological difficulties

It is trite that the owner of a corporeal moveable can, in principle, **10.02** assert his right and recover possession from one who holds without a right available against him. There is, however, some difficulty as to how this right is labelled and classified. This is not simply a semantic issue, but one which may have implications from the point of view of the nature and scope of the right.[4]

The Institutional treatises and earlier case law refer to the vindicatory action (or *rei vindicatio*) available to an owner to recover

---

[1] *e.g.* the delictual remedy protecting against unlawful damage to property which is more appropriately dealt with in the context of the law of delict.

[2] See, *e.g.* Gloag and Henderson, para. 14.1. On the issue of the classification of the remedy of restitution see Birks, "Restitution: a view of the Scots law" (1985) 35 C.L.P. 57 at pp. 58–65.

[3] I.vii.1.

[4] See, *e.g.* below para. 10.13 concerning prescription.

possession of a moveable thing.[5] In most modern legal writings, however, one does not find this term,[6] but, broadly speaking, what it would cover seems to be subsumed under "restitution."

Stair's exposition recognises a distinction between two senses of the right of vindication. On the one hand, one has the pure proprietary sense of a claim in and to the thing with the defender/possessor's position only of incidental relevance to the claimant's right to recover; on the other hand, one has the case of a claim based upon the possessor's obligation to restore—to make restitution.

In Stair's analysis restitution is preferred to vindication: both, it would seem, from the point of view of fitting appropriately into his general scheme and, as it were, on the dogmatic merits. Stair's system, which has been influential in the development of the law, gives emphasis to restitution—a remedy encompassing what amounts to a right of vindication.[7] Vindication proper, in the civilian sense of a property-derived action, is expressly excluded by Stair.[8]

The preference shown by Stair for restitution needs to be looked at in some detail. It seems that Stair[9] took the view that the right of vindication was of limited utility on account of what he perceived to be its passivity, in that: "the conclusion of delivery does not properly arise from vindication, which concludes no such obligation on the haver, but only to be passive, and not to hinder the proprietor to take possession of his own."

Probably for this reason, Stair emphasised the obligation of restitution as the basis of the right to recover possession of moveable property. According to Stair[10] this obligation derived not from agreement or wrongful act, but "whereby that which is another's coming into our power, without his purpose to gift it to us, and yet without our fault, ought to be restored, as thing straying, or found, or recovered from pirates, thieves etc., or bought *bona fide*, or the like."

In these passages Stair identifies two distinct concepts. First, the right, based upon the owner's interest, to recover the thing—a right seen by Stair not to encompass an obligation upon the holder to restore. Secondly, Stair recognises an obligation of restitution on the basis of which a holder, in certain circumstances, is obliged to restore to the owner. The distinction is philosophically valid but, when applied

---

[5] See below, para. 10.03.

[6] Walker, *The Law of Civil Remedies in Scotland* (1974) does not mention the remedy. On the disappearance of the use of the label "vindication," see Scot. Law Com., Memo. No. 31, *Corporeal Moveables: Remedies* (1976), para. 6.

[7] Generally on Stair's scheme see Professor David Walker's introduction to the tercentenary edition of Stair, pp. 32–35; see also Birks, "Restitution: a view of the Scots law" (1985) 35 C.L.P. 57 at pp. 58–65 and MacDonald, "Restitution and Property Law," 1988 S.L.T.(News) 81.

[8] IV.iii.45.

[9] *Ibid.*

[10] I.vii.1.

to the practical matter of legal remedies, it is probably open to criticism on the basis of artificiality. While the conception of vindication proper as a claim in and to a thing is unexceptionable it seems an unduly restrictive theory to question its applicability from the point of view of recovering the thing. Arguably, a simple Hohfeldian analysis would see as implicit in the right to the thing a complementary duty, owed by the possessor without right against the owner, to release the item concerned to the owner. In any event, the law, it is submitted, needs no more than a basis upon which to order that the claimant is entitled to the thing; thereafter, assuming that the possessor does not allow the claimant to recover, the issue is one of enforcement.

It seems that the scope of restitution, from the point of view of recovery of a moveable, is the same as would apply to vindication to the extent that one can see the likelihood of tautology. What is understood by vindication—the owner's right to recover from one who holds without right against him—implies a duty to restore and, in the result, vindication and restitution appear to be no more than different ends of the same equation. This, it is submitted, is borne out by the description of the scope of restitution applicable in the case of things "belonging to others coming into our hands without delinquence, which we acquire *bona fide*" given by Stair[11]: "[I]n such cases we are bound to restore them to the owner, though thereby we lose what we gave, except in some cases, wherein positive law secures the buyer, and leaves the owner to seek the seller."[12]

This passage describes a proprietary remedy. It involves three parties: the owner, the seller and the buyer. Restitution as envisaged by Stair encompasses the owner's basic right to recover from a third party in the sense of one who obtained the thing in question from someone other than the owner. That this right is given effect to on the basis of an obligation to restore does not detract from its quality of universality; a feature inherent in the fact that restitution, providing for recovery of the thing, is available against any party who holds without a right binding upon the owner.

It would appear that what Stair's analysis comes down to is the argument that the owner's overriding right to recover is more appropriately classified as deriving from an obligation to make restitution rather than a right to recover property.

The implications of the above from the point of view of a possible distinction between real and personal rights is dealt with below.[13]

---

[11] I.vii.4.

[12] *Ibid. Cf. International Banking Corporation* v. *Ferguson, Shaw, & Sons*, 1910 S.C. 182 at p. 191, where Lord Low identified the following in the defender's argument: "The reason why a person in the *bona fide* possession of the goods of another is bound to restore them to that other is that the possessor has power to dispose of the goods, and is bound to exercise that power for the purpose of restoring them." Although this analysis of the basis of restitution appears to have been accepted, the matter before the court was distinguished because *specificatio* had occurred.

[13] See below, para. 10.04.

However, a passage concerned with the distinction between real and personal actions is especially relevant to Stair's analysis of the relationship between vindication and restitution, to the extent, it would seem, that the earlier passages must probably be read in the context of it. After pointing out that the law does not follow the general distinction of Roman law between real and personal actions and that, properly speaking, only certain actions relating to land are "real," Stair[14] goes on to explain his emphasis upon restitution to the exclusion of vindication.

> "But we make not use of the name or nature of Vindication,[15] whereby the proprietor pursues the possessor, or him who, by fraud, ceases to possess, to suffer the proprietor to take possession of his own, or to make up his damage by his fraud. This part of the action is rather personal than real, for reparation of the damage by the fraudulent quitting possession; yea, the conclusion of delivery doth not properly arise from vindication, which concludes no such obligation to the haver, but only to be passive, and not to hinder the proprietor to take possession of his own."

The gist of this passage is that the possessor's obligation to deliver to the owner is not a feature of vindication which is simply concerned with the owner's claim to the thing based upon his right of property.[16] SStair[17] shows that Roman law saw the right to vindicate as synonymous with ownership, but did not recognise "any personal obligation upon the haver." In Scots law, on the other hand, "there is a real obligation upon possessors, not having a title sufficient to defend their possession, to restore or re-deliver, not only to the proprietor, but to the lawful possessor."[18] The emphasis upon the holder's duty to restore to the rightful owner—rather than upon an overriding right to vindicate—seems to be consistent with the recognition of the importance of possession in the case of corporeal moveables: a position provided for in the presumption of ownership arising from possession.[19] This presumption is given effect to by requiring a claimant to show not only his ownership, but also how he came to lose possession.[20] The latter

---

[14] IV.iii.45.

[15] It may be noted that Stair uses a capital "V" to denote vindication in the Roman sense.

[16] See below, para. 10.03, n. 30.

[17] IV.iii.45.

[18] *Ibid.*

[19] See above, para. 1.12.

[20] See *Prangnell-O'Neill* v. *Lady Skiffington* 1984 S.L.T. 282 at p. 284 where Lord Hunter adopted the following statement from Dickson, *Evidence* (3rd ed.), s.150: "In overcoming the presumption by proving the property, it must be shown not only that the moveables once belonged to the person seeking to recover them, but that his possession terminated in such a way that the subsequent possessor could not have acquired a right of property in them."

requirement is consistent with the recognition of a category of circumstances of deprivation on the basis of which a party proving a right of ownership should be restored—that the item concerned was stolen, lost, handed over in error, and so on.[21] But the policy of the protection of possession of moveables means that the issue of the owner's right to get a thing back is looked at from the point of view of a duty of restoration on the part of the possessor. In the result the right of vindication is given effect to through the obligation of restitution. As Erskine[22] put it, "whatever comes into our power or possession which belongs to another, without an intention in the owner of making a present of it, ought to be restored to him."

From the point of view simply of the owner's right to recover a moveable which has come into the hands of another, the only significant distinction between vindication and restitution would appear to be that the latter is a binary remedy, in that it applies not only to give a right to recover the thing but also the right to compensation in the case of *mala fide* disposition.[23]

Recognition in sources of principle of owner's right to recover

Stair recognised as implicit in the notion of ownership the owner's **10.03** right to recover possession; a right in and to property in the sense of being a right deriving from the owner's relationship with the thing but, of course, at the same time, and most importantly according to Stair's analysis, a right leading to an obligation to restore (to make "restitution") as a duty binding a party holding the thing without right against the owner. These features emerge from a passage in Stair[24] which, being concerned with the obligation of restitution, commences from the point of view of the duty of restitution rather than the right of vindication. "Restitution of things belonging to others, may seem to be an effect of property, whence cometh the right of vindication or repetition of any thing."

Regarding the case of a special legacy, Stair[25] points out that the legatee has not only a personal action against the heir for delivery or payment but also—in so far, presumably, as the legacy is over a corporeal moveable—an action of vindication. The right of vindication is also mentioned in the context of Stair's[26] treatment of the action of

---

[21] See Stair, I.vii.3–9.

[22] III.i.10.

[23] See below, para. 10.07.

[24] I.vii.2. Regarding "repetition" see Birks "Restitution: a view of the Scots law" (1985) 35 C.L.P. 57 at p. 63: "Within 'restitution' there is an obvious difference between the *res* which is returnable not only exactly but specifically, and the sum of money which is returnable exactly but, almost invariably, only by substitution of other money to the same value. Reflecting this distinction between the two types of benefit received, 'restitution' *strictissimo sensu* is made to indicate the claim to the *res*, while the claim to the money is denoted 'repetition.' "

[25] III.viii.23.

[26] See IV.xxx.8: "though there were no injury in the entry, yet so soon as the owner claims his goods, and they are refused, the possessor becomes a wrongous intromitter."

"wrongous intromission," in that even if there is no wrong in attaining or retaining possession both a duty to restore and a right to vindicate will apply. In this regard, Stair[27] notes that the vindicatory action is competent "for recovery of all goods to the true owner, where there is no special title competent for recovery thereof."

It is important to note that in the cases of legacy and "wrongous intromission" Stair is concerned with the right of vindication applying as a corollary of a duty to restore. Neither case is an instance of the exercise of a right of vindication, in the classic sense of a claim in and to the thing not necessarily involving any particular party in a duty to deliver. As shown above,[28] Stair[29] draws a distinction between an action of vindication in this classic sense and a right of vindication in the sense of a right to claim delivery from a particular party owing a duty to deliver.

The essential point is that a vindicatory claim, in and to the thing concerned, does not involve the holder (the "haver") in an obligation to deliver—"the conclusion of delivery doth not properly arise from vindication"[30]—and, to this extent, Stair sees the vindicatory action as inappropriate, hence the emphasis upon restitution providing for "a real obligation . . . to restore or re-deliver."[31]

Erskine's[32] statement that the right of property "necessarily excludes every other person but the proprietor" implicitly recognises a right of vindication for, plainly, without a right to recover there could be no such feature.[33] In considering the distinction between real and personal actions Erskine[34] acknowledges that, in principle, a right of property—"the highest right that one can have in a subject"—necessarily implies a right to vindicate from whomsoever may hold the thing (without a right against the owner to do so): "every action founded on a right in any subject, though it should be moveable, is, in a legal sense, real, and therefore may proceed against every person who holds the possession or custody thereof."

Hume,[35] in considering the position of the *bona fide* purchaser of a moveable from a non-owner, takes for granted the existence of a vindicatory action based upon the owner's title. "The nature of a proper *rei vindicatio*, or real action for recovery of property is that it

---

[27] *Ibid.*

[28] para. 10.02.

[29] IV.iii.45.

[30] *Ibid.*

[31] *Ibid.*

[32] II.i.1.

[33] The primary criterion as to whether a right excludes others must be the extent to which legal means of exclusion exist. Moreover, the recognition of a duty of restitution on the basis of the possessor's power over the property of another (Erskine, III.i.10) must necessarily imply a right of vindication—in effect enforcement—because otherwise the owner's right would be hardly more than nominal.

[34] IV.i.10.

[35] III, p. 235.

attaches to and follows the thing as the possession shifts from hand to hand." In another passage the recognition of the principle of vindication appears from the denial of its applicability to the circumstances of sale and delivery by the owner to a fraudulent party.

"But then what is the shape and substance of the complaint which the seller has to make on such an occasion? He cannot, in strict form, bring an immediate real action, or *rei vindicatio*, setting forth that the thing is still his, and assuming that it shall therefore be restored to him as such."[36]

Bell[37] speaks of a summary action which "comes in place of the *rei vindicatio* of the Roman law" whereby "the owner is by civil process entitled to follow and recover his property."[38] Bell[39] is clear that this action requires, "as a title to pursue, the right of ownership" and, as a result, items bought but not yet delivered "cannot be so vindicated by the owner in a summary process."[40] It seems that Bell sees the Scottish counterpart of the civilian vindicatory action as a summary process to recover possession.[41]

In earlier case law one finds a number of examples of recognition of the principle of vindication. An express instance of this is to be found in the case of *Ramsay* v. *Wilson*[42] where the Lords sustained the pursuer's argument for the right to vindicate jewels: "though the jewels had gone per *mille manus*, the haver always is liable, who should know better the condition of the party he deals with." In another seventeenth-century case[43] a claim to vindicate a horse was sustained against a *bona fide* purchaser from a party to whom the owner had lent it. The Lords accepted the pursuer's submission that the princple that the property of moveables is presumed from possession was excluded by his "offering to prove the horse his own, and that he did not sell him, but set him for hire, and, therefore, hath *rei vindicationem* against any haver thereof, whether he acquire *bona fide* or *mala fide*."[44]

---

[36] III, p. 236.

[37] *Prin.*, § 1320.

[38] *Prin.*, § 1318.

[39] *Prin.*, § 1320.

[40] See also Bell, *Comm.*, I, 299: "Moveables sold by a thief, for example, may be claimed or *vindicated* by the owner, wherever he may find them."

[41] As to the notion of vindication as a summary process, see also *Scottish Central Ry. Co.* v. *Ferguson & Co.* (1863) 1 M. 750 *per* Lord Ardmillan at p. 758: "In Scotland we have a very valuable summary remedy for the vindication of property." *Cf.* spuilzie (below, para. 10.24), a summary remedy based upon the assertion of a right of possession which, of course, although not exclusive to an owner would be available to an owner in possession.

[42] (1666) Mor. 9113.

[43] *Forsyth* v. *Kilpatrick* (1680) Mor. 9120.

[44] See also the cases of *Findlay* v. *Monro* (1698) Mor. 1767 and *Russel* v. *Campbell* (1699) 4 Brown's Supp. 468, in which the principle of vindication is recognised.

In *Scot* v. *Low*[45] S sold sheep to B but P, S's delivery agent, fraudulently sold the flock to L who bought in good faith. After B had obtained repetition of the price paid by him S sought restitution from L. The Lords found that S's claim was not relevant because it did not allege that L was in possession at the time of citation. The court, in effect, upheld the argument that the only action available to the pursuer was vindicatory but that this was not competent in the circumstances because the defender had disposed of the flock.

In *Walker* v. *Spence and Carfrae*[46] a party who had received the pursuer's sheep on a grazing contract sold them, as his own, to the defenders who purchased *bona fide*. In the circumstances of the defenders' having disposed of the sheep, there could be no vindicatory action against them.[47] In approaching the matter from the point of view that liability required either *mala fide* disposition or enrichment the court appears to have accepted this.

Instances of the recognition of the principle of vindication are also to be found in later case law although, in the more recent case law, the designation "restitution," or the description "action for delivery" or something similar, tends to supplant the label "vindication"[48]—a tendency which may be explained on the basis of the influence of Stair's analysis.[49] However, this is not to suggest that the civilian terminology dies out,[50] far less the principle concerned.[51] Indeed, in the mid-to late nineteenth century—a most important era in the development of Scots private law—one finds judicial dicta which take for granted the availability of the owner's vindicatory action. A dictum of Lord Mackenzie in *Duff* v. *Snare*[52] is an example: "I can imagine a case so pregnant with suspicion of theft, as to justify the detention of the property of an innocent person, during a process of *rei vindicatio*; but it must be far stronger and more specific than anything we have here."

In *Scottish Central Railway Co.* v. *Ferguson & Co.*[53] Lord President McNeill acknowledged the owner's proprietary interest as the basis of the action to recover moveable property. "But this action is an action for vindication of property, not on the alleged breach of the contract of carriage, but on the allegation of the wrongful withholding of the goods from the true proprietor."

---

[45] (1704) Mor. 9123.

[46] (1765) Mor. 12802.

[47] Had the sheep still been in the defenders' possession, their *bona fides* would have been irrelevant, for: "*rem meam vindicare possum ubicumque inveniam*"—what is mine I can vindicate wherever I find it.

[48] See, *e.g. Mitchell* v. *Heys & Sons* (1894) 21 R. 600 at p. 608; *Morrisson* v. *Robertson*, 1908 S.C. 332 at p. 335.

[49] See above, para. 10.2.

[50] See, *e.g. Henderson* v *Gibson*, June 17, 1806, F.C.; *Wylie and Lochhead* v. *Mitchell* (1870) 8 M. 552 *per* Lord President Inglis at p. 556: "they may be entitled to recover possession of it *rei vindicatione*."

[51] See, *e.g. Pride* v. *St. Anne's Bleaching Co.* (1838) 16 S. 1376.

[52] (1849) 11 D. 1119 at p. 1122.

[53] (1863) 1 M. 750 at p. 754.

Occasionally the right to vindicate has been recognised in the context of the rule that theft is a *vitium reale* which prevents ownership from passing against the interests of the true owner deprived by the act of theft. An example is the dictum of Lord Craighill in *Todd* v. *Armour*[54]: "by the law of Scotland, as I have been taught, and as I regard that law, stolen property, wherever stolen, can be vindicated."

In *International Banking Corporation* v. *Ferguson, Shaw, & Sons*[55] one finds the terminology of "restitution" and "vindication" used interchangeably by two judges. First, *per* Lord Low[56]: "the property still remaining in the true owner . . . he being entitled to follow the goods and demand restitution"; and, secondly, *per* Lord Justice-Clerk MacDonald[57]: "The pursuers, without doubt, could have vindicated their proprietary right and enforced delivery."

That an owner has an action to recover his property from one who holds, without a right against him to the same, is not in doubt. How this action is designated is unimportant,[58] although from the point of view of consistency of usage and meaning it is clearly desirable that the law adopt uniform terminology.[59]

Owner's right to recover: a real or personal right?

The fundamental civilian distinction between a proprietary right or **10.04** action and a mere obligation—the former being available against "the whole world": the latter only against a particular party—is recognised by Scots law as a matter of general jurisprudence.[60] Moveable property is particularly susceptible to competing claims and, where these occur, whether a right is proprietary or merely personal may well be in issue, especially if the insolvency factor is present.

---

[54] (1882) 9 R. 901 at p. 908.

[55] 1910 S.C. 182.

[56] at pp. 191–192.

[57] at p. 193.

[58] What, of course, is crucial here is that a given label may identify a specific remedy and any particular features the remedy may have.

[59] Various formulations meaning the same thing can only lead to confusion. See, *e.g. Gorebridge Co-operative Society Ltd.* v. *Turnbull*, 1952 S.L.T.(Sh.Ct.) 91, where the owner's civil remedy to recover stolen property was described as an "action of restitution brought against the present possessor." *Cf. George Hopkinson Ltd.* v. *Napier & Son*, 1953 S.C. 139 *per* Lord President Cooper at pp. 148–149, where the "true owner's remedy . . . to get delivery" is identified as a right of "vindication." As indicated, a tendency to use these terms interchangeably appears in the case law; see also, *e.g. Faulds* v. *Townsend* (1861) 23 D. 437 *per* Lord Ordinary (Ardmillan) at p. 439: "This is not an action for vindication or restitution of the stolen horse."

[60] See Erskine, III.i.2: "the essential difference may be perceived between rights that affect a subject itself, which are called *real*, and those which are founded in obligation, or, as they are generally styled, *personal*. A real right, or *jus in re*, whether of property or of an inferior kind—as servitude—entitles the person vested with it to possess the subject as his own; or, if it be possessed by another, to demand it from the possessor, in consequence of the right which he hath in the subject itself; whereas the creditor in a personal right or obligation has only a *jus ad rem*, or a right of action against the debtor or his representatives, by which they may be compelled to fulfil that obligation, but without any right in the subject which the debtor is obliged to transfer to him."

Stair,[61] in his treatment of actions, points out that the law does not follow the general real/personal distinction of Roman law and that, properly speaking, only certain actions relating to land are "real." In a poinding of the ground "there is nothing decerned against the possessors personally," but "in all other cases, we proceed upon the personal obligation."[62] In the same text Stair goes on to explain his emphasis upon restitution to the exclusion of vindication.[63] What are the implications of this from the point of view of the standing of an owner's right to moveable property? More especially, is Stair saying that the right of an owner to recover a moveable is a personal right in the sense of being available only in respect of a particular party owing an obligation to restore the thing to the claimant?

"Personal" in Stair's treatment seems to signify no more than that the rationale of the action is a personal obligation in that, given the nature of moveable property, the holder must necessarily be seen as subject to an obligation to restore. One may contrast Stair's[64] use, in relation to land, of the label "real." In this case the rationale is simply the owner's right in the land concerned; a right which can be given effect to by an order that the claimant is entitled to possession.

The real/personal distinction, as applied by Stair in this context, does not mean that the right to the restitution of a moveable is personal rather than proprietary in the sense of deriving from a *jus ad rem* rather than a *jus in re*.[65] Clearly, the right of ownership in a moveable is a real right in the sense of being a proprietary right. Moreover, the action protecting this right—whether styled "restitution" or "vindication"—is a real action because it avails against any party who holds without a right to which the owner is subject; as a modern writer has put it: "Restitution was the personal remedy by which the owner asserted his real right."[65a] Stair's[66] somewhat uncomfortable label "real obligation" demonstrates this hybrid quality: "there is a real obligation upon possessors, not having a title sufficient to defend their possession, to restore or re-deliver."

Of course, the obligation of restitution is personal to the extent that it comes to an end when the party bound parts with the thing in good

---

[61] IV.iii.45.

[62] *Ibid.* The basis of this distinction seems to be that in the case of land no more is needed than an order that the claimant is entitled to possession whereas, in respect of a moveable, there must be an order to restore.

[63] See above, para. 10.02, n. 14, where part of the relevant passage is quoted.

[64] IV.iii.45.

[65] The distinction between a claim to a thing and a right in it is well recognised; see, *e.g.* the *obiter dictum* of Lord Dunpark in *Sloans Dairies Ltd.* v. *Glasgow Corpn.* 1977 S.C. 223 at pp. 241–242: "if the original contract had specified particular barrels by their numbers, the defenders would have acquired their *jus ad rem* in relation to the specified barrels on completion of the contract, although they would not have acquired a *jus in re* until they had intimated their document of title to the third party custodiers."

[65a] MacDonald, "Restitution and Property Law," 1988 S.L.T. (News) 81.

[66] IV.iii.45.

faith.[67] From the point of view of the protection of an owner's interest, however, the material consideration is that, in principle, he can recover the item from any subsequent holder and, to this extent, his right is real.[68]

Relevance of circumstances in which claimant lost or parted with thing

The right to vindicate and its correlative the duty of restitution only **10.05** prevail in circumstances in which an owner has retained his right to the thing; put another way, one may say that there can be no claim to restitution where ownership has passed. Stair,[69] after identifying various ways "by which the things of others may come to our hands," notes that: "In all these, the obligation of restitution is formally founded upon the having of things of others in our power, and therefore, that ceasing, the obligation also ceaseth."[70]

The situation of an owner delivering a thing on the basis of a *causa*, void for turpitude, but nonetheless intending to pass ownership,[71] is an example of the case in which there is no obligation of restitution because, in principle, in these circumstances, ownership passes[72]: "But there is not the same ground for things given for an unjust cause, as *ob turpem causam*; in which the will of the owner, and his purpose to transfer the property is effectual, though his motive was not good."[73]

A claim to possession, on the basis of an alleged right of ownership in a thing held by another, raises the issue of the claimant's ownership. However, the circumstances under which he lost or parted with custody of the thing are material to this issue. Plainly enough, a claimant will succeed only if these circumstances are consistent with his retention of the right of ownership. The importance of the circumstances in which physical possession was lost or parted with follow also from the law's emphasis upon the significance of the possession of moveable property. Effectively, possession is protected to the extent that a claimant to ownership can succeed only by overcoming a presumption that the possessor is owner; this involves the claimant in

---

[67] See Smith, *Short Commentary*, at p. 625.

[68] But, in identifying the nature of the owner's right, one must distinguish "title to sue" and the nature of a particular claim in a given case. Regarding the former, the owner's right is by definition the most extensive. As Lord Dunedin noted in *D. & J. Nicol* v. *Dundee Harbour Trustees*, 1915 S.C.(H.L.) 7 at p. 12: "The simplest case of all is where the person is owner of something. The legal relation of ownership gives him the right to sue all actions which deal with the vindication or defence of his property."

[69] I.vii.3.

[70] I.vii.11.

[71] See above, paras. 8.08–8.09.

[72] However, as Stair (I.vii.8) points out, positive law may, as a matter of policy, determine that ownership does not pass, in which case there will be an obligation of restitution.

[73] I.vii.8. *Cf.* Erskine, III.i.10, who does not make the important distinction between ownership passing as a matter of principle and policy-based rules which may determine otherwise.

demonstrating that in the circumstances he has retained his right of ownership.[74]

Stair identifies various situations in which there would be an obligation of restitution—all cases in which the circumstances are consistent with the retention of a right of ownership. In the case of strayed animals, "if the owner make them appear to be his, he may have them."[75] Likewise in the analogous case of lost property.[76]

More importantly, Stair[77] refers to the case of the *bona fide* acquisition of a thing which in fact belongs to a third party—this is not so much a distinct fact-situation as a statement of the principle *nemo dat quod non habet*.[78] Erskine[79] is equally clear that the loss must be the innocent purchaser's: "And though the possessor should have purchased the subject for a price *bona fide*, still the owner must have it restored to him, in consequence of his property, without the burden of repaying that price to the possessor." If a *bona fide* purchaser must give the thing up, *a fortiori*, this must apply in respect of things recovered from thieves.[80]

The final cases mentioned by Stair are situations in which the owner delivered the thing but, because ownership did not pass, an obligation of restitution arises. The first case is that of property handed over subject to a condition which fails—a gift in contemplation of a marriage which the parties call off[81]; the second is that of delivery made in error, to a party to whom it was not due ("*indebiti.*")[82]

THE OWNER'S RIGHT TO RESTITUTION

Essentials of claim

10.06   It is readily apparent that the essential ingredients of an owner's action to recover what is his, are the pursuer's right of ownership and the defender's possession. In *Scot* v. *Low*,[83] where the action was

---

[74] See above, para. 1.12.

[75] I.vii.3. Stair, it may be noted, goes on to point out that even if the owner does not emerge, the possessor will not acquire because the principle of *occupatio—quod nullius est, fit occupantis*—applies only to "things which were never known to have an owner." See above, para. 2.03. See also Erskine, II.i.10. The Winter Herding Act 1686 provided for the right of an occupier of land to detain straying animals pending payment of compensation for any damage done, but this legislation was repealed by the Animals (Scotland) Act 1987.

[76] Stair, I.vii.3. The Civic Government (Scotland) Act 1982 now controls: see above, para. 2.08.

[77] I.vii.4.

[78] See below, para. 10.15.

[79] III.i.10.

[80] Stair, I.vii.5. Regarding things taken in war—an issue of public international law—Stair (I.vii.6) inclines to the view that an obligation of restitution to the deprived owner arises on recovery by his nation.

[81] I.vii.7. See also Erskine, III.i.10.

[82] I.vii.9.

[83] (1704) Mor. 9123.

designated "*vindicatio*," the Lords upheld the defender's argument that the two things which must be proved were "property on the pursuer's part, and possession on the defender's."

Because the question of recovery by an owner only arises when another has natural possession,[83a] this aspect may be considered first.

Erskine[84] emphasises the feature of possession adverse to the owner's right: "As this obligation is founded on the power which the possessor hath by his possession over the property of another, therefore, if he shall cease to possess, by sale, donation, etc., the obligation to restore ceaseth also."[85]

The prerequisite of a defender in possession is shown in the case of *Faulds* v. *Townsend*,[86] where a manufacturing chemist bought a stolen horse, destroyed it and put the carcass to use in the normal course of his business. The judgment of the Lord Ordinary, upheld by the First Division, commenced from the position that, in the circumstances, there could be no claim to restitution.

> "This is not an action for vindication or restitution of the stolen horse. That has been rendered impossible by the act of the advocator. If the horse had still been alive, and in possession of the advocator, he must have restored it, and *bona fides* in the purchase would, in that case, have been no defence."[87]

In *Gorebridge Co-operative Society Ltd.* v. *Turnbull*,[88] a claim to restitution was dismissed as incompetent in the absence of an averment of "present possession by the defender of the property said to have been stolen."

While the preliminary issue of the defender's possession is a question of fact, the method of proof of the pursuer's claim to the thing is subject to certain requirements which stem from the protection of the possession of a moveable.[89] The law gives effect to the presumption that the possessor of a moveable thing is the owner by requiring a claimant to discharge a particular burden in establishing his right to the thing. Hume[90] explains that it is not enough for the pursuer

---

[83a] For the distinction between natural and civil possession, see above, para. 1.14.

[84] III.i.10.

[85] See *International Banking Corporation*. v. *Ferguson, Shaw, & Sons*, 1910 S.C. 182 *per* Lord Low at p. 191: "The reason why a person in the *bona fide* possession of the goods of another is bound to restore them to that other is that the possessor has power to dispose of the goods, and is bound to exercise that power for the purpose of restoring them."

[86] (1861) 23 D. 437.

[87] *per* Lord Ardmillan at p. 439. See also *International Banking Corporation*. v. *Ferguson, Shaw, & Sons*, 1910 S.C. 182 *per* Lord Low at pp. 191–192.

[88] 1952 S.L.T.(Sh.Ct.) 91.

[89] See above, para. 1.12.

[90] III, pp. 228–229.

to show that he had once been proprietor of the thing. To avoid damage to commerce by inhibiting the free flow of goods the law does not require the possessor to prove the soundness of his title. For this reason, and also as a matter of justice, Hume[91] notes that the law "lays the burden of proof on the former owner, vindicating his subject":[92]

> "We do not require of the present possessor to show, even how he himself acquired the moveable, much less how it came to any intermediate person between him and the pursuer: we presume in his favour from his possession alone, *qua dominus*, in character of owner, that the thing came fairly to him on some just and lawful title of acquisition; and this presumption it lyes upon the pursuer or complainer, to overcome. Which to do he must prove, not only that the thing once belonged to him, but also *quomodo desiit possedere*—the matter of the departure of the thing out of his hands. He must show, that the thing passed from him either utterly without his consent (as by stealth, or robbery or being lost); or, at least, without any intention on his part to transfer the property of the thing, as by loan or pledge, on deposit, or on some other and like limited and defeasible title of possession consistent with the right of property remaining in him."[93]

In *Forsyth* v. *Kilpatrick*,[94] a claim for the restitution of a horse, the defender alleged *bona fide* purchase and relied upon the principle that the property of moveables is presumed from possession. The Lords accepted the pursuer's position, which was that the presumption could be overcome by proof that he was the owner of the horse and that he had not sold it but had handed it over on the basis of a contract of hire."[95]

Some dicta tend to suggest that the presumption of ownership operating in favour of a possessor may be less far-reaching than might be thought from a reading of the Institutional writings. A well-known instance of this theme is the comment of Lord Cockburn in the case of *Anderson* v. *Buchanan* that the presumption "is one liable to be rebutted, and perhaps liable to be rebutted easily."[96] However, in

---

[91] III, p. 229.

[92] See also Stair, II.i.42.

[93] Hume, III, p. 229. For a concise statement see *Russel* v. *Campbell* (1699) 4 Brown's Supp. 468 at p. 469: "ere you can recover them, you must first prove that you lost the possession, *clam vi*, or *precario*, or by some title not alienative of the property, as loan or the like." See also *Hariot* v. *Cuningham* (1791) Mor. 12405.

[94] (1680) Mor. 9120. See above, para. 10.03, n. 43.

[95] *Pride* v. *St. Anne's Bleaching Co.* (1838) 16 S. 1376 is another example of property handed over in circumstances which could not be construed to indicate an intention to transfer ownership. Here a bleaching company, through error, delivered to a customer a larger quantity of cloth than had been received.

[96] (1848) 11 D. 270 at p. 284. See also *George Hopkinson Ltd.* v. *Napier & Son*, 1953 S.C. 139 *per* Lord President Cooper at p. 147. See generally above, para. 1.12.

Prangnell-O'Neill v. *Lady Skiffington*,[97] a recent decision of the Second Division, Lord Hunter qualified this statement in observing: "Whether it may be easy or difficult to rebut the presumption depends on circumstances, which may vary greatly." Lord Hunter went on to clarify the scope of the presumption by adopting the statement in Dickson on *Evidence*[98] as to the method by which it might be rebutted:

> "In overcoming the presumption by proving the property, it must be shown not only that the moveables once belonged to the person seeking to recover them, but that his possession terminated in such a way that the subsequent possessor could not have acquired a right of property in them."

Making the claimant subject to a presumption in this form is consistent with the emphasis placed by the common law upon the *vitium reale* of theft.[99] In principle a claimant able to identify the thing as his property and show that his possession was terminated by an act of theft will rebut the presumption that the present possessor is owner. The effect of this will be to remove the obstacle to vindication. On the other hand, where the circumstances under which the claimant's original possession was terminated are consistent with an intention to transfer ownership, the presumption will not be overcome and the claim will fail. It is suggested that this result is in keeping with the notion that ownership passes on the basis of an act of delivery accompanied by the requisite intention—the abstract approach— regardless of the circumstances as to any underlying contract.[1]

Binary nature of restitution

As indicated,[2] the obligation of restitution gives not only a right to recover the thing but also a claim to compensation available against the holder who parts with it knowing of the owner's right. Stair,[3] explaining how this right is concomitant with the owner's right to demand his thing, goes on to urge that recognition of the right follows more appropriately from the basis of an obligation to make restitution than the notion of a right of vindication: **10.07**

> "not only when it is in the possession of the haver, but if he hath fraudfully put it away; and yet it is his once having it that obliges

---

[97] 1984 S.L.T. 282 at p. 284.
[98] (3rd ed.), s.150.
[99] See, *e.g.* Stair, IV.xl.21: "because moveables must have a current course of traffic, and the buyer is not to consider how the seller purchased, unless it were by theft or violence which the law accounts as *labes reales*, following the subject to all successors, otherwise there would be the greatest encouragement to theft and robbery."
[1] See above, paras. 8.08–8.09.
[2] Above, para. 10.2.
[3] I.vii.2.

him, and his fraudulent away-putting, though it be a delinquency, yet it gave not the rise to the obligation, but only continues it in the same condition as if he yet had it; so in that case his obligation is more palpable; for vindication of the thing, where it is not, cannot take place, though *pro possessore habetur qui dolo desiit possidere*, that is only *fictione juris*; but the obligation to restore is direct and proper."[4]

In short, Stair's point is that the obligation of restitution theory accommodates a claim for payment of the value of the thing in the event of a *mala fide* disposition because liability on the basis of the obligation to restore simply continues in this case. As Erskine[5] puts it, "if he has given up the possession fraudulently, he continues bound." By contrast, vindication can only be competent where the thing is,[6] and accordingly a claim for value in the event of *mala fide* disposition can only be justified on the basis that the act amounted to a delict.

Hume,[7] commencing from the premise that a *bona fide* purchaser of the property of another who disposes of it believing that he has a right to do so is not liable, notes that this will not be the position "where the owner can instruct something materially wrong in the conduct of the purchaser, to create a personal ground of claim against him,—one that is good against him personally, by reason of the circumstances of his own conduct." Hume's[8] concluding remarks seem to be consistent with the notion of a continuing obligation. "As he cannot restore the thing itself, he must therefore pay the value to the owner. In such a case *dolo desiit possidere*, and he must account as if he were still in possession."

In case law, the owner's right to recover value in the event of a *mala fide* disposition is fully recognised. In *Scot* v. *Low*[9] the court accepted that failing recovery on the basis of the defender's possession there could be liability for value following the principle *qui dolo desiit possidere pro possessore habetur*. In *Faulds* v. *Townsend*[10] this maxim is quoted in support of an obiter statement to similar effect.

"If, on the other hand, the advocator had, in *mala fide* or by dole, or by such fault as is equivalent to dole, parted with or put an end to possession of the horse, he would be liable in the proved value

---

[4] Stair expressly rejects any implied contract theory in explaining the basis of this aspect of restitution; see Birks "Restitution: a view of the Scots law" (1985) C.L.P. 38, 57 at pp. 60–61.

[5] III.i.10.

[6] Stair, I.vii.2: "for vindication of the thing, where it is not, cannot take place."

[7] III, p. 234.

[8] *Ibid*.

[9] (1704) Mor. 9123.

[10] (1861) 23 D. 437, *per* Lord Ordinary (Ardmillan) at p. 439.

of the animal, *si dolo desiit possidere, dolus pro possessione habetur.*"

The distinct character of the two remedies which have come to travel together under the label "restitution" is most markedly manifested by the fact that the owner's right in and to the thing itself is a real right, whereas the right to compensation is a personal right—the correlative of an obligation by which a particular party is bound to the owner. Stair[11] makes this important point in distinguishing the petitory action based upon a personal right from the declaratory action deriving from the real right of ownership. "The action for delivery of moveables, is also upon the personal obligation of the haver, which is distinct from the right of property, which is rather a declaratory action, as *rei vindicatio* in the Roman law did chiefly declare the pursuer's right of moveables."

Proof of mala fides

The states of good and bad faith are the opposite conditions of the **10.08** same matter—the issue of a possessor's state of mind in relation to the property of another. The present inquiry is concerned with the circumstances in which an owner can recover value on the basis that the defender parted with the thing in bad faith. The principles applying to this question are the same as those applicable to determine a possessor's right to fruits.[12] As indicated, two separate but related issues are raised: first, the question of the communication—by one means or another—of the fact of the claim to the possessor and, secondly, whether this knowledge caused a realisation by the possessor that his right was defective. While the former issue is a matter of fact, the latter—in principle a subjective question—is determined by the necessarily objective test whether "upon the smallest reflection"[13] the possessor should realise that he was not owner.

Erskine's[14] comment concerning the commencement of *mala fides* in the case of a possessor's right to fruits[15] is also applicable to the present issue.

"*Bona fides* necessarily ceaseth, when the possessor can have no longer a probable opinion that the subject is his own; for it is that opinion that the essence of *bona fides* consisteth. *Mala fides is*

---

[11] IV.xxi.5. See also Smith, *Short Commentary*, p. 625: "The true owner's right of vindication of the thing itself (*rei vindicatio*) is a right *in rem*, but in addition the person in possession of another's goods is bound by the obligation of restitution. This is a *jus in personam*."
[12] See above, para. 6.05.
[13] Erskine, II.i.25.
[14] II.i.28.
[15] See above, para. 6.08, n. 62.

therefore induced by the conscientia rei alienae, though such consciousness should not proceed from legal interpellation, but barely from private knowledge; for private knowledge necessarily implies consciousness."

Hume[16] regards a possessor's conduct as *mala fide* "if he has disposed of the thing in question after citation in the real action for recovery of the thing." The merits aside, this "was a warning to him and he does wrong, and is not in *bona fide* when he thus attempts to extricate himself from the claim which lies against him as possessor at the time." This is consistent with Stair's[17] use of the word "fraud" in identifying the touchstone of the action applicable to one who parts with the thing *mala fide*: "or him who, by fraud, ceases to possess, to suffer the proprietor to take possession of his own, or to make up his damage by his fraud."[18]

The better view is that while notice of the commencement of legal proceedings may be an obvious example of a communication sufficient to induce *mala fides*, this is not the only way in which the state of *bona fide* possession may come to an end; arguably, the requisite change from an assumption of right to an awareness of another's claim can be induced by any means—whether direct or on the basis of inference.[19]

While it is clear that one who disposes of a thing following intimation of a claim of ownership acts *mala fide*,[20] a more difficult issue is whether, on the basis of objective reasoning, bad faith can be inferred from the circumstances in which the thing was acquired. In *Faulds* v. *Townsend*[21] Lord President McNeill, delivering the opinion of the First Division, confirmed the position taken by the Lord Ordinary (Ardmillan) to the effect that there could be liability on the basis of a failure to exercise reasonable care. An employee of the defender, a manufacturing chemist who used animal carcasses, had purchased a horse which was immediately destroyed. In the view of the Lord Ordinary, while there was no active *mala fides*, the circumstances of the purchase demonstrated a want of care sufficient to infer bad faith, because "on grounds of public policy, an unusual degree of care

---

[16] III, p. 234.

[17] IV.iii.45.

[18] See also I.vii.2: "and his fraudulent away-putting."

[19] An arguable case would be the situation of the *bona fide* purchaser of a horse seeing a "lost property" advertisement describing an animal and referring to circumstances which would cause him "upon the slightest reflection" to realise that the horse he had bought had in fact been stolen from the advertiser.

[20] The intimation of a claim to the thing by the owner is sufficient to justify an action for value where the goods are disposed of—assuming, of course, that the owner can prove his right. Stair, IV.xxxi.8, notes that "so soon as the owner claims his goods, and they are refused, the possessor becomes a wrongous intromitter," but if retention is wrongful in these circumstances, *a fortiori* disposition must be.

[21] (1861) 23 D. 437; see above, para. 10.06, n. 87.

and caution is required from a person who carries on a business which must afford temptation to theft."[22]

In *F.C. Finance Ltd.* v. *Langtry Investment Co. Ltd.*[23] the court accepted the possibility of equating negligence and intentional conduct with regard to an act of disposition of moveable property belonging to another.

> "This decision would seem to warrant the proposition that if a person buys stolen goods under circumstances in which ordinary prudence would require him to satisfy himself as to the seller's right to sell them, and he makes no inquiries to that end, he may be held liable to the true owner for their value if recovery of the goods themselves has been made impossible by his actings."

As indicated, the right approach would appear to be that the state of mind appropriate to *mala fide* disposition may be established in any way; in particular, "notice" need not be express but may be inferred from the circumstances. Of course, the circumstances must point to knowledge of the true facts on the part of the possessor—the inquiry being, in principle, a subjective one—but where this is arrived at by inference, objective criteria must necessarily be applied.

Owner's right following recovery from mala fide party

Meeting the owner's claim for value satisfies the obligation of a party **10.09** who *mala fide* disposed of the property of another but, in principle, does not affect the owner's right to claim the thing from a subsequent party. This possibility follows as a consequence of the basis of restitution as an obligation due by the possessor of a moveable belonging to another.[24] The obligation to restore the owner, deriving from his right in the thing, comes into being afresh immediately a subsequent party obtains possession.

The Scottish Law Commission[25] have commented upon the unsatisfactory nature of the common law in this regard. Noting that while no further obligation can be due once the owner has recovered

---

[22] at p. 439. It may be noted that the court founded upon a requirement of due care, commensurate with the circumstances: "If the advocator purchased the horse, not merely in good faith, and without knowledge that it was stolen, but with due care and caution under the circumstances, and then disposed of the horse by slaughtering and using it up, also with the due care and caution which the law requires in the prosecution of his business, then he would only be liable in *quantum lucratus*" (at p. 439). It may be noted that the Scot. Law Com., Memo. No. 31, *Corporeal Moveables: Remedies*, para. 9, accept that the principle of liability for value where the thing is unlawfully disposed of "was extended in *Faulds* v. *Townsend* to comprehend cases where *culpa* could be equiparated with *dolus*."

[23] 1972 S.L.T.(Sh.Ct.) 17 *per* Sheriff-Substitute Peterson at p. 18.

[24] See above, para. 10.07.

[25] Memo. No. 31, *Corporeal Moveables: Remedies*, para. 9.

his property, the Commission point out that: "A successful claim for value of the property against a *mala fide* possessor would not seem to bar a subsequent claim for delivery from a third party actually in possession. In this situation the owner would have been over-compensated." As the Commission[26] indicated, this result would be contrary to the principle behind the dictum of Lord Wright in *Spence* v. *Crawford*,[27] to the effect that the victim's unjust enrichment—"if he got back what he had parted with and kept what he had received in return"—would be unfair, even if the party affected had acted fraudulently. Certainly, the recovery of property from a *bona fide* possessor—who has given value for the thing—after obtaining compensation from an interim *mala fide* possessor, would seem to be an instance of the unjustified enrichment of the owner at the expense of the *bona fide* possessor.

The Scottish Law Commission[28] point to the possible application of the principle of recompense as the most appropriate solution[29] to this problem:

> "if an owner, having received value from a *mala fide* former possessor, subsequently concludes for delivery in an action against a third party, that party should in the same proceedings be entitled to recover from the owner, on principles of recompense, the amount by which the owner would have been enriched by recovering his property in addition to the money already received."

Given that the possible unjustified enrichment of an owner is the difficulty envisaged it would seem only appropriate that the solution should be on the basis of the application of the principle of recompense.[30] But it is beyond the scope of the present work to examine the application of the principle of recompense as a counter to the owner's claim.

---

[26] *Ibid.*

[27] 1939 S.C.(H.L.) 52 at p. 77.

[28] Memo. No. 31, *Corporeal Moveables: Remedies*, para. 9.

[29] Two other possible solutions are mentioned. First, that the claim to the thing by an owner, who has recovered value from an intermediate party, be barred; secondly, that the right to recover the thing should be retained but made conditional upon the handing over to a *bona fide* party in possession what was recovered from a *mala fide* intermediate party. It seems that there are drawbacks to both these possibilities: in the first case the change would involve a major departure from principle; the second would seem to be no more than an *ad hoc* device based upon the presupposition that the owner would be unjustifiably enriched.

[30] The Scot. Law Com., *loc. cit.*, while indicating a preference for this solution, note their reservation in that its effect would be to set off a money payment against a claim for a specific *res*. The answer to this would appear to be that as a matter of justice it should be open to a *bona fide* possessor, required to restore a thing to its true owner, to raise the issue of the possible unjustifiable enrichment of the owner.

Problem of act of specification or consumption

In the case of a possessor who *mala fide* disposes of another's thing, **10.10** the difficulty is not in finding justification for the recognition of a right to recover value but rather in determining an appropriate basis for liability.[31] Where a party uses another's property, and in doing so makes recovery *in specie* impossible, the issue of the owner's remedy is a matter of some controversy.[32]

In principle the problem is the same whether one is concerned with specification or consumption. Specification is a kind of consumption involving the creation of a new thing in an act of making which ends the separate existence of the constituent elements.[33] Both specification and consumption involve the problem of the possible termination of the owner's right of ownership, consequent upon the termination of the existence of the thing, and the issue as to what rights—necessarily of a personal nature—remain available to the deprived owner.

The better view is that *specificatio*—being a matter of proprietary consequence—may occur even if the specificator is in bad faith.[34] In the case of consumption it is clear that the owner loses his interest in the thing consumed whether the consuming party is in good or bad faith. However, from the point of view of rights remaining available to a deprived owner, the question whether the specificator or consumer acted in good or bad faith is important.

In the cases of both *specificatio* and consumption there will be potential liability for what would amount to a *mala fide* act of disposition.[35] Where, however, the maker of a *res nova* acts in good faith the better view, as a matter of principle, is that no proprietary remedy is open to the owner; but, of course, relief may be available if the remedy of recompense can be applied to the circumstances.[36] It would appear that the cases of both *bona fide* specification and *bona fide* consumption are covered by the opinion of Lord Low in *International Banking Corporation* v. *Ferguson, Shaw, & Sons*[37]:

> "If, therefore, the possessor, in good faith, exercises his power as possessor in such a way that it is no longer possible for him to

---

[31] See above, para. 10.7.

[32] See Scot. Law Com., Memo. No. 31, *Corporeal Moveables: Remedies*, paras. 12–17.

[33] See above, para. 4.01.

[34] See above, para. 4.04.

[35] See *Faulds* v. *Townsend* (1861) 23 D. 437 *per* the Lord Ordinary (Ardmillan) at p. 439.

[36] This is a matter of unjustified enrichment rather than property; however, one may note that the Scottish Law Commission favoured the solution of recompense: "the *bona fide* specificator who uses another's materials in manufacturing a new species should be liable only on principles of recompense, and only to the extent that he is *lucratus*." See Memorandum No. 31, *Corporeal Moveables: Remedies*, para. 17; this solution, the Commission noted (para. 16), was in accordance with the dictum of Lord Ardmillan in *Faulds* v. *Townsend* (1861) 23 D. 437 at p. 439: see above, para. 10.08, n. 22.

[37] 1910 S.C. 182 at p. 191.

restore the goods to the true owner, the latter has no claim for the value, but only for any profits which the possessor may have made. It is admitted that that would be the result if the possessor, in good faith, sold or otherwise transferred the article *in forma specifica* to a third party, and it makes no difference if the impossibility of restoring arises from the way in which the possessor has, in good faith, dealt with the article still in his possession. The right of the true owner (apart from the question of profits, which depends upon a different principle), is limited to a demand for restitution of the goods themselves, and if the person against whom the demand is made has, in the *bona fide* exercise of his right as possessor, put it out of his power to restore the goods, the owner has no claim against him."

It may be noted that in *Oliver & Boyd* v. *Marr Typefounding Co. Ltd.*,[38] a previous Outer House decision, Lord Stormonth Darling did not accept the effect of "the conversion of the article into another shape, by the act of the defenders" as an act "terminating their possession, and consequently their obligation to restore." In this case stolen type had been melted down and made into new type. The view taken was that a logical extension of Stair's[39] recognition of the owner's right to recover value from the *mala fide* seller as "a variety or extension of restitution" would cover the case of specification. "Surely, if this be so, when possession has been absolutely transferred to another, the duty of restitution may very well cover the case of possession being retained, though in an altered shape." It does seem incontrovertible that in so far as a right to recover value, on the basis of a duty to make restitution, applies in the case of *mala fide* disposition,[40] it should also be available against a possessor who, acting in bad faith, consumes the thing, whether absolutely or in the process of creating a new item.

General position of defences to claim for restitution

10.11   The right to recover the thing or its value, being a right of ownership, may be challenged on the basis that the claimant is no longer owner. While conceding that the pursuer was formerly owner, the defender may contend that this is no longer the case because the right of ownership has passed to him. Clearly, it is open to the defender to allege, in answer to the pursuer's claim, that he in fact received transfer of the thing directly from the pursuer. More importantly, however, a defender may deny the claimant's alleged right on the basis that he—the defender—acquired a right effective against the

---

[38] (1901) 9 S.L.T. 170 at p. 171.
[39] 1.vii.2.
[40] See above, para. 10.7.

pursuer on one of the various bases under which property is taken to pass against the owner even though there was no act of transfer on his part.

In that the defender founds upon circumstances on the basis of which it is contended that ownership passed to him in the absence of an act of transfer by the owner, these cases may amount to exceptions to the *nemo dat quod non habet* rule. The recognition of the passing of ownership, without any positive act of transfer from the owner, may also be seen as an exception to the owner's right to restitution (or vindication) in that proof that ownership has passed, on one or other of these bases, would be grounds for the denial of a right to restitution. These matters will be considered in this context.[41]

We are here concerned with the defences to restitution which do not go to the fundamental issue of the claimant's right of ownership in the above sense. Besides the obvious possibilities of defences on the facts—for instance, that the defender, is no longer in possession, and that he parted with the the thing *bona fide* believing in his right to do so—the defences of turpitude and prescription are applicable in this more limited sense.

Turpitude

Stair[42] makes clear that in the case of "things received *ex turpi causa*, **10.12** if both parties be *in culpa, potior est conditio possidentis*; so there is no restitution."[43] The point for present purposes is that in the case of property obtained on the basis of a *causa* void for illegality, the position of the possessor is stronger because the law does not sanction the recovery of property in so far as this would involve reliance upon an illegal act.[44] The general test is whether the pursuer must rely upon an illegal act to establish his case. It is, of course, significant that, by reason of the presumption in favour of the possessor,[45] the pursuer must prove the circumstances under which he parted with the thing; in so far as these circumstances amount to an illegal act recovery will be barred.

---

[41] See below, para. 10.15.

[42] I.vii.8.

[43] *Cf.* Erskine, III.i.10: "What is given *ob turpem causam* must be restored if the turpitude was in the receiver, and not in the giver, whether the cause of giving was performed or not."

[44] But the illegality must impinge upon the right relied upon. Arguably the act of acquisition or conveyance must be illicit; see *Burns* v. *Forbes and Boyd*, 1807 Hume 694 at p. 695. Although this issue was not raised in *Scott* v. *Everitt* (1853) 15 D. 288, the facts illustrate the scope for the recognition of a distinction between an illegal act actually affecting a proprietary right and illegality proximate to the right but not affecting it. In *Scott*, the Second Division decided that an illegal possessor of game was entitled to claim restitution from a procurator fiscal who had seized the game because, as Lord Cockburn noted at p. 293, the statute which imposed a fine for unlawful possession of game "does not say that the game is not the property of that party, or that any one may seize and retain it." See above, para. 2.03, n. 26.

[45] See above, para. 1.12.

The effect of the maxim *in turpi causa melior est conditio possidentis* is that an act otherwise invalid and unenforceable is given partial effect because any interference with the *status quo* would involve the recognition of an illegal transaction.[46]

If the illegal purpose relates to a temporary right—such as hire—then: "it is conceived that the illegality of the purpose for which the temporary possession of the property was given would not prevent the owner from recovering it when the temporary title had expired."[47]

Prescription

10.13   Although it is open to conjecture whether there is a common law rule providing for the acquisition of moveable property by prescription[48] there does appear to be a relevant rule of negative prescription in modern law. Section 8 of the Prescription and Limitation Scotland Act 1973[49] provides that if an exercisable or enforceable right relating to heritable or moveable property subsists for a continuous period of 20 years unexercised or unenforced, and without any relevant claim in relation to it having been made, then, upon the expiry of that period, the right is extinguished. It would appear from Schedule 3, listing imprescriptible rights, that the reference to rights in section 8 covers the right of ownership in moveable property.[50] This conclusion follows from the fact that the right to recover stolen property "from the person by whom it was stolen or from any person privy to the stealing thereof"[51] is excluded as imprescriptible. It would seem that this regulation of the effect of the defect of theft would only occur in the context of a rule providing for the extinctive prescription of the owner's vindicatory right.

There is, however, a possible difficulty with the above interpretation in that the Act makes express provision for the prescription of the obligation of restitution in five years. Indeed, the Scottish Law Commission[52] state that a claim to delivery of a corporeal moveable

---

[46] See the answers in *A* v. *B*, 21 May 1816, F.C. which the court appears to have accepted: "Hence a distinction arises, as to the validity of such an obligation, between the case where performance has not taken place upon it, and the case where it has. In the former case, the pursuer insisting for implement cannot be heard, neither can he be heard in the latter case insisting to be restored against performance, as in both cases he must libel his own turpitude."

[47] Gloag, *Contract*, pp. 586–587.

[48] See above, paras. 7.02–7.03.

[49] See generally, Walker, *The Law of Prescription and Limitation of Actions in Scotland*.

[50] Sched. 3(*a*) lists "any real right of ownership in land" as imprescriptible leaving a real right of ownership in moveable property covered by s.8.

[51] Sched. 3(*g*). For the purposes of the legislation theft does not produce a *vitium reale*; accordingly, a subsequent party, innocent of the theft, may, in appropriate circumstances, resort to s.8 and defeat the claim of an owner originally deprived by theft.

[52] Memo. No. 30, *Corporeal Moveables: Usucapio, or Acquisitive Prescription*, para. 3.

prescribes in this shorter period, and this is seen as a departure from the prior rule: "the obligation of restitution, which in practice justifies a conclusion for delivery of corporeal moveables, now prescribes in 5 years instead of 20 as formerly." The basis of this conclusion is paragraph 1(*b*) of Schedule 1 providing for the application of the five-year period of extinctive prescription under section 6 "to any obligation based on redress of unjustified enrichment, including without prejudice to that generality any obligation of restitution, repetition or recompense."[53] It should be noted that the system of the Act—provided for in section 8(2)—is that the shorter period of prescription applying to an obligation under section 6 in effect displaces a potentially longer period under section 8, at least in so far as the right concerned falls within section 6 "as being a right correlative to an obligation" to which section 6 applies.

The difficulty is that while the express reference to restitution—in Schedule 1 applying to section 6—points to the five-year period, a reading of section 8 and its concomitant Schedule 3 suggests that the real right of ownership in moveable property is subject to the 20-year period of extinctive prescription. It is submitted that the better view is that the Prescription and Limitation (Scotland) Act 1973 gives effect to the difference between real and personal rights. While the real right of ownership is subject to the 20-year prescriptive period the obligation of restitution—as a matter of unjustified enrichment—prescribes in five years. This would be consistent with the common law distinction alluded to above.[54]

Moreover, it is submitted that the owner's real right to recover his thing from whomsoever has possession is not a right—as envisaged in section 8(2)—correlative to the obligation to make restitution provided for in section 6 read with Schedule 1, paragraph 1(*b*). So to hold would amount to contending that the lesser encompasses the greater because the effect of this interpretation is to rank equally a mere obligation or personal right, prevailing against a particular party, and a proprietary or real right, prevailing against the whole world. Rather, the correlative of the obligation of restitution referred to is a personal right to recover compensation on the basis of unjustified enrichment.[55]

As shown above,[56] the word "restitution" has two distinct spheres of operation. It is a term of art of both unjustified enrichment—as a

---

[53] It seems that the intention of the legislature, in Sched. 1(*b*) under s.6, was to make the five-year period of prescription applicable to all obligations based on unjustified enrichment. This was consistent with the approach advocated by the Scot. Law Com. in a report which preceded the Prescription and Limitation (Scotland) Act 1973; see Scot. Law Com. No. 15, *Reform of the Law Relating to Prescription and Limitation of Actions* (1970), para. 63: "We recommend that the new short prescription should apply to all obligations based upon unjustified enrichment."

[54] See above, para. 10.07, n. 11.

[55] See above, para. 10.07.

[56] *Ibid.*

matter of obligation, beyond the scope of this book—and of property. It is used in Schedule 1 to section 6 of the Prescription and Limitation (Scotland) Act 1973 to mean unjustified enrichment.

Warrant to search as concomitant of decree for delivery

10.14   Stair[57] describes an action "of exhibition and delivery" arising from the right to restitution. An action for delivery must be available to give effect to the owner's right to restitution and, as Stair[58] puts it: "The exhibition is but preparatory to the delivery, that thereby the thing in question may be known to the parties, judge and witnesses."[59]

In modern law the court has power to grant a warrant to search for moveable property as an adjunct to a crave for delivery and, of course, the basis of the claim could be restitution.[60] In *United Dominions Trust (Commercial) Ltd.* v. *Hayes*[61] it was held incompetent for the sheriff court to grant warrant to search at the same time as granting decree in an action for delivery, but this decision was not followed in *Merchants Facilities (Glasgow) Ltd.* v. *Keenan.*[62] In the latter decision the view taken was that it was well established for the sheriff court to entertain, as part of an action for delivery of goods, a crave to grant warrant to

> "officers of Court to search such premises in the occupancy or tenancy of the defender and to take possession of and deliver to the pursuers the said articles, and for the purpose of carrying the warrant into lawful execution, to grant warrant to officers of Court to open, if necessary, shut and lockfast places."[63]

EXCEPTIONS TO OWNER'S RIGHT TO RESTITUTION

Relevance of principles of derivative acquisition

10.15   There are certain circumstances in which the law recognises the passing of ownership in the absence of any positive act of transfer on the part of the owner. These cases are exceptions to the basic principle of derivative acquisition to the effect that no party, other than the owner, can give a good title—*nemo plus juris ad alium transferre potest quam ipse habet*, or simply *nemo dat quod non habet.*[64]

---

[57] I.vii.14.

[58] *Ibid.*

[59] Stair (I.vii.14) goes on to say "*majori inest minus*, he that hath right to crave delivery hath much more right to crave the production, or the inspection." The right of exhibition is merely a facilitating right which must, on the basis of the greater including the lesser, be open to an owner who has a right to claim restitution.

[60] See Graham Stewart, *Diligence*, pp. 274–275.

[61] 1966 S.L.T.(Sh.Ct.) 101.

[62] 1967 S.L.T.(Sh.Ct.) 65.

[63] at p. 65.

[64] See above, paras. 8.03–8.04.

As indicated,[65] the recognition of the passing of ownership, without any act of transfer on the part of the owner, amounts to an exception to the owner's right of recovery because proof that ownership has passed, on one or other of the bases in question, would be grounds for the denial of a right to vindicate the thing concerned.

A feature of the various situations in which the right to recover moveables may be denied in this manner is that the party entitled to rely upon an exception to the general principle is normally one who has obtained the thing in good faith and for value. However, this said, it must be emphasised that there is no general basis in terms of which the right of a *bona fide* possessor is elevated above that of the owner. The common law tendency is the other way; one may note the pervasive quality of the *vitium reale* of theft[66]—effectively protecting the owner of stolen goods from being deprived of his interest through acquisition by a subsequent *bona fide* party—and the absence of any doctrine of market overt.[67] Even the protection accorded a *bona fide* acquirer under the Sale of Goods Act 1979 is by way of a number of special exceptions to the acknowledged foundation principle that: "where goods are sold by a person who is not their owner, and who does not sell them under the authority or with the consent of the owner, the buyer acquires no better title to the goods than the seller had."[68]

The only general form of protection of an acquirer in good faith is through the rebuttable presumption that the possessor of a moveable thing is owner.[69] But, of course, the effect of this is no more than to provide a measure of protection for the *status quo* of possession. An owner who proves his title and demonstrates that he lost or parted with possession in circumstances inconsistent with an intention to convey ownership will overcome the presumption.

The particular common law and statutory provisions which have potential effect upon the right to vindicate may now be considered.

The common law protection of a bona fide acquirer for value

Stair,[70] in the context of a general discussion of defences, refers to **10.16** the *exceptio doli*, available where "the pursuer's title and right was obtained by fraud." But, Stair[71] notes, in respect of moveables:

---

[65] See above, para. 10.11.

[66] See Stair, II.xii.10: "Things stolen, whereunto, for utility's sake, to repress that frequent vice, the law hath stated an inherent and real vitiosity, that passeth with the thing stolen to all singular successors; and therefore though such things be acquired by a just title, though for a cause onerous, and an equivalent price, and by continuation of possession *bona fide*; yet prescription taketh no effect because of the inherent vitiosity."

[67] *Todd* v. *Armour* (1882) 9 R. 901 *per* Lord Craighill at p. 908: "If there is a *vitium reale* by the law of Scotland, a sale in open market, has no effect in destroying the right of the real owner." See also s.22(2) of the Sale of Goods Act 1979.

[68] s.21(1).

[69] See above, para. 1.12.

[70] IV.xl.21.

[71] *Ibid.*

"purchasers are not quarrellable upon the fraud of their authors, if they did purchase for an onerous equivalent cause. The reason is, because moveables must have a current course of traffic, and the buyer is not to consider how the seller purchased, unless it were by theft or violence which the law accounts as *labes reales*, following the subject to all successors, otherwise there would be the greatest encouragement to theft and robbery."

Reading this passage alone, the following points emerge: (1) the accepted premise is the basic principle of property that by derivative process no party can give a better title than he has[72]; (2) in relation to moveables, however, an exception applies to the purchaser in good faith, who acquires a good title regardless of the position of his transferor; (3) the exception protecting a *bona fide* purchaser does not apply where the thing concerned was stolen or removed by violence from the true owner. But did Stair intend to write a prescription for the general protection of the *bona fide* purchaser of a moveable, including the circumstances of acquisition *a non domino*, or was his treatment limited to the case of an owner parting with property under some form of fraudulent inducement?

Bell, in his *Commentaries*,[73] reads Stair's passage as authority for the general protection of an innocent purchaser: "As possession presumes property in moveables, the general rule is, that the purchaser of moveables at market or otherwise in *bona fide*, acquires the right to them, although they may have been sold by one who is not the owner." John McLaren, later Lord McLaren, as editor of Bell's *Commentaries* regards this statement as too wide and an inaccurate rendering of its source. Stair's passage, according to McLaren, "treats solely of right and title acquired by *fraud* from the true owner, not of purchase *a non domino*."[74]

Taking Stair's passage in isolation, it is possible to understand Bell's interpretation; Stair, indeed, does seem to be saying that the instance of fraud, instrumental in the owner's having parted with his thing, is not a defect which should be allowed to prejudice the position of a subsequent *bona fide* acquirer for value. However, significantly, the apparently overriding scope of this protection seems to be emphasised by the statement that only the defect of deprivation by theft would follow the thing to all successors. The rationale of "a current course of traffic for moveables" is policy-based and its logical application is in the form of the recognition of a *bona fide* purchaser's general protection, failing only where the greater policy interest in protecting

---

[72] See above, para. 8.04.

[73] I, 305.

[74] *Idem*, n. 1. One may note that Scot. Law Comm., Memo. No. 27, *Protection of the Onerous Bona Fide Acquirer of Another's Property*, para. 15, draws attention to the view that Bell's statement goes too far.

an owner against criminal deprivation prevails. Acquisition *a non domino* would not, however, be protected by the interpretation which limits Stair's rule to the circumstances of an owner's having parted with his thing through fraud. From the point of view of the principles governing the passing of property, a different result is justified depending upon whether the owner participated in an act of transfer or was subject to involuntary dispossession,[75] but the point of the general policy protection of a *bona fide* acquirer is that it avoids the uncertainty of a possible defect in title.

Another passage casts doubt upon whether, in the text quoted above, Stair intended a general rule of the "*mobilia non habent sequelam*" type providing that, in principle, moveable goods cannot be followed.[76] Having noted that the efficacy of the possession of moveables justifies a presumption of disposition by the owner, Stair[77] goes on to show that the possessor's protection is only through a presumption—rebuttable by an owner able to show that acquisition was in fact *a non domino*:

"so that it will not be sufficient to any claiming right to moveable goods, against the lawful possessor, to allege he had a good title to these goods, and possession of them, but he must condescend, *quomodo desiit possidere*, as by spuilzie, stealth etc., or that he gave them only in grazing and custody, and continued to use acts of property."[78]

Bell, in his *Principles*, does not maintain the position taken in his *Commentaries* on this issue. In the former[79]—a later work—one finds reference to a rebuttable presumption arising from possession rather than an infrangible rule based upon commercial policy.

The common law in effect requires the claimant to ownership against a *bona fide* possessor to rebut a presumption that he parted with the thing intending to transfer title. Moreover, as Stair[80] makes clear, at this stage it is too late to invoke, against an innocent party, an act of fraud by the party to whom transfer was first given:

---

[75] From this point of view the critical difference is that in the first case the owner intended to transfer ownership to the fraudulent party, whereas of course, in the second case, he parted with the moveable concerned on a basis inconsistent with the transfer of ownership. See above, para. 8.08.

[76] See Carey Miller, *The Acquisition and Protection of Ownership*, p. 263.

[77] III.ii.7: "In moveables possession is of such efficacy, that it doth not only consummate the disposition thereof, but thereupon the disposition is presumed without the necessity to prove the same." See also Erskine, II.i.24: "And, indeed, commerce could not have a free course if it behoved the possessors of moveables, which often pass from hand to hand without either witnesses or writing, to prove the titles of their possession."

[78] III.ii.7.

[79] § 1314.

[80] IV.xl.22.

"it is a relevant reply . . . that it is a purchase of moveables, by commerce, for an equivalent cause: to which the relevant duplies are, that the defender was partaker of the fraud, and at least knew of it before he purchased; or that a decreet was pronounced upon the fraud before his acquisition."

The better view, it would appear, is that there is no overriding policy-based general preference for the innocent acquirer for value at common law. One may note the comment of the Scottish Law Commission[81]:

"The main protection for the *bona fide* onerous acquirer in possession by the common law is the presumption of ownership which arises from possession. Since at common law a buyer acquired a real right only when possession was transferred to him, the presumption was usually efficacious,[82] and favoured by the law in the interests of commerce."

The various particular exceptions to the principle *nemo dat quod non habet*, effecting the scope of the right of restitution, may now be considered. These involve a combination of common law principles and statutory provisions, the latter emanating from the factors and sale of goods legislation. The exceptions fall into three groups: reducible title, personal bar, and purchase from an ostensible owner.

Reducible title at common law

10.17   Stair[83] recognised that a buyer in good faith obtains a good title where, although, on account of fraud, the owner has the right to avoid the consequences of the handing over of a thing, he fails to do so before acquisition by an innocent subsequent party. As indicated,[84] Stair[85] states that, in the case of moveables, purchasers "for an onerous

---

[81] Memo. No. 27, *Corporeal Moveables: Protection of the Onerous Bona Fide Acquirer of Another's Property*, para. 12.

[82] The point here is that the fact of possession in a particular party will tend to mean that he has received delivery and, accordingly, has become owner. The statement that the presumption is usually efficacious does not mean that the owner's proprietary right is usually subject to the interest of a *bona fide* possessor who has given value by reason of the fact that, at common law, the transmission of the right of ownership is by the transfer of possession. Any such meaning would be incompatible with the emphasis on the protection of the right of ownership; in particular, the fact that a party seeking to rebut the presumption arising from possession need go no further than establish the basis of his claim to ownership and that he gave up or lost possession in circumstances inconsistent with an intention to transfer his right. What the claimant to ownership must prove is all within the circumstances of his own relationship with the thing prior to its coming into the hands of the defender and, given this, it is clear that the presumption could not be "usually efficacious" in any sense of a tendency to prefer the *bona fide* possessor.

[83] IV.xl.21, 22.

[84] See above, para. 10.16.

[85] IV.xl.21.

equivalent cause" are not vulnerable on account of the fact of a merely fraudulent act of acquisition by the party from whom the thing was purchased. Dealing with the case of a purchaser who claims a thing but is met by an allegation of fraud, Stair[86] notes that a relevant reply is that it was a purchase of moveables "by commerce, for an equivalent cause." This defence will prevail unless it can shown that the party relying upon it "was partaker of the fraud, and at least knew of it before he purchased; or that a decreet was pronounced upon the fraud before his acquisition."[87]

This approach would seem to be consistent with an abstract theory of the transfer of ownership[88] in that an intention to pass ownership, albeit one induced by fraud, will be effective to the extent that the right obtained on the basis of a voidable *causa* may be transmitted to an innocent third party whose position will be unimpeachable.

Bell[89] explains the difference between the presence and the absence of an intention to pass ownership in cases of defective consent with reference to the rights of creditors of the transferee.

"Although, lawful consent and actual delivery once concurring, the real right to the subject sold is vested in the purchaser, and the seller has no privilege of restitution as a resource against the bankruptcy of the buyer, yet where the consent is only apparent, there is no effectual transference; but the seller is entitled to restitution against the creditors of the buyer. Restitution will therefore be given, not only against the buyer, but even against purchasers from him, where the seller is incapable of full and legal consent; or where the sale has proceeded from such fear and compulsion as in law annuls and makes it void. Where the sale has been induced by fraud, the seller is to be considered as having given his consent; but in consequence of the deceit, that consent is held to be revocable to the effect of grounding an action for reduction and restitution, which, though not available against purchasers *bona fide*, is good against the buyer and his general creditors."

It is questionable, from a point of view of dogmatic accuracy, whether the case of a voidable title should be seen as an exception to the owner's right to recover his property. The better view may well be that the result in this case is simply a matter of the proper application of the principles of derivative acquisition. On this basis, and given that one is concerned with a voidable rather than a void act of disposition,

---

[86] IV.xl.22.
[87] *Ibid.*
[88] See above, para. 8.08.
[89] *Comm.*, I, 261.

the issue is whether ownership has passed to the innocent party or whether this consequence was prevented by the claimant to ownership acting timeously to set aside a reducible cause. The issue whether the thing concerned was handed over on the basis of a radical defect[90] or merely one which was reducible[91] must be determined as a matter of contract.[92] This, moreover, is so whether one is proceeding on the basis of the causal or abstract theories.[93] In the case of the causal approach the issue will simply be whether the underlying transaction was void or voidable. Where the analysis is abstract, the issue will be whether the notional "agreement" inferred from the circumstances under which the thing was handed over—including, of course, appropriate inferences drawn from the circumstances of the parties' antecedent contract—is fundamentally defective and, accordingly, void or affected only to the extent of being voidable and, therefore, effective pending reduction.[94]

The logical consequence that in the case of a merely voidable title a third party acquires where he receives transfer prior to any challenge to the basis of his transferor's right is recognised in the case law. The fundamental point is that the acquisition of the right of ownership puts the acquirer in a position to transfer title in the thing to a third party.[95] As Lord McLaren observed in *Morrisson* v. *Robertson*,[96] although the claimant

> "might have had an action for reducing the sale, yet if in the meantime the property of the cows had passed by lawful subsale

---

[90] The *vitium reale* of theft is a defect which permeates all subsequent transactions; see Stair, II.xii.10 (see above, para. 10.15, n. 66), IV.xl.21. Incapacity of the transferor is also a radical defect which would affect the handing over and all subsequent transfers. See Scot. Law Comm., Memo. No. 27, *Corporeal Moveables: Protection of the Onerous Bona Fide Acquirer of Another's Property*, para. 17.

[91] Fraud and error are the most usual causes of defective consent on the basis of which the tainted act of handing over the thing may be reduced. The better view is that force and fear also give rise to no more than a right on the part of the transferor to reduce the act of transfer to the wrongful transferee. See Scot. Law Comm., Memo. No. 27, *Corporeal Moveables: Protection of the Onerous Bona Fide Acquirer of Another's Property*, paras. 17–19.

[92] See, *e.g.* Gloag, *Contract*, pp. 488–489, 492.

[93] See above, para. 8.06.

[94] The primary significance of the abstract approach is that it seeks to establish, as an independent fact, the mutual intention of the parties concerning the passing of ownership. The causal approach controls this issue by reference to the parties' underlying contract. While defects of consent may be applicable to the "agreement" as to the passing of ownership in the usual way, circumstances intervening between the underlying contract and delivery may support a conclusion that, even though the underlying contract was defective, the parties' "agreement" to pass ownership is unimpeachable. Moreover, in the obvious case where one party intended sale and the other understood the transaction to be gift, ownership will pass on the basis of the mutual intention to that effect despite the absence of an underlying contract. The abstract approach, accordingly, allows somewhat greater scope for the passing of ownership and, as a result, gives more extensive protection to subsequent parties who are less likely to be affected by the defective state of the initial parties' underlying contract.

[95] See generally, *Bryce* v. *Ehrmann* (1905) 7 F. 5.

[96] 1908 S.C. 332 at p. 336.

to a third person, then the right of that third person . . . would be indefeasible. Having acquired the property by purchase from someone who had a lawful title, he would have had a good defence to an action of this nature."[97]

The position is comprehensively dealt with in a dictum of Lord Kinnear in the case of *Price & Pierce Ltd.* v. *Bank of Scotland*[98]:

"It is well settled that a contract induced by fraud is not void, but voidable at the option of the party defrauded. In other words it is valid until it is rescinded.[99] It follows that when third parties have acquired rights in good faith and for value, these rights are indefeasible. Buchanan & French, therefore, at the time of the transaction with the other claimants . . . had acquired the goods under a valid contract of sale, and until the defrauded seller had intimated his intention to rescind, they had a good and valid title to sell or pledge, and to give a valid title to a purchaser or to a pledgee—titles which would remain valid although their own title was subject to rescission, provided always the persons so dealing with them were ignorant of the fraud and gave value for the goods."

What are the bases of the requirements of good faith and onerosity given that, in principle, a party with a valid, if voidable, title should be in a position to transfer ownership, or some lesser real right, regardless? The essential of good faith can be more easily explained than the onerosity requirement.

Where the party receiving the thing from a transferee who obtained through fraud is in bad faith—at any rate, to the extent that he is aware that his transferor's title is reducible—his intention to acquire ownership is tainted by his knowledge of the fraud. In these circumstances he acquires subject to the defect affecting his transferor and, accordingly, is also vulnerable to reduction at the instance of the deprived owner. It would appear that the requirement of good faith is compatible with the abstract system of the transfer of ownership,[1] in

---

[97] See also the dictum of Lord Kinnear at p. 338: "The principle is that a contract obtained by fraud is not void but voidable; and since it follows that it is valid until it is rescinded, the rescission may come too late if in the meantime third persons have acquired rights in good faith and for value." This statement was quoted with approval by Lord President Clyde in *Macleod* v. *Kerr*, 1965 S.C. 253 at p. 256; see also Smith, "Error and transfer of title," 1967 S.L.T. (News) 206.

[98] 1910 S.C. 1095 at pp. 1106–1107. This decision was affirmed in 1912 S.C.(H.L.) 19. See also *A. W. Gamage Ltd.* v. *Charlesworth's Tr.*, 1910 S.C. 257 *per* Lord Kinnear at p. 266.

[99] On what is required to avoid a voidable contract and prevent property passing to a *bona fide* subsequent party, see also below, para. 10.18.

[1] See above, n. 94.

that the "agreement" on the basis of which the thing concerned is delivered and received is affected by the transferee's knowledge of the initial act of fraud and, on this basis, the subsequent act of transfer is also reducible.

The requirement of onerosity, it is submitted, can only be satisfactorily explained as a matter of policy. In principle, provided the acquiring transferee is in good faith, it should be irrelevant whether he gives value or not. If the transferor is in a position to pass ownership, this should follow regardless as to whether the transferee gives value. However, as a matter of policy, it is more difficult to justify the resulting situation in which an owner is deprived through the transfer of property to a gratuitous party, as distinct from one who has given value.

Of course, it may well be that a *bona fide* onerous third party does not acquire from a fraudulent party because, in the circumstances, there has been no transmission of the right to the latter from the true owner. In principle, at common law, if an owner delivered property on the basis of a contract in terms of which the transfer of ownership to the purchaser was suspended, there could have been no question of acquisition by a third party.[2] Under the Sale of Goods Act 1979 the answer may be otherwise,[3] but the point is that the principles of derivative acquisition determine the outcome of the competing claims of an owner, deprived of possession by fraud, and a subsequent *bona fide* acquirer. Clearly, where the owner inserted a condition suspending the passing of ownership, it could hardly be said that he intended ownership to pass and in these circumstances the fraudulent party would simply not acquire a proprietary right and, accordingly, could not transmit ownership to a third party.[4] Similarly, where the transaction involving a fraudulent act was merely intended to transfer possession, without ownership passing, there can be no question of the transmission of title to a third party.

Reducible title under the Sale of Goods Act 1979

10.18   Section 23 of the Sale of Goods Act 1979 protects a *bona fide* acquirer against an owner in a position to reduce a title obtained in circumstances amounting to defective consent.

> "When the seller of goods has a voidable title to them, but his title has not been avoided at the time of the sale, the buyer acquires a good title to the goods, provided he buys them in good faith and without notice of the seller's defect of title."[5]

---

[2] See *Murdoch & Co. Ltd.* v. *Greig* (1889) 16 R. 396 at pp. 401–402.

[3] See below, para. 10.21.

[4] See *Murdoch & Co. Ltd.* v. *Greig*, above, at pp. 402–403.

[5] s.61(3) provides that "[a] thing is deemed to be done in good faith within the meaning of this Act when it is in fact done honestly, whether it is done negligently or not." This in effect precludes the argument that *mala fides* can be imputed to a subsequent purchaser on the basis that, in the circumstances, he acted unreasonably in accepting that his seller had the right to transfer ownership.

The law of contract identifies the cases of voidable title[6] providing for the availability of reduction, but a controversial issue is the problem of what is envisaged by the requirement that "his title has not been avoided at the time of the sale." The issue will arise where A (or his trustee on sequestration[7]) claims ownership in goods on the basis that B's right was rescinded prior to transmission of title in the goods from B to C. Given that it is accepted that C bought in good faith it will be for A to show that at the time of sale from B to C, he had already acted to reduce his transfer to B. But what facts must A prove to show that B's title had been avoided at the time of the sale by B to C?

In *A. W. Gamage Ltd.* v. *Charlesworth's Tr.*[8] Lord Johnston noted a difference between rescission effective only between the immediate parties and with regard to the interests of third parties. "The remedy of rescission and recovery of the property is an equitable remedy, and, though as between seller and buyer a *brevi manu* operation may be effectual, it requires, where other interests are concerned, the inter-position of the Court." On this basis, given that section 23 is specifically concerned with the protection of the interests of third parties, one would expect the conclusion to be that a decree of court was required. The section does speak of the buyer's title not having been avoided in a manner which suggests that the completion of an act of avoidance is contemplated. Moreover, section 23 is concerned with the situation in which title has passed, and the fact that the circum-stances under which title was acquired makes it voidable at the instance of the transferor does not detract from its efficacy pending reduction. To this extent a voidable title is not distinguishable from an unimpeachable title. In these circumstances, as a matter of principle, it is hardly conceivable that title could be restored to the first party ("A" above) on any basis other than by way of judicial act. This approach would seem, also, to be consistent with the apparent policy-based purpose of section 23 to protect the position of an onerous *bona fide* third party.

In *MacLeod* v. *Kerr*[9] the First Division rejected the contention that the voidable title to a car had been avoided pending sale and delivery to an innocent party. Lord President Clyde commented as follows:

"the only fact relied upon to justify the argument that there was any rescission of the contract by Mr. Kerr is that on 13th February—the day before the resale—Mr. Kerr informed the police that the cheque with which Galloway had purported to pay

---

[6] See above, para. 10.17, nn. 90, 91 and 92.
[7] Regarding gratuitous alienations and unfair preferences see below nn. 18 and 19.
[8] 1910 S.C. 257 at p. 267.
[9] 1965 S.C. 253.

him for the car had been stolen. There is no suggestion of any
intimation to Galloway, prior to the resale on 14th February, of
any rescission of the contract, far less any suggestion that proceedings were by then initiated by Mr. Kerr against Galloway. By no
stretch of the imagination could we treat an intimation to the
police as of any materiality to found a plea of rescission of the
contract."[10]

The implication of this dictum is that an owner—entitled to rescind
and recover property handed over—must, at very least, give notice to
the party who has obtained title on the basis of defective consent prior
to delivery to an innocent third party.

It may be noted, however, that in the English decision in *Car &
Universal Finance Co. Ltd.* v. *Caldwell*[11] Lord Denning M.R. recognised as effective rescission an intimation to the police and the
Automobile Association that a motor vehicle had been handed over on
the basis of a fraudulent inducement to sell.[12]

The better view would appear to be that in Scots law "avoided" in
section 23 requires, at very least, actual notice to the party who has
acquired a voidable title. One may note the comment of Professor Sir
Thomas Smith[13] concerning the decision in *Car & Universal Finance
Co. Ltd.* v. *Caldwell*[14]:

> "The Scottish courts, construing the same section in *MacLeod* v.
> *Kerr*,[15] have expressly declined to recognise this interpretation of
> avoidance, and it is thought that even notification of rescission to
> the fraudulent party in possession of goods would not bar the
> rights of a *bona fide* purchaser from him."[16]

In practice, of course, it is likely to be difficult for the deprived owner
to give timeous notice to his transferee, because the party who obtains
on the basis of a voidable title frequently acts with fraudulent intent
and will very probably dispose of the thing for value at the earliest
opportunity.[17]

---

[10] at p. 257.
[11] [1965] 1 Q.B. 525 at p. 532.
[12] But see *Newtons of Wembley Ltd.* v. *Williams* [1965] 1 Q.B. 560, in which it was
held that, on the basis of the principle of ostensible ownership in s.25(1) of the Sale of
Goods Act 1979, an innocent third party would acquire title notwithstanding the fact that
the true owner had avoided the voidable title obtained from him by a fraudulent party.
[13] *Property Problems in Sale*, p. 168.
[14] [1965] 1 Q.B. 525.
[15] 1965 S.C. 253.
[16] See also Wilson, "999 for Rescission" (1966) 29 M.L.R. 442.
[17] See Atiyah, *Sale of Goods*, p. 370: "Where the contract is fraudulently induced, it
was generally thought that in practice there was little that the innocent party could do to
defeat a bona fide purchaser."

The policy behind section 23 of the Sale of Goods Act 1979 extends to another situation—also unexceptionable from the point of view of derivative acquisition—where there is a title on the face of it good but potentially open to reduction given certain provisions of the law of bankruptcy. What would otherwise be an unimpeachable act of disposition may, because of the circumstances of the transferor's insolvency, be reducible at the instance of a trustee on bankruptcy or a creditor of the bankrupt estate. The Bankruptcy (Scotland) Act 1985 repealed the Bankruptcy Acts of 1621 and 1696 but left intact the common law rules providing for the reduction of gratuitous alienations and fraudulent (or "undue") preferences. The Act introduced new provisions to govern the question of possible reduction under the two heads[18]; what is significant for present purposes is that both at common law and under the 1985 Act an onerous third party who has acquired in good faith is protected.[19]

Personal bar

In principle, the defence of personal bar may be applicable against **10.19** an owner claiming restitution of a thing on the basis that he allowed, or acquiesced in, a state of affairs which led the defender to conclude, not unreasonably, that the owner intended ownership to pass.[20] When moveable property has been delivered, by a party apparently vested with the right to dispose of it, the plea of personal bar may be available to the transferee as a defence against a vindicatory action by one asserting a right of ownership.[21] In this context personal bar is essentially a defence on the basis that the owner be precluded from denying that his intention that ownership should pass be inferred from the circumstances. One may note the tenor of the general definition of Lord Chancellor Campbell in *Cairncross* v. *Lorimer*[22]:

> "If a man, either by words or by conduct, has intimated that he consents to an act which has been done, and that he will offer no

---

[18] See the Bankruptcy (Scotland) Act 1985, ss.34–36; McBryde, *Bankruptcy*, pp. 157–168. See also Coull, *Bankruptcy in Scotland*, paras. 11.01–11.06.

[19] Regarding gratuitous alienations, see *Hay* v. *Jamison* (1672) Mor. 1009; *Williamson* v. *Sharp* (1851) 14 D. 127; s.34(4)(*b*) of the Bankruptcy (Scotland) Act 1985 and McBryde, *Bankruptcy*, p. 160. Regarding fraudulent preferences see *Drummond* v. *Watson* (1850) 12 D. 604; s.36(5) of the Bankruptcy (Scotland) Act 1985 and McBryde, *Bankruptcy*, pp. 167–168.

[20] See the definition of Lord Chancellor Birkenhead in *Gatty* v. *Maclaine*, 1921 S.C.(H.L.) 1 at p. 7: "Where A has by his words or conduct justified B in believing that a certain state of facts exists, and B has acted upon such belief to his prejudice, A is not permitted to affirm against B that a different state of facts existed at the same time." Lord Justice-Clerk Thomson adopted this dictum in *Dealest Finance Ltd.* v. *Steedman*, 1961 S.L.T. 61.

[21] On the authority of Rankine, *Personal Bar*, pp. 55–57, 225–227, it would appear that although personal bar cannot be the basis of a transfer of title to heritage it may apply to the acquisition of moveable goods.

[22] (1860) 3 Macq. 827 at p. 829.

opposition to it, although it could not have been lawfully done without his consent, and he thereby induces others to do that from which they otherwise might have abstained—he cannot question the legality of the act he had so sanctioned—to the prejudice of those who have so given faith to his words or to the fair inference to be drawn from his conduct."

On the above basis, it is suggested, one may tentatively identify a rôle for personal bar, as a defence against a claim to ownership, by way of an assertion that the right of ownership has in fact passed from claimant to defender in possession. There is, however, no direct authority for this: only possibly persuasive authority in English case law in which the concept of "estoppel" has been applied to a proviso to the Sale of Goods Act 1979.

Section 21 of the Sale of Goods Act states the fundamental tenet of derivative acquisition, that there can be no transfer of ownership in goods by a party who is neither owner nor invested with the owner's authority to convey title. But this iteration of the *nemo dat quod non habet* principle is subject to the proviso: "unless the owner of the goods is by his conduct precluded from denying the seller's authority to sell."

Brown[23] quotes the explanatory dictum of Blackburn J. in *Cole* v. *North Western Bank*[24]:

"If the owner of the goods had so acted as to clothe the seller or pledger with apparent authority to sell or pledge, he was at common law precluded, as against those who were induced *bona fide* to act on the faith of that apparent authority, from denying that he had given such an authority, and the result as to them was the same as if he had really given it."

Brown[25] comments: "In other words, the owner is prevented by estoppel, or, in Scottish phraseology, barred *personali exceptione*, from denying that he had been given authority to sell or pledge."

It is plain, and generally accepted, that the *raison d'être* behind this exception is the doctrine of estoppel. Benjamin,[26] indeed, suggests that the wording of the proviso "may have been intended to render the principle intelligible in Scots law where the specific term 'estoppel' is unknown." Professor Sir Thomas Smith,[27] responding to this, commented as follows:

---

[23] *Sale of Goods*, p. 144.
[24] (1875) L.R. 10 C.P. 354 at p. 363.
[25] *Sale of Goods*, p. 144.
[26] *Benjamin's Sale of Goods*, para. 456.
[27] *Property Problems in Sale*, pp. 162–163.

"In fact, Scots law recognises the principle of 'personal bar' which is the equivalent of 'estoppel'—at least as a rule of evidence barring a party from proving that facts are in truth different from what his conduct led others to suppose. The rule is a *personal* exception barring only a particular party and those claiming through him. If the legislators chose language in the hope of enlightening the Scots, they have sadly failed in that objective, and, so far as I am aware, the Scottish courts have never ruled on the meaning of 'precluded by his conduct.' "

The formulation of the general exception to the *nemo dat quod non habet* principle in section 21 of the Sale of Goods Act does no more than make possible a defence against the claimant owner, available by invoking the circumstances deriving from his conduct, which induced the transferee to believe that the transferor had authority to dispose of the thing.[28] Accordingly, where owner A allowed B to hold the thing and C bought from B, C may have a defence against A's claim to recovery based upon the impression created by A's conduct in the circumstances.[29]

But what would be the position of a subsequent party—D, E or, indeed, Y or Z—whose acquisition could be traced back to the initial sale to C? In an English case[30] Lord Denning M.R. spoke of "proprietary estoppel" and went on to define its incidence and effect:

"There are many cases where the true owner of goods or of land has led another to believe that he is not the owner, or, at any rate, is not claiming an interest therein, or that there is no objection to what the other is doing. In such cases it has been held repeatedly that the owner is not to be allowed to go back on what he has led the other to believe. So much so that his own title to the property, be it land or goods, has been held to be limited or extinguished, and new rights and interests have been created therein."[31]

In principle, if estoppel has proprietary effect, the party in a position to rely upon it should be in a position to transfer title to a third party,

---

[28] Atiyah, *Sale of Goods*, p. 343, points out that the provision "appears to be merely a restatement of the common law doctrine of estoppel." Likewise in Scots law, the exception is no more than an invocation of the common law device of personal bar: see Gow, *Mercantile Law*, pp. 116–117. As Professor Sir Thomas Smith (*Property Problems in Sale*, p. 162) has pointed out, the limited nature of the device means that "the buyer in good faith does not necessarily acquire clear title but only the title of the person who by his conduct is precluded from objecting."

[29] In *Gall* v. *Murdoch* (1821) 1 S. 75, G consigned goods to L as his agent but allowed L to send them on to H on a sale or return basis.

[30] *Moorgate Mercantile* v. *Twitchings* [1975] 3 All E.R. 314 at p. 323.

[31] This decision was reversed by a majority in the House of Lords ([1976] 2 All E.R. 641) but on grounds not relevant to the present issue and without any challenge to Lord Denning's description of proprietary estoppel.

even one aware of the true original situation who would not, himself, have had the option of the "precluded by conduct" defence. In the view of the Scottish Law Commission such a result would be unacceptable given the limited scope of the doctrine of personal bar. Moreover, as the Commission pointed out,[32] it could lead to the protection of a *mala fide* subsequent acquirer.

> "If personal bar is given its normal meaning, it could not create a proprietary right, extinguishing title. Someone fully aware from the outset of a defect in title might eventually acquire from a *bona fide* mediate possessor. Would the original owner be barred *personali exceptione* from reclaiming his property?"[33]

The short answer to this fear would appear to be that a *mala fide* party cannot himself invoke the "precluded by conduct" provision because, if he had known the true facts, he would not be in a position to claim that the owner should be barred from relying on them.[34] Assuming that the claimant can prove his original title, a subsequent party could only rely upon the transmission of a right of ownership from one whose right was founded upon personal bar.[35] But would such a defence in fact be open to an acquirer in bad faith? Not, it would appear, on the basis of the exception to *nemo dat quod non habet* provided for in section 21(1) of the Sale of Goods Act. This proviso is only open to one who can establish a personal justification, from the point of view of the owner's act or omission, for relying upon

---

[32] See Scot. Law Comm., Memo. No. 27, *Corporeal Moveables: Protection of the Onerous Bona Fide Acquirer of Another's Property*, para. 28.

[33] This concern would appear to be about the exceptional case and it is questionable whether it should weigh heavily in determining the system. As a matter of policy, as far as moveable property is concerned, one may well contend that an owner who by conduct creates the impression that he will be bound by an act of disposition by the party holding the goods should be bound not only to the immediate transferee, who relies upon the impression created, but to subsequent parties as well. Arguably, it is inappropriate to speak of a "defect of title" in the context of the owner's acquiescence in the circumstances under which the thing was held and the fact that steps could have been taken to avoid the risk involved in the continuation of the *status quo*.

[34] Rankine, *Personal Bar in Scotland*, p. 234, refers to the good faith of a party taking under a disposition from a mercantile agent as a prerequisite to the owner being barred, under the Factors Acts, from denying authority. This, it is submitted, is simply an instance of the requirement of good faith which necessarily applies to all situations in which a party claims to have been induced to rely upon some apparent state of affairs. One may note the comment of Spencer Bower and Turner, *Estoppel by Representation*, para. 97: "reliance necessarily involves the belief of the representee in the truth of the representation. If the representee does not believe the representation to be true how can he be said to have been induced by it?"

[35] The practical difficulty facing a subsequent party in establishing personal bar between the original owner and a prior party aside, as a matter of theory it should be open to a subsequent party to claim a derivative title in this way and, in principle, the fact of his own knowledge of the true original position as to ownership should be irrelevant.

the seller's authority.[36] What then is the point of the label "proprietary estoppel"?

Another English Court of Appeal case throws some light on this. In *Eastern Distributors Ltd.* v. *Goldring*[37] a subsequent *bona fide* purchaser from the original owner was held estopped from asserting his title against an earlier purchaser from an agent who had apparent authority to sell, on the grounds that the original owner would have been estopped. Devlin J., as he then was, described the operation of section 21(1) as follows:

> "This section expresses the old principle that apparent authority to sell is an exception to the maxim *nemo dat quod non habet*; and it is plain from the wording that if the owner of the goods is precluded from denying authority, the buyer will in fact acquire a better title than the seller."

The learned judge went on to question the accuracy of referring to this principle as an embodiment of the common law of estoppel; in his view it is distinguishable in the "vital respect, that the effect of its application is to transfer a real title and not merely a metaphorical title by estoppel."[38]

In this case the better title accorded the buyer over his seller amounted to a proprietary right in so far as it defeated the subsequent transfer of the vehicle by the true owner to a *bona fide* purchaser. But, of course, this was no more than an instance of a buyer in good faith relying upon his seller's authority, and the owner being precluded by his conduct from denying that he gave authority to sell.

Purchase from an ostensible owner: seller in possession

The exceptions to the principle *nemo dat quod non habet* in favour **10.20** of the purchaser from an ostensible owner—the cases of a party in possession delivering a thing with the apparent right to convey ownership—are based on an extended notion of personal bar,[39] justified from the point of view of the interests of commerce in the protection of *bona fide* purchasers. There are two distinct cases under this head: first, that of the seller who retains possession notwithstanding an earlier sale—hence, "seller in possession"—and secondly, that of the seller who has possession but has in fact not yet obtained title

---

[36] The legislation does not provide for any other possibility and given that the exception is in derogation of the section's founding principle, that a buyer obtains no better title than his seller had, there would not appear to be scope for an extension by interpretation.

[37] [1957] 2 Q.B. 600 at p. 611.

[38] *Ibid.*

[39] See Gow, *Mercantile Law*, p. 113.

from the seller to him—hence "buyer in possession." The second case will be dealt with in the following section. The first case is provided for in section 8 of the Factors Act 1889, extended to Scotland by the Factors (Scotland) Act 1890. The section was reproduced in section 25(1) of the Sale of Goods Act 1893 and repeated in slightly modified form,[40] as section 24 of the Sale of Goods Act 1979.

Section 24 reads as follows:

> "Where a person having sold goods continues or is in possession of the goods, or of the documents of title to the goods, the delivery or transfer by that person, or by a mercantile agent acting for him, of the goods or documents of title under any sale, pledge, or other disposition thereof, to any person receiving the same in good faith and without notice of the previous sale, has the same effect as if the person making the delivery or transfer were expressly authorised by the owner of the goods to make the same."

As the Scottish Law Commission pointed out,[41] prior to the Sale of Goods Act 1893 the situation covered by the then applicable legislation "could not have arisen in the Scots law of sale, since only by tradition would a seller have been divested of his real right." This would, of course, be so on the basis that a seller, continuing in possession, had not divested himself of title but had only given a contractual right to the first buyer and, accordingly, would remain in a position to transfer a real right to a subsequent party by delivery.[42]

The intended meaning of the word "owner," at the end of the section, is an important issue of interpretation. There are two possibilities. First, the ordinary meaning without any link with what is stated earlier in the section. On this basis "a person having sold" would not necessarily be owner and, under the basic system of the Act, would not be in a position to pass ownership by the conclusion of a contract of sale. But a person receiving in good faith would get a good title regardless of the fact that the seller (continuing in possession) was not in a position to pass ownership.[43] This interpretation would amount to an exception to the *nemo dat quod non habet* principle, which would

---

[40] The anomalous result is that slightly different versions of the same text coexist in separate sources. See Atiyah, *Sale of Goods*, p. 371, n. 116.

[41] Memo. No. 27, *Corporeal Moveables: Protection of the Onerous Bona Fide Acquirer of Another's Property*, para. 29.

[42] See Brown, *Sale of Goods*, pp. 158–159.

[43] As Professor Sir Thomas Smith pointed out (*Property Problems in Sale*, p. 166): "As the word 'owner' is not defined, if it is given its ordinary legal meaning the result might be that the seller in possession who had only a defective title to transfer to the original buyer, could confer an unqualified right of ownership by his subsequent wrongful disposition."

appear to be difficult to justify. On what basis could a subsequent buyer acquire from one who could not have given a good title to an earlier buyer?

A second possible meaning of the word "owner" is the buyer from "a person having sold goods" who continues in possession. This interpretation is consistent with the system of the Act whereby ownership passes on the basis of the parties' intention and without any necessary act of delivery.[44] Moreover, the general construction of the section is consistent with the application of the principle of personal bar and, of course, this would only be possible on the basis of the first purchaser being owner.[45] Accordingly, the better view would appear to be that the word "owner" refers to the first buyer, that is to the one who would be owner under the Act on the basis of purchase from the seller/owner.[46]

The latter interpretation received support in the House of Lords, decision in *National Employers Insurance* v *Jones*.[47] Here Lord Goff, in an *obiter dictum*, rejected the proposition that

"when A has sold goods to B1, and B1 allows A to remain in possession of the goods after the sale, a subsequent sale by A to B2 will be effective to divest the title of a person from whom the goods have previously been stolen before they came into the hands of A. [The learned judge continued:] In truth, the whole section proceeds on the assumption that the relevant owner of the goods, who is deemed to have authorised their delivery and transfer, is B1, the person to whom the goods have been sold by A and who has allowed A to remain in possession of them."[48]

English case law has tended towards a restrictive interpretation of this section with regard to the protection of a *bona fide* subsequent

---

[44] See above, para. 9.05.

[45] See Gow, *Mercantile Law*, p. 113: "The foundation of the statutory fiction that the disposition is with the express authority of the true owner is that the circumstances of possession are such as to bar the owner from pleading want of authority. There is no element of personal bar where the possession is taken against the will of the owner and is *ab initio* unlawful."

[46] Supporting this interpretation see Gloag and Henderson, para. 17.21; *Benjamin's Sale of Goods*, para. 519.

[47] [1988] 2 All E.R. 425 at p. 432.

[48] The legislature only intended to give priority to B2 where there was *delivery* to him following a sale or other disposition. In Lord Goff's treatment of the intended scope of s.8 of the Factors Act 1889 (s.24 of the Sale of Goods Act 1979) it seems that this may have been overlooked: "Assuming B1 to have acted in good faith, why should not A, whom I will assume to be the thief, give as good a title to B1 as to B2? Each is relying equally on the possession of A of the goods" (at p. 432). Even if this piece of reasoning is erroneous it is submitted, with respect, that the conclusion arrived at by the learned judge remains valid in that the more plausible interpretation is that "owner" refers to the buyer (B1) from "a person having sold goods" who continues in possession.

purchaser. The approach has been to require a claimant to show that "the seller was in possession as seller, and not in some other capacity."[49] On this basis a third party purchaser would not benefit from section 24 where, for example, the seller held the thing as a hirer from the first buyer. In what would appear to have been an aberrant approach to the section the courts required a claimant to show, not that his seller had an ostensible right to sell, but rather that the basis upon which he actually held was consistent with such a right.[50] However, in *Pacific Motor Auctions Pty. Ltd.* v. *Motor Credits (Hire Finance) Ltd.*[51] the Privy Council, interpreting the counterpart provision of the New South Wales Sale of Goods Act, concluded that the section referred to the circumstances of a continuity of physical possession regardless of the actual basis upon which the seller held.

> "There is therefore the strongest reason for supposing that the words 'continues in possession' were intended to refer to the continuity of physical possession regardless of any private transactions between the seller and the purchaser which might alter the legal title under which the possession was held."[52]

Purchase from an ostensible owner: buyer in possession

10.21   This variation of purchase from a party with an ostensible right to convey title is provided for in section 9 of the Factors Act 1889, extended to Scotland by the Factors (Scotland) Act 1890. The section was reproduced in section 25(2) of the Sale of Goods Act 1893[53] and repeated, in slightly modified form,[54] as section 25(1) of the Sale of Goods Act 1979.

Section 25(1) reads as follows:

> "Where a person having bought or agreed to buy goods obtains, with the consent of the seller, possession of the goods or the documents of title to the goods, the delivery or transfer by that person, or by a mercantile agent acting for him, of the goods or

---

[49] Atiyah, *Sale of Goods*, p. 371 citing, *inter alia, Staffs Motor Guarantee Ltd.* v. *British Wagon Co. Ltd.* [1934] 2 K.B. 305; *Eastern Distributors Ltd.* v. *Goldring* [1957] 2 Q.B. 600.

[50] On this approach a third-party purchaser would only be protected where the seller actually held as seller but, for one reason or another, was not in a position to pass ownership.

[51] [1965] A.C. 867.

[52] at p. 888. See also *Worcester Works Finance Ltd.* v. *Cooden Engineering Co. Ltd.* [1972] 1 Q.B. 210.

[53] For a history of the two parallel provisions from the point of view of their intended interpretation, see *National Employers Insurance* v. *Jones* [1988] 2 All E.R. 425, *per* Lord Goff at pp. 427–433.

[54] See above n. 40.

documents of title, under any sale, pledge, or other disposition thereof, to any person receiving the same in good faith and without notice of any lien or other right of the original seller in respect of the goods, has the same effect as if the person making the delivery or transfer were a mercantile agent in possession of the goods or documents of title with the consent of the owner."

The broad effect of this section is to give priority to one who buys in good faith from a party who holds the thing, or the relevant documents of title, but has in fact not yet obtained title from his seller.[54a]

Subsection 2 of section 25 deals with the exclusion of conditional sale agreements under the Consumer Credit Act 1974 from the ambit of the principal provision in section 25.[55] Section 25(2)(a) of the Sale of Goods Act 1979 provides that the buyer under a conditional sale agreement is to be taken not to be a person who has "bought or agreed to buy goods" for the purposes of section 25(1). Section 25(2)(b) gives the meaning of a "conditional sale agreement" as

"an agreement for the sale of goods which is a consumer credit agreement within the meaning of the Consumer Credit Act 1974 under which the purchase price or part of it is payable by instalments, and the property in the goods is to remain with the seller (notwithstanding that the buyer is to be in possession of the goods) until such conditions as to the payment of instalments or otherwise as may be specified in the agreement are fulfilled."[56]

Accordingly the protection, under section 25(1), of a *bona fide* acquirer of goods from one in possession, against the circumstances of the retention of a right or interest by a party no longer in possession, does not extend to the various forms of credit agreement falling within the category of conditional sale agreements under the Consumer Credit Act 1974—legislation which was intended to provide comprehensive regulation of the debtor/creditor relationship in matters within its scope.

It may be noted that on a strict interpretation a third party acquiring from a hire-purchase[57] possessor would not obtain a good title under

---

[54a] See below, para. 12.03, n. 30.

[55] s.9 of the Factors Act 1889 is also subject to the exclusion of conditional sale agreements under the Consumer Credit Act 1974.

[56] See s.189(1) of the Consumer Credit Act 1974. Also relevant are certain limits to the scope of the Act. The amount of credit involved may not exceed a prescribed amount: at time of writing £15,000; see the Consumer Credit (Increase of Monetary Limits) Order 1983 (S.I. 1983 No. 1878) and the buyer must be an "individual"—including a partnership or other unincorporated body but not a body corporate: s.189(1).

[57] Defined in s.189(1) of the Consumer Credit Act 1974, as "an agreement, other than a conditional sale agreement"—broadly, an agreement of hire providing for the possible transmission of property to the buyer in certain circumstances.

section 25(1) because one who possesses on this basis is not a person who has bought or agreed to buy.[58] However, if the terms of an agreement labelled "hire-purchase" bind the hirer to purchase the subject concerned, the contract may be one of sale[59] and section 25(1) will be potentially applicable, but of course its operation may be excluded in so far as the parties' agreement amounts to a "conditional sale agreement" under the Consumer Credit Act 1974.[60]

The general effect of section 25(2) of the Sale of Goods Act 1893, precursor of the essentially identical section 25(1) of the present Act, was examined in *Thomas Graham & Sons* v. *Glenrothes Development Corporation*.[61] On the liquidation of a building company, which had contracted to erect houses for a development corporation, its suppliers claimed materials which had been delivered on the basis of a contract in terms of which ownership was retained pending full payment. The development corporation, however, contended on the basis of section 25(2) of the Sale of Goods Act 1893 that the building company had been in possession of the materials with the consent of the owner/ sellers and that, acting in good faith without notice of the supply contracts, it had paid a substantial part of the value of the materials to the builders. The First Division allowed proof before answer on this issue. Lord President Clyde noted the following requirements for protection under the legislation.

"The first requirement of that subsection is that a person, having bought or agreed to buy goods, obtains, with the consent of the seller, possession of the goods . . . The second requirement of the subsection is the delivery or transfer by that person . . . of the goods under any sale or other disposition thereof to any person receiving the same in good faith and without notice of any right of the original seller in respect of the goods . . . The final provision of the subsection is that, if these requirements are satisfied, they will have the same effect as if the person making the delivery or transfer was a mercantile agent in possession of the goods with the consent of the owner. In my view, this just means that he will have the ostensible authority of a mercantile agent to pass the property in the goods."[62]

The potential sphere of operation of section 25(1) is partly control-led by the interpretation of the phrase "having bought or agreed to buy goods." Professor Atiyah[63] has questioned the rôle of the words

---

[58] See *Helby* v. *Matthews* [1895] A.C. 471 at p. 475.
[59] See *Murdoch & Co. Ltd.* v. *Greig* (1889) 16 R. 396 at pp. 400, 402.
[60] See generally, Gloag and Henderson, paras. 17.21 and 17.52.
[61] 1967 S.C. 284.
[62] at pp. 293–294.
[63] *Sale of Goods*, pp. 376–377.

"having bought" on the argument that, under the scheme of the Act, there would be no need to protect a third party purchasing from a buyer in possession—as opposed to a party who has merely agreed to buy. The point made by Atiyah is that, under the Act, property would have passed to a buyer who would, in the normal course of events, then be in a position to pass transfer. While it is true that the normal operation of the subsection will be in the case of a contract envisaging the delayed transfer of property in the goods to the buyer,[64] another possible application is the case in which property has passed to the buyer but subject to "any lien or other right of the original seller."[65] Moreover, according to Benjamin,[66] the word "bought" is intended to cover the case "where the buyer has obtained both property in and possession of the goods under the contract of sale, but his title has subsequently been avoided by the seller."

In *National Employers Insurance* v. *Jones*[67] Lord Goff rejected the argument that section 9 of the Factors Act 1889 and its counterpart section 25(1) of the Sale of Goods Act 1979 were intended to give a good title to stolen goods.[68] Commenting on section 9, the learned judge noted that when it was incorporated as section 25(2) of the Sale of Goods Act 1893 Parliament "expressly maintained the fundamental principle *nemo dat quod non habet* in s.21(1) of the Act (now s.21(1) of the 1979 Act)." Lord Goff continued:

> "The succeeding sections enact what appear to be minor exceptions to that fundamental principle; yet, if the appellant's contention were to be correct, s.25(2) would have made not so much an exception to the principle, but would have substantially amounted to a reversal of it."[69]

Private purchase of a motor vehicle from a party holding under hire-purchase or a conditional sales agreement

As explained above,[70] the exception to the principle *nemo dat quod* **10.22** *non habet* provided for in section 9 of the Factors Act 1889 and section 25(1) of the Sale of Goods Act 1979 does not extend to goods held under a conditional sale agreement within the meaning of the Consumer Credit Act 1974. However, the sale of a motor vehicle held on the basis of hire-purchase or subject to a conditional sales agreement

---

[64] As in *Thomas Graham & Sons* v. *Glenrothes Development Corpn.*, 1967 S.C. 284.
[65] s.25(1). See *Benjamin's Sale of Goods*, para. 523.
[66] *Ibid.*
[67] [1988] 2 All E.R. 425.
[68] The conclusion arrived at on this is consistent with the position of Scots law which is to prefer the owner to an innocent party in the case of property tainted by the *vitium reale* of theft. See above, para. 10.17, n. 90.
[69] [1988] 2 All E.R. 425 at p. 432.
[70] para. 10.21.

is, potentially, an exception to *nemo dat quod non habet* in that a good title may, in certain circumstances, be passed to a buyer.

Part III of the Hire-Purchase Act 1964,[71] substantially re-enacted in Schedule 4 to the Consumer Credit Act 1974, provides for this. The first two subsections of section 27 are relevant:

> "(1) This section applies where a motor vehicle has been bailed or (in Scotland) hired under a hire-purchase agreement, or has been agreed to be sold under a conditional sale agreement, and before the property in the vehicle has become vested in the debtor, he disposes of the vehicle to another person.
>
> (2) Where the disposition referred to in subsection (1) is to a private purchaser, and he is a purchaser of the motor vehicle in good faith without notice of the hire-purchase agreement or conditional sale agreement . . . that disposition shall have effect as if the creditor's title to the vehicle had been vested in the debtor immediately before that disposition."

A limit upon the scope of this exception to *nemo dat quod non habet* is that it can only apply in favour of a "private purchaser," being a purchaser who, at the time of the disposition made to him, does not carry on business as a "trade or finance purchaser."[72] A "trade or finance purchaser" is more precisely defined as one who carries on a business which consists, wholly or partly:

> "(*a*) of purchasing motor vehicles for the purpose of offering or exposing them for sale, or
>
> (*b*) of providing finance by purchasing motor vehicles for the purpose of bailing or (in Scotland) hiring them under hire-purchase agreements or agreeing to sell them under conditional sale agreements."[73]

The exclusion of a "trade or finance purchaser" does no more than preclude the acquisition of a good title under section 27(2) by such a purchaser[74]; a subsequent party who qualifies as a "private purchaser"

---

[71] Pt. III of this Act was not repealed by the Hire-Purchase Act 1965 but was amended by s.59(4) of and Sched. 5 to the 1965 Act. Further amendments were effected by s.63 and Sched. 2, para. 4 of the Sale of Goods Act 1979.

[72] s.29(2). In *North-West Securities Ltd.* v. *Barrhead Coachworks Ltd.*, 1976 S.C. 68 at p. 70 Lord MacDonald explained this distinction as "intended to protect the interests of private purchasers who have no ready means of checking whether or not a vehicle is the subject of a current hire-purchase agreement as distinct from those of trade purchasers who do have access to certain facilities in this respect."

[73] s.29(2).

[74] It would appear that the question is one of the status of the buyer rather than the capacity in which he makes the purchase: *Stevenson* v. *Beverley Bentinck Ltd.* [1976] 2 All E.R. 606 at p. 609. A car dealer would be denied protection regardless of the fact that he purchased the vehicle entirely for his own use. But the class of "trade or finance purchaser" is limited to trade in motor vehicles, and the fact that a vehicle is purchased for business use does not bar the purchaser from the protection of s.27(2). See Atiyah, *Sale of Goods*, p. 389.

and satisfies the conditions of section 27(2) will acquire a good title. Section 27(3) repeats the protection accorded a "private purchaser" in section 27(2) in the situation in which a "trade or finance purchaser" is an intervening party between the hirer or conditional sale buyer and the subsequent "private purchaser."[75]

In the situation in which a "private purchaser" acquires a good title from an intervening "trade or finance purchaser" under section 27(3) the deprived original owner has no proprietary remedy—his proprietary interest comes to an end upon acquisition by the "private purchaser." However, although there is no possible proprietary remedy, an intermediate trade purchaser who acted *mala fide*—in knowledge of the hire-purchase or conditional sale agreement—is liable to the deprived owner for his loss: in the case of one who acted *bona fide*, only to the extent of his enrichment.[76]

SPUILZIE

As a proprietary remedy

Possession in its strongest sense[77] of a party holding a thing "in his own name as his own property"[78] is a real right even though of a lesser sort than the right of ownership.[79] As such it is protected by a proprietary remedy, in principle available on the basis of possession, whether that of an owner or a party holding as owner. Spuilzie is the term applied by the common law to an act of unlawful dispossession of moveable property. The same word is used to identify the remedy applicable to such an act: somewhat confusingly whether one is concerned with the rights of an owner or those of a party who possesses as owner but, in fact, has no title.[80] As Stair[81] put it "In spuilzies the pursuer needs no other title but possession, from whence in moveables a right is presumed."[82] **10.23**

It seems that the remedy is the broad counterpart of the possessory interdict of Roman law or the brieve of dissasine of feudal law.[83]

---

[75] See *North-West Securities Ltd.* v. *Barrhead Coachworks Ltd.*, 1976 S.C. 68.

[76] *Idem* at p. 70. Lord MacDonald speaks of liability for the value of the thing in the case of a *mala fide* interim party; the better view, however, is that a deprived owner's claim is limited to his actual loss and he would have to account for payments received under the hire-purchase or conditional sale agreement. See below, para. 10.26, n. 24.

[77] See above, para. 1.13.

[78] Erskine, II.i.20.

[79] See Stair, II.i.8.

[80] See below, paras. 10.24, 10.25.

[81] I.ix.17.

[82] See also Stair, IV.xxx.1: "spuilzie is the dispossession of the possessor in moveables."

[83] See Craig, II.xvii.25. See also Scot. Law Comm., Memo. No. 31, *Corporeal Moveables: Remedies*, paras. 19, 24 where the comparability of the remedy to the canonical *actio spolii* and the Roman-Dutch *mandament van spolie* is noted.

It may be noted that the protection accorded possession is concerned with the *status quo* and, in principle, it should not matter how the possessor came to possess; once the state of possession exists it is protected regardless of the manner in which it commenced. A passage from Stair's[84] treatment of actions makes this clear.

"Possessory actions or judgments are these, wherein an absolute right is not insisted for, but possession is claimed to be attained, retained, or recovered; such as actions of spuilzie, or wrongous intromission with moveables; where the pursuer needs not prove an absolute right but a lawful possession; or, though the possession at the first was *vi, clam* or *precario*, yet it is a good title against any dispossession, except by law or consent."[85]

The circumstances of possession in respect of which the remedy is sought must be that of an owner; accordingly relief by way of spuilzie will not be available to one who holds on the basis of a contract—such as loan or hire—from which one would infer a continuing acknowledgment of the right of ownership of another.[86]

Spuilzie is a remedy against an act amounting to some form of deprivation or denial of the right of possession, but must the pursuer have been in actual physical possession to have access to the action? Not necessarily so, because the remedy is available to an owner who has parted with physical custody but remains the legal possessor.[87] But it does not extend to an owner against a liferenter in possession because the owner—in this case no more than a title holder—can no longer be said to "hold as owner."[88] In this situation the liferenter would have an action to recover possession on the basis of a real right. A party not in physical possession and not in a position to establish

---

[84] IV.iii.47.

[85] See also Stair, IV.xxviii.2: "though the possession itself had been violent, or clandestine, it will not warrant a dispossession any other way." This passage is concerned with dispossession from heritable subjects but, as Stair (IV.xxx.1) notes, the principle involved is the same.

[86] The formulation *nec vi, nec clam, nec precario* is simply a statement of this point. One who holds neither by force, nor by stealth, nor on sufferance holds as owner.

[87] See *Laird of Durie* v. *Duddingston* (1549) Mor. 14735 regarding the right of a landlord to an action of spuilzie in respect of the unlawful ejection of a tenant. The decision was qualified to the extent that in respect of "steelbow" goods—items for the use of the tenant who was subject only to an obligation to return a like amount—the tenant was in possession and accordingly had the action. In *F.C. Finance Ltd.* v. *Brown & Son*, 1969 S.L.T.(Sh.Ct.) 41, an undecided issue was the right of an owner, who had parted with a vehicle under a hire-purchase agreement, to an action on the grounds of spuilzie. Rodger, "Spuilzie in the modern world," 1970 S.L.T. (News) 33 at p. 35 commented: "There seems to be no good ground for saying that the H.P. company did not have civil possession to maintain the action here."

[88] See *Drummond* v. *Forrest* (1581) Mor. 14727 where an owner of land was held not to be in possession for the purposes of an action of spuilzie against a liferenter in possession.

title will, it is submitted, have some difficulty in maintaining that he "held as owner," not least on account of the presumption that, in the case of moveables, possession points to ownership.[89]

Application and tendency to blur with restitution

The fundamental basis of the remedy is to provide for the restora- **10.24** tion of the *status quo ante* of possession where a thing has been removed without consent and in the absence of overriding authorisation.[90] Stair[91] defined spuilzie as "the taking away of moveables without consent of the owner or order of law"; Erskine[92] is to similar effect: "Spuilzie is the taking away or intermeddling with moveable goods in the possession of another, without either the consent of that other, or the order of law."[93]

Arguably spuilzie is the next logical stage in a possessor's right to defend against deprivation which is violent in the sense of the dispossessor having taken the law into his own hands.[94] Once possession is actually lost, the law cannot condone reciprocation by the deprived party, but the remedy of spuilzie is available to obtain restoration of the *status quo*.[95] Erskine[96] notes the bar to a right of self-help once the act of deprivation is completed, because it is then no longer possible to justify a possessor's right to defend against a current and continuing wrong: "But after he has lost possession, however unwarrantably, he cannot use force to recover it . . . but must apply to the judge, that he may be restored by the order of law."

The character of spuilzie as a remedy intended to give immediate protection against an interference with the *de facto* circumstances of possession was recognised in the short (three-year) period of extinctive prescription applied by the Prescription Act of 1579 c. 21.[97] One may contrast the 40-year period applying to the right of restitution deriving from the right of ownership under the statute of 1579.[98] But in modern law this distinction is not maintained.[99]

---

[89] See above, para. 1.12.
[90] On this basis the fact that the dispossessor obtained a title after the act of dispossession is no defence. See *Somerville* v. *Hamilton* (1541) Mor. 14737.
[91] I.ix.16.
[92] III.vii.16.
[93] See the reply for the pursuers in *Brodie* v. *Watson* (1714) Mor. 11757: "No person can *sibi jus dicere*."
[94] See Erskine, II.i.23: "Violent possession is when one turns another masterfully, or by force, out of possession, and puts himself in his place . . . the possessor against whom the violence is used may also use force on his part to maintain his possession, in the same manner that he might in defence of his life."
[95] It is no defence for the defender to allege that the pursuer had taken as much from him; see *More* v. *McPhaderick* (1678) Mor. 14729.
[96] II.i.23.
[97] Repealed by the Prescription and Limitation (Scotland) Act 1973, Sched. 5, Pt. 1.
[98] See Erskine, III.vii.16.
[99] See below, para. 10.28.

Accepting the underlying relevance of the notion expressed in the maxim *spoliatus ante omnia est restituendus*,[1] it follows that any question of superior title is irrelevant.[2] While restitution applied to the recovery of possession involves proof of the pursuer's right of ownership,[3] the remedy applicable to spuilzie requires no more than proof that the claimant was in possession.[4] But, this said, one can see the potential for the blurring of the two concepts by reason of the presumption that the possessor of a moveable is the owner.[5] Moreover, the very fact that spuilzie is available to an owner—as possessor—may have tended towards an unjustified identification of spuilzie and restitution as tautologous terms. Stair[6] gives a definition of spuilzie which speaks of the absence of the "consent of the owner" and the obligation "to restitution of the things taken away." This text may well have been productive of a certain amount of confusion,[7] but Stair's final book, on actions and procedure, makes it clear that restitution and spuilzie are distinct. Here Stair[8] divides actions into declaratory, petitory and possessory. An action for "the restitution or delivery of moveables" is given as an example of a petitory action in which something is "claimed to be done or permitted by the defenders"—in this instance the restoration of a thing in respect of which the pursuer has established his right of ownership. Spuilzie, however, leads to a possessory action "where the pursuer needs not prove an absolute right but a lawful possession."[9]

This important distinction was recognised in the early case of *Brown* v. *Hudelstone*.[10] In an action of spuilzie in respect of a cow, the defender contended that he had poinded the animal from the posses-

---

[1] To the effect that the deprived party must be restored before anything else is done. The point is well made in *A* v. *B* (1677) Mor. 14751: "The defender in a spuilzie having alleged, that the goods were his own, and that, having given them to the pursuer to be grazed, he must have taken away his own goods, it was replied, that the pursuer was not obliged to debate the right and property of the said goods; but *in spolio*, he needed libel no more but that the goods were upon his ground and in his possession, and taken away *vi* and in manner libelled; and *spoliatus ante omnia restituendus*." See the general application of this maxim in early case law: Mor. 14737–14740; see also Scot. Law Comm., Memo. No. 31, *Corporeal Moveables: Remedies*, para. 19.

[2] See Stair, I.ix.17.

[3] See above, para. 10.6.

[4] Stair, I.ix.17. See also *Montgomery* v. *Hamilton* (1548) Mor. 14731, where it was held that the essentials of possession and violent ejection must be proved, "[b]ut if he libels a title with his possession, it is not necessary to prove the same."

[5] See above, para. 1.12. Stair, 1.ix.17, it may be noted, could be interpreted as reasoning that possession is a sufficient basis not *qua* possession, but rather by reason of the title to moveables being presumed from possession.

[6] I.ix.16.

[7] See, *e.g. Gorebridge Co-op. Soc. Ltd.* v. *Turnbull*, 1952 S.L.T.(Sh.Ct.) 91 which seems, on the basis of Stair, I.ix.16, to confuse the owner's right to restitution and the possessor's remedy to recover possession.

[8] IV.iii.47.

[9] *Ibid.*

[10] (1625) Mor. 11748.

sion of his debtor who, it seems, had held it for the preceding two years. In these circumstances the action of spuilzie was denied the pursuer/owner but his right to restitution was recognised. While spuilzie was not appropriate in that the defender could not be said to have dispossessed the pursuer by a violent act, yet there was no reason why the latter should not recover his cow on the basis of proof of his right of ownership. As the pursuer replied: "the exception might have appearance to put the defender in *bona fide*, and to assoilzie him from violence and spuilzie, yet it ought not to be sustained, to free him from delivery of the cow to the just owner."

Availability against subsequent parties; nature of right protected by spuilzie

It is important to distinguish between an act of spuilzie involving, on **10.25** the one hand, the deprivation of an owner in possession and, on the other, the case of a mere possessor dispossessed. In the former situation, an owner on proof of his right of ownership may, as a matter of restitution, recover the thing from any subsequent party.[11] In the latter case a deprived possessor—who, notwithstanding the presumption applying to the possession of a moveable, cannot establish a right of ownership—can only recover from his immediate dispossessor. Given that the basis of his claim is the wrongful act of dispossession, it follows that relief can only be available against the dispossessor and not any subsequent possessor.[12] Accordingly, where Stair[13] notes that: "Spuilzie *inurit labem realem*, whereby the goods may be recovered from purchasers *bona fide*"—he is referring to the owner's right to recover possession on the basis of his proprietary right.[14]

As indicated,[15] the assimilation of possession to ownership in the case of moveables[16] tends to a mode of thinking in which what, in principle, is a purely possessory remedy is identified as an owner's remedy. A possessor is presumed to be owner and, on this basis, the

---

[11] See above, para. 10.4.

[12] The possessory remedy is restricted to application against a party who has disturbed the *status quo* of possession and, on this basis, it would not be available against even a *mala fide* subsequent party, provided, of course, that the act of deprivation of possession was completed before transmission to the party concerned. This fact explains why the possessory remedy should be an expedited form of relief, to facilitate the restoration of a dispossessed party and to minimise the risk of the transmission of the thing to another; see Stair, IV.xxx.4: "for restoring the possession summarily." Stair is here referring to ejection, but having previously noted (IV.xxx.1) that ejection, as the dispossession of heritable rights, and spuilzie, as the dispossession of moveables, are, in principle, the same. As to the summary nature of the action in modern law see below, para. 10.27.

[13] I.ix.16.

[14] The case of *Hay* v. *Leonard* (1677) Mor. 10286 which is cited does no more than make the obvious point that an act of spuilzie is no different from an act of theft from the point of view of a *vitium reale*, but, clearly, only the owner can rely upon the fact that the thing is tainted by an unlawful act of dispossession.

[15] Above, para. 10.24.

[16] See above, para. 1.12.

possessory remedy is seen primarily as an owner's remedy. The consequence of this thinking is the unjustified tendency to identify the possessory remedy as a proprietary action from the point of view of availability against third parties.[17] Where a party seeks to recover possession *qua* owner he does assert a right potentially applicable against the world at large; where he does not claim to be owner but simply proceeds on the basis of unlawful deprivation of possession, the claim can only lie against his dispossessor.

Spuilzie leading to a right of reparation

10.26   The dispossessed party is not limited to a claim to restoration of his possession under the remedy applying to spuilzie. The action also has a compensatory side which would appear to be more a matter of delict than property.[18] As Erskine[19] noted:

> "When a spuilzie is committed, action lies against the delinquent, not only for restoring to the former possessor the goods or their value, but for all the profits he might have made of these goods, had it not been for the spuilzie. These profits are estimated by the pursuer's own oath, and get the name of *violent*, because they are due in no other case than of violence or wrong."[20]

The pursuer's claim to profits would appear to be simply a matter of reparation for his loss in being deprived of the possession, and hence the use, of the thing.

Accordingly, where the wrongful dispossessor cannot restore the thing he is potentially liable for the deprived possessor's total loss, made up of his actual loss in the loss of the thing plus his consequential loss (of "profits") on the normal delictual basis. In *F.C. Finance Ltd.*

---

[17] See, *e.g.* Walker, *Civil Remedies*, p. 1039, under the subtitle "spuilzie": "A *vitium reale* attaches to the goods by virtue of their wrongful acquisition and it is not purged by any kind, or number, of transmissions. It is independent of knowledge or good faith, and a third, or subsequent, party, however innocent, must restore or pay damages." Professor Walker is describing the owner's remedy in the case of an unlawful deprivation of possession, and of course in principle, in this situation, the owner can recover from a subsequent innocent party; but, it is respectfully submitted, the basis would be the intact right of ownership rather than the unlawful act of deprivation. The case of *Morrisson* v. *Robertson*, 1908 S.C. 332 (see above, para. 8.09, n. 62), cited by Professor Walker, is authority for the owner's right to recover the thing, from a subsequent innocent party, where title did not pass to the initial transferee from the owner. The case is relevant in that one can say *a fortiori* ownership would not pass, and so could not be transmitted, in the event of an unlawful act of deprivation. But the point remains that the basis of recovery from a third party is the right of ownership and the means by which possession was lost by the owner is only relevant to show that there could be no transmission of title in the circumstances.

[18] Scot. Law Comm., Memo. No. 31, *Corporeal Moveables: Remedies*, para. 19: "it combines elements of restitution and reparation."

[19] III.vii.16.

[20] See also Stair, I.ix.16.

v. *Brown & Son*[21] the defenders, car dealers acting as agents for a factoring company, sold a vehicle which they knew to be subject to a hire-purchase agreement. When the factoring company went into liquidation the hire-purchase owners, being unable to recover the vehicle,[22] claimed damages on the basis of unlawful dispossession. On the grounds that the pursuers did not have possession, the lower court rejected the argument that spuilzie applied. On appeal, however, the view taken was that the defenders were liable in reparation and that damages were due, not simply as a matter of actual loss, but because "deprivation of ownership" was involved on the basis of "the value of the article lost."[23] In the circumstances of certain payments made to the pursuer prior to dispossession, this was more favourable to him than reparation on the basis of his actual loss. It seems that the question of the basis upon which damages should be arrived at was wrongly decided in this case. If a deprived possessor, whether owner or not, cannot be put back in possession there is no good reason why he should recover any more than his actual loss.[24]

Form of remedy available to dispossessed party

The principle that the *status quo* of possession should be restored **10.27** following any unlawful interference, and pending a determination of the merits of the matter, is provided for in the powers accorded the Court of Session under the Court of Session Act 1868. Section 91 provides for the competence of an order, in response to an application by summary petition, to provide for

"the Restoration of Possession of any Real or Personal Property of the Possession of which the Petitioner may have been violently or fraudulently deprived."[25]

---

[21] 1969 S.L.T.(Sh.Ct.) 41.
[22] Because of the protection accorded the innocent buyer from a hire-purchaser; see above, para. 10.22.
[23] *per* Sheriff McDonald at pp. 44–45.
[24] See Rodger "Spuilzie in the Modern World," 1970 S.L.T. (News) 33. As the learned writer pointed out, the cases of *Faulds* v. *Townsend* (1861) 23 D. 437 and *Mackintosh* v. *Galbraith* (1900) 3 F. 66 are not authority for the proposition that the measure of damages should be the value of the item lost regardless: "in both the measure of the pursuer's loss was clearly the entire value of ownership, but in the instant case it is equally clearly not." See above, para. 10.22, n. 76.
[25] See also Maxwell, *Practice of the Court of Session*, p. 354: "Possessory actions are those grounded, not upon absolute right, but upon a claim to lawful possession, and may be brought for attaining, retaining or recovering possession. The process now generally used to determine questions of possession is the process of suspension and interdict, initiated by petition; and application may be made to the Court by summary petition to order the restoration of any real or personal property of the possession of which the petitioner has been violently or fraudulently deprived." See also Maclaren, *Court of Session Practice*, p. 639; McBryde and Dowie, *Petition Procedure in the Court of Session*, p. 161. The Sheriff Courts (Scotland) Act 1971 provides in s.35(1)(c) for the form of process known as "summary cause" to be applied to "actions for the recovery of possession of heritable or moveable property, other than actions in which there is claimed in addition, or as an alternative . . . a decree for payment of money exceeding two hundred and fifty pounds in amount (exclusive of interest and expenses)."

Where a respondent in any application or proceeding in the Bill
Chamber has, whether before or after the institution of proceedings,
done any act which the court might have prohibited by interdict, then
the court is empowered to "ordain such Respondent to perform any
Act which may be necessary for reinstating the Complainer in his
Possessory Right."[26]

Defences to spuilzie

10.28   Stair[27] considers various defences to spuilzie, but without distinguishing the distinct causes of action of, on the one hand, wrongful
deprivation of possession and, on the other, reparation for the loss
involved.

Certain defences are directed towards the rebuttal of any inference
that the dispossession was an unjustified act of violence. That the deed
was "warrantably done, at least *bona fide* by a colourable title,"[28] that
it was a case of voluntary delivery[29] and that it was a lawful poinding
not perpetrated *mala fide*,[30] are instances of this. The implication, in
these defences, is that the defender did not take the law into his own
hands and that, in view of this, there is no justification for restoring the
status quo ante as an interim measure pending a final resolution of the
question of the right of possession.

According to Stair,[31] there is a defence of restitution *re integra* within
24 hours or without time limit, if the return of the goods is accepted by
the pursuer. But this defence could only have meaningful application
to a claim for violent profits. In modern law it is doubtful whether any
set time limit would apply. The issue would simply be whether
patrimonial loss was suffered as a result of the temporary deprivation
of possession.

Regarding prescription,[32] in modern law the better view is that the
right to claim restoration of possession is subject to the 20-year period
of negative prescription applying to proprietary rights.[33] The obligation
to make reparation for loss arising from an unlawful act of deprivation

---

[26] s.89 of the Court of Session Act 1868.
[27] I.ix.19–24.
[28] Stair, I.ix.19.
[29] Stair, I.ix.20.
[30] Stair, I.ix.21.
[31] I.ix.23.
[32] Formerly provided for by the Prescription (Ejections) Act 1579 (c. 21) which was
repealed by the Prescription and Limitation (Scotland) Act 1973, Sched. 5, Pt. 1.
[33] See my argument (above para. 10.13) as to the applicability of s.8 of the
Prescription and Limitation (Scotland) Act 1973. But *cf.* Walker, *The Law of Prescription and Limitation in Scotland*, p. 53, where the five-year period under s.6 is taken to
apply to spuilzie in general. Given the nature of the right as a device to obtain
immediate restoration of the *status quo*, the shorter period of extinctive prescription
would seem appropriate (see above, para. 10.24, n. 97), but it would appear that the
better interpretation is that this is the case only in respect of the reparation aspect of the
action; see below, n. 34.

of possession is, however, subject to the five-year period of extinctive prescription.[34]

---

[34] The right to reparation arising from an act of deprivation of possession would appear to be a "right relating to property . . . correlative to an obligation" (see s.8(2))—in this case one to make reparation. An obligation to make reparation prescribes in five years under s.6 (see Sched. 1, para. 1(*d*)) and the correlative right is subject to potential loss in the same period. Walker, *The Law of Prescription and Limitation of Actions in Scotland*, p. 53, regards Sched. 1, para. 1(*d*) as applying to spuilzie; see above, n. 33.

CHAPTER 11

SECURITY

GENERAL MATTERS

Present coverage

11.01   Consistent with the object of this book to cover the general principles of property applying to corporeal moveables, the treatment of security interests is restricted to matters of general import. Accordingly, the general conventional forms of security based on the common law principle requiring possession by the creditor are dealt with. On the same basis the legal (or implied) forms deriving from the common law and from the Sale of Goods Act 1979 are covered. There is no treatment of the various special and general possessory liens which apply in particular cases. The relevant general issues would not be taken any further by a consideration of these limited instances of security. Likewise, regarding instances of security which amount to exceptions to the principle that the creditor must have possession, there is no coverage of the diverse particular conventional and legal forms. Hire-purchase is not covered because it is a self-contained subject which does not have general property implications. The floating charge is a matter of company law and beyond present scope. The decision to limit the present treatment on the above basis would seem to be valid in terms of the aim of this book.[1] From the point of view of exposition it may be noted that other works bring together the diverse forms of security potentially applicable to moveable property.[2]

Credit reservation of title—not security in the technical sense—is dealt with in Chapter 12.

Definition of security

11.02   Security is a wide term; as the definition of Gloag and Irvine[3] shows, denoting:

---

[1] The *Report by Working Party on Security over Moveable Property* (the Halliday Report), Scottish Law Commission (1986), would appear to support this approach. Para. 7 refers to the general rule that possession is required for security over moveable property, with this "possession in security" described as pledge when it is created by agreement and lien when it comes into being by operation of law. The report goes on to note that: "Both common law and statute have admitted exceptions to the general rule but these exceptions are not numerous and do not substantially detract from the general rule" (para. 7).

[2] See, *e.g.* Gloag and Henderson, Chap. 20; Wilson, *The Law of Scotland Relating to Debt*, Chap. 7.

[3] *Rights in Security*, p. 1.

228

"any right which a creditor may hold for ensuring the payment or satisfaction of his debt, distinct from, and in addition to, his right of action and execution against the debtor under the latter's personal obligation."

The present treatment is concerned with the general forms of rights in security which may be created over corporeal moveables and which provide the creditor with a real right in the moveable concerned.

An agreement providing for the furnishing of security is, in principle, no different from any other contractual obligation and while potentially binding between the parties involved does not, as such, give the creditor a real or proprietary interest.[4] The "giving of security" denotes something more[5] and, in the case of corporeal moveables, envisages the creditor obtaining or retaining an actual proprietary—or "real"—interest in the thing or things to which the security applies. This interest is designated a *"jus in re"*—a right "in the thing," as opposed to a *"jus in personam"*—a right "against a person" or a *"jus ad rem"*—a right "to a thing."[6] It is a species of real right equal, in principle, to ownership and only distinct from ownership in so far as it does not extend to the sum total of rights in the item concerned.[7]

The present treatment, being concerned with property and proprietary rights, is limited to forms of security which amount to a real or proprietary interest. The mark of the right of ownership is its general superiority over other lesser rights, on the basis of which a particular thing is held. In the same way the criterion of a right of security is its superiority over the claims of other creditors who only hold lesser rights. The circumstances in which this priority is tested is the debtor's bankruptcy; upon the sequestration of the debtor's estate, the security[8]

---

[4] See Gloag and Irvine, *Rights in Security*, p. 5: "Since the main characteristic of a right in security over property lies in its conferring on the creditor, who is entitled to it, the right to vindicate a particular subject, and, consequently, a preference over that subject on the bankruptcy of the debtor, it is clear at the outset that a merely personal pecuniary obligation by the debtor himself is not in any legal sense a right in security."

[5] See the submission of counsel (subsequently Lord Gillies) in *Bow* v. *Spankie*, 1 June 1811, F.C.: "Where nothing more is granted than the personal obligation of the debtor, it can never be understood that a security is given."

[6] See *Pochin & Co.* v. *Robinows and Marjoribanks* (1869) 7 M. 622 at p. 629; where the designations *jus in re* and *jus ad rem* are used.

[7] If it did, it would amount to the acquisition of a right of ownership by the creditor—a not unknown device; see below, para. 11.10; see also the *ex facie* absolute disposition of heritable property of Scots common law: Gordon, *Scottish Land Law*, para. 20.86. In this regard one may note a distinction between the limited interest of security proper—predicated on the condition of ownership vesting in a party other than the holder of the right of security—and credit reservation of title, intended to serve a "security" purpose but not technically security because the creditor is owner. See below, para. 12.01.

[8] In the Bankruptcy (Scotland) Act 1985, s.73 provides that "security" means "any security, heritable or moveable, or any right of lien, retention or preference" and "secured creditor" means "a creditor who holds a security for his debt over any part of the debtor's estate."

in question should accord to the creditor concerned a preference[9] against other creditors in the sense of a prior call on the property over which the security is held.[10]

Common law emphasis on possession

11.03   Erskine[11] notes the limited scope for the hypothecation[12] of moveables without physical possession by the creditor

> "because the impignoration of moveable goods without their delivery to the creditor cannot but prove a heavy weight on the free currency of trade, it being impracticable to keep a record for moveables, by which purchasers may be ascertained of their danger."[13]

Bell,[14] on the premise of the significance of possession in the case of moveables, shows the irrelevance of any formal instrument of conveyance in the conferring of a real right.

> "While delivery alone, accompanied by an intention to transfer, is without any written conveyance sufficient to pass the property of ordinary corporeal moveables, the most formal and solemn written conveyance of them will confer no real right without such delivery, either actual, or at least the best which the circumstances will allow. The general rule respecting moveables is, that possession presumes property. A mere instrument of possession, then, is not sufficient to transfer moveables assigned or disponed in security."[15]

---

[9] See Gloag and Irvine, *Rights in Security*, p. 4: "Where, as is usually the case, the property over which the creditor has a real right in security belongs to the debtor, the practical effect of the security is to confer on the creditor holding it a preference over the other creditors of the debtor in the debtor's sequestration."

[10] The common law followed a technically correct approach in treating the secured interest as a real right separate and additional to the creditor's personal claim against the debtor; see *University of Glasgow* v. *Yuill's Tr.* (1882) 9 R. 643 *per* Lord President Inglis at p. 650. On this basis a secured creditor was entitled to his secured interest and could also claim the full amount due to him in the sequestration, provided that this did not result in the recovery of more than the total liability. Under the bankruptcy legislation, however, a secured creditor is required to deduct the value of any security in calculating the claim to be made against the debtor's estate; see the Bankruptcy (Scotland) Act 1985, s.22(9), Sched. 1, para. 5. See generally, McBryde, *Bankruptcy*, pp. 195–196. See also Coull, *The Law of Bankruptcy in Scotland*, para. 14.11.

[11] III.i.34.

[12] The only tacit or legal hypothecs are those in favour of a landlord (or superior) and a solicitor and those applying in certain maritime contexts. See Gloag and Henderson, paras. 20.8–20.12. See also Wilson, *The Law of Scotland Relating to Debt*, pp. 120–123.

[13] See also Stair, I.xiii.14, rejecting the wide use of security over moveables without delivery on the basis of the general interests of commerce: "that commerce may be the more sure, and every one may more easily know his condition with whom he contracts: and therefore goods sold were not found under any hypothecation for the price."

[14] *Comm.*, II, 11.

[15] See also Gow, *Mercantile Law*, p. 272, pointing out that "the possessor would have a misleading fund of credit" because "at common law corporeal moveables are currency, and possession the badge of *dominium* upon the faith of which business is transacted."

Throughout the case law, from the earliest reported decisions,[16] there are dicta to the effect that there can be no security—amounting to a real right—over a corporeal moveable without possession of the thing by the creditor. A frequently quoted statement is that of Lord President Inglis in *Clark* v. *West Calder Oil Co.*[17]: "A mere assignation of corporeal moveables *retenta possessione* is nothing whatever but a personal obligation and creates no preference of any kind."[18] This firm conclusion was reiterated, from a positive point of view, by Lord Trayner in *Pattison's Tr.* v. *Liston*[19]: "Now it is quite certain that an effectual security over moveables can only be effected by delivery of the subject of the security."

Possession must be retained by the creditor for the security to continue. As Erskine[20] noted: "In a pledge of moveables, the creditor who quits the possession of the subject loses the real right he had upon it." But this requirement does not mean that the creditor must necessarily continue to have actual physical control. However, if another obtains natural possession, the pledge will only survive if the circumstances support the retention of the right of possession by the creditor. The case of *North-Western Bank* v. *Poynter, Son, and Macdonalds*[21] illustrates this. To secure a bank loan, merchants delivered by way of pledge a bill of lading on the basis of an absolute power of sale in favour of the bank. The bill was later returned by the bank to the merchants, to hold "as trustees," with a request that they obtain delivery of the goods; at the same time, the bank gave authority to the merchants to sell and to credit the proceeds to the loan. Lord Chancellor Herschell considered Erskine[22] and Bell[23] and concluded that, in the circumstances, the priority of the pledgee was not lost by the return of the bill of lading to the pledgor. "Where it is a pledge, as here, with a power of sale, I cannot think that anything I have yet read warrants the assertion that the delivery to the pledgor, who is a broker, for the purposes of sale would destroy all the right of the pledgee."[24]

The dominating requirement of possession manifests itself in two broad general classes of security. First, there is the category of security founded upon agreement—the "intention based" forms—and, secondly, there are those forms, of general application, implied or provided for by the law in certain circumstances.

---

[16] *e.g. Thomsone* v. *Chirnside* (1558) Mor. 827.

[17] (1882) 9 R. 1017 at p. 1024.

[18] See also *Gavin's Tr.* v. *Fraser*, 1920 S.C. 674 *per* Lord President Clyde at p. 683: "a security over moveables *retenta possessione* is bad by the law of Scotland."

[19] (1893) 20 R. 806 at p. 813.

[20] III.i.33.

[21] (1895) 22 R.(H.L.) 1.

[22] III.i.33.

[23] *Comm.*, II, 22.

[24] *North-Western Bank* v. *Poynter, Son, and Macdonalds* (1895) 22 R.(H.L.) 1 at p. 9.

SECURITY BASED ON AGREEMENT

Pledge

11.04   The most simple and obvious form of security applicable to a corporeal moveable is the actual handing-over of the thing into the possession of the creditor. The justification for the recognition of a real right of security can be seen in the primative form of the device with the creditor empowered to sell the thing in satisfaction of his claim in the event of the debtor's failure timeously to pay his debt. This feature of the creditor's power over the very thing emerges from Stair's[25] description:

> "a kind of mandate whereby the debtor for his creditor's security gives him the pawn, or thing impignorated, to detain or keep it for his own security, or in case of non-payment of the debt, to sell the pledge, and pay himself out of the price, and restore the rest, or restore the pledge itself upon payment of the debt."

Stair[26] goes on to qualify this general definition by noting that the custom of Scots law "allows not the creditor to sell the pledge," the position being that the creditor's right in this regard can only be exercised through the court.[27] As Lord Curriehill noted in *Hamilton* v. *Western Bank of Scotland*[28]: "if the right had been merely a pledge, the defenders could not have sold the goods without judicial authority."

Pledge involves an *animus* or mental element in the parties' respective intentions to pass and to receive possession for the purposes of security, and a *corpus* or physical element in the actual transfer of possession to the creditor. Clearly enough, these two elements co-exist in the straightforward case of an agreement to pledge followed by delivery of the subject concerned to the creditor. The presence of the two elements—necessary to constitute a real right—in a completed act of pledge was noted by Lord Neaves in *Moore* v. *Gleddon*[29]:

> "If there be a contract for the constitution of a real right in favour of a creditor, such as would naturally produce and justify an *animus possidendi*, then the removal of the articles to the ground of the creditor is, I think, sufficient to perfect and complete the real right so contemplated."

---

[25] I.xiii.11.
[26] *Ibid.*
[27] See Bell, *Prin.*, § 207: "But with us . . . the subject of the pledge cannot be sold without the order of a judge, which is obtained on a summary application to the Sheriff."
[28] (1856) 19 D. 152 at p. 164.
[29] (1869) 7 M. 1016 at p. 1021.

In this case the majority of an eight-judge appeal court treated a contract, in terms of which a railway company obtained a right over plant left on its premises by a creditor, as giving rise to a pledge.

The intention element in pledge

The intention or *animus* element is a prerequisite to the constitution **11.05** of the real right of pledge but, of course, it is not possible to determine intention as a matter isolated from the circumstances as to the actual holding of the moveable concerned. Indeed, as in the case of an outright change of ownership[30] the parties' mutual intention may be inferred from the circumstances of a change of natural possession.[31]

While a declaration of intent—even if reduced to writing—cannot supply "the outward or visible fact of possession"[32] it may be possible to infer the parties' intention from their actions in relation to possession. The circumstances of an alteration of the *status quo* of natural possession may support the inference of an intention to possess on the part of the creditor or the correlative of an intention no longer to possess on the part of the debtor. As Lord Neaves put it: "Paction cannot supply the place of possession; but when there is an outward change of possession, paction supplies the *animus possidendi* of the one party, or the *animus desinendi possidere* of the other party."[33]

Pledge is a particular form of security constituted by a transfer of the right of possession to the creditor; a transfer of the right of ownership—whatever else this may amount to[34]—does not constitute pledge. Moreover, whether a security interest amounts to pledge or to some other right may be important from the point of view of the scope of the right; differences in the way in which matters are arranged may "result in a contract of a different kind from pledge, and, of course, giving different rights, and leading to different consequences."[35] Given this, it is necessary to identify the type of security interest created. In the case of pledge the circumstances must point to the conclusion that the parties intended to transfer possession for the purpose of creating a security interest. If this intention is not manifest from the terms of the

---

[30] See above para. 8.08.

[31] To the extent that the change of possession is a prerequisite to any claim that the necessary *animus* is present. See the dictum of Lord Neaves quoted below, n. 33.

[32] *Moore* v. *Gleddon* (1869) 7 M. 1016 *per* Lord Neaves at p. 1020.

[33] at p. 1021.

[34] See below, para. 11.10.

[35] *Hamilton* v. *Western Bank of Scotland* (1856) 19 D. 152 *per* Lord President McNeill at p. 160. In the case of pledge a creditor cannot sell the subject pledged without judicial authority (see above, n. 27), whereas in the case of a transfer of ownership in security this would, in principle, be competent. See *Hamilton, per* Lord Curriehill at p. 164: "if the right had been merely a pledge, the defenders could not have sold the goods without judicial authority. But there can be no doubt that the right which was transferred to the defenders was such as would have enabled them to sell the goods without any such authority."

parties' agreement—and supported by the circumstances—it may, as already stated, be inferred. In this event what is required is a basis from which the inference of an intention to transfer possession may be drawn.

Where the basis of a claimed right of security is contractual, the terms agreed must be consistent with the coming into being of a real security interest. In *Mackinnon* v. *Max Nanson & Co.*[36] the parties' contract reserved to the debtor the right to remove items from the goods in question "for engraving or other purposes requisite to carry on his business." Lord President Inglis found that it was "quite inconsistent with the nature of the bargain disclosed on the face of that document, that Max Nanson and Company should have a *jus in re*," and accordingly, that it was "not such a document as creates in the party to whom it is given that *jus in re* which is essential to make a good security."[37]

Frequently the parties seek to arrange matters so that the creditor obtains a right of security while natural possession is retained by the debtor. The usual means of effecting this is to transfer title to the creditor.[38] In these circumstances there is unlikely to be room for any possible inference that the parties intended possession to pass to the creditor and, accordingly, such cases would not normally be treated as pledge. Where, however, physical possession remains with a neutral third party, it may be that the parties intended no more than to transfer the right of possession. In such cases a central question will usually be what intention may most plausibly be inferred from the circumstances.

In *Hamilton* v. *Western Bank of Scotland*[39] a bank had made an advance to one M on a bill of exchange. As "collateral security," 300 cases of brandy in a bonded warehouse were transferred—by delivery order to the warehouse keeper—from M to the bank. On M's bankruptcy the question arose whether the security applied to a subsequent advance by the bank and on this issue it was necessary to determine whether the parties had intended pledge or outright transfer in security; in the former case a subsequent advance would not be covered, while in the latter it would. It was held that the arrangement was not "a transaction of pledge, but a transference of property," even though "it may not have been the intention of the parties that the property should permanently or ultimately remain with the defender."[40] The extent to which the parties' intention is determined on the basis of an objective consideration of the circumstances is shown by this dictum. In effect the court said that intention in the

---

[36] (1868) 6 M. 974.
[37] at p. 976.
[38] See below, para. 11.09.
[39] (1856) 19 D. 152.
[40] *per* Lord President McNeill at p. 160.

subjective sense of what the parties sought to achieve could not prevail over intention inferred on the basis of what the parties had actually done.

The physical element in pledge

The general emphasis upon the central importance of the require- **11.06** ment of possession by the creditor in the constitution of security over moveable property[41] manifests itself strongly in the case of pledge. Actual delivery, or what in particular circumstances amounts to its practical equivalent, is required. The entrenched nature of this requirement is indicated by dicta in uncompromising terms. In *Stiven* v. *Scott and Simpson*,[42] for example, Lord President Inglis—in reject-ing, as pledge, a mere marking in favour of the creditor of parcels of flax retained by the debtor—commented as follows:

> "Now, it is needless for me to say that as matter of law that made no security at all. If it was intended to be a contract of pledge we all know that that real contract cannot be completed or made available without actual delivery of the subject pledged by the pledger to the pledgee."[43]

The simple case of the actual transfer of physical possession in completion of an agreement to pledge is effective in the constitution of a real right. However, because it deprives the owner of the use of the thing concerned, this unexceptionable form of pledge has limited utility. Accordingly, what is of interest is the extent to which the law allows the physical element to be constituted by something less than an out-and-out delivery to the creditor.

The notion of "actual" delivery extends to any form—there is no *numerus clausus* of forms of actual delivery[44]—in which the creditor obtains power and control over the thing sufficient to justify the conclusion that he is in possession. The discussion of delivery in the context of derivative acquisition[45] is relevant here and, indeed, a number of the cases referred to there are concerned with delivery for the purpose of the creation of a real right of security.[46]

Delivery of the subject of the security to a warehouse or other premises, to be held there in the creditor's name and subject to his control, "is as effectual delivery as if made into the buyer's own

---

[41] See above, para. 11.03.

[42] (1871) 9 M. 923.

[43] at p. 930.

[44] See above, para. 8.16.

[45] See above, paras. 8.15–8.19.

[46] See, *e.g. Gibson* v. *Forbes* (1833) 11 S. 916; *West Lothian Oil Co.* v. *Mair* (1892) 20 R. 64.

cellar."[47] Even if there is no physical removal of the items pledged, the creditor may obtain a real right on the basis of being given control by the debtor, the classic situation being the handing over of the key giving access to the premises in which the goods are kept or stored. Delivery of a key may be relevant to a debtor's intention to give possession to his creditor but, from the point of view of the actual transfer of possession, its rôle lies in the fact that it gives access.[48] However, neutral storage in the name of the creditor will not be effective if the debtor retains a degree of control inconsistent with the transfer of possession to the creditor.[49]

The mere marking of goods could hardly amount to a sufficient physical element based upon a transfer of the right of possession to the creditor—on the argument that what remained with the debtor was only natural possession.[50] Of course, in certain circumstances, it may be possible to transfer a right of ownership by marking[51] and, in principle, it should be competent, by this means, to create a security based upon an absolute transfer to the creditor but this would be something distinguishable from pledge.[52]

Given that the criterion of a sufficient transfer of power and control to the creditor applies to all cases, it is arguably unnecessary to distinguish on the basis of the labels of "actual," "constructive" and "symbolical" delivery. However, the sources do identify these forms,[53] and to a certain extent special rules have been developed in the case law.[54] Accordingly, the forms of "constructive" and "symbolical" delivery warrant special consideration.

Security created by constructive delivery

11.07   The device of a transfer of possession, on the basis of intimation to a neutral third party who holds the goods, is frequently applied as a means of delivery to achieve an outright transfer of ownership.[55] It is

---

[47] Bell, *Comm.*, I, 185. See also *Strachan* v. *Knox & Co.'s Tr.*, 21 June 1817, F.C.

[48] See *Pattison's Tr.* v. *Liston* (1893) 20 R. 806. In this case a majority of the Second Division declined to recognise a transfer of possession because the creditor already had the key in his capacity as house agent for the defender (see at pp. 813–814). Lord Young (diss.) saw no reason why the defender's possession of the keys should not suffice for the purpose of the coming into being of the security intended by the parties, even though he also held them for another purpose (see at p. 818). See also above, para. 8.16, n. 16.

[49] See *Mackinnon* v. *Max Nanson & Co.* (1868) 6 M. 974 at p. 976.

[50] In *Orr's Tr.* v. *Tullis* (1870) 8 M. 936 at p. 944 the Lord Ordinary (Gifford) did not consider that the affixing of a label to printing machinery, which remained with the seller/debtor, amounted to the delivery of possession. See Gloag and Irvine, *Rights in Security*, p. 192.

[51] See above, para. 8.16.

[52] See below, para. 11.09.

[53] See, *e.g.* *Pochin & Co.* v. *Robinows & Marjoribanks* (1869) 7 M. 622, *per* Lord President Inglis at pp. 628–629.

[54] For a summary of the rules applying to the various forms, see Marshall, *Scots Mercantile Law*, paras. 8.82–8.91.

[55] See above, para. 8.20.

also potentially applicable to the creation of a right of security.[56] Moreover, the rules which have been developed to govern its application[57] are the same whether it is used to transfer title pursuant to sale or to create security, either by outright or limited transfer of interest to the creditor. Given that the subject concerned is in the hands of a third party, there is no greater potential for misleading creditors in the transfer—without change in the *status quo* of natural possession—of a real interest for the purpose of security.[58]

Where goods are held on a basis independent of the owner,[59] intimation to the party vested with control[60] is a potentially effective means of creating a security interest whereby the goods are held no longer for the debtor but henceforth for the creditor as pledgee. The critical requirement, from the point of view of the creation of a real right, is intimation by the owner to the custodier, to the effect that the goods are no longer held on his behalf, but henceforth on behalf of a named party as pledgee. In *Inglis* v. *Robertson & Baxter*,[61] Lord Watson emphasised the importance of this "delivery" aspect to create an effective right of pledge:

"by the common law of Scotland the indorsation and hypothecation of delivery-orders, although it may give the pledgee a right to retain the documents, does not give him any real right in the goods which they represent. He can only attain to that right by presenting the delivery-orders to the custodier by whom they were granted, and obtaining delivery of the goods from him, or by making such intimation of his right to the custodier as will make it the legal duty of the latter to hold the goods for him."

Before any right in particular goods can come into being, there must be identification of the goods concerned. Given that the security comes about through a transfer of possession, it is clearly a prerequisite to identify the items in respect of which it is intended to create the interest. Lord MacLaren noted this in contrasting the case of a pledge created by constructive delivery, through the handing over of a delivery order, and the transfer of a bill of lading in security. "It is perfectly true that a delivery-order is worthless as passing specific

---

[56] See, *e.g. Pochin & Co.* v. *Robinows & Marjoribanks*, above.

[57] See above, para. 8.22.

[58] *Ibid.*

[59] In *Anderson* v. *McCall* (1866) 4 M. 765 an attempt to create a security interest failed because the wheat concerned was not held by an independent party but by a storekeeper employed by the debtor.

[60] In *Rhind's Tr.* v. *Robertson & Baxter* (1891) 18 R. 623, *per* Lord Trayner at p. 628 intimation to an excise officer, holding a key to the bonded warehouse containing the stocks of liquor concerned, was held not to amount to constructive delivery because "the goods were in no sense whatever in his custody."

[61] (1898) 25 R.(H.L.) 70 at p. 74.

property until the goods have been ascertained, but that is exactly the distinction between the effect of a delivery-order for goods on shore and a bill of lading."[62]

The case of *Price & Pierce Ltd.* v. *Bank of Scotland*[63] illustrates the possibility of the creation of a security interest over moveables held by a storekeeper.[64] Here a creditor intimated to the storekeeper concerned—and the latter acknowledged—the holding of delivery-orders for a quantity of logs identified by marks stamped on them. It may be noted that this case reflects the essential features of (i) identification of the goods involved, and (ii) intimation to the storekeeper concerned.

Security created by symbolical delivery

11.08   In view of the importance of the actual delivery of the thing pledged to give a change of possession,[65] it is not surprising that symbolical delivery has only a limited rôle. In general it will not suffice merely to hand over a symbol of the property intended to be made subject to the security, and this is consistent with the limited scope of the transfer of ownership in moveables on the basis of the handing over of a symbol of the thing to be conveyed.[66]

The handing over of keys will not necessarily be an instance of symbolical delivery, because possession of the keys may amount to possession of the goods pledged on the basis that access and control fall to the party who holds the keys to the premises in which the moveables concerned are kept. The relevant dicta show that possession of keys will tend to be looked at primarily from this point of view.[67]

From early times[68] the courts have consistently disallowed attempts to create security interests in moveable subjects by an act symbolic of the transfer of possession backed up by a written instrument—"on the

---

[62] *Hayman & Son* v. *McLintock*, 1907 S.C. 936 at p. 952. Regarding the delivery of a bill of lading see above, para. 8.27; see also below, para. 11.09.

[63] 1910 S.C. 1095 at p. 1117. The appeal to the House of Lords is reported in 1912 S.C.(H.L.) 19.

[64] The better view is that this is not a case of *constititum possessorium*; see above, para. 8.24.

[65] See above, para. 11.06.

[66] See above, para. 8.26.

[67] See *Rhind's Tr.* v. *Robertson & Baxter* (1891) 18 R. 623 *per* Lord Trayner at p. 628: "The excise officer was not a warehouseman; the goods were in no sense whatever in his custody at any time either as being held by him for Rhind or anybody else. He has a key of the warehouse where the goods were stored, but that only for the purpose of enabling him to protect the interests of the excise." See also *Pattison's Tr.* v. *Liston* (1893) 20 R. 806 *per* Lord Trayner at pp. 813–814: "if the bankrupt . . . had delivered to the defender the keys of the house where the furniture was situated for the purpose of giving thereby delivery and control of the furniture to the defender to the exclusion of the bankrupt, such a proceeding would have been delivery sufficient to make the security effectual."

[68] See *Ker* v. *Scott & Elliot* (1695) Mor. 9122. See also *Carse* v. *Halyburton* (1714) Mor. 9125.

analogy of the conveyance of heritable property by giving sasine."[69] In *Stiven* v. *Cowan*[70] a symbolic act of handing over keys and locking the premises—the keys were subsequently returned to the owner (*i.e.* the debtor)—followed by recording the act in the Register of Sasines, was held not to amount to a real security; the Lord Ordinary (Curriehill) emphasised that the recording of what had been done did not take the matter any further: "on principle, so far as the moveables are concerned, such an infeftment, even though recorded, would not effectually divest the granter or confer any real right upon the grantee so long as the moveables remained in the possession of the granter." On the basis that the symbolic acts were insufficient to create a real right, it followed that the official recording of the acts concerned had no effect.

Delivery of documents of title

The handing over of a bill of lading is the most important instance of **11.09** symbolical delivery applicable to the creation of a real security interest—as of course it is in respect of an out-and-out transfer of ownership.[71] However, as noted in relation to the transfer of ownership,[72] the bill of lading is more appropriately seen as a transferable document of title to moveables—a special device appropriate to commercial needs in the case of goods in shipment—rather than a prime example of symbolical delivery. The significance of the bill of lading as a document of title was emphasised in a case[73] in which a quantity of bags of flour—subject to a security interest based upon the holding of a bill of lading—were, after shipment, mixed with other identical bags in a store. In rejecting the argument that a change of ownership had occurred on the basis of mixing[74] Lord President Dunedin observed that "when a person gives a document which transfers moveable property he can make a perfectly good security," and that where this occurs: "You cannot lose possession of the moveables unless you lose the document."[75] Plainly enough, identified in this way, the bill of lading is a document of title facilitating the transfer of real rights, rather than an instance of symbolical delivery.

---

[69] Gloag and Irvine, *Rights in Security*, p. 190. In *Fraser* v. *Frisby* (1830) 8 S. 982 the court regarded as ineffective an attempt to give possession by the transmission, to the creditor's agent, of an inventory of the debtor's furniture. In *Paul* v. *Cuthbertson* (1840) 2 D. 1286 the sale of a stand of trees, followed by the symbolic cutting of a few of them, supported by a minute that the buyer had entered into the bargain, was rejected as a means of delivery. In *Roberts* v. *Wallace* (1842) 5 D. 6 a symbolic act of delivery supported by an instrument of possession was held not to confer a preferential right over farm moveables.
[70] (1878) 15 S.L.R. 422 at p. 424.
[71] See above, para. 8.27.
[72] *Ibid.*
[73] *Hayman & Son* v. *McLintock*, 1907 S.C. 936.
[74] See above, para. 5.01.
[75] *Hayman & Son* v. *McLintock*, 1907 S.C. 936 at pp. 949–950.

As indicated above,[76] Lord McLaren in *Hayman & Son* v. *McLin-tock*[77] contrasts a delivery order and a bill of lading from the point of view that the former can only be applied to transfer property in ascertained goods, whereas the object of the latter is to facilitate the transfer of goods in shipment[78]—necessarily including an unascertained part, by weight or measure, of a bulk cargo.[79] Lord McLaren's observations on this are entirely plausible; however, it should be noted that his dictum was *obiter* because in the matter before the court the disputed security related to the entire cargo. Moreover, as indicated above,[80] the English decisions are to the effect that section 16 of the Sale of Goods Act 1979—barring the passing of property pending the ascertainment of goods[81]—operates to prevent the creation of a real right in an unascertained quantity of bulk goods, and the Scottish Law Commission has accepted this as the correct position.[82]

Under the provisions of section 25(1) of the Sale of Goods Act 1979, following section 8 of the Factors Act 1889, an effective pledge may be created by a mercantile agent on the basis of the transfer of the documents of title to goods. The requirements relating to the outright transfer of ownership under this section also apply to the creation of a security interest.[83]

Ex facie absolute transfer in security

11.10   Pledge proper is constituted by the transfer of possession to the creditor with the parties intending to create a security interest. A debtor may, however, agree to an *ex facie* absolute transfer to the creditor, and where followed by some sufficient form of delivery this will give the creditor a title for the purpose of security. In *Hamilton* v. *Western Bank*[84] the creditor bank received as security from its debtor— a firm of merchants—a delivery order on the basis of which a specified quantity of liquor in a bonded warehouse was transferred, in the books of the warehouse keeper, to the bank manager. The First Division held

---

[76] para. 11.07, n. 62.

[77] 1907 S.C. 936 at p. 952.

[78] See above, para. 8.27 n. 34 for the initial part of Lord McLaren's dictum.

[79] See *Hayman* v. *McLintock* 1907 S.C. 936 *per* Lord McLaren at p. 952, as quoted above, para. 8.27, n. 37.

[80] para. 8.27.

[81] See above, para. 9.05, n. 31.

[82] Discussion Paper No. 83, *Bulk Goods* (1989), para. 3.2. See also Gloag and Henderson, para. 20.22: "But, at least so far as sale is concerned, this dictum [*i.e.* Lord McLaren's: above, n. 79] seems inconsistent with the provisions of section 16 of the Sale of Goods Act."

[83] See above, para. 10.21.

[84] (1856) 19 D. 152.

that the transaction was not pledge but a security device which gave the bank an *ex facie* absolute title to the goods.[85]

In *National Bank of Scotland* v. *Forbes*[86] Lord Justice-Clerk Inglis, as he then was, distinguished the cases of pledge and *ex facie* absolute transfer in security from the point of view of the nature of the title "on which the party has attained the possession which he proposes to hold till his debt is paid," noting that "this title of possession furnishes the precise measure of the right of retention."[87] In the case of the creditor obtaining a title of possession limited to a security interest the transaction is pledge, where it is unlimited "as a title of property"[88] the transaction is an *ex facie* absolute transfer in security.

Ex facie absolute transfer in form of sale

A familiar form of *ex facie* absolute transfer in security is a "sale" by **11.11** the debtor to the creditor with the "price" reflected in the amount advanced to or due by the debtor; the object being that the creditor's interest will be protected by his acquisition of ownership of the subject of the sale.[89]

In cases of this type, where the intention of the parties is to create a security interest, there must be delivery to the creditor. Section 62(4) of the Sale of Goods Act 1979,[90] excludes the operation of the Act, in respect of the passing of property,[91] from transactions "intended to operate by way of mortgage, pledge, charge or other security."[92] In the Second Division case of *Robertson* v. *Hall's Tr.*[93] Lord Moncreiff explained the basis of the subsection:

> "This is in effect a statutory declaration that a pledge of or security over moveables cannot be created merely by completion

---

[85] The grounds of this decision have been identified by Alan Rodger, "Pledge of bills of lading in Scots law," 1971 J.R. 193 at p. 194: "(1) There can be no pledge unless the pledgee has custody of the goods, and this the bank never had because it was never intended that they should present the delivery-order, pay the duty and carry off the goods. Nor could they carry off the goods without paying the duty. (2) By presenting the delivery-order and having the goods transferred to their name in the storekeeper's books, the bank obtained merely constructive delivery of the goods and that is insufficient to constitute pledge, which requires actual delivery. (3) The delivery-order was absolute in terms. Its effect was therefore always to transfer property and this effect could not be removed by reference to any agreement between the bank and the merchants, although (4) sufficient notice would be taken of that agreement to make the bank's title merely a security title and to give the merchants a personal right to its reconveyance."

[86] (1858) 21 D. 79.

[87] at p. 85.

[88] *Ibid.*

[89] See, *e.g. Robertson* v. *Hall's Tr.* (1896) 24 R. 120.

[90] s.61(4) of the 1893 Act.

[91] See above, para. 9.02.

[92] See below, para. 12.06 where the subsection is considered from the point of view of credit reservation of title.

[93] (1896) 24 R. 120 at p. 134.

of what professes to be a contract of sale. If the transaction is truly a sale, the property will pass without delivery. But the form of the contract is not conclusive. The reality of the transaction must be inquired into; and if, contrary to the form of the contract, and even the declaration of the parties, it appears from the whole circumstances that a true sale was not intended, it will be held that the property has not passed and that no effectual security has been acquired."

Accordingly, where section 62(4) applies there must be delivery, actual or constructive, to the "purchaser"—the creditor—before a real right of security can come into being.

In *Jones & Co.'s Tr.* v. *Allan*[94] a cycle dealer purported to sell to his creditor a number of cycles specified in a receipt handed over to the "purchaser" together with a promissory note relating to the amount advanced. In fact the "purchaser" did not make any payment as the price of the bicycles, nor were the items specified on the receipt actually delivered to the lender. The majority of the Second Division took the view that the parties had intended security but, because of section 61(4) of the Sale of Goods Act 1893,[95] this could only be achieved through a transaction taking the form of sale if there was delivery of the subjects concerned to the "purchaser." In this respect what had occurred between the parties was regarded as insufficient: "The debtor retained possession of the goods, they not having been in any way delivered or set aside or even identified."[96] Lord Young, dissenting, took a different view. Commencing from the premise that "whatever the motive and intention might be it was as clear a contract of sale as anything could possibly be in its inception," Lord Young observed that "it is no objection to the contract of sale that the only purpose of it was a security to the *ex facie* buyer."[97] Lord Young did not see section 61(4) of the Sale of Goods Act 1893[98] as presenting any difficulty in this regard:

"This language indicates unmistakeably, I think, that in the opinion of the Legislature a transaction in the form of a contract of sale may be intended to operate by way of mortgage, pledge, charge or other security, and lawfully may so operate, and the

---

[94] (1901) 4 F. 374.

[95] s.62(4) of the 1979 Act.

[96] *Jones & Co.'s Tr.* v. *Allan* (1901) 4 F. 374, *per* Lord Justice-Clerk MacDonald at p. 382.

[97] at p. 384. See also *McBain* v. *Wallace & Co.* (1881) 8 R.(H.L.) 106, *per* Lord Chancellor Selborne at p. 109: "whether in some sense security was the object or not, there was here a sale in fact and in intent."

[98] s.62(4) of the 1979 Act.

only purpose of the clause in which it occurs is to leave the law applicable to every such transaction as it stood before the Act."[99]

The point of departure between Lord Young and the rest of the court would appear to be simply what was required at common law by way of delivery. The fact that the parties intended to create a security arrangement by their contract of sale is relevant in this regard. To say that there may be a valid sale, intended to operate by way of security, is unexceptionable but the better view, subscribed to by the majority, is that the form of delivery must then comply with what is required for the creation of a security interest.[1]

Where the transaction concerned falls within the scope of section 62(4) of the Sale of Goods Act 1979, more recent case law does not depart from the requirement of delivery to create an effective security. In *Newbigging* v. *Ritchie's Tr.*,[2] a contract of sale of scheduled livestock was followed by a hire-purchase agreement on the basis of which the "seller" retained possession of the animals purchased by his creditor. The approach of the court was to determine the true nature of the transaction for: "If the transaction was one of loan, the pursuer must admittedly fail, for there was no change in possession of the stock."[3] Lords Ormidale and Anderson[4] both approved the statement of the Lord Ordinary (Kincairney) in *Robertson* v. *Hall's Tr.*[5]:

"I am disposed to think that a conveyance of moveables has been sustained to the effect of constituting a security for an advance where the transaction has been in reality a pure sale, although the whole object of it has been to effect a security, and although there may be an understanding that the ownership shall revert to the borrower when that purpose has been served."

In the circumstances it was held that the contract was truly one of loan and that the creditor, not having obtained possession of the stock, did not have a real right of security.

In *Scottish Transit Trust* v. *Scottish Land Cultivators*[6] a debtor company purported to sell to its creditor company certain earth-moving equipment and vehicles. Possession was retained on the basis of hire-purchase with the debtor company given a right to repurchase,

---

[99] *Jones & Co.'s Tr.* v. *Allan* (1901) 4 F. 374 at p. 385. Lord Young's dissenting judgment in *Rennet* v. *Mathieson* (1903) 5 F. 591 at pp. 597–598 is another instance of his readiness to regard the delivery requirement as satisfied by a formal change of title.

[1] See generally above, para. 11.03.

[2] 1930 S.C. 273.

[3] *per* Lord Justice-Clerk Alness at p. 285.

[4] at pp. 288 and 290 respectively.

[5] (1896) 24 R. 120 at p. 127.

[6] 1955 S.C. 254.

for a nominal amount, when all the hire-purchase instalments had been paid. Lord Russell took the view that, despite the contrary assertion of the pursuer's witnesses, the reality of the transaction was security and that this conclusion did not confuse "the motive with the contractual intention of the parties."[7] In short, not only was it the parties' motive to create a security interest, but this was also the manifest intention behind their actings. Put another way, one could not say that, disregarding the parties' ulterior motive to create a security interest, the circumstances were none the less consistent with an intention to enter into a genuine sale. In *Ladbroke Leasing (South West) Ltd.* v. *Reekie Plant Ltd.*[8] an earth-moving shovel was sold and delivered on the basis that the seller retained ownership pending full payment. To facilitate the provision of finance the purchasers resold the shovel but it was never removed from their premises. Lord Grieve took the view that the transaction was a scheme to raise finance using the shovel as security for the advance of funds and that, as such, it was struck down by section 62(4) of the Sale of Goods Act 1979.

The possibility of the circumstances supporting an intention to conclude a genuine contract of sale, regardless of an ulterior motive to create a security interest is demonstrated in the case of *Gavin's Tr.* v. *Fraser.*[9] A contractor retained the possession and use of plant which he had sold to a timber merchant to whom he was in debt. Two agreements formed the basis of the parties' relationship. The first was an unequivocal sale of the plant with the price made up partly of sums already advanced and partly in cash; the second was an option in favour of the seller/debtor to repurchase the plant—*a pactum de retrovendendo.* Lord President Clyde regarded as significant the fact that there was no personal obligation, due by the seller, to be secured. In this regard the circumstances were distinguishable from most of the earlier authorities in which the sale was usually linked to the acknowledgment of a loan to the seller.[10] Moreover, the *pactum de retrovendendo* was seen by Lord President Clyde as consistent with an out-and-out sale in that "it proceeds on the assumption that the rights flowing from the sale are effective."[11]

Scope of security in giving priority to the creditor

11.12   The pledge of a corporeal moveable gives the creditor a real right in the thing amounting to a preference in the event of the debtor's insolvency or in the circumstances of multiplepoinding. But the

---

[7] at p. 262. In *G. and C. Finance Corp. Ltd.* v. *Brown*, 1961 S.L.T. 408 a hire-purchase company claimed ownership of a vehicle which it had purported to purchase and give back on hire-purchase. But the "sale" price was paid before the transaction was concluded and at no relevant stage was there any change in the *status quo* of possession of the vehicle. This case is a strong example of an attempt to create a security interest by a simulated sale without transferring possession.

[8] 1983 S.L.T. 155.

[9] 1920 S.C. 674.

[10] See at p. 684.

[11] at p. 683.

creditor's priority does not extend beyond the amount of the debt in respect of which the security was granted.[12] Where, however, the security is granted in the form of an *ex facie* absolute transfer the creditor's right is more extensive than it would be in the case of a simple pledge. In this regard one may note the remarks of Lord Deas in *Hamilton* v. *Western Bank of Scotland*[13]:

"In a case of pledge the property remains with the pledger, and, consequently, if the article be pledged for a specific debt, the right to withhold it is limited to that debt. But in a transference like this the property passes to the transferee, subject only to a personal obligation to recover, and consequently the right of retention for the general balance, competent by the law of Scotland to a party in whose favour the property has been transferred, comes to be applicable—just as happens in the case of an absolute disposition to heritage, or an intimated assignation to a debt qualified by a back-bond."[14]

The case of *Laurie* v. *Denny's Tr.*,[15] although concerned with a right of retention[16] rather than a security interest created by agreement, illustrates the difference between, on the one hand, an interest limited to the particular debt applying to the goods held and, on the other hand, a more extensive interest whereby the goods are considered to be held as security in respect of any debt arising from the relevant relationship. In this case it was held that, on the bankruptcy of a grain merchant, a storekeeper was only entitled to retain grain deposited by the grain merchant in respect of rents due for the particular parcels of grain held and not in respect of any general balance owing from the course of dealings between the parties.

---

[12] The straightforward case is that of a pledge given as security for the repayment of an existing debt—or one about to be incurred—of fixed or at least finite amount. For example, A agrees to lend B £1000 repayable in 12 months with interest at 1 per cent. over the maximum bank rate in the period and, by way of security, B hands over in pledge to A a pair of diamond earrings. In this example A's priority over the earrings will be limited to the capital amount of the debt plus the interest due at the time of repayment. A subsequent additional advance of £500, not provided for in the parties' original agreement and made without reference to the pledge, will not be secured.

[13] (1856) 19 D. 152 at p. 166.

[14] See also *National Bank of Scotland* v. *Forbes* (1858) 21 D. 79 *per* Lord Justice-Clerk Inglis at p. 85: "If the title of possession be unlimited, as a title of property, the party is entitled to retain till every debt due by the party demanding delivery of the subject is paid. If his title be limited, he can retain only for the payment of the particular debt which is secured by his possession."

[15] (1853) 15 D. 404.

[16] See below, para. 11.16.

Scope of security regarding a right of sale

11.13   In the case of pledge the creditor does not have any implied power of sale in the event of the debtor failing to comply with his obligation.[17] As Stair[18] notes, given the protection inherent in pledge, the creditor must proceed by one or other of the applicable means of diligence: "there being a real right of the pledge, no other diligence will affect it further, than as to the reversion of it, on payment of the creditor's debt." But although there is no implied right of sale "a power to sell is not inconsistent with the contract of pledge, and is frequently conferred."[19]

While pledge merely gives the creditor a real security interest, the device of *ex facie* absolute transfer of title has the potential to make the creditor owner and, in this situation, a right of sale is implied. Arguably, by its nature an absolute transfer must produce this result. There is unequivocal authority that a disposition *ex facie* absolute applying to heritable property gives a power of sale,[20] and there is no reason in principle why moveable property should be subject to any different dispensation. If the relatively stringent requirements of the law which govern the validity of *ex facie* absolute dispositions in security are satisfied,[21] there should be no difficulty concerning an implied power of sale where the parties have not expressly provided for such a power.

The unavoidable consequence of *ex facie* absolute disposition is such that even if the parties agree that the creditor should not have a power of sale this will be ineffective from the point of view of the standing of a third-party acquirer from the creditor—although, of course, it may be the basis of a right of action against the creditor by the debtor.[22]

---

[17] See Bell, *Prin.*, § 207: "with us . . . the subject of the pledge cannot be sold without the order of a judge, which is obtained on a summary application to the Sheriff." See also § 1363: "a power over the subject, to retain it in security of the debt for which it is pledged: and, if necessary, to have it sold judicially for payment."

[18] I.xiii.11.

[19] Gloag and Irvine, *Rights in Security*, p. 213.

[20] See *Baillie* v. *Drew* (1884) 12 R. 199 at p. 202; *Aberdeen Trades Council* v. *Ship-constructors and Shipwrights Association*, 1949 S.C.(H.L.) 45 *per* Lord Simonds at p. 51: "The first question, which I conceive to be of general importance, is whether a disponee under an *ex facie* absolute disposition qualified by a duly recorded back letter has a power of sale of the subjects conveyed limited only by such restrictions upon that power as may be contained in the back letter. I speak here of title and disregard any contractual obligation that may be founded upon an unrecorded back letter or other instrument. In spite of the strenuous argument of the learned counsel for the appellant I have no doubt what the answer to this question must be. It is that such a disponee has such a power."

[21] See above, para. 11.11.

[22] See *Baillie* v. *Drew* (1884) 12 R. 199 *per* Lord Justice-Clerk Moncreiff at p. 202: "In regard to the limitations of the creditor's right, it has been well settled that, in the first place, an absolute disposition will give the purchaser under it—where the sale is by virtue of powers to the granting of which the debtor has been a party—an absolute right, and that it will not be in the power of the original proprietor, the debtor, to quarrel that disposition, if the powers of the creditor have been duly and properly exercised. It is

Application of Consumer Credit Act 1974 to security founded on possession

The Consumer Credit Act 1974 repealed the Pawnbrokers Acts of **11.14** 1872 and 1960[23] and now regulates pawnbroking.[24] The provisions concerned do not apply to "non-commercial agreements."[25] Such an agreement is defined as

> "a consumer credit agreement or a consumer hire agreement not made by the creditor or owner in the course of a business carried on by him."[26]

The relevant sections of the Consumer Credit Act 1974 use the word "pawn," meaning "any article subject to a pledge."[27] In the terminology of the Act the debtor/pledgor is "pawner" and the creditor/pledgee is "pawnee." The concept of pledge—defined as "the pawnee's rights over an article taken in pawn"[27a]—is in accordance with the common law.

Section 114(1) requires the party taking an article in pawn under a regulated agreement[28] to give to the person from whom he receives it "a receipt in the prescribed form (a 'pawn-receipt')."[29]

A pawn is redeemable at any time within six months after it was taken[30] or, subject to this maximum period, within the period agreed upon by the parties for the duration of the credit secured by the pledge or within such longer period as they may have agreed.[31] If the pawn is not redeemed by the end of the period determined on the above basis it nevertheless remains redeemable until realised by the pawnee under section 121 unless, under section 120(1)(*a*) relating to low-value credit,[32] property in the pawn has passed to the pawnee.[33] Unless the

---

another matter where the question is between the debtor himself and the creditor, for if the creditor has not exercised this right—absolute as it is where third parties are concerned—in a fair, reasonable, and equitable manner, the Court will give a remedy, and that remedy will not be by setting aside the sale, but by giving the pursuer, the debtor, an opportunity of proving damage, arising from reckless or inequitable use of the powers which the disposition gave him."

[23] See Sched. 5 to the Consumer Credit Act 1974. Generally on the Act see *Stair Memorial Encyclopaedia* (Vol. 5) paras. 801–965.

[24] See ss.114–122.

[25] s.114(3)(*b*).

[26] s.189(1).

[27] *Ibid.*

[27a] *Ibid.*

[28] Defined in s.189(1) as "a consumer credit agreement, or consumer hire agreement, other than an exempt agreement."

[29] Regarding the form of receipt, see the Consumer Credit (Pawn-Receipts) Regulations 1983 (S.I. 1983 No. 1566); where the receipt is combined with the regulated agreement the Consumer Credit (Agreements) Regulations 1983 (S.I. 1983 No. 1553).

[30] s.116(1).

[31] s.116(2).

[32] At the time of writing under £25.

[33] See s.116(3).

pawnee knows, or has reasonable cause to suspect, that the bearer of the pawn-receipt is neither the owner nor authorised by the owner, he shall, on surrender of the pawn receipt and payment of the amount due, deliver the pawn to the bearer of the pawn-receipt.[34]

Redemption is possible even though the claimant does not have the pawn-receipt. Section 118 provides that in this situation redemption can be achieved by tendering to the pawnee a statutory declaration or, in the case of a low value loan,[35] a written statement.[36]

If on termination of the redemption period the pawn has not been redeemed it becomes redeemable by the pawnee[37]; in the case of low value credit[38] the property in the pawn simply passes to the pawnee.[39] Section 121 prescribes the process of realisation.[40] The pawnor is entitled to notice of the pawnee's intention to sell and where a sale occurs details as to proceeds and expenses must be given. If the proceeds of the sale exceed the sum which would have been payable for redemption, the debt secured by the pawn is discharged and any surplus shall be paid by the pawnee to the pawnor[41]; if there is a shortfall the debt is reduced by the net proceeds of the sale.[42] The onus is on the pawnee to show that reasonable care was used to ensure that the true market value was obtained and that the expenses of the sale were reasonable.[43]

Section 122 provides for the case of an article stolen or obtained by fraud being pawned. The Act empowers the court convicting a person of theft or fraud to order delivery of the pawn to the owner or the party entitled to it. Such an order may be made subject to appropriate conditions as to the payment of the debt secured by the pawn.[44]

SECURITY IMPLIED BY LAW

Basis of implied possessory security

11.15   In certain circumstances the law allows a creditor to retain a thing in security where otherwise he would be required to hand it over. The rationale behind this device is that a creditor is justified in retaining

---

[34] s.117. It may be noted that s.119(1) provides that it is an offence to refuse without reasonable cause to allow a pawn to be redeemed.

[35] See above, n. 32.

[36] Regarding the form of these documents, in lieu of a pawn-receipt, see the Consumer Credit (Loss of Pawn-Receipt) Regulations (S.I. 1983 No. 1567).

[37] s.120(1)(b).

[38] See above, n. 32.

[39] s.120(1)(a).

[40] See also the Consumer Credit (Realisation of Pawn) Regulations 1983 (S.I. 1983 No. 1568).

[41] s.121(3).

[42] s.121(4).

[43] s.121(6).

[44] This section applies exclusively to Scotland; in England the Theft Act 1968 is applicable.

property belonging to, or claimed by, his debtor pending satisfaction of the debt. Esrkine[45] observes that a right of retention does not extinguish obligations but merely suspends them "till he who pleads it obtains payment or satisfaction from his counter claim." Erskine, of course, is referring to the suspension of what is due by the creditor to the debtor; but from the point of view of the creditor it is not only a matter of the suspension of his obligation to restore the thing but also the fact that he obtains a real right of security in the moveable concerned.

Distinction between retention and lien

Stair[46] defines retention in broad terms to include the act whereby **11.16** and the right on the basis of which what is due may be retained "till satisfaction be made to the retained." Subsequent to Stair, it seems, the term "lien"—meaning a tie over—came into the Scottish legal vocabulary.[47]

More, in his notes to the 1832 edition of Stair,[48] attempted to resolve any possible tautology by arguing that retention applied where a creditor had a right of diligence: on the basis that he could not arrest or poind what he had possession of, the right of retention was allowed in lieu. Lien, on the other hand, was seen to be based upon an implied agreement allowing, in particular cases, a right to retain the debtor's property.[49]

Later in the nineteenth century the juxtaposition of retention and lien was resolved in a manner consistent with the basic principles of property.[50] In Hamilton v. *Western Bank of Scotland*[51] Lord Curriehill explained the position as follows:

> "This right of *retention* is *sua natura* different from a right of *lien*; inasmuch as retention entitles a party who is the owner, or

---

[45] III.iv.20. See also Stair, I.xviii.7.

[46] *Ibid.*

[47] See the argument in *Harper* v. *Faulds* (1791) Mor. 2666. Gloag and Irvine (*Rights in Security*, p. 329) cite this case in support of the following statement: "Originally, indeed, it would appear that the doctrine of retention is a part of the law of Scotland, derived from the civil law, while lien is an equitable right introduced from the law of England."

[48] cxxxi.

[49] Gloag and Irvine (*op. cit.*, p. 329) are critical of this theory on the basis that it supports an unduly wide notion of retention—but so, it would appear, does Stair. Brown (*Sale of Goods*, p. 310) also contends that—until the mid-19th century—retention signified "a right to retain property in the lawful custody of a person other than the owner until a counter obligation due by the owner to the holder had been duly implemented."

[50] Given the requirement of delivery to convey property in Scots law, one can see the scope for retention on the basis of withholding delivery pending receipt of the price. This point was noted by Lord President Inglis in *Black* v. *Incorporation of Bakers, Glasgow* (1867) 6 M. 136 at p. 140. On Scottish retention and English lien see Brown, *Sale of Goods*, p. 313.

[51] (1856) 19 D. 152 at p. 163.

dominus of property, to withhold performance of some personal obligation to transfer his right of ownership to another, until the latter perform a counter obligation; whereas lien entitles a party who is in possession of what is another party's property, to continue to withhold it from its real owner, until the latter perform a counter obligation. And, on the other hand, the corresponding right to demand possession of the property, on the counter obligation being performed, is, in the former case, merely a personal right, or *jus crediti*; while, in the latter case, it is the real right of property."[52]

In the result the law recognises, on the one hand, the obvious right of retention based upon a proprietary interest in the thing concerned and, on the other hand, a right merely based upon the fact of possession of one holding the thing on the basis of or for the purposes of a contract.[53] These forms are respectively designated "retention" and "lien." Gloag and Irvine[54] define retention as a right which exists "when the owner of property is under a personal obligation to transfer it to a party who is in debt to him"; and lien as applying "where a person is in possession or is the custodier of property which belongs to a party who is in debt to him."[55]

Retention at common law

11.17   A right of retention in favour of an owner is implied at common law where a claimant to the subject concerned is bound to the owner in an unsatisfied obligation. Retention applies as a basis upon which an owner may withhold the transfer of title—due in terms of an agreement with the other party—pending performance of what is due by

---

[52] See also the dictum of Lord Justice-Clerk Hope in *Melrose* v. *Hastie* (1851) 13 D. 880 at p. 887 contrasting liens "arising out of special contracts, and founded on possession given for a specific purpose and on a limited title—or rather, on a temporary delegation of title" and "the right of retention of the undivested owner of moveables, subject to a contract of sale." See also the dictum of Lord Moncreiff at p. 900 (quoted with approval by Lord President McNeill in *Robertson's Tr.* v. *Baird* (1852) 14 D. 1010 at p. 1014) explaining the basis of the right of retention as something distinct from lien.
[53] As Lord President Inglis urged in *Black* v. *Incorporation of Bakers, Glasgow* (1867) 6 M. 136 at p. 140, the difference is so fundamental that there is no justification for "an identity between the seller's right of retention in Scotland and the seller's lien in England." The learned Lord President observed: "The seller's right of retention thus being grounded on an undivested right of property, cannot possibly be of the nature of a lien, for one can have a lien only over the property of another."
[54] *Rights in Security*, p. 330.
[55] Smith, *Short Commentary*, p. 477, n. 87, is critical of the definition in s.62(1) of the Sale of Goods Act 1893 to the effect that "Lien in Scotland includes right of retention"—not, it may be noted, repeated in the definition section (s.61(1)) of the Sale of Goods Act 1979. The learned author comments: "The right of lien is a right to remain in possession; and this may be contrasted with a right of retention, which is founded upon property." See also Gloag and Henderson, para. 20.29.

way of counter obligation.[56] Implied retention is essentially similar in its effect to retention created by agreement whereby a debtor makes an *ex facie* absolute transfer of title to his creditor on the basis of an undertaking by the creditor to reconvey upon the debtor meeting his obligation.[57] This said, implied retention must necessarily be in accordance with the contractual context within which it operates. Accordingly, whereas in the case of a cash sale the owner can withhold delivery pending payment it is otherwise if the sale is a credit transaction. Lord Young noted this distinction in *Fleming* v. *Smith & Co.*[58]:

"Now, there is no doubt that by our law the undivested seller, unless he bargains otherwise, is entitled to retain for the price. If he sells on credit he is of course bound to deliver according to the contract to the buyer, having waived his right to payment before delivery."

Clearly enough, the seller's right of retention prevails only provided that property has not already passed to the buyer. The possibility, at common law, that there could be a conveyance of title without actual delivery to the buyer[59] meant, that there could be no question of the assertion of a right of retention by the seller after an act amounting to constructive delivery on his part. As Lord Mackenzie put it in *Melrose* v. *Hastie*[60]: "A seller may refuse delivery of goods until he gets payment, or until something has been done equivalent to a transmission of the property." On a bill of exceptions relating to a new trial in the same matter it was held that the issuing of a delivery order by the seller amounted to no more than a revocable mandate and was incapable of proprietary effect in the manner of a bill of lading.[61] Where the circumstances of the granting of a delivery order did not amount to constructive delivery to the immediate purchaser there could be no question of the indorsee acquiring a proprietary interest which would defeat the owner's right of retention.[62] Where the

---

[56] See Stair, I.x.16. See also *Wright* v. *Mitchell* (1871) 9 M. 516 *per* Lord President Inglis at p. 518: "In one sense every sale is conditional on payment of the price, for the seller is not bound to deliver the article sold except upon payment of the price, and the buyer is not bound to pay until delivery, no matter though it is stipulated that the price is to be paid in a particular way, or that the goods are to be delivered in a particular place."
[57] See above para. 11.10.
[58] (1881) 8 R. 548 at p. 552.
[59] See above, paras. 8.14 and 8.20.
[60] (1850) 12 D. 665 at p. 670.
[61] See *Melrose* v. *Hastie* (1851) 13 D. 880 at pp. 884–885; see also *McEwan* v. *Smith* (1849) 6 Bell's App. 340 at p. 352.
[62] See *McEwan* v. *Smith* (1847) 9 D. 434 at pp. 460–461; affd. (1849) 6 Bell's App. 340. See also *Distillers Co. Ltd.* v. *Russell's Tr.* (1889) 16 R. 479.

circumstances did amount to constructive delivery a seller would lose the right to retain goods held on his behalf.[63]

As developed in nineteenth-century decisions, the seller's right of retention came to be a wide and far-reaching device.[64] Two features, in particular, show its scope. First, the right applied not only against the immediate purchaser in respect of whom it was intended to provide security but also against a sub-purchaser who contracted in good faith on the basis of a valid delivery note endorsed in his favour.[65] Secondly, the seller's right was not restricted to the amount due to him by way of price, but extended to all debts due by the purchaser. Although of questionable validity from a point of view of principle—because it tends to blur the distinction between separate obligations—the extension appears to be well established.[66]

Seller's right of retention modified by legislation

11.18   The common law position relating to a seller's right of retention and, in particular, the problem of the scope of the right against a subsequent purchaser was modified by the Mercantile Law Amendment (Scotland) Act 1856.[67] The relevant sections of the 1856 Act were recast in the provisions of the Sale of Goods Act 1893 which continue to apply in the Sale of Goods Act 1979.[68]

The Sale of Goods Act 1893 introduced a general departure from the requirement of delivery to transfer title and substituted, as the primary basis for the transmission of property, the notion of ownership passing on the conclusion of the contract of sale.[69] A consequence of this was that the basis of retention was eliminated in respect of the usual contract of sale—by far its most important sphere of operation. However, Part V of the Sale of Goods Act to some extent maintains

---

[63] In *Bovill* v. *Dixon* (1854) 16 D. 619, concerned with a warrant drawn in the form of a promise to deliver iron "to the party lodging this document with me," the right of retention was held to be lost (see *per* Lord Wood at p. 638). See Gloag and Irvine, *Rights in Security*, p. 261.

[64] See the summary in Gloag and Henderson, para. 17.5.

[65] This rule is based upon an unqualified application of the principle *nemo dat quod non habet*. If the circumstances did not amount to constructive delivery to the original purchaser there could be no question of the acquisition of a proprietary right by a *bona fide* sub-purchaser and, indeed, the particular equities, as between original seller and sub-purchaser, could be taken to be irrelevant—even in the circumstances of the insolvency of the first purchaser; see *Wyper* v. *Harveys* (1861) 23 D. 606 in particular *per* Lord Deas (dissenting) at pp. 623–631. *Cf.* the decision in *Fleming* v. *Smith & Co.* (1881) 8 R. 548, where recognition was given to the sub-purchaser's rights in the circumstances of the first purchaser's insolvency.

[66] See *Robertson's Tr.* v. *Baird* (1852) 14 D. 1010 *per* Lord President McNeill at p. 1014: "It is not necessary that these counter obligations should arise out of the same contract." See also *Landale & Co.'s Tr.* v. *Bogle & Co.* (1828) 6 S. 360.

[67] See *Wyper* v. *Harveys* (1861) 23 D. 606 at pp. 611–615.

[68] On this legislative development see Gloag and Irvine, *Rights in Security*, pp. 262–272.

[69] See above para. 9.02.

the balance between the unpaid seller and the buyer with a right to possession of the subjects sold.[70] Under the heading "rights of unpaid seller against the goods" the Act provides for three devices which may be seen as forms of security interest: the unpaid seller's lien, stoppage in transit and a right of resale. These forms of protection which, the merits of the evolution aside, may be seen as successors to the common law right of retention in the context of sale,[71] will be considered in the following sections.

Unpaid seller's protection under the Sale of Goods Act 1979: prelimin- **11.19**
ary matters

Definition of unpaid seller. The recipient of the three security interest **11.19a**
devices provided for in Part V of the Act is the unpaid seller and this condition is defined in the first part of section 38 which provides as follows:

"(1) The seller of goods is an unpaid seller within the meaning of this Act—
(*a*) when the whole of the price has not been paid or tendered;
(*b*) when a bill of exchange or other negotiable instrument has been received as conditional payment, and the condition on which it was received has not been fulfilled by reason of the dishonour of the instrument or otherwise."

In the second subsection "seller" is defined as including: "any person who is in the position of a seller, as, for instance, an agent of the seller to whom the bill of lading has been indorsed, or a consignor or agent who has himself paid (or is directly responsible for) the price."[72] It should be noted that this is an extended notion of "seller" from the general definition of "a person who sells or agrees to sell goods."[73] The

---

[70] See *Hostess Mobile Catering* v. *Archibald Scott Ltd.*, 1981 S.C. 185 *per* Lord MacDonald at p. 187 regarding the change brought about by the Sale of Goods Act 1893: "Counsel for the defenders argued that the unpaid seller's right of lien was introduced into the law of Scotland for the first time by the 1893 Act. He said this was done because the Act altered the common law by providing that the property in the goods sold passed when the parties intended and not on delivery. Thus an unpaid seller in possession had, at common law, no need for a right of lien, because he owned the goods until he delivered them to the purchaser. When the law was altered to make ownership dependent on intention it was thought proper to give him a right of lien so long as he remained in possession and was unpaid. Thus far the argument is sound."
[71] But some would reject this as a superficial and uncritical view; see Gow, *Mercantile Law*, p. 108: "the Sale of Goods Act, 1893, created even more distortion by imposing the unpaid seller's lien and by making the conveyance depend upon the intention of the parties."
[72] s.38(2).
[73] s.61(1). But this general definition already includes as a person who "agrees to sell" the case of a buyer who resells goods before obtaining ownership. That such a party is covered follows from s.2(4) and (5) of the Act which distinguishes a "contract of sale" whereby property passes and an "agreement to sell" envisaging the passing of property at some stage in the future.

inclusion of a party "in the position of a seller" is intended to cover those who are *de facto* sellers of goods even if, technically speaking, the party in question is an agent or factor. The qualification applying to the example of a consignor or agent as one "who has himself paid (or is directly responsible for) the price"[74] is significant in that it indicates the thrust of the subsection towards the circumstances of *de facto* sale.[75] It is only logical that the protective devices provided for should extend to a party who, as part of the commercial chain of supply of goods, bears the risk of non-payment on insolvency. The two examples given in the subsection are merely illustrative and do not exhaust the cases of a person "in the position of a seller."[76]

A buyer who, after the justifiable rejection of goods, is left with a claim for repayment of the purchase price is not, however, a party "in the position of a seller" for the purposes of retaining the goods, on the basis provided for in the Act,[77] pending repayment of the price.[78] Although the buyer in this situation has paid the price he cannot, in any sense, be seen as a seller involved in the chain of supply. Rejection of the goods leaves the buyer with only a contractual remedy and thus subject to the risk of the seller's insolvency.[79]

Turning to the statutory criteria of "unpaid seller," the effect of section 38(1)(*a*) is that the condition of "unpaid" prevails until payment is made in full or there is a tender of full payment.[80] Regardless of whether the sale was for cash or on a credit basis, the seller remains "unpaid" until full or final payment is made. Even where, on the basis of the parties' contract, payment is not yet due the seller can be "unpaid" within the meaning of section 38(1); both the seller's lien and the right of stoppage in transit are available in the

---

[74] s.38(2).

[75] According to Brown (*Sale of Goods*, p. 307), s.38(2) is consistent with the English decision in *Feise* v. *Wray* (1802) 3 East 93 at pp. 102–103. In this case a commission agent who bought in his own name but for consignment to a principal was held to be a seller for the purpose of stopping goods in transit to his insolvent principal.

[76] Benjamin (*Sale of Goods*, para. 1114) contends that a surety for the buyer who has paid the seller qualifies on the basis that he is "subrogated to the rights of the seller against the defaulting buyer." It does seem arguable that a cautioner could be "in the position of a seller" in so far as he has assumed responsibility for payment of the price to the original seller and in lieu thereof obtained the original buyer's right to the goods.

[77] s.39(1)(*a*).

[78] *J. L. Lyons & Co.* v. *May and Baker Ltd.* [1923] 1 K.B. 685 *per* Shearman J. at p. 689: "I am unable to say that a person who has bought and paid for and afterwards rejected goods is a person like an unpaid seller."

[79] In *Kwei Tek Chao* v. *British Traders and Shippers Ltd.* [1954] 2 Q.B. 459 at p. 483, Devlin J. noted that: "faced merely with an unsecured claim for the recovery back from the seller of the price which he had originally paid" the seller did not opt to reject the goods.

[80] This would appear to be consistent with the common law right of rejection available pending payment of the full price. See *Landale & Co.'s Tr.* v. *Bogle & Co.* (1828) 6 S. 360 *per* Lord Gillies at p. 362: "The fact of the full price not having been paid is sufficient to decide the case, because Landale and Company, at the date of their bankruptcy, could not have demanded possession of the goods. "

circumstances of the buyer's insolvency[81] and the exercise of these rights, in the context of insolvency, is not dependent upon payment being due.

The seller is also an "unpaid seller" where under section 38(1)(*b*) a negotiable instrument has been received as conditional payment and, "by reason of the dishonour of the instrument or otherwise," the condition has not been fulfilled. This is in accordance with the common law position that payment by negotiable instrument is "subject always to the condition that the cheque will be met when presented."[82] In *McDowall & Neilson's Tr.* v. *J. B. Snowball Co. Ltd.*[83] it was contended that the buyers had paid for a cargo of timber by accepting bills for the price in favour of the sellers and that the sellers, accordingly, did not have the rights of "unpaid sellers." Lord Moncreiff did not accept this argument:

> "In my opinion the payment so made was conditional, and as the acceptances were immediately found to be worthless owing to the insolvency of the buyers, Snowball Company, Limited, were unpaid sellers in the sense of section 44 of the Sale of Goods Act, and were entitled to stop the goods *in transitu*, and resume possession of them."

Section 38(1)(*b*) uses the words "by reason of the dishonour of the instrument or otherwise" to identify the condition of "unpaid" where payment is by negotiable instrument. The accepted view is that the "or otherwise" refers to the circumstances of an insolvent buyer.[84] Although, in principle, the seller cannot claim the price, and accordingly has no lien pending the maturity of a bill of exchange, these remedies become available upon the buyer's insolvency.[85]

Definition of state of insolvency. Because the protection accorded an **11.19b** "unpaid seller" by the rights of lien or stoppage prevails in the circumstances of the buyer's insolvency[86]—in the latter case only in these circumstances—it is necessary to define the state of "insolvency." Section 61(4) provides that

> "A person is deemed to be insolvent within the meaning of this Act if he has either ceased to pay his debts in the ordinary course of business or he cannot pay his debts as they become due,

---

[81] ss. 41(1)(*c*) and 44.

[82] *Leggat Brothers* v. *Gray*, 1908 S.C. 67 *per* Lord President Dunedin at p. 74.

[83] (1904) 7 F. 35 at p. 46.

[84] See Benjamin, *Sale of Goods*, para. 1119.

[85] See Brown, *op. cit.*, p. 305, n. (g): "The non-fulfilment of the condition may arise from the buyer's insolvency during the currency of the bill, and before actual dishonour."

[86] ss.39(1)(*b*), 41(1)(*c*) and 44.

whether he has committed an act of bankruptcy or not, and whether he has become a notour bankrupt or not."[87]

11.19c Summary of unpaid seller's rights. Section 39 gives a summary of the unpaid seller's rights as provided for in this part of the Act, but the importance of the section lies in certain fundamental matters which it aims to settle. The section reads:

> "(1) Subject to this and any other Act, notwithstanding that the property in the goods may have passed to the buyer, the unpaid seller of goods, as such, has by implication of law—
> (a) a lien on the goods or right to retain them for the price while he is in possession of them;
> (b) in case of the insolvency of the buyer, a right of stopping the goods in transit after he has parted with the possession of them;
> (c) a right of re-sale as limited by this Act.
> (2) Where the property in goods has not passed to the buyer, the unpaid seller has (in addition to his other remedies) a right of withholding delivery similar to and co-extensive with his right of lien or retention and stoppage in transit where the property has passed to the buyer."

The scope of the unpaid seller's rights against the buyer in a competition with a subsequent party who has obtained a right in the goods is dealt with in section 47.[88]

The present work is not concerned with the consequences from a contractual point of view of the exercise by an unpaid seller of his right of lien, retention or stoppage in transit.[89] From a property point of view it may be noted that section 48(2) provides that the unpaid seller who resells pursuant to his right of lien, retention or stoppage gives a good title against the original buyer.[90]

What is the significance of the identification, in section 39(1), of an unpaid seller's rights as prevailing "by implication of law"? The answer is to be found in section 55—under the heading "supplementary"—providing that what arises under a contract of sale "by implication of law" may be departed from by the parties.[91] The subsection provides that where a right, duty or liability arises as an implied term it may be "negatived or varied by express agreement, or by the course of dealing between the parties, or by such usage as binds both parties to the contract."[92]

---

[87] In questions between a debtor and his creditors, insolvency normally means "apparent" or "practical" insolvency—the inability to pay debts. The Bankruptcy (Scotland) Act 1913 (s.5) referred to the state of "notour bankruptcy," but now see s.7 of the Bankruptcy (Scotland) Act 1985 and McBryde, *Bankruptcy*, pp. 5–6.
[88] See below para. 11.25.
[89] See s.48(1), (3) and (4) regarding contractual implications.
[90] See below, para. 11.25 regarding priorities.
[91] s.55(1).
[92] *Ibid.*

Section 39(2) is concerned with the seller's rights in the situation in which property has not passed to the buyer. In so far as the seller is undivested he has a right of retention.[93] Indeed, whatever the consequences from a contractual point of view between himself and the buyer, it must be the case that in so far as he retains his proprietary right the seller has the power to deal with the goods. The statutory recognition of an undivested owner's proprietary power over his goods would seem to be no more than confirmatory.[94] But the subsection is open to an interpretation relating solely to the position between the seller and the buyer.[95] As the section is concerned with the seller's position *vis-à-vis* a non-paying buyer, it is unexceptionable that the scope of subsection (2) should be so limited. The better view, it is submitted, is that the subsection does no more more than provide the unpaid seller with a clear right to resist the buyer's contractual claim for delivery without risk of breach of contract. The subsection does not mention the undivested seller's right of resale because this is a right independent of the contractual position between the parties.[96]

Arrestment or poinding by seller. Until its repeal by the Debtors (Scotland) Act 1987,[97] section 40 of the Sale of Goods Act 1979 gave the seller of goods—the property of which had passed to the debtor— the power to arrest the goods concerned "in his own hands or possession." There was no counterpart process in English law. Given the seller's right of lien under section 41 it is difficult to see the object of section 40; one suggestion is that it was intended to extend to the sphere of the Act the common law right of retention to enable the seller "to obtain a right over the goods in security of other debts due to him by the buyer."[98] **11.19d**

---

[93] See above, para. 11.16.

[94] See Atiyah, *Sale of Goods*, pp. 431–432.

[95] Benjamin, *Sale of Goods*, § 1111: "The 'right' of withholding delivery under section 39(2) is a right as against the buyer, *viz.* an entitlement to withhold delivery without committing a breach of the contract. Before the property passes to the buyer, the seller, as owner of the goods, clearly enjoys the legal power to withold delivery from the buyer . . . But although at common law the seller who retained the property would have the *power* to pass a good title to a third person, it would not necessarily be a *right* or entitlement to do so as against the original buyer (*i.e.* without breach of the original contract)."

[96] Brown (*Sale of Goods*, p. 309), referring to *Muir* v. *Rankin* (1905) 13 S.L.T. 60 follows Blackburn on *Sale* in interpreting the clause "in addition to his other remedies" on the basis that "the owner may, in defiance of his contract, sell to some third person and give him a perfectly good title." The modern English authorities point to s.48(3) as providing for a right of resale whether or not ownership in the goods has passed (see *R. V. Ward Ltd.* v. *Bignall* [1967] 1 Q.B. 534 at p. 545; Benjamin, *Sale of Goods*, § 1111): however, Brown (*loc. cit.*), with some plausibility, contends that the common law right of resale, applicable in principle where ownership is retained by the seller, is more extensive than the statutory right provided for in s.48.

[97] s.108(3), Sched. 8.

[98] Gloag and Henderson, para. 17.48. See generally, Brown, *Sale of Goods*, pp. 314–318, esp. at p. 318: "It does not appear that, during the sixteen years which have now elapsed since the passing of the Act there has been any attempt to make use of the section, and it is submitted that it should be repealed."

11.20 *The unpaid seller's lien*

11.20a Preliminary matters. Section 41(1) of the Sale of Goods Act 1979 provides for the unpaid seller's[99] lien as follows:

> "Subject to this Act, the unpaid seller of goods who is in possession of them is entitled to retain possession of them until payment or tender of the price in the following cases:—
> (*a*) where the goods have been sold without any stipulation as to credit;
> (*b*)where the goods have been sold on credit but the term of credit has expired;
> (*c*) where the buyer becomes insolvent."

As indicated[1] this statutory model is open to variation on the basis of the parties' agreement.

A preliminary question concerns the meaning of "possession" in the premise phrase "the unpaid seller of goods who is in possession of them." It is trite that the context is important to the shade of meaning of the word possession. That the emphasis in this case is upon *de facto* control by the seller seems to be borne out by section 41(2): "The seller may exercise his lien or right of retention notwithstanding that he is in possession of the goods as agent or bailee or custodier for the buyer."[2] In *Paton's Trs.* v. *Finlayson*[3] the Second Division emphasised the importance of "possessory control" in addressing the issue whether a seller had lost his right of lien on the basis of section 43(1)(*b*)— "when the buyer or his agent lawfully obtains possession of the goods." In this case a merchant who had purchased a potato crop lifted the crop and pitted it on the farmer's land. It was held that although property passed to the buyer on the lifting, the seller retained possession for the purposes of his lien because "that possessory control which gives them their right of retention"[4] was never lost.[5]

While it would appear to be correct to say that the retention, to a sufficient degree, of *de facto* control by the seller constitutes possession

---

[99] For the meaning of "unpaid seller" see above, para. 11.19a.

[1] Above para. 11.19c, n. 92.

[2] Given this approach, the fact that the seller is extracting a storage or warehousing charge from the buyer does not preclude the former from being a possessor for the purpose of s.41; see *Grice* v. *Richardson* (1877) 3 App.Cas. 319 at pp. 323–324.

[3] 1923 S.C. 872.

[4] *per* Lord Hunter at p. 879.

[5] The Court of Session referred with approval to the following dictum of Fletcher Moulton L.J. in *Lord's Tr.* v. *Great Eastern Ry. Co.* [1908] 2 K.B. 54 at p. 72: "A lien is impossible except under circumstances which place the goods in what I may call the possessory control of the holder of the lien, that is to say, where they are so far in his actual possession that he can prevent their being taken away and dealt with by the owner." It may be noted that this statement was made in a dissenting judgment which was given effect to by the House of Lords on appeal: see *Great Eastern Ry. Co.* v. *Lord's Tr.* [1909] A.C. 109 at p. 115.

for the purpose of section 41 it is probably not possible to formulate a more precise criterion. The particular circumstances of individual cases are all important.[6]

The lien applies in the circumstances of a cash sale or, in the case of a credit sale, where the terms of credit have expired or in the event of the buyer's insolvency. Insolvency, for this purpose, has been defined,[7] but the aspects of the requirement of payment and the incidence of credit must be examined.

Cash sale. The applicability of the lien in the circumstances of a sale not on credit—*i.e.* a cash sale—is straightforward enough. Under the Act property in the goods, as yet undelivered, may have passed to the buyer, but from the point of view of the parties' contractual relationship payment and delivery are concurrent conditions.[8] The lien gives a right to the undivested seller, who satisfies the requirement of being "unpaid,"[9] to retain the goods pending payment by the buyer.[10] **11.20b**

The right prevails until the entire price has been paid or tendered.[11] Moreover, where delivery is staggered the seller is, in principle, entitled to exercise his lien over any part of the goods remaining in his possession provided, of course, that a part of the contract price is outstanding. Section 42 is relevant to this:

"Where an unpaid seller has made part delivery of the goods, he may exercise his lien or right of retention on the remainder, unless such part delivery has been made under such circumstances as to show an agreement to waive the lien or right of retention."

Provided there is only one contract involved, the lien is not restricted to those goods over which an outstanding balance of the price can be attributed.[12] Where goods are sold by instalments the general presumption is that the contract is a single indivisible entity and, on this basis, the seller's lien is applicable to any part of the goods remaining

---

[6] See the range of cases referred to in Benjamin, *Sale of Goods*, §§ 1138–1139.

[7] See above, para. 11.19.

[8] See s.28: "Unless otherwise agreed, delivery of the goods and payment of the price are concurrent conditions, that is to say, the seller must be ready and willing to give possession of the goods to the buyer in exchange for the price and the buyer must be ready and willing to pay the price in exchange for possession of the goods."

[9] See above, para. 11.19a.

[10] Operating in this manner the seller's lien "possesses the characteristics common to all liens, of being a right over the property of a person other than the person seeking to enforce it": Brown, *Sale of Goods*, p. 321.

[11] See the definition of "unpaid seller" in s.38, above, para. 11.19a.

[12] See *Ex p. Chalmers* (1873) L.R. 8 Ch.App. 289, *per* Mellish L.J. at p. 291: "the seller, notwithstanding he may have agreed to allow credit for the goods, is not bound to deliver any more goods under the contract until the price of the goods not yet delivered is tendered to him; and that, if a debt is due to him for the goods already delivered, he is entitled to refuse to deliver any more till he is paid the debt due for those already delivered, as well as the price of those still to be delivered." See also *Longbottom (H.) & Co. Ltd.* v. *Bass, Walker & Co.* [1922] W.N. 245 at p. 246.

undelivered in respect of whatever balance of the price remains due.[13] But where the relationship between the parties is constituted by two or more separate contracts—or, at least, severable instances of specified correlative delivery and payment[14]—the seller's lien must necessarily be restricted to goods in respect of which payment is due, in whole or in part, under the relevant contracts or severable sub-contracts.[15]

Section 42 provides for part delivery "made under such circumstances as to show an agreement to waive the lien or right of retention." As indicated,[16] the unpaid seller's rights are suppletive rules which may be departed from by the parties; moreover, what the parties intend may be established not only by reference to their express agreement but also on an inferential basis. Accordingly, the proviso to section 42 does no more than acknowledge the possibility of waiver being inferred from the circumstances of part delivery.[17] As Lord Blackburn put it in *Kemp* v. *Falk*[18]: "If both parties intend it as a delivery of the whole, then it is a delivery of the whole; but if either of the parties does not intend it as a delivery of the whole, if either of them dissents, then it is not a delivery of the whole."

11.20c Credit sale. In the case of a credit sale the Act proceeds upon the basis that, unless otherwise agreed, the granting of credit will be intended to have the same effect as payment of the price—*i.e.* the assumption will be that the granting of credit and delivery are concurrent conditions.[19] Accordingly, just as the normal inference would be against the seller having a lien where the price has been paid in full, so, equally, in the case of a credit sale a lien will not normally be inferred. However, given that the rights of an unpaid seller provided for by the Act are suppletive rather than prescriptive rules—and so open to variation by the parties[20]—one can do no more than speak in terms of what would apply in the absence of contrary agreement. In view of this, section 41

---

[13] See *Ex p. Chalmers* (1873) L.R. 8 Ch.App. 289 at p. 292.

[14] As envisaged by s.31(2).

[15] See *Merchant Banking Co. of London* v. *Phoenix Bessemer Steel Co.* (1877) 5 Ch.D. 205 at pp. 219–220.

[16] See above, para. 11.19c, n. 92.

[17] See *Bunney* v. *Poyntz* (1833) 4 B. & Ad. 568. At p. 571 the court recognised that "the intention of both parties was to separate the part delivered from the residue" and, on this basis, the seller's permission to take away part of the hay crop was held not to be delivery of the whole.

[18] (1882) 7 App.Cas. 573 at p. 586.

[19] This simply reflects the common law position which is the relevant background to the Act; Brown, *Sale of Goods*, p. 320, quotes the dictum of Bayley J. in *Bloxam* v. *Sanders* (1825) 4 B. & C. 941 at p. 948 that: "If goods are sold upon credit, and nothing is agreed upon as to the time of delivering the goods, the vendee is immediately entitled to the possession, and the right of possession and the right of property vest at once in him."

[20] See above, para. 11.19c, n. 92.

should not be taken to imply that a lien cannot come into being in the circumstances of a credit sale.[21]

Part delivery. Section 42 provides that an unpaid seller who has made **11.20d** part delivery may exercise his right of lien or retention over the undelivered goods "unless such part delivery has been made under such circumstances as to show an agreement to waive the lien or right of retention."[22]

Termination of the seller's lien   **11.21**

General observations. Clearly enough, the seller's lien is terminated by **11.21a** full payment or tender of full payment[23] by the buyer but section 43 identifies other circumstances in which the unpaid seller's lien is terminated:

> "(a) when he delivers the goods to a carrier or other bailee or custodier for the purpose of transmission to the buyer without reserving the right of disposal of the goods;
> (b) when the buyer or his agent lawfully obtains possession of the goods;
> (c) by waiver of the lien or right of retention."

It is also provided in section 43(2) that an unpaid seller does not lose his lien "by reason only that he has obtained judgment or decree for the price of the goods."

Delivery to carrier. Subsection (a) is consistent with the position under **11.21b** section 32(1) of the Act whereby "delivery of the goods to a carrier . . . for the purpose of transmission to the buyer is *prima facie* deemed to be a delivery of the goods to the buyer." Delivery to a carrier or interim custodier for the purpose of transmission to the buyer is the commencement point of the act of handing over possession to the buyer; to be consistent with the notion of a possessory lien the effect of such an act must, in principle, be to terminate the lien. But section 19(1) provides for the possibility of the conditional reservation by the seller of the right of disposal and, where parties have contracted on this basis, property does not pass "until the conditions imposed by the seller are fulfilled."[24]

Where goods are handed over for shipment the taking out of a bill of lading by the seller in his own name may be taken to amount to a

---

[21] See Benjamin, *Sale of Goods*, § 1134. On this basis Atiyah (*Sale of Goods*, p. 435) does not appear to be wholly accurate in stating that "the Act appears to assume that an agreement as to credit necessarily means an agreement that the buyer shall be entitled to the goods before payment." Rather, the position of the Act is that in the absence of contrary indication the inference will be that the granting of credit by the seller presupposes the existence of an obligation to deliver.

[22] See below, para. 11.21.

[23] See s.38(1)(a); see above, para. 11.19a, n. 80.

[24] s.19(1); see above, para. 9.15.

reservation of property in the goods and, *a fortiori*, of the right of disposal for the purposes of section 43(1)(*a*).[25] But it is questionable whether the unpaid seller's lien is applicable where the seller has taken out a bill of lading in his own name; the better view would appear to be that this is a situation in which a right under the Act is varied by usage.[26] In this case the fact that the seller, holding a bill of lading, retains full rights over the shipped goods would appear to be overriding; by like token endorsement and delivery of the bill of lading to the buyer or his agent will effectively divest the seller, leaving no possible room for a lien.

11.21c Transmission to buyer. If the lien is lost by delivery to a carrier for transmission to the buyer it follows that it will also be lost, as provided by section 43(1)(*b*), "where the buyer or his agent lawfully obtains possession of the goods." The word "possession" refers to natural or actual possession[27]; under the scheme of the Act the normal position would be that title and the right of possession will pass to the buyer prior to actual delivery of the goods.[28] The issue here is whether the seller's natural possession—sufficient for the purpose of maintaining a right of lien[29]—has passed to the buyer or his agent. In the event sections 41(1) and 43(1)(*b*) are correlative, and the issue is whether the critical degree of control over the goods has passed from the seller. A dictum of Lord Hunter in *Paton's Trs.* v. *Finlayson*[30] is in point:

> "It is no doubt true that lien or right of retention depends on possession by the seller, and that transference of possession to the buyer or his agent brings the right to an end. But the possession by the buyer necessary to defeat the seller's right of retention must be actual and absolute."[31]

The qualification of the "lawfully" obtaining of possession by the buyer or his agent in section 43(1)(*b*) implies that a lien will not terminate in the case of an unlawful removal of goods by the buyer. But what does this mean? Professor Atiyah[32] contends that "lawfully" in section 43 means possession obtained "with the consent of the seller" on the basis that harmony with section 25(1)—where the phrase is used—must have been intended. The argument is that section 25(1)

---

[25] See Atiyah, *Sale of Goods*, p. 439.
[26] See s.39(1) ("by implication of law") read with s.55(1); see above, para. 11.19c, n. 91.
[27] See above, para. 1.14.
[28] See above, para. 9.02.
[29] See above, para. 11.20, on the meaning of possession for the purpose of s.41(1).
[30] 1923 S.C. 872 at p. 878.
[31] The word "absolute" would appear to be intended to mean no more than that possessory control has passed from the seller to the buyer. Although, of course, there may be degrees of possessory control, one may say that possessory control has passed absolutely when the degree of control obtained by the buyer is sufficient to justify the conclusion that he has obtained possessory control.
[32] *Sale of Goods*, p. 440.

provides that a buyer in possession "with the consent of the seller" may pass a good title to a third party who has received delivery "without notice of any *lien* or other right of the original seller."[33] On this basis the lien is terminated by the buyer obtaining possession of the goods "with the consent of the seller" except to the extent that a subsequent acquirer may be held bound on the basis of the doctrine of notice. On the other hand, where the buyer obtains possession unlawfully—without the seller's express or implied consent—the lien prevails and any subsequent transfer of title in the goods will remain subject to it.[34]

Revival. It may be noted that once terminated by the loss of possession **11.21d** the seller's lien does not revive merely by reason of the regaining of natural possession of the goods. In *London Scottish Transport Ltd.* v. *Tyres (Scotland) Ltd.*[35] the unpaid sellers, anticipating the buyer's insolvency, repossessed goods already delivered. While questioning Bell's[36] view that once lost a lien remains "extinct beyond revival," the court (Sheriff Bryden) expressed the opinion that, "before it could be argued that a lost lien had revived it would be necessary . . . to show that the goods had been handed back to the sellers by the purchasers with the particular intention that the sellers' lien should revive."

In *Hostess Mobile Catering* v. *Archibald Scott Ltd.*[37] a refreshment trailer was sold and delivered but subsequently returned to the sellers for repairs under warranty. The sellers refused to redeliver until the outstanding balance of the purchase price was paid. It was accepted that a lien could be revived if the goods were restored by the purchaser to the seller with the intention that the lien should revive.[38] Moreover, Lord MacDonald indicated approval for the argument that an intention to revive the lien might be inferred on the basis of the principle of mutuality.

> "If the unit was restored to the possession of the defenders so that they could fulfil their obligations under the original contract this meant that the pursuers' obligation to pay the contracted price remained and they must be taken to have assented to the revival of the defenders' rights in connection therewith, including their right of lien."[39]

Waiver. The essential requirements for a lien to come into being have **11.21e** been discussed above[40]; waiver under section 43(1)(c) is concerned with the circumstances in which a seller may be taken to have waived an

---

[33] See above, para. 10.21.
[34] See s.47(1).
[35] 1957 S.L.T.(Sh.Ct.) 48 at p. 49.
[36] *Comm.*, II, 91.
[37] 1981 S.C. 185.
[38] at p. 187.
[39] *Ibid.*
[40] See above, paras. 11.19–20.

existing lien. Given that section 43 provides, in subsections 1(*a*) and (*b*), for termination by delivery to a carrier and by the buyer lawfully obtaining possession, it follows that subsection (1)(*c*) is concerned with waiver in the circumstances of the seller remaining in possession.[41]

Clearly, there may be express waiver but waiver may also be implied; for example, where the parties negotiate new terms which are inconsistent with the continuation of the lien.[42] Although the unpaid seller's lien has the potential to prevail notwithstanding that the seller is in possession merely as agent for the buyer,[43] it may be shown to have been waived in the particular circumstances. Waiver of the lien is to do with a waiver by the seller of his right to payment prior to or on delivery; section 41(2), on the other hand, is concerned with the potential continuation of the lien even though ownership has passed to the buyer, leaving the seller with no more than a right of possession. But whether or not ownership has passed to the buyer does not determine the existence of a lien, including the question of the waiver of an existing lien.

Given that lien is intended as a means of securing payment of the price and that this purpose is achieved by the seller retaining possessory control, it follows that in these two areas there is scope for implied waiver. Waiver of the right to require payment pending delivery may be implied where the seller deals with the goods in a manner inconsistent with such a right. Accordingly, where the seller does some act which is inconsistent with his obligation to deliver, he may be taken to have waived his right to withhold delivery pending payment. The resale or consumption of the goods by the seller, in breach of his obligation to the buyer, would *prima facie* amount to such a waiver.[44] As indicated, if the effect of a departure by the parties from their original contract is that the seller will no longer have sufficient possessory control to justify the continuation of the lien it will be taken to have been waived. There may be a waiver on the basis of part delivery, although section 42 states the basic position that in the case of part delivery the lien is preserved over the undelivered goods.[45]

11.21f Lien not terminated by judgment in favour of seller. Section 43(2) provides that the unpaid seller's lien will not be terminated "by reason only that he has obtained judgment or decree for the price of the

---

[41] If, *e.g.* it was agreed that the seller would retain the thing for a period as hirer or borrower there would, arguably, be implied waiver on the basis that holding the thing as hirer or borrower was inconsistent with a right of lien.

[42] Where an agreed cash sale basis is renegotiated to provide for credit, a lien which had come into being on the basis of the original terms might be taken to be waived by the new terms. See *Bank of Africa* v. *Salisbury Gold Mining Co.* [1892] A.C. 281 *per* Lord Watson at p. 284: "a right of lien may be discharged by a new arrangement between creditor and debtor the terms of which are incompatible with its retention, or by any other arrangement which sufficiently indicates the intention of the parties that the right shall no longer be enforced."

[43] s.41(2); see above, para. 11.20a, n. 2.

[44] See *Mulliner* v. *Florence* (1878) 3 Q.B.D. 484 *per* Brett L.J. at p. 492: "in the case of a wrongful sale the lien is destroyed."

[45] See above, para. 11.20b, n. 17.

goods."[46] The security of a lien would not be very satisfactory if it terminated upon the issuing of a judicial decree which might not be complied with. Clearly, a creditor holding security sufficient to meet his claim is in a stronger position than one with no more than a judicial decree in his favour.[47]

While the obtaining of a decree will not *per se* affect the lien, it would seem that the removal of the goods concerned, by an officer of the court for the purpose of sale in execution of a decree, would terminate the lien by ending the seller's possessory control.[48]

Stoppage in transit

The seller's right to resume possession—usually from a carrier—of **11.22** goods in the course of delivery to an insolvent buyer was recognised in 18th-century English mercantile law[49] and provided for in section 44 of the Sale of Goods Act 1893. The section was retained in essentially the same form in the 1979 Act:

> "Subject to this Act, when the buyer of goods becomes insolvent the unpaid seller who has parted with the possession of the goods has the right of stopping them in transit, that is to say, he may resume possession of the goods as long as they are in course of transit, and he may retain them until payment or tender of the price."

In Scotland the common law allowed the unpaid seller to recover the goods from the buyer on the basis of presumptive fraud; the developed form of the rule requiring the seller to act within three days of delivery—the *inter triduum* rule.[50] Given that the seller's protection

---

[46] To cover the terminology of both English and Scots law the subsection speaks of the unpaid seller retaining his "lien or right of retention" despite obtaining "judgment or decree."

[47] Brown (*Sale of Goods*, pp. 325–326) explains the subsection from the point of view of the potential effect of a judgment upon the passing of property in English law, but the primary justification for the provision would appear to be to obviate any doubt concerning the continuation of the lien pending full payment by the buyer.

[48] See Benjamin, *Sale of Goods*, § 1159.

[49] See *Wiseman* v. *Vandeputt* (1690) 2 Vern. 203; *Lickbarrow* v. *Mason* (1793) 4 Bro.Parl.Cas. 57. For an account of the development of the doctrine see the dissenting judgment of Lord Abinger in *Gibson* v. *Carruthers* (1841) 8 M. & W. 321 at pp. 337–348.

[50] *Inglis* v. *Royal Bank* (1736) Mor. 4936. It may be noted that this was by way of exception to the basic position that property passed despite non-payment because Scots law did not receive the rule of Roman law (Inst. 2.1.41; see Thomas, "Institutes 2.1.41 and the passage of property on sale" (1973) 90 S.A.L.J. 150) which, in the case of sale, made the passing of ownership subject to payment of the price, or to the granting of credit or the giving of security. See Stair, I.xiv.2: "Sale being perfected, and the thing delivered, the property thereof becomes the buyer's, if it was the seller's, and there is no dependence of it, till the price be paid or secured, as was in the civil law." Erskine (III.iii.8: "But whether this would be held for the law of Scotland remains in doubt") leaves the matter open, but the better view is that Scots law did not adopt the Roman rule; this would, of course, have been inconsistent with the *inter triduum* rule which presupposes that ownership has passed to the buyer.

took this form, it seems that there was no right of stoppage *in transitu*.[51] However, in *Allan, Steuart & Co.* v. *Stein's Creditors*[52] although the Court of Session gave effect to the *inter triduum* rule the House of Lords held, in effect, that it had given way to stoppage *in transitu*.[53]

Different explanations have been given as the policy justification for stoppage in transit. An unconvincing generalisation is that "one man's goods shall not be applied to the payment of another man's debt."[54] Benjamin[55] prefers the rationale of delivery to a carrier as only amounting to delivery to the buyer subject to an implied condition of solvency, but this is more of an explanation as to the technical basis of the rule than a policy justification for it. Atiyah[56] suggests that it is consistent with commercial reality that a seller should be able to look to the goods as security pending their coming into the possession of the buyer. The difficulty with this is that it accords a secured position to a seller who has opted not to protect himself by recourse to one of the forms of security which would put him in a position of priority *vis-à-vis* other creditors. Arguably, the better view is that pending delivery to the buyer the expectations of the buyer's creditors would not be raised and, on this basis, it is possible to allow the seller to obtain restoration of the *status quo ante*.

The right of stoppage in transit is available to an unpaid seller, in the circumstances of the buyer's insolvency, provided of course the goods are in transit. The circumstances which constitute an "unpaid seller" and an "insolvent buyer" have been examined,[57] but it is necessary to consider the meaning of the phrase "in the course of transit."

Duration of transit

11.23   Various rules—essentially the product of English common law development—applying to the determination of the state of "the course of transit" have been brought together in section 45. The essential feature of the goods being in the possession of "some person intervening between the vendor who has parted with and the purchaser who has not yet received them"[58] is reflected in section 45(1).

---

[51] See *Prince* v. *Pallat* (1680) Mor. 4932.
[52] (1788) Mor. 4949.
[53] See *Jeffrey* v. *Allan, Stewart & Co.* (1790) 3 Pat.App. 191 *per* Lord Chancellor Thurlow at p. 196: "But within the last hundred years, a rule has been introduced, from the customs of foreign nations, that in the case of the vendee's bankruptcy, the vendor might stop and take back the goods *in transitu*, or before they came into the hands of the vendee: and this is certainly now a part of the law of England, and I understand it to be the law likewise of Scotland." See also Bell, *Prin.*, § 1307.
[54] See *Booth Steamship Co. Ltd.* v. *Cargo Fleet Iron Co. Ltd.* [1916] 2 K.B. 570 *per* Lord Reading at p. 580 following *D'Aquila* v. *Lambert* (1761) 2 Eden 75 at p. 76.
[55] *Sale of Goods*, § 1164.
[56] *Sale of Goods*, p. 442.
[57] See above, paras. 11.19b & c.
[58] *Schotsmans* v. *Lancashire & Yorkshire Ry. Co.* (1867) L.R. 2 Ch.App. 332 *per* Cairns L.J. at p. 338.

"Goods are deemed to be in course of transit from the time when they are delivered to a carrier or other bailee or custodier for the purpose of transmission to the buyer, until the buyer or his agent in that behalf takes delivery of them from the carrier or other bailee or custodier."

For the purposes of the right to stop goods, the most important question is when the transit ends. Section 45(2) is to the effect that the criterion is not arrival at the intended destination but the obtaining of delivery by the buyer: "If the buyer or his agent in that behalf obtains delivery of the goods before their arrival at the appointed destination, the transit is at an end." This subsection will apply either when the buyer himself obtains early delivery or when this occurs through delivery to an agent for the buyer. For the latter case to amount to delivery to the buyer, the agent must necessarily have the buyer's authority to take delivery.[59]

Transit comes to an end when the goods arrive at their appointed destination and the carrier or custodier acknowledges to the buyer that they are held on his behalf.[60] Moreover, the state of transit is not revived if, on the buyer's instructions, the goods commence transit for another destination.[61] These related rules are together provided for in section 45(3):

"If, after the arrival of the goods at the appointed destination, the carrier or other bailee or custodier acknowledges to the buyer or his agent that he holds the goods on his behalf and continues in possession of them as bailee or custodier for the buyer or his agent, the transit is at an end, and it is immaterial that a further destination for the goods may have been indicated by the buyer."

Section 45(3) provides for the termination of the transit where the arrival of the goods has been intimated to the buyer and, in these

---

[59] See *Mechan & Sons Ltd.* v. *North-Eastern Ry. Co.*, 1911 S.C. 1348 *per* Lord Dundas at pp. 1357–1358: "McLarens were just in the ordinary position of an independent firm of carting contractors, and were not acting as servants or agents of the vendees to obtain anticipated delivery of these boats. It is not shown that they had any power or authority from the vendees."

[60] *A fortiori*, in *Muir* v. *Rankin* (1905) 13 S.L.T. 60 at p. 62, it was held that transit had ended where the consignee signed for goods which had arrived at their station of destination even though he did not uplift them.

[61] See *Bethell* v. *Clark* (1888) 20 Q.B.D. 615 *per* Lord Esher M.R. at p. 617: "if the goods are not in the hands of the carrier by reason either of the terms of the contract or of the directions of the purchaser to the vendor, but are *in transitu* afterwards in consequence of fresh directions given by the purchaser for a new transit, then such transit is no part of the original transit, and the right to stop is gone. So also, if the purchaser gives orders that the goods shall be sent to a particular place, there to be kept till he gives fresh orders as to their destination to a new carrier, the original transit is at end when they have reached that place, and any further transit is a fresh and independent transit."

circumstances, the buyer's intention to receive can be inferred—the intention element is implicit in the requirement that the carrier continues in possession "for the buyer or his agent," because clearly he could only do this with the concurrence of the buyer. Where, however, section 45(3) does not apply it remains open to the buyer to decline to receive the goods, and in these circumstances the course of transit and the seller's option to stop delivery continue. Section 45(4) provides for this eventuality:

> "If the goods are rejected by the buyer, and the carrier or other bailee or custodier continues in possession of them, the transit is not deemed to be at an end, even if the seller has refused to receive them back."[62]

The motive behind a buyer's rejection is irrelevant from the point of view of proprietary effect. The central point is that delivery to the buyer only occurs on the basis of his accepting actual or constructive physical control with the intention to receive the goods. Accordingly, whether he declines to receive because he intends first to satisfy himself that the goods are of contract standard or whether he does so to protect the seller from the circumstances of his own insolvency is irrelevant.

The situation of goods being delivered to a ship chartered by the buyer is open to the argument that stoppage is henceforth incompetent because delivery to the ship amounts to delivery to the buyer. Section 45(5) makes this a matter to be determined according to the circumstances.

> "When goods are delivered to a ship chartered by the buyer it is a question depending on the circumstances of the particular case whether they are in the possession of the master as a carrier or as agent to the buyer."

This subsection makes clear that the criterion is whether the goods, having been delivered to the ship, are in the possession of the master

---

[62] The better view is that subss. 3 and 4 are complementary: see Brown, *Sale of Goods*, p. 336. Atiyah (*Sale of Goods*, p. 445) is of the view that the relationship between the subsections is not clear: "If the carrier informs the buyer that the goods have arrived and that he holds them on his behalf and, subsequently, the buyer inspects the goods and rejects them, does the transit continue or not?" The answer to this must depend upon the buyer's intention inferred from his response to the carrier's intimation that the goods have arrived. If the buyer reserves the right to inspect the goods the transit continues. If, however, he unreservedly assents to the carriers continuing in possession on his behalf his intention to receive the goods may be inferred and, on this basis, he can be taken to have waived any right of rejection for purposes of stoppage rules.

"as a carrier or as agent to the buyer." The determination of this
question is straightforward enough in the case in which the vessel is
"demised"—in effect, leased—to the buyer so that he has control over
it, *a fortiori* in the exceptional case in which the buyer is owner of the
vessel. In principle, where the buyer has control over the vessel, the
master is not an independent carrier but rather the buyer's agent, and
in the result, on delivery to the ship, the goods can no longer be said to
be "in the course of transit." But even in the case of a charter by
demise to the buyer the terms of the bill of lading may operate to
retain the seller's control to the extent that the right of stoppage is
preserved. In the more usual case of the ship chartered for a particular
voyage the master will not normally become the agent of the charterer
and, in these circumstances, delivery to the ship will not terminate the
seller's right of stoppage.[63]

Where there is a right of stoppage in the circumstances the issue
may be whether the right was exercised before the ship reached its
destination and, of course, where successive carriers are involved there
may be dispute as to when this occurred.[64]

The law favours the buyer's creditors in the circumstances in which
the carrier wrongfully refuses to deliver the goods to the buyer or his
agent. Section 45(6) provides for this situation.

"Where the carrier or other bailee or custodier wrongfully refuses
to deliver the goods to the buyer or his agent in that behalf, the
transit is deemed to be at an end."

Where the buyer is ready and willing to receive delivery—of goods
which have reached their destination—and, in the circumstances, there
is no reason why the carrier should not deliver, it would be anomalous
if the right of stoppage remained available to the seller.[65]

The counterpart of section 42, providing for the preservation of a
lien over the undelivered balance where part delivery has occurred[66] is
provided for in section 45(7) in respect of stoppage in transit.

"Where part delivery of the goods has been made to the buyer or
his agent in that behalf, the remainder of the goods may be
stopped in transit, unless such part delivery has been made under

---

[63] See *Berndtson* v. *Strang* (1868) L.R. 3 Ch.App. 588 at p. 590.
[64] See, *e.g. McLeod & Co.* v. *Harrison* (1880) 8 R. 227 *per* Lord Gifford at p. 232:
"The goods were just as much *in transitu* when on their way to Moscow as at Leith,
though necessarily they went into the hands of successive carriers, and some one must
carry them; the sellers were in good time in stopping them before they reached their
destination."
[65] See *Dunlop* v. *Scott* (22 Feb. 1814, F.C.) where, following an arrestment by a
creditor of the buyer, the carrier refused to deliver.
[66] See above, paras. 11.20d, n. 22 and 11.21e, n. 45.

such circumstances as to show an agreement to give up possession
of the whole of the goods."[67]

Exercise of right of stoppage in transit

11.24   Section 46(1) provides that the seller may exercise his right of
stoppage "either by taking actual possession of the goods or by giving
notice of his claim to the carrier or other bailee or custodier in whose
possession the goods are." Notice may be given either to the person
"in actual possession of the goods or to his principal."[68] If given to the
principal it will be ineffective unless given "at such time and under
such circumstances that the principal, by the exercise of reasonable
diligence, may communicate it to his servant or agent in time to
prevent a delivery to the buyer."[69] The carrier or custodier in possession of goods in transit, upon receipt of a stoppage notice, "must re-
deliver the goods to, or according to the directions of, the seller"[70]; the
expenses of re-delivery to be borne by the seller.[71]

It may be noted that while the provision for the method of exercise
of the right of stoppage by the seller is permissive, the carrier or
custodier, upon receiving intimation of the right, is subject to an
imperative duty to redeliver. Notice of the seller's intention to stop the
goods may take any form, but clearly a seller will be advised to use a
means which facilitates subsequent proof. The seller's extensive power
to implement the right of stoppage is subject to a correlative duty to
exercise care in doing so which is manifested in the rule that the seller
assumes the risk of the stoppage being unjustified.[72] Of course, if the
carrier or custodier is in any serious doubt as to the seller's right he
may resort to multiplepoinding. Given that the carrier or custodier is a
neutral party—the issue being one between seller and buyer—it makes
sense that the duty to redeliver is peremptory. However, because, as
between seller and buyer, the question of possession is critical the
stoppage is defeated if the carrier or custodier disregards the notice
and delivers to the buyer. In this situation the goods will fall to the

---

[67] In *Mechan & Sons Ltd.* v. *North-Eastern Ry. Co.*, 1911 S.C. 1348 at p. 1356 Lord
Justice-Clerk MacDonald rejected the argument that s.45(7) applied in the circumstances
of the delivery of one boat from a consignment of two (see below, n. 73): "I cannot see
any ground for holding that there was, between the builders and the Laings' firm, any
understanding of the delivery of one boat being held to be a delivery of both boats. And
unless that was proved to be the case, then, as the second boat was not in any view a
delivered boat, the builders were quite entitled to stop delivery while the second boat
was still at the railway station, and therefore *in transitu* between their yard and that of
Laings."
[68] s.46(2).
[69] s.46(3).
[70] s.46(4).
[71] *Ibid.*
[72] See *The Tigress* (1863) 32 L.J. Adm. 97 at p. 101.

benefit of the buyer's creditors and the seller's only remedy is a claim for damages against the carrier or custodier.[73]

Priorities accorded to an unpaid seller

Section 47 deals with the problems of the competing interests of the **11.25** unpaid seller and a party who has, or may have, acquired a subsequent interest in the goods concerned. The basic priority which must necessarily be accorded an unpaid seller, as against a subsequent party, if the right of lien or stoppage is to be effective, is provided for in subsection (1).

> "Subject to this Act, the unpaid seller's right of lien or retention or stoppage in transit is not affected by any sale or other disposition of the goods which the buyer may have made, unless the seller has assented to it."

Complementing this, section 48(2) provides that:

> "Where an unpaid seller who has exercised his right of lien or retention or stoppage in transit re-sells the goods, the buyer acquires a good title to them as against the original buyer."

The potentially contentious aspect of section 47(1) is the question as to what amounts to assent by the seller. The better view is that this is not a matter of personal bar because there is no requirement that the seller's assent must be communicated to the subsequent party. Indeed, it seems that there is no room for a defence of personal bar on the basis of the seller's knowledge of a subsequent transaction. What must be shown, to avoid the priority, is that the seller assented to the disposition made by the buyer—in effect waived his right[74]—because section 47(1) is clear that otherwise the unpaid seller's rights stand. However, the seller's assent to waive his rights does not have to be express but may be inferred from the circumstances.

---

[73] *Mechan & Sons Ltd.* v. *North-Eastern Ry. Co.*, 1911 S.C. 1348, was concerned with a contract for the sale of two lifeboats which the sellers had agreed to deliver to the buyer's yard. The boats were dispatched by rail and arrived at the station local to the yard. A firm of carriers who habitually took goods from the yard delivered one of the boats to the yard. Before delivery of the second boat the sellers gave notice of stoppage in transit to the railway company; subsequently, however, the company delivered the boat to the liquidator of the buyer's insolvent estate. The Second Division upheld the judgment of the sheriff-substitute (Mackenzie), the relevant part of which is as follows: "For these reasons, I am of opinion that the second boat had not been delivered either actually or constructively before the notice of stoppage *in transitu* was received by the defenders, and that the defenders were, therefore, in fault in delivering the second boat to the liquidator. It follows that they are liable in damages" (at p. 1352).

[74] See the comment in a contributed book review in (1895) 7 J.R. 384 at p. 386: "Must there not be something amounting to waiver?"

The case of *Mordaunt Bros.* v. *British Oil and Cake Mills Ltd.*[75] was
concerned with the buyer's resale of oil to the plaintiffs, the circumstances being that the plaintiffs paid the buyer and received the
relevant delivery orders which were transmitted to the sellers—the
defendants—who accepted them without comment. The defendants
commenced delivery to the plaintiffs but, upon the buyer falling into
arrears, refused to continue with delivery. Pickford J. held that the
defendants had not assented to resale in the circumstances.

> "the assent which affects the unpaid seller's right of lien must be
> such an assent as in the circumstances shews that the seller intends
> to renounce his rights against the goods. It is not enough to shew
> that the fact of a sub-contract has been brought to his notice and
> that he has assented to it merely in the sense of acknowledging the
> receipt of the information."[76]

Arguably this is the correct approach because it cannot be in accordance with principle that a party should be divested of a substantive
right on the basis of what would amount to no more than mere notice
of a subsale.[77] It would be inconsistent with the premise that the unpaid
seller's rights prevail regardless of a subsequent disposition by the
original seller to hold that waiver of protection could be inferred from
a neutral reaction to notice of a subsequent sale.[78]

But the situation is probably different where the unpaid seller, in a
credit transaction, retains possession of goods—the property in which
has passed to the buyer—for and on behalf of the buyer. In this
situation the seller's acceptance of the purchaser's delivery order in

---

[75] [1910] 2 K.B. 502.

[76] at p. 507. *Cf. D. F. Mount Ltd.* v. *Jay & Jay (Provisions) Co. Ltd.* [1960] 1 Q.B.
159 *per* Salmon J. at p. 167: "In my view, the true inference is that the defendants
assented to Merrick reselling the goods, in the sense that they intended to renounce their
rights against the goods and to take the risk of Merrick's honesty. The defendants are
reputable merchants and I am sure that it was not their intention to get rid of their goods
on a falling market through Merrick on the basis that, if he defaulted, they could hold
the goods against the customers from whom he obtained the money out of which they
were to be paid."

[77] *Cf. Distillers Co. Ltd.* v. *Russell's Tr.* (1889) 16 R. 479 *per* Lord President Inglis at
p. 486: "No doubt the subvendee, having received a delivery—order from the original
purchaser, intimated that delivery-order to the original seller, in whose hands the goods
were. What is the effect of that? Nothing but this, so far as I can see, that it is an
intimation to the original seller that the original purchaser has parted with the right he
had to demand delivery. He could give no more to the subvendee than he had himself. If
he himself had only a *jus ad rem*, he could not convey to the subvendee a *jus in re*."

[78] See Brown, *Sale of Goods*, p. 352 n. 1 where, regarding "intimation . . . given with
a view to render the sub-sale complete," the learned author comments: "It seems
illogical to infer therefrom a consent on the part of the seller to waive his remedies in
respect of the unpaid price."

favour of a sub-purchaser very probably amounts to assent to the subsequent disposition.[79]

Section 47(2) provides, in the case of goods to which a document of title applies, for an exception to the general priority accorded the unpaid seller.

> "Where a document of title to goods has been lawfully transferred to any person as buyer or owner of the goods, and that person transfers the document to a person who takes it in good faith and for valuable consideration, then—
> (*a*) if the last-mentioned transfer was by way of sale the unpaid seller's right of lien or retention or stoppage in transit is defeated; and
> (*b*) if the last-mentioned transfer was made by way of pledge or other disposition for value, the unpaid seller's right of lien or retention or stoppage in transit can only be exercised subject to the rights of the transferee."[80]

The expression "document of title to goods" has "the same meaning as it has in the Factors Acts."[81]

The subsection refers to a document of title to goods having been "lawfully transferred to any person as buyer or owner of the goods." The implication would appear to be that a seller delivering on the basis of a document of title should be subject to the priority of a subsequent party receiving the relevant document in good faith and for value. In handing over a potentially negotiable document of title the seller may be taken to run the risk of losing his priority to a subsequent party. But the subsection has been interpreted in a manner not wholly consistent with this rationale. It has been held that the buyer may initiate a document of title himself—the typical case being a delivery order addressed by the buyer to the seller requiring delivery to a sub-

---

[79] In *Fleming* v. *Smith & Co.* (1881) 8 R. 548 at p. 552 Lord Young noted that while the unpaid credit seller's right to withhold delivery revived upon the buyer's bankruptcy, "it is the law of England, and I think the law of Scotland also, that if a seller has received intimation of a sub-sale, and has assented thereto, that deprives him of all right to retain against the original purchaser."

[80] In the 1893 Act the part corresponding to subs. 2 was by way of proviso to the basic rule and is referred to as such in the relevant case law.

[81] s.61(1). It may be noted that s.10 of the Factors Act 1889 (extended to Scotland by the Factors Act 1890) is substantially the same as s.47(2) of the Sale of Goods Act 1979. The relevant definition of the Factors Act (s.62(1) read with s.1(4)) is "any bill of lading, dock warrant, warehouse keeper's certificate, and warrant or order for the delivery of the goods, and any other document used in the ordinary course of business as proof of the possession or control of goods, or authorising or purporting to authorise, either by endorsement or by delivery, the possessor of the document to transfer or receive goods thereby represented."

buyer.[82] Arguably this goes beyond the intended scope of the subsection from the point of view of protecting the interests of an innocent subsequent purchaser. In another decision, however, it has been held that the same document must be transferred to the buyer and then on to a subsequent party,[83] and this would appear to be more consistent with the wording of the subsection.

---

[82] See *Ant. Jurgens Margarine Fabrieken* v. *Louis Dreyfus & Co.* [1914] 3 K.B. 40 *per* Pickford J. at p. 44: "A delivery order is not the less a document of title because it is created by the owner of the goods. It would be a curious result if the document by which the owner gets a title can, if passed on by him, give a title to some one else, but that a document created by himself cannot give a title when passed on because it is not a transfer but is only a delivery or issue. I cannot narrow the meaning of the word transfer in the way suggested."

[83] See *D. F. Mount Ltd.* v. *Jay & Jay (Provisions) Co. Ltd.* [1960] 1 Q.B. 159 *per* Salmon J. at p. 168: "It is clear that the person who transfers the document of title to the buyer may originate it himself and need not have received it from some third party in order to 'transfer' it within the meaning of the proviso . . . In my judgment, however, on the plain language of the section, it must be that very document which is transferred by the buyer for the proviso to operate. I am conscious that this construction leads to a very artificial result, but I cannot avoid it without doing violence to the plain language of the section."

CHAPTER 12

RESERVATION OF TITLE

GENERAL MATTERS

Nature of device

Reservation of title is a contractual device available to a seller **12.01**
seeking to retain title in goods sold and delivered pending payment by
the buyer. Although reservation of title is brought into being by
contract, its *raison d'être* is proprietary. The aim is to protect the seller
against what would otherwise be the consequences of delivery intended
to pass ownership to the buyer: first, by preventing an effective
disposal of the subject by the buyer and, secondly, by keeping the
subject out of the reach of the buyer's creditors. Because the effectiveness of reservation of title turns on its standing against third parties,
the legal issues which are raised are questions of property rather than
contract.

Viewed from different positions, and applying different criteria,
reservation of title may be classified, on the one hand, as a matter
distinct from security, on the other hand, as a form of security. From a
technical point of view reservation of title prevents ownership from
passing to the buyer. Although seller and buyer are in a creditor/
debtor relationship one cannot say that the seller has retained a
security interest because, clearly enough, this could only be the case
where title has passed from the seller.[1] Viewed, however, in terms of
consequences, reservation of title is at least analogous to a real right of
security.[2] This is so because its effect is to protect the personal right of

---

[1] See *Armour* v. *Thyssen Edelstahlwerke A.G.* (H.L) 1990 S.L.T. 891 *per* Lord Keith
at p. 895: "I am, however, unable to regard a provision reserving title to the seller until
payment of all debts due to him by the buyer as amounting to the creation by the buyer
of a right of security in favour of the seller. Such a provision does in a sense give the
seller security for the unpaid debts of the buyer. But it does so by way of a legitimate
retention of title, not by virtue of any right over his own property conferred by the
buyer." See also Reid and Gretton, "Retention of title in Romalpa clauses," 1983
S.L.T. (News) 77 at p. 79: "a clause of retention of title cannot be a species of hypothec.
It is in the nature of a hypothec that both debtor and creditor have real rights in the
subject of the security. The debtor is owner, the creditor has a real right of security. In
the case of a sale subject to a retention of title it is the creditor (the seller) who is the
owner. The right of the debtor (the buyer) is purely personal."

[2] See Gloag and Irvine, *Rights in Security*, p. 241: "The effect of such conditions when
validly stipulated is practically to create a security over moveables without possession in
favour of a seller of goods." See also Smith, *Property Problems in Sale*, p. 107: "where
the seller transfers property to a buyer under reservation to the seller of the right of
ownership until payment, his preference again resembles a security right." See the same
author's "Retention of title: Lord Watson's legacy," 1983 S.L.T. (News) 105: "far from
treating reservation of title in isolation, the law should treat it functionally as part of the
overall problem of creditor competition and security devices."

the creditor, in a creditor/debtor relationship, by means of a real right—although by leaving the creditor's real right of ownership intact rather than by investing him with a real right of security in the property of his debtor. Moreover, importantly, the policy implications are similar in that in both reservation of title and real security the dominating issue is the problem of a fair adjustment between the interests of the party accorded a real interest and other creditors who may justifiably rely upon the circumstances of the debtor's possession.

Reservation of title, in its simplest form, is a device to protect the seller's interest in obtaining payment. Looked at in another way, it is a means by which the seller may strengthen his position[3] given that, in a particular case, credit must necessarily be extended to the buyer and in view of the fact that the granting of credit amounts to a waiver by the seller of his right to withold delivery pending payment.[4]

Reservation of title, suspending the passing of ownership, should not be confused with a resolutive condition intended to restore the *status quo ante* in the event of the buyer failing to meet his credit obligation within a stipulated period. This, the so-called *pactum de retrovendendo*,[5] is no more than an option in favour of the seller to repurchase the subject sold at a stated price—usually the sale price—within an agreed period.[6] From a property point of view the important point is that a *pactum de retrovendendo* produces no more than a contractual obligation.[7] Accordingly, in the context of a credit sale the seller may enforce the option against the buyer and recover the thing sold where the price is not paid within the agreed period. But, of course, this right will be meaningless if the buyer has transferred ownership to a third party unaware of the option. Moreover, even if the thing concerned is retained by the buyer, the seller's claim is subject to the potential detrimental effect of the buyer's insolvency.[8]

Recognition of reservation of title at common law

12.02 The reservation of title device is well established in Scots common law. Stair[9] noted the use of a condition

---

[3] In this non-technical sense it clearly is "security."

[4] See above, para. 11.17.

[5] See Stair, II.x.1; Erskine, II.viii.2 and III.iii.12.

[6] See *Gavin's Tr.* v. *Fraser*, 1920 S.C. 674 *per* Lord President Clyde at p. 683: "Notwithstanding its reversionary character, such a paction is quite consistent with a genuine contract of sale; indeed it proceeds on the assumption that the rights flowing from the sale are effectual." See also *Latta* v. *Park and Co.* (1865) 3 M. 508 at pp. 512–513.

[7] See Stair, I.xiv.4: "this paction is no real quality or condition of the sale, however it be conceived, but only a personal obligement on the buyer, which therefore doth not affect the thing bought, nor a singular successor." This passage was quoted with approval by Lord President Clyde in *Gavin's Tr.* v. *Fraser*, 1920 S.C. 674 at p. 683.

[8] See Bell, *Comm.*, I,260: "It is settled as law in Scotland, that an express paction, made by the seller when delivering the property, that the property shall be reinstated to him if the price be not paid against an appointed day, is quite ineffectual against the buyer's creditors."

[9] I.xiv.4.

"so conceived and meant, that thereby the bargain is truly conditional and pendant, and so is not a perfect bargain, till the condition be existent, neither doth the property of the thing sold pass thereby, though possession follow, till it be performed, as if the bargain be conditional, only upon payment of the price at such a time, till payment, the property passeth not unto the buyer."[10]

The common law position, in respect of all forms of underlying contract, was that title only passed on the basis of the parties' intention that the transferee become owner upon delivery to him of the subject concerned.[11] Given the two distinct requirements of delivery and intention to convey title,[12] it follows that delivery unaccompanied by the necessary *animus* will not transfer ownership—*a fortiori* where the parties have expressly agreed that title shall remain with the transferor. In these circumstances, the rebuttable presumption that the possessor of a moveable is the owner of it[13] will apply to the transferee; but this does not gainsay the possible conclusion that, in the circumstances, ownership has been retained by the selling transferor pending payment of the price.[14]

Bell[15] states that the effect of a reservation of title condition is that the transferee "will be held to possess as a mere depositary."[16] This, it need hardly be said, is not intended to suggest that the transferee holds on the basis of the contract of deposit,[17] but that the transferee's possession, like that of a depositee, is possession on a contractual basis rather than as owner.

Recognition of the potential effectiveness of the reservation of title device is to be found in the case law.[18] In *Murdoch & Co. Ltd.* v.

---

[10] See the comment of Erskine, III.iii.11: "if a sale should be entered into under condition that the price shall be paid on or before a day prefixed, such condition, before it be purified, is, as Stair justly observes . . . truly suspensive of the sale, which is not understood to be perfected till the condition exists; insomuch that though the subject should be delivered to the buyer, the property continues in the seller till the price be paid."

[11] See above, para. 8.03.

[12] See Erskine, II.i.18.

[13] See above, para. 1.12.

[14] Bell, *Comm.*, I, 258 notes the tension between a condition suspending the transfer of ownership and the presumption arising from possession: see below, n. 37.

[15] *Ibid.*

[16] Smith, "Property problems in sale: three footnotes," 1987 S.L.T. (News) 241 at p. 244 notes that Bell identified the transferee's position in this way.

[17] But the statement that the transferee holds as depositee with a right of use would be broadly accurate. See *Murdoch & Co. Ltd.* v. *Greig* (1889) 16 R. 396 *per* Lord Shand at p. 402: "the harmonium was held by the purchaser only as deposited with her with a right to use it."

[18] But there is some authority the other way; in *Cropper & Co.* v. *Donaldson* (1880) 7 R. 1108, printing machinery was delivered on the basis of a contract of "hire" in terms of which property was only to pass on full payment. The court treated the contract as sale and gave preference to a poinding creditor of the buyer over the seller on the basis that the reservation of title agreement amounted to an attempt to create a security over moveables without possession.

Greig[19] a harmonium was sold on a contract purporting to be hire but construed by the court as sale. Lord President Inglis had no hesitation in recognising the effectiveness of what amounted to a condition of reservation of title.[20]

> "The contract declares in so many words that the property shall not pass until the full price is paid. Therefore while thinking that the contract is one of sale, and negativing the idea of hire, I am still for deciding for the pursuers, on the ground that Mrs Taylor never had any right of property in the harmonium, and therefore could not sell it or give a good title to it."[21]

That the standing of reservation of title is beyond question has been confirmed by the House of Lords.[22]

> "It is well settled in the law of Scotland that a condition in a contract for the sale of corporeal moveables which provides that, notwithstanding delivery, ownership of the goods shall not pass to the buyer until the price has been paid is valid and effective."

Relevant statutory provisions

12.03   Section 19(1) of the Sale of Goods Act 1979 provides for the reservation by the seller of goods of a right of disposal pending the fulfilment of one or more conditions.[23] As Brown[24] points out, prior to

---

[19] (1889) 16 R. 396.

[20] Contrary dicta are unsound. See, *e.g. Clarke & Co.* v. *Miller & Son's Tr.* (1885) 12 R. 1035 *per* Lord Young at p. 1042: "With us the contract of sale does not pass the property without delivery, and I am unable to understand the idea of a condition in a contract of sale in Scotland suspensive of the property passing notwithstanding delivery,—that is to say, I cannot conceive a contract of sale in Scotland, followed by *bona fide* delivery, yet leaving the property unpassed." This reasoning fails to recognise the rôle of intention in delivery, for clearly there can be no question of the parties intending that ownership should pass where they expressly contract on the basis that it shall not.

[21] At p. 402. In *Hogarth* v. *Smart's Tr.* (1882) 9 R. 964 at p. 968 Lord Justice-Clerk Moncreiff recognised that the buyer never became proprietor but, it would appear, on the basis that "the contract never grew into a contract of sale" rather than on the more correct view that ownership did not pass by delivery because the parties did not intend this. See the more accurate dictum of Lord Rutherfurd Clark at p. 969: "Property cannot pass by mere possession contrary to the wish of both giver and receiver." The effectiveness of reservation of title was recognised by Lord Mayfield in *Archivent Sales & Development Ltd.* v. *Strathclyde Regional Council*, 1985 S.L.T. 154 at p. 156: "In this case there was an agreement between the parties that property should not pass until payment was made . . . as the goods remained the property of the seller they could have been reclaimed from the liquidator or receiver." See also *Armour* v. *Thyssen Edelstahlwerke A.G.*, 1989 S.L.T. 182 at p. 185.

[22] *Armour* v. *Thyssen Edelstahlwerke A.G.* (H.L.), 1990 S.L.T. 891 *per* Lord Keith at p. 893.

[23] For the text and a comment see above, para. 9.15.

[24] *Sale of Goods*, p. 135.

the Sale of Goods Act 1893 conditions reserving title to the seller "were necessarily attached to delivery, as it was only by delivery that the property in goods sold could be transferred." The Act, in providing in section 17(1) for the passing of property on the basis of the parties' agreement,[25] accommodated the reservation of title device.[26] Moreover, the Act was drafted to include a section providing for the conditional reservation of the right of disposal by a seller and confirming that in such a case

"notwithstanding the delivery of the goods to the buyer, or to a carrier or other bailee or custodier for the purpose of transmission to the buyer, the property in the goods does not pass to the buyer until the conditions imposed by the seller are fulfilled."[27]

Two possible limitations upon reservation of title are present in the Sale of Goods Act 1979. First, in section 62(4), by excluding the operation of the provisions on sale from what is in fact a security arrangement purporting to be a contract of sale, the Act might be seen to limit the scope of the device. This exclusion of simulated sales— intended to preserve the rôle of the common law in requiring delivery to the creditor to give an effective security over moveable property[28]— is dealt with in the context of a consideration of the development of the reservation of title device in modern law.[29]

The second limitation relates to the standing of a reservation of title condition against a *bona fide* acquirer from the buyer in possession. In this regard the effectiveness of a reservation of title is subject to section 25(1) of the Sale of Goods Act 1979[30] on the basis of which a buyer in possession—but not yet owner by reason of a reservation of title—may give a good title to a *bona fide* purchaser. As Lord President Clyde put it in *Thomas Graham & Sons* v. *Glenrothes Development Corporation*[31]: "Section 25 is a statutory recognition of an exception to the general rule that only an owner of goods can transfer the property in them. The section enables an apparent owner to transfer someone else's goods to a third party in certain specified circumstances."

---

[25] See above, para. 9.01.

[26] One may note the comment of Gloag and Irvine, *Rights in Security*, p. 243: "The Sale of Goods Act, 1893, by which, as has already been stated, the property in goods sold passes to the buyer at the time when the parties to the contract intend it to pass, would seem, in this particular, to be merely a statement of the common law as to sales under suspensive conditions."

[27] s.19(1). See above, para. 9.15 for the full text and a discussion of the scope of the subsection.

[28] See above, para. 11.11.

[29] See below, para. 12.06.

[30] See above, para. 10.21.

[31] 1967 S.C. 284 at p. 293.

The two other sub-sections of section 19 of the Sale of Goods Act 1979 provide for particular instances of the reservation of the right of disposal. Section 19(2) provides a statutory basis for the proposition—which, it is submitted, would be supported at common law[32]—that a seller of shipped goods "is prima facie to be taken to reserve the right of disposal" where "by the bill of lading the goods are deliverable to the order of the seller or his agent."

Section 19(3) provides for the reservation of the title to goods to a seller where a bill of exchange drawn on the buyer for the price is transmitted to him together with the relevant bill of lading. In these circumstances the Act provides that "the buyer is bound to return the bill of lading if he does not honour the bill of exchange, and if he wrongfully retains the bill of lading the property in the goods does not pass to him."[33]

Difference between security and reservation of title

12.04   Security and reservation of title are technically distinct in that the former is predicated upon the debtor having title whereas the basis of the latter is to withhold title from the debtor. Moreover, while it may be true that the *raison d'être* of both is to secure the creditor's position in a debtor/creditor relationship, the technical difference is significant in the way in which the respective devices work.

In the case of security the creditor's right is no more than to obtain satisfaction of what is due to him by giving effect to his real right. This, of course, means that: "The creditor, having realised out of that subject matter a sufficient sum to meet the debt, is obliged to account to the debtor for any surplus."[34]

Where a seller reserves title to goods pending payment by the buyer his full interest is retained and this is reflected in the seller's rights in the event of the buyer's failure to meet his credit obligation. On this basis reservation of title has the potential for consequences quite distinct from security.

> "Where, however, the seller of goods retains title until some condition has been satisfied, and on failure of such satisfaction repossesses them, then he is not obliged to account to the buyer for any part of the value of the goods. Where the condition is to

---

[32] See *Arnots* v. *Boyter* (1803) Mor. 14204.

[33] As Brown (*Sale of Goods*, p. 137) notes, the principle given effect to in this subsection was established in Scots law prior to the Sale of Goods Act 1893. See Bell, *Comm.*, I, 238–239; *Brandt and Co.* v. *Dickson* (1876) 3 R. 375 *per* Lord Ormidale at pp. 385–386: "The acceptance of the draft was a suspensive condition of the sale, and it never was purified." See also *Clarke & Co.* v. *Miller & Son's Tr.* (1885) 12 R. 1035 at pp. 1041–1042.

[34] *Armour* v. *Thyssen Edelstahlwerke A.G.* (H.L.), 1990 S.L.T. 891 *per* Lord Keith at p. 895.

the effect that the price of the goods shall have been paid and it has not been paid, then in the situation where the market price of the goods has risen, so that they are worth more than the contract price, the extra value belongs to the unpaid seller."[35]

PROBLEM OF SIMULATED SALE

At common law

The problem of simulated sale arises where what is in fact a security **12.05** device masquerades as a conventional sale. The argument is that the common law rule, requiring delivery to the creditor to constitute an effective security over moveable property,[36] should not be evaded by the use of reservation of title to cloak what is in fact a security arrangement.

Given the position of the common law regarding property in moveables, it is not surprising that the reservation of title device is seen as involving a certain compromise. Thus Bell[37] comments: "These are admitted to the effect of preventing the delivery from passing the property; although, perhaps, it is to be regretted that sanction should have been given to any latent real right controlling the apparent ownership which arises from possesion." An attitude such as this tends towards limiting the scope of reservation of title to genuine sales rather than allowing the device to be applied to the constitution of what in fact amounts to a security arrangement. Scots common law is generally alert to the danger of allowing what would amount to a security interest in moveables without possession by the party in the position of creditor.[38] In *Cropper & Co.* v. *Donaldson*[39] the court disallowed a hire-purchase arrangement in which the price was secured by a reservation of ownership condition in favour of the seller.[40] But, as indicated, in general the courts recognise the validity of a reservation of title where the circumstances amount to an actual sale.[41]

---

[35] *Armour*, above, *per* Lord Keith at p. 895.

[36] See above, paras. 11.03, 11.11.

[37] *Comm.*, I, 258.

[38] See, *e.g. Cabbell* v. *Brock* (1831) 5 W. & S. 476 *per* Lord Chancellor Brougham at p. 503 quoting the judgment of the Court of Session to which the matter had been remitted for clarification of the Scottish position: "the case plainly resolves itself into a collusive device to create a latent security over a real right, without change of possession, either naturally, civilly, or symbolically; an attempt at variance with the first principles of the law of Scotland, and which, if it could be accomplished, would give rise to mischievous consequences."

[39] (1880) 7 R. 1108.

[40] One may note the dictum of Lord Gifford at p. 1114: "The law of Scotland does not recognise such a security as this, and no stipulation or contract between the parties can create such a security in competition with the rights of creditors. If a seller delivers to the purchaser the articles sold, and parts with its possession, all he has is a personal claim for the balance of the price. The written contract here is a mere device, by means of which it is sought to hide the real nature of the contract, and to change its name without altering its nature."

[41] See above, para. 12.02.

Under section 62(4) of the Sale of Goods Act 1979

12.06   In any event, the policy position of an unreceptive attitude towards
security in the form of sale was reflected in a general disallowing
provision in the Sale of Goods Act 1893[42]:

> "The provisions of this Act about contracts of sale do not apply to
> a transaction in the form of a contract of sale which is intended to
> operate by way of mortgage, pledge, charge or other security."[43]

What is important from the point of view of modern law is the way this
subsection has been interpreted and applied.

In the leading case of *Gavin's Tr.* v. *Fraser*[44] Lord President Clyde
distinguished "the motive which may have inspired the transaction,
and the contractual intention with which the actual transaction was
made." In the learned Lord President's view the relative clause (*viz.*
"which is intended to operate by way of mortgage, pledge, charge or
other security") on which the meaning of the subsection turns, was not
designed to exclude what was intended as a contract of sale—even if its
effect was to provide security—but only to disallow what was cast in
sale form but actually intended to create security[45]: "The exclusion
applies in terms, not to transactions which, while they employ sale
form, *actually* operate by way of security, but to transactions which,
while they employ sale form, are *intended* so to operate."[46] This dictum
is consistent with the statement of Lord Moncreiff in *Robertson* v.
Hall's Tr.[47] quoted in full in Chapter 11.[48] Regarding the means by
which the determining intention factor is to be ascertained, Lord
Moncreiff concluded that "the whole circumstances" must be examined, for the "reality of the transaction" might be "contrary to the
form of the contract, and even the declaration of the parties."[49]

---

[42] s.61(4); s.62(4) of the Sale of Goods Act 1979.

[43] See generally above, para. 11.11.

[44] 1920 S.C. 674 at p. 687.

[45] In *Lawrence's Tr.* v. *Lawrence* (1899) 6 S.L.T. 356 at p. 357 Lord Kincairney was of
the view that the parties intended more than a simple outcome in a case in which a
bankrupt had sold furniture and the buyer had let it back for five years: "The parties
intended the contract to have some part of the operation as a pledge or security, but to
have other effects. I think they intended that it should operate in law as a transference of
the property, although whether they intended that it should have the effect of depriving
the bankrupt of the enjoyment of his furniture may be doubted."

[46] *Gavin's Tr.* v. *Fraser*, 1920 S.C. 674 *per* Lord President Clyde at p. 686. As Reid
and Gretton ("Retention of title in Romalpa clauses," 1983 S.L.T. (News) 77 at p. 80)
point out: "Although widely drafted, the subsection has been interpreted narrowly" in
that the word "intended" was interpreted in *Gavin's Tr.* v. *Fraser* (1920 S.C. 674) "as
referring, not to the parties' motives, but strictly to their contractual intentions."
Consequently, the learned authors point out: "So long as the parties intend to enter into
a sale, therefore, s.64(2) does not operate, and it is irrelevant that the motive behind the
transaction was to create a security." See also *McBain* v. *Wallace & Co.* (1881) 8
R.(H.L.) 106 at p. 109; *Jones & Co.'s Tr.* v. *Allan* (1901) 4 F. 374 at p. 382.

[47] (1896) 24 R. 120.

[48] See above, para. 11.11, n. 93.

[49] at p. 134.

As Reid and Gretton[50] note, section 62(4) has been held to apply to instances of *ex facie* absolute disposition in security where "the owner purports to sell goods to a creditor in order to raise secured finance." While cases of this type[51] have been treated as security transactions, requiring delivery to give an effective real right, it is significant that a device reserving title pending payment in the case of sale is not necessarily disallowed because, in principle, the parties may well intend sale subject to reservation of title and it is immaterial that this provides what amounts to a security interest in favour of the seller. That this is the better view has been confirmed by the House of Lords in *Armour* v. *Thyssen Edelstahlwerke A.G.*[52]

In so far as section 62(4) of the Sale of Goods Act 1979 affects arrangements which while cast in sale form are intended to operate as security, one may say that the subsection applies to transactions "where the sale itself is a sham."[53] Moreover, it is probably accurate to say that the subsection applies to transactions "only where the sale itself is a sham."[54] However, one view is that the subsection applies to an overt security provision provided for as a term in a genuine contract of sale.[55] On this basis Lord Ross in the Second Division decision in *Armour* v. *Thyssen Edelstahlwerke A.G.*[56] took the view that there was "no reason why the transaction should not be treated both as being a genuine sale and as an attempt to create security without possession." But, because the offending clause could not be severed from the contract as a whole the result which was held to apply was that section 62(4) excluded the application of the Sale of Goods Act. In the result, ownership in the goods concerned was held to have passed on the basis of the fact of delivery with no indication by the court as to how the intention to pass ownership was satisfied in the circumstances.[57] This decision has been overruled by the House of Lords.[58] Lord Keith,[59] in a speech concurred in by the other Lords, expressed the opinion that it

---

[50] "Retention of title in Romalpa clauses," 1983 S.L.T. (News) 77 at p. 80–81.

[51] For examples see above, para. 11.11.

[52] (H.L.) 1990 S.L.T 891.

[53] Gretton and Reid, "Romalpa clauses: the current position," 1985 S.L.T. (News) 329 at pp. 330–331.

[54] *Ibid.*

[55] See below, para. 12.07.

[56] 1989 S.L.T. 182 at p. 187.

[57] To declare that an "all sums" reservation of title amounts to security may leave the transaction in limbo from the point of view of proprietary consequences; see McBryde, *The Law of Contract*, para. 13.77: "The seller originally owned the goods. He has attempted, unsuccessfully to create a security over the goods. Does he still own them? If he does not own the goods, what has passed property to the buyer and when did this happen?" There can be no question of ownership having passed in the absence of an intention to give title on the part of the seller. Accordingly, ownership cannot be taken to have passed unless it is possible to say that the particular facts support the necessary intention despite the failure of what may be termed the security aspect.

[58] *Armour* v. *Thyssen Edelstahlwerke A.G.* (H.L.), 1990 S.L.T. 891.

[59] at p. 895.

could not be said that the contractual clause in question was itself "a transaction in the form of a contract of sale." Rather it was simply "one of the conditions of what is a genuine contract of sale." In the case of a reservation of title clause in a contract of sale it is indeed difficult to see that it could itself amount to a "transaction in the form of a contract of sale" and so, as a contract rather than a contractual provision, be potentially subject to section 62(4) of the Sale of Goods Act 1979.

The decision of the House of Lords in *Armour* v. *Thyssen Edelstahlwerke A.G.*[60] means that there will be no need to argue severability in respect of an appropriately drafted reservation of title clause.[61] The decision also reduces the likelihood of an artificial construction which recognises an intention to pass ownership despite the failure of the provision that this will not occur pending full payment by the buyer.[62]

"ALL SUMS" RESERVATION CLAUSES

An extension of reservation of title

12.07   A simple reservation of title clause does no more than reserve to the seller the title to goods sold and delivered to the buyer pending payment of the agreed sale price. Technically, in this form, the device is not security because there is no fragmentation of *dominium* to give a separate security interest. Although, as indicated, it has been argued that reservation of title amounts to *de facto* security,[63] the House of Lords[64] has now made clear that a seller reserving title is not in the position of a debtor "seeking to give a right of security to a creditor."

A variation of the simple form seeks to extend the reservation of title to the seller to have effect beyond the buyer's liability for the price. The object is to apply the reservation of title, founded upon the buyer's liability to pay the sale price, to his liability arising from other aspects of the parties' relationship. A common form is to "all sums due by the buyer to the seller." The practical objective of such a clause is

---

[60] (H.L.), 1990 S.L.T. 891.

[61] Severance has been resorted to as a means of preserving provisions supporting the parties' intention that ownership should be retained by the seller while striking out what is seen to be unenforceable. See the opinion of Lord Clyde in *Glen* v. *Gilbey Vintners Ltd.*, 1986 S.L.T. 553 at p. 555. See generally, St Clair and Drummond Young, *The Law of Corporate Insolvency in Scotland*, para. 10.18.

[62] In *Emerald Stainless Steel Ltd.* v. *South Side Distribution Ltd.*, 1982 S.C. 61 and *Deutz Engines Ltd.* v. *Terex Ltd.*, 1984 S.L.T 272, the sellers were refused interim interdict against the receivers of the buyers. In both cases, the court must have concluded that ownership had passed to the buyers. It would appear to be implicit in this conclusion that although the true intention of the parties was to pass ownership subject to a security arrangement, this intention was severable in the sense that it could be taken to prevail even though the security aspect failed.

[63] See above, para. 12.01.

[64] *Armour* v. *Thyssen Edelstahlwerke A.G.* (H.L.), 1990 S.L.T. 891 at p. 894.

to allow the seller to repossess "all goods supplied during the whole period down to insolvency during which a debt of any sort has been outstanding."[65] The question whether such extensions of the seller's priority, to include liability arising from causes no more than ancillary to the transaction giving rise to the reservation of title, has arisen in modern law as a somewhat controversial issue.[66] The development seems to reflect the claimed interests of commerce leading but the law hesitating in its response because of concern to maintain the integrity of established principles of property.[67]

The issue of the possible extension of reservation of title to the general relationship between a seller/supplier and a buyer/manufacturer came to prominence in the English case of *Aluminium Industrie B.V.* v. *Romalpa Ltd.*,[68] which also raised the question of the extension of a seller's interest to new products in which the independent identity of the materials supplied was subsumed in the manufacturing process.[69]

The matter may be looked at first from the point of view of the difficulties involved in the recognition of "all sums" clauses and, secondly, with reference to the possible means of accommodating the concept.

The difficulties of "all sums" clauses

In the sense that there is no fragmentation of ownership involved, a **12.08** reservation of title purporting to extend beyond the relevant purchase price is no more a security than the simple form of reservation restricted to the price. But, from another point of view, it is difficult to resist the argument that an "all sums" clause amounts to a security device. The point here is that the clause aims to protect the seller's position in respect of claims over and above his claim to the purchase price of the goods in which the priority is given. Put another way, an effective "all sums" clause would mean that the goods sold remain potentially subject to a real interest in favour of the seller even though the purchase price has been paid in full.

While it is clear that, provided the parties intend sale, a simple reservation of title is not hit by section 62(4) of the Sale of Goods Act 1979,[70] the view taken in a line of Scottish cases was that the "all sums" form amounts to a security arrangement and so falls foul of the subsection. Although this matter has been settled by the House of Lords,[71] it is worth examining the reasoning behind the overruled decisions.

---

[65] St. Clair and Drummond Young, *The Law of Corporate Insolvency in Scotland*, para. 10.9.
[66] See, *e.g.* McBryde, *The Law of Contract*, para. 13.73.
[67] St Clair and Drummond Young, *op. cit.*, para. 10.2.
[68] [1976] 1 W.L.R 676. For a perceptive summary see Smith, *Property Problems in Sale*, pp. 126–140.
[69] See below, para. 12.14.
[70] See above, para. 12.04.
[71] *Armour* v. *Thyssen Edelstahlwerke A.G.* (H.L.), 1990 S.L.T. 891.

In *Emerald Stainless Steel Ltd.* v. *South Side Distribution Ltd.*,[72] Lord Ross regarded it as significant that "security is sought not only for the purchase price of the goods but also 'for all and any other monies for the time being owed by the customer to the company.' " The learned Lord Ordinary, as he then was, without specifying non-compliance with section 62(4), held that the clause in question was an attempt to obtain security without possession.[73]

In *Deutz Engines Ltd.* v. *Terex Ltd.*[74] the sale was subject to an "all sums" reservation of title condition which Lord Ross interpreted as having the potential to "include sums which had nothing whatsoever to do with the particular transaction of sale in question."[75] The view taken was that:

> "the transaction appears both to have been a genuine sale (provided that the buyer did not remain indebted to the seller) and an attempt to create security without possession (in the event of any sum being due and unpaid by the buyer to the seller)."[76]

On this basis it was held that:

> "although in the form of a contract of sale . . . the contracts here were intended to operate by way of security of sums over and above the purchase price of the goods sold under the particular contract."[77]

In *Armour* v. *Thyssen Edelstahlwerke A.G.*[78] the Second Division refused a reclaiming motion against an Outer House decree of Lord Mayfield.[79] The principal issue in this case concerned the validity of an

---

[72] 1982 S.C. 61 at p. 64.

[73] Reid and Gretton ("Retention of title in Romalpa clauses," 1983 S.L.T. (News) 77 at pp. 79–81) criticised this decision on the basis that it was incorrect to apply the principle of s.62(4) of the Sale of Goods Act 1979, because "a clause retaining title in a sale is not primarily a security" (at p. 79). Professor Sir Thomas Smith ("Retention of title: Lord Watson's legacy," 1983 S.L.T. (News) 105 at p. 106), however, expressed reservations as to the view that "s.62(4) does not apply even though the debt 'secured' far exceeds the purchase price of the thing sold." Reid and Gretton ("Retention of title for all sums: a reply," 1983 S.L.T. (News) 165 at p. 166) replied to the effect that, on a functional analysis, an "all sums" reservation of title sale involved both sale and security and that it was settled that s.62(4) did not apply "where a transaction is functionally both a sale and a security." In this regard the learned authors cited *Lawrence's Tr.* v. *Lawrence* (1899) 6 S.L.T. 356 and *Gavin's Tr.* v. *Fraser*, 1920 S.C. 674—see above, para. 12.04.

[74] 1984 S.L.T. 273.

[75] at p. 274.

[76] at p. 275.

[77] *Ibid.*

[78] 1989 S.L.T. 182.

[79] Reported in *Armour* v. *Thyssen Edelstahlwerke A.G.*, 1986 S.L.T. 452. See also the report of the original hearing, on relevancy, in 1986 S.L.T. 94.

"all sums" reservation of title arrangement. All three judges recognised the difficulty in the extension of a reservation of title beyond the amount due by the buyer by way of price. Lord Justice-Clerk Ross did not depart from his earlier position to the effect that in so far as the seller's priority extended beyond the sale price of the goods concerned it inevitably amounted to a security without possession.

> "The clause purports to retain ownership 'until all debts owed to us including any balances existing at relevant times—due to us on any legal grounds—are settled.' Some of these debts might be unconnected with the contract of sale. They might be debts which arose on legal grounds arising independently of the contract of sale altogether. That being so, I am of opinion that the intention of the contracting parties must have been to create a security over moveables without possession."[80]

The Second Division decision in *Armour*,[81] and the line of authority leading up to it, was overruled by the House of Lords[82] on the simple basis that a provision reserving title to the seller until payment of all debts due to him by the buyer is not security and is, accordingly, not subject to the rule requiring possession by the creditor. As Lord Keith[83] noted:

> "Such a provision does in a sense give the seller security for the unpaid debts of the buyer. But it does so by way of a legitimate reservation of title, not by virtue of any right over his own property conferred by the buyer."

Means of Extending Scope of Reservation of Title

Reservation of title creating a trust

12.09 Reservation of title in its simple common law form is subject to a number of limitations from the point of view of the protection of the seller's interest. Section 25(1) of the Sale of Goods Act 1979 makes it possible for a buyer in possession—by reason of a reservation of title clause, not yet owner—to give a good title to a *bona fide* purchaser.[84] The seller's interest may be at risk from the quarter of other creditors of the buyer if specification or accession occurs.[85] Moreover, the

---

[80] at pp. 186–187. See also dicta of Lord McDonald at p. 190 and Lord Wylie at p. 191.
[81] 1989 S.L.T. 182.
[82] *Armour* v. *Thyssen Edelstahlwerke A.G.* (H.L.), 1990 S.L.T. 891.
[83] at p. 895.
[84] See above, paras. 10.21, 12.03.
[85] See below, paras. 12.14, 12.15.

likelihood of this may well be the rule rather than the exception in the circumstances of goods supplied for use in the manufacturing process.

Difficulties of this kind have led to attempts to strengthen the seller's interest in two ways. First, to provide for its extention to include a right to the proceeds of any sale by the buyer to a third party. Secondly, to extend its scope so as to encompass both new and composite items: the former made in a process involving the consumption of the original goods, and the latter involving the identity of the original goods being subsumed under the identity of a principal thing on the basis of accession.

Different forms of the trust device have been used in attempts to extend the seller's interest in this way and, indeed, it is open to argument that the doctrine of constructive trust may apply to the proceeds of the sale of goods subject to reservation of title. The trust solution will be considered under the headings of (i) express trust, (ii) constructive trust, and (iii) agency.

Express trust

12.10   The parties to a sale subject to reservation of title may agree that the proceeds of any subsequent sale of the items concerned by the buyer shall be held in trust for and on behalf of the seller. As indicated,[86] the need for this arises because purchase of the goods subject to reservation of title by a *bona fide* third party may well give a good title at the expense of the title of the original seller. Potentially, the creation of a trust protects the original seller because trust property is protected— for transmission to the beneficiary—and does not form part of the insolvent estate of a trustee.[87]

To achieve the desired objective of the protection, as trust property, of the proceeds of the sale of reserved property, it must be possible to say that the original buyer made himself a trustee of a trust established for the benefit of the original seller, the trust property being the proceeds of the sale of items subject to reservation of title in favour of the original seller.

In principle it is competent to establish a trust relationship on this basis, but the actual constitution of the trust requires some form of delivery to the trustee. In *Clark Taylor & Co. Ltd.* v. *Quality Site Development (Edinburgh) Ltd.*[88] the First Division answered questions of law arising from a clause—accompanying a reservation of title— which provided that payments received for the goods concerned would be held in trust by the buyer for the seller, until full payment of the contract price by the buyer. The goods were bricks and given their intended use in building work—to be carried out by the buyer for third

---

[86] See above, paras. 10.21, 12.03.
[87] *Heritable Reversionary Co. Ltd.* v. *Millar* (1892) 19 R.(H.L.) 43.
[88] 1981 S.C. 111.

parties—it was clear that the seller could only be protected by achieving the transfer of his interest in the actual bricks to the proceeds of their sale. The court did not accept that there was constructive delivery of the proceeds to the buyer, as trustee for the benefit of the seller. The argument in this regard was that there was a "continuing intimation" in the parties' contract "equivalent to an intimation of the creation of a trust over each payment" received by the buyer on resale of the bricks.[89]

Following an analysis of the decisions concerned with the constitution of trusts the court in *Clark Taylor* concluded that

> "in order to bring about the successful constitution of a trust recognised as such by our law, where the truster and the trustee are the same persons, there must be in existence an asset, be it corporeal or incorporeal or even a right relating to future acquirenda; there must be a dedication of the asset or right to defined trust purposes; there must be a beneficiary or beneficiaries with defined rights in the trust estate, and there must also be delivery of the trust deed or subject of the trust or a sufficient and satisfactory equivalent to delivery, so as to achieve irrevocable divestiture of the truster and investiture of the trustee in the trust estate."[90]

On the question of delivery the court had earlier stated that a person making himself a trustee can demonstrate the establishing of an irrevocable trust in a variety of ways.

> "The person in question can, for example, execute a deed or declaration of trust over defined trust subjects in favour of his intended beneficiary and proof of a validly created trust will be complete when he has done something which can be regarded as equivalent to the delivery of the subjects of the trust which would be required to constitute a valid trust with a third party as trustee. Intimation to the beneficiary of the execution of the deed or declaration of trust and of its terms, would clearly suffice for this purpose. In each case, however, it will be a matter of circumstances whether the truster has done enough to establish the necessary constructive delivery of the trust subjects to himself as trustee of an irrevocable trust."[91]

It may be noted that in the Second Division decision in *Export Credits Guarantee Department* v. *Turner*[92] it was held that the intima-

---

[89] at p. 118.
[90] *Ibid.* See *Tay Valley Joinery Ltd.* v. *C. F. Financial Services Ltd.*, 1987 S.L.T. 207, at p. 212.
[91] at p. 115.
[92] 1979 S.C. 286 at p. 294.

tion of the declaration of a trust was ineffective if, in the circumstances, the trust fund was not in the hands of the truster at the time.
In *Allan's Tr.* v. *I.R.C.*[93] Lord Reid had explained why, in the case of
the creation of a trust in which the truster is sole trustee, there must be
intimation to the beneficiary of the establishing of the trust. This was
necessary because if

> "mere proved intention to make a trust coupled with the execu-
> tion of a declaration of trust can suffice . . . it would be easy to
> execute such a declaration, keep it in reserve, use it in case of
> bankruptcy to defeat the claims of creditors, but if all went well
> and the trustee desired to regain control of the fund simply
> suppress the declaration of trust."[94]

Professor W. A. Wilson,[95] it may be noted, submits that the mischief
which Lord Reid alluded to "is avoided by intimation of the declaration of trust even although the trust fund is not in existence at the date
of intimation." Accordingly, the learned writer urges: "There would
seem to be no reason in principle for a requirement that the trust fund
must be in existence at the time of intimation of the declaration of
trust."

Even if it is accepted that the trust fund does not need to be in
existence at the time of the declaration of trust, it remains necessary
for the party relying on the trust to prove the necessary constructive
delivery of the trust subjects to the truster as trustee.[96] In this regard
Professor McBryde[97] has made an apposite comment.

> "It would be possible to create a trust, but the mechanics for
> doing so, and in particular the need for delivery or an equivalent
> suggest that it would be easier for the buyer to pay over the sale
> proceeds to the seller."

In practice, of course, the question of the entitlement of a seller who
has reserved title usually arises in the context of the buyer being in
parlous financial circumstances. Any new act apparently putting the
seller in a better position in the context of other claims against the
buyer may well attract the attention of the other creditors as a
unjustified preference.[98]

---

[93] 1971 S.C. (H.L.) 45.
[94] at p. 54.
[95] "Romalpa and trust," 1983 S.L.T. (News) 106 at p. 108.
[96] See *Clark Taylor & Co. Ltd.* v. *Quality Site Development (Edinburgh) Ltd.* 1981
S.C. 111 at p. 115.
[97] *The Law of Contract*, para. 13.80. The learned author goes on to comment that
money due to the seller may be deposited in a separate bank account, but: "In practice it
is highly unlikely that the buyer will create a trust if he mixes resale proceeds with his
other funds."
[98] See s.36 of the Bankruptcy (Scotland) Act 1985. The granting of security may
amount to an unfair preference see McBryde, *Bankruptcy*, p. 164.

It is not possible to create a trust as a simple adjunct to a sale subject to reservation of title. While title in the goods sold is reserved to the seller there can be no question of a trust with the seller as beneficiary; as Lord Clyde observed in *Glen* v. *Gilbey Vintners Ltd.*[99]: "If a trust is created then the property and title must be in the trustee with the beneficiary having merely a right of action against him." Moreover, seemingly, the steps necessary to be taken to create a trust over the proceeds of a sale are entirely up to the buyer, with the seller having no more than a contractual right to require the buyer to take the necessary steps. From the seller's point of view this is unsatisfactory. A possible solution which should strengthen the seller's position would be to constitute a trust over the goods sold as soon as possible after their acquisition by the buyer. The advantage of an existing trust would be that upon resale the seller would be automatically protected as the beneficiary of trust property. It would appear that this could be provided for by an outright sale subject to a resolutive condition providing for the cancellation of the sale—and of the passing of ownership pursuant to it—in the event of the buyer failing to comply with an obligation to create a trust over the goods sold, with himself as trustee and the seller as beneficiary, within a stated period. Clearly, to protect the seller's position the resolutive condition would have to require the more or less immediate creation of a trust. Of course, in so far as there may be other claims against the buyer there is always the risk that a subsequent act, apparently strengthening the position of a particular creditor, may be open to challenge as an unfair preference.

Constructive trust

Although there has been no judicial recognition of a constructive **12.11** trust over the proceeds of the sale of goods subject to reservation of title, this possibility has been argued in a journal article. Professor Wilson,[1] commenting on the requirements prescribed by the courts in respect of the creation of an express trust by a truster making himself trustee, raised the issue of the recognition of a constructive trust.

> "One wonders whether . . . it is necessary to resort to elaborate trust-creating provisions to protect the seller in the *Romalpa* situation. If the contract of sale contains a retention of title clause and the proceeds of a sub-sale of the goods can be identified in the original buyer's estate, can it not be argued that the proceeds are held in a constructive trust because the buyer has sold goods which are not his property?"[2]

---

[99] 1986 S.L.T. 553 at p. 554.

[1] "Romalpa and trust," 1983 S.L.T. (News) 106 at p. 108. See also Reid, "Constitution of trust," 1986 S.L.T. (News) 177, at pp. 180–181.

[2] *Cf.* Cusine, "The Romalpa family visits Scotland" (1982) 27 J.L.S. 147, 221 at p. 223: "Even if an express trust does not exist, a person might be the subject of a constructive trust. This is, of course, implied by law, but none of the categories of constructive trust would seem to be an appropriate analogy."

As the learned writer points out, in the leading case of *Clark Taylor &
Co. Ltd* v. *Quality Site Development (Edinburgh) Ltd.*[3] nothing was
made of the fact that the bricks disposed of for value by the buyer
were still the property of the seller. Taking this point further, one
might say that were the courts less zealous in protecting the interests of
general creditors, against what is seen to amount to a particular
creditor obtaining preferential treatment, there would be a greater
prospect of the recognition of a constructive trust.

In relation to a constructive trust, however, no less than in respect of
an expressly constituted trust, one has the problem of the identification
of the property or fund constituting the trust.[4]

Agency

12.12   Another possible method of protecting the seller—who has reserved
title to the goods delivered—against resale by the buyer, is to arrange
matters so that the buyer is an agent of the seller.[5] In principle, the
seller would then be entitled to the proceeds of the resale, provided, at
any rate, that the proceeds were identifiable.[6] Reid and Gretton[7]
explain the use of agency as an indirect means of constituting a trust,
for the benefit of the original seller, over the proceeds of a sub-sale:
"The effect of this arrangement is that, since the buyer is acting in a
fiduciary capacity, the proceeds of subsale are automatically held in
trust (constructive trust) for the agent's principal, who is the original
seller."

The requirement of identification of the proceeds is critical if the
seller subject to reservation of title is to retain his interest as principal.
Bell[8] states the general doctrine that "where goods sent by the
principal . . . are found in the hands of the factor, distinguishable from
the general mass of his property, they are not part of the factor's
estate." Moreover, as Bell[9] notes, where the principal's goods are
disposed of the price paid remains the property of the principal,
provided it is kept distinct.[10]

---

[3] 1981 S.C. 111.

[4] See above, para. 12.10 and below, para. 12.12.

[5] In respect of the subject sold the creation of a trust proper, with the buyer as trustee,
would be incompatible with reservation of title; but this difficulty may be avoidable if the
buyer holds as agent of the seller. See *Glen* v. *Gilbey Vintners Ltd.*, 1986 S.L.T. 553 at
pp. 554–555.

[6] See *Michelin Tyre Co. Ltd.* v. *Macfarlane (Glasgow) Ltd.*, 1917 (2) S.L.T. 205.

[7] "Retention of title in Romalpa clauses," 1983 S.L.T. (News) 77.

[8] *Comm.*, I, 279.

[9] *Comm.*, I, 284.

[10] In this regard Bell (*loc. cit.*) quotes a relevant dictum of Lord Kenyon in *Tooke* v.
Hollingworth, (1973) 5 Term.Rep. 215 at pp. 226–227: "If goods be sent to a factor to be
disposed of . . . who afterwards becomes a bankrupt, and the goods remain distinguishable from the general mass of his property, the principal may recover the goods in
specie, etc. Nay, if the goods be sold and reduced to money, provided that money be in
separate bags, and distinguishable from the factor's other property, the law is the same."

An important difference between constructive and express trust concerns the manner in which the requirement of the identification of trust property applies. In the case of an express trust it is required for the very purpose of the constitution of the trust because of the requirement of constructive delivery by truster to trustee. Moreover, where a trust situation exists, there may well be the further question of the identification of the trust property because some fundamental change has occurred. In the case of a constructive trust, based upon agency, the fiduciary relationship comes into being with the original buyer constituted the agent of the original seller. In this form the identification of the subject-matter of the ensuing constructive trust is relevant—not from the point of view of recognising the seller's right but merely for purposes of implementation.

Whether the reservation of title employs the concept of trust, or that of agency, to protect the seller's interest in the goods sold, the question may well arise as to the extent to which the relevant property or fund can be identified—or, indeed, traced where some change in identity has occurred.

Tracing and entitlement to proceeds

Where there is an express or constructive trust and the goods subject **12.13** to the trust are disposed of, there should be no difficulty in the seller having recourse to the proceeds provided these have been deposited in a separately identified account. Arguably, the seller would only need to show (i) that the goods disposed of by the buyer were held on the basis of a fiduciary relationship under which the seller was entitled as beneficiary; and (ii) that the proceeds of the sale are separately identifiable within the original buyer's estate.[11]

What is the position where the proceeds of the sale are mixed with other funds by the buyer? In the cases of *Macadam* v. *Martin's Tr.*[12] and *Jopp* v. *Johnston's Tr.*[13] the Court of Session recognised that funds held or obtained by a party subject to a fiduciary duty in favour of another—in these cases the relationship was law agent and client— could be separated from private funds. In the latter case Lord Moncreiff[14] stated the applicable law leading to this conclusion.

> "First, where a trustee or agent, with or without authority, sells trust property and lodges the proceeds of the sale in bank in his

---

[11] In *Aluminium Industrie B.V.* v. *Romalpa Ltd.* [1976] 1 W.L.R. 676 at pp. 687, 691 the Court of Appeal accepted the dicta of Sir George Jessel M.R. in *Re Hallett's Estate* (1880) 13 Ch.D. 696 at pp. 708–711 to the effect that the identifiable proceeds of the sale of property by a person in a fiduciary position could be claimed by the party entitled to the property disposed of.

[12] (1872) 11 M. 33.

[13] (1904) 6 F. 1028.

[14] at p. 1036.

own name, the money so lodged can be followed and vindicated by the truster provided it can be traced with reasonable certainty.

Secondly, this holds good not only as between the truster and the trustee but also as between the truster and the trustee's trustee or asignee in bankruptcy acting for the general body of his creditors.

Thirdly, the proceeds of the sale can be vindicated although they may have been blended with moneys belonging to the trustee. And

Fourthly, if after the proceeds of trust property are so lodged and blended with the trustee's own funds, the trustee, for his own purposes, draws out part of the mixed funds he will be held to have drawn out his own funds, and not those which represent the proceeds of the trust-estate."

Where, however, the party subject to a fiduciary obligation depletes a mixed fund beyond the limit of his personal funds it is unavoidable that the trust funds are affected,[15] and the question then arises as to whether the trust interest can be traced to assets acquired by the use of trust funds. In *Borden (U.K.) Ltd.* v. *Scottish Timber Products Ltd.*[16] Buckley L.J. described the limits of tracing as follows:

"it is a fundamental feature of the doctrine of tracing that the property to be traced can be identified at every stage of its journey through life, and that it can be identified as property to which a fiduciary obligation still attaches in favour of the person who traces it."

It may well be clear that in principle a seller has a right to the proceeds of property sold subject to reservation of title. It is another matter, in any given case, to identify, within the estate of the buyer, assets which may be said to have been derived from the original items subject to reservation of title. Where the goods—and their proceeds—have been dealt with by the buyer, without being separated or distinguished from other assets in his estate, it will almost certainly be difficult to make the necessary connection with any reasonable degree of accuracy.

One may contrast the circumstances of two leading English cases reflecting the critical difference between, on the one hand, the proceeds kept entirely separate and, on the other, their being dealt with as assets indistinguishable from other assets in the estate. In *Aluminium Industrie B.V.* v. *Romalpa Ltd.*[17] Roskill L.J. had no

---

[15] See *Jones Roscoe (Bolton) Ltd.* v. *Winder* [1915] 1 Ch. 62 at p. 68.
[16] [1981] 1 Ch. 25 at p. 46.
[17] [1976] 1 W.L.R 676 at p. 687.

difficulty in identifying the proceeds of sales to subsequent purchasers
because by the time they came in a receiver had been appointed and
he had kept the relevant sums separate from other assets: "we were
told that there is no complication arising of those moneys having
become mixed with other moneys, because they were always kept
separate." In *Borden (U.K.) Ltd*. v. *Scottish Timber Products Ltd*.[18] a
very different position was noted by Templeman L.J.:

> "No one knows how the defendants, going about their business,
> no doubt blissfully unconscious of any fiduciary duty, employed
> the proceeds of sale of chipboard. They may have paid part to
> discharge their debt to the plaintiffs; they may have paid the
> money into their bank in reduction of an overdraft; they may have
> paid their taxes; they may have bought and consumed other goods
> and paid other creditors."

EFFECTIVENESS OF RESERVATION OF TITLE WHERE PROPERTY DEALT WITH BY BUYER

Effect of accession, specification or consumption

An act of accession, specification or confusion may bring about a **12.14**
change of ownership[19]; consumption, resulting in the termination of
existence, necessarily ends the right of ownership. In principle, the
effect of accession, specification, confusion or consumption upon a
right based upon reservation of title is that recovery *in specie* is
impossible where the thing or things concerned no longer exist.[20]

Where goods are supplied on credit to a manufacturer or processor
subject to a reservation of title in favour of the supplier/seller, the
reserved right is subject to the risk of being affected by the use of the
goods in a manner which leads to a change of ownership on the basis
of original acquisition. The most likely bases are accession and
specification; and the contract under which the goods are supplied will
not infrequently include a clause intended to protect the seller against
changes which may affect his reserved title. The intention behind such
terms is to carry forward the seller's reservation of title from the
original to the new goods. But can a contractual term achieve the
desired effect in controlling the proprietary consequences which would
otherwise follow, as a matter of law, from a fundamental change in the
nature of the subjects concerned?[21]

---

[18] Above, at p. 43.

[19] See above, paras. 3.01, 4.01, 5.04.

[20] See above, para. 10.10.

[21] The efficacy of provisions of this sort was one of the issues in *Aluminium Industrie
B.V.* v. *Romalpa Ltd.* [1976] 1 W.L.R 676, a case which was the point of commencement
of modern developments concerned with the extension of a seller's real rights under a
reservation of title.

From a point of view of principle the difficulty is to see how the usual proprietary effect could be avoided by a contractual term.[22] The rationale behind the principle that property prevails over contract is the protection of the legitimate interests of parties who may not be privy to the contractual arrangements. But, arguably, the recognition of reservation of title in favour of a seller who has parted with possession already departs from this, in so far as the law recognises an exceptional situation in which what has been agreed between the parties prevails over the circumstances as they would appear to a third party. Why should it be incompetent to go a stage further and extend the exception by giving priority to a contractual term to the effect that the seller's reservation of title continues even though the original subjects are processed into new items?

In so far as the matter is viewed in terms of the legitimate interests of third parties, there does not seem to be a compelling case for disallowing a clause avoiding the possible consequences of accession or specification as an extension of a contract-based reservation of title in favour of a seller who has transferred possession to his buyer.

Whereas derivative acquisition operates on the basis of the mutual intentions of the parties to give and receive ownership,[23] accession and specification are original modes of acquisition.[24] By accession the right of ownership in an accessory item passes to the owner of a principal item where the circumstances are consistent with a sufficient degree of finality to justify the conclusion that the accessory element has become part of the principal item.[25] Specification is an original mode of acquisition in which, at any rate in certain circumstances, ownership passes to the maker of a new thing as a matter of proprietary consequence.[26] A reservation of title clause, being "intention based," is perfectly acceptable in the context of derivative acquisition. It is consistent with the principle of both the common law and the Sale of Goods Act 1979[27] that property cannot pass on a derivative basis contrary to "the will of both giver and receiver."[28] A contractual extension of reservation of title intended to cover the circumstances of *accessio* and *specificatio* is, however, inconsistent with this principle. But, of course, this is not to say that the option of making accession

---

[22] Reid and Gretton ("Retention of title in Romalpa clauses," 1983 S.L.T. (News) 77) are of the view that "a declaration in the Romalpa clause that the finished products are to belong to the seller, is an attempt to transfer ownership of moveables nudis pactis, and is therefore ineffectual."

[23] See above, paras. 8.03, 8.06.

[24] See above, para. 1.17.

[25] See above, para. 3.01.

[26] See above, para. 4.01. This, it would appear, is the basis of the *nudis pactis* point made by Reid and Gretton (above, n. 22). If the maker of a new thing *ipso facto* becomes owner, it can only be by derivative transfer that title is vested in another—in this case the seller of materials or components.

[27] s.17.

[28] *Hogarth* v. *Smart's Tr.* (1882) 9 R. 964 *per* Lord Rutherfurd Clark at p. 969.

and specification subject to contractual control for the purposes of reservation of title is beyond the law. It clearly is not, but arguably such control would be at the expense of the integrity of established principles of property.

A procedure roll decision is authority supporting the view that it is within the power of the parties to depart from what would otherwise follow on the basis of accession. In *Zahnrad Fabrik Passau GmbH* v. *Terex Ltd.*[29] the parties' contract incorporated article 947(1) of the West German BGB which provides for joint value-based ownership in the case of the accession of moveable objects. Moreover, it was specifically agreed that accession would only occur in the event of the components supplied being installed in a manner which precluded removal without destruction. Lord Davidson appears to have at least acknowledged the possibility of a term in the parties' contract being decisive over proprietary consequences[30] which would otherwise follow on the basis of the common law principle of accession.[31]

There is, however, authority to the effect that it is not open to the parties to a contract to alter or adjust what would otherwise follow as a matter of proprietary consequence. In *Deutz Engines Ltd.* v. *Terex Ltd.*[32] Lord Ross, as he then was, commented that a contractual condition went "far beyond a mere reservation of title in respect of the goods delivered" and purported "to alter the law of accession and specification." In *Shetland Islands Council* v. *BP Petroleum Development*[33] Lord Cullen observed that "a contractual arrangement between owner and occupier is ineffective to prevent what is annexed to the heritage being treated as such." The learned Lord Ordinary went on to refer to the "universality" of a right of property, stating—with respect, perfectly correctly—that "no agreement between owner and occupier can affect the matter of ownership of heritable fixtures."[34]

Possible distinction between accession and specification

Although accession and specification are both instances of original **12.15** acquisition, a closer investigation of their respective bases reveals a difference which may be material to the problem of extending a contractual reservation of title to subsequent events involving either of the two concepts.

---

[29] 1986 S.L.T. 84.

[30] Lord Davidson, at p. 88, indicated that he "would prefer the pursuers' arguments" on the basis of which "a Scottish buyer of their goods might succeed in proving accession . . . but be defeated by the pursuers' contractual condition which imposes a stiffer test for accession."

[31] What is significant here is that this would give the contractual term proprietary effect in that it would have the potential to defeat the claims of third-party creditors who might otherwise be entitled on the basis of the accession of the goods concerned.

[32] 1984 S.L.T. 273 at pp. 274–275.

[33] 1990 S.L.T. 82 at p. 94.

[34] *Ibid.*

In the case of accession it is clear that an irreversible annexation of accessory to principle—as in the case of paint applied to a table or bricks built into a house—is not affected by proof that the parties intended some other result.[35] The principles relating to "fixtures" are apposite here, and as demonstrated in the leading case of *Scottish Discount Co. Ltd.* v. *Blin*[36] the test is an objective one based upon the circumstances of annexation with reference to the parties' intention having no more than a confirmatory rôle.

It is submitted that the better view is that the proprietary consequences of accession—as opposed to matters of compensation—are not open to adjustment on the basis of the parties' contract. Provided, however, that it is not inconsistent with the physical circumstances, what the parties agreed may have a rôle in determining the proprietary consequences.[37]

Specification, however, does not involve a philosophically determined result in the manner of the accession of accessory to principal.[38] Accession takes precedence over specification in so far as an existing principal item precludes the coming into being of a new thing—a mural belongs not to the painter but to the owner of the house.[39] But what is the basis of specification? Arguably, that reason dictates that the maker of a new—and therefore unowned—thing[40] should acquire where there has been no prior determination as to how rights are to be allocated. As distinct from accession, the proprietary consequence is not unavoidable but open to control at the instance of the owners involved.[41]

Accordingly, the distinct bases of accession and specification would appear to show that while it is probably incompetent to attempt to extend a reservation of title to the circumstances of accession, this is not necessarily so in respect of specification.[42]

---

[35] See Gretton and Reid "Romalpa clauses: the current position," 1985 S.L.T. (News) 329 at p. 333: "It seems clear that a Romalpa clause cannot be used to prevent the operation of accession." In the English case of *Borden* (*U.K.*) *Ltd.* v. *Scottish Timber Products* [1981] 1 Ch. 25 at p. 44, Templeton L.J. noted that: "When the resin was incorporated in the chipboard, the resin ceased to exist, the plaintiff's title to the resin became meaningless and their security vanished."

[36] 1985 S.C. 216 at pp. 235, 240.

[37] See above, para. 3.15.

[38] The tendency of Scottish Institutional writers—*e.g.* Erskine, II.i.16—to identify specification as a form of accession is artificial and potentially misleading.

[39] Erskine, II.i.16.

[40] See above, para. 4.02.

[41] See the unsuccessful argument of counsel in *Re Peachdart Ltd.* [1984] 1 Ch. 131 at p. 142.

[42] See Carey Miller, "Logical consistency in property," 1990 S.L.T. (News) 197 at pp. 198–199.

INDEX

[References are to page numbers]

ACCESSION
basis of,
a matter of natural law, 30
accessorium sequitur principale, 31
accretion of parts, 30
distinct from *confusio/commixtio*, 32
distinct from specification, 32, 299–300
original acquisition, 15–16, 30
principal and accessory, 30, 31
sufficient connecting factor, 31
forms of,
acquisition of fruits, 31, 75
alluvio, avulsio, 32
borderline cases, 31, 32
fixtures. *See* FIXTURES.
industrial or artificial, 31, 32
mussel-scalps, 31, 32
natural, 31
growing things,
basis of accession of, 33
alternative view of, 36, 37
connection and dependence, 33
continuation of accessory status after detachment excludes occupation, 21
partes soli, 33
pendentes, 34
plantatur solo, solo cedit, 40 (n. 77)
cultivated crops, excluded,
basis of exclusion, 34
bona fide producer favoured, 34
case of hay crop, 35
case of undersown grass, 35
messis sementem sequitur, 34
pendentes, 34
relevance of status as crop,
bankruptcy implications, 38
heritable creditors rights subject to, 38
implications for tenant, 38
open to *bona fide* cultivator to claim, 38
open to poinding, 38
ownership of land and crop distinct, 37, 38
sale of crop facilitated, 37, 38
trees,
basic position: *partes soli*, 35
destinatione, 36
distinct from annual crops, 35
nursery stock as heritable, 35, 36
nursery stock not *partes soli*, 35, 36

ACCESSION—*cont.*
to moveables,
annexor's *animus* irrelevant to property consequences, 62
by constructive annexation, 62
car jack, 62
car sunroof, 61, 62
car tyres, 61, 62
contexture, 68
distinguishable from accession to land, 59
drawings made for employer, 61
identification of principal and accessory, 59–60, 61
materials woven into cloth, 60, 68
not open to control through contract, 62
picture, 60, 61
right to compensation arising from, 62
separation without damage, 61
stone set in ring, 60
test of, 60, 61
writing or printing, 61
ACQUISITION OF FRUITS BY BONA FIDE POSSESSOR
basis of,
belief in right, 78
consumption theory, 77, 81–83
contribution theory, 77, 78
equity theory, 77
presumed from possession, 78
general,
circumstances in which question arises, 75–76, 76(n. 11), 80–81
classes of fruits, 76
fructus consumpti, 77
fructus pendentes, 76
fructus percepti, 76
fruges bona fide perceptae et consumptae, 82(n. 55)
natural, industrial and civil fruits, 76
original acquisition, 75
usus, fructus, abusus division, 81(n. 42)
when *bona fide*,
apparently good title, 79
circumstances incompatible with, 80
denied in mistake of law, 80
mala fides not necessarily inferred from dispute, 80
subjective/objective considerations, 79
when possession becomes *mala fide*, 79